# KNOWLEDGE MANAGEMENT AND MANAGEMENT LEARNING:
Extending the Horizons of Knowledge-Based Management

# INTEGRATED SERIES IN INFORMATION SYSTEMS

*Series Editors*

Professor Ramesh Sharda
*Oklahoma State University*

Prof. Dr. Stefan Voß
*Universität Hamburg*

**Other published titles in the series:**

E-BUSINESS MANAGEMENT: *Integration of Web Technologies with Business Models/* Michael J. Shaw

VIRTUAL CORPORATE UNIVERSITIES: *A Matrix of Knowledge and Learning for the New Digital Dawn/* Walter R.J. Baets & Gert Van der Linden

SCALABLE ENTERPRISE SYSTEMS: *An Introduction to Recent Advances/* edited by Vittal Prabhu, Soundar Kumara, Manjunath Kamath

LEGAL PROGRAMMING: *Legal Compliance for RFID and Software Agent Ecosystems in Retail Processes and Beyond/* Brian Subirana and Malcolm Bain

LOGICAL DATA MODELING: *What It Is and How To Do It/* Alan Chmura and J. Mark Heumann

DESIGNING AND EVALUATING E-MANAGEMENT DECISION TOOLS: *The Integration of Decision and Negotiation Models into Internet-Multimedia Technologies/* Giampiero E.G. Beroggi

INFORMATION AND MANAGEMENT SYSTEMS FOR PRODUCT CUSTOMIZATION/ Blecker, Friedrich, Kaluza, Abdelkafi & Kreutler

MEDICAL INFORMATICS: *Knowledge Management and Data Mining in Biomedicine/* Chen, Fuller, Friedman & Hersh

# KNOWLEDGE MANAGEMENT AND MANAGEMENT LEARNING:
## Extending the Horizons of Knowledge-Based Management

Edited by

## Walter Baets
*Euromed Marseille – Ecole de Management*
*E$^c$KM : Euromed Center for Knowledge Management*

 Springer

Walter Baets
Euromed Marseille

Library of Congress Cataloging-in-Publication Data

Knowledge management and management learning : extending the horizons of
  knowledge-based management / edited by Walter Baets.
      p. cm. – (Integrated series in information systems ; 9)
      Includes bibliographical references.
      ISBN-10: 0-387-25819-1
      ISBN-13: 978-0-387-25819-5
      ISBN-10: 0-387-25846-9 (e-book)
      ISBN-13: 978-0-387-25846-1 (e-book)
      1. Knowledge management. 2. Organizational learning. 3. Management.
  I. Baets, W.R.J. (Walter R.J.) II. Series.

      HD30.2.K636846  2005
      658.4'038—dc22

                                              2005044154

Printed in the United States of America.

9 8 7 6 5 4 3 2 1          SPIN  11053903

springeronline.com

Wanderer, your footprints are
the path, and nothing more;
Wanderer, there is no path,
it is created as you walk.
By walking,
you make the path before you,
and when you look behind
you see the path which after you
will not be trod again.
Wanderer, there is no path,
but the ripples on the waters.

Antonio Machado

A very great musician came and stayed in our house.
He made one big mistake…
He was determined to teach me music,
and consequently, no learning took place.
Nevertheless, I did casually pick up from him
a certain amount of stolen knowledge.

Rabindranath Tagore

**For Erna**, without whom my writings would be stone and my thinking
frozen;
Now, you only see little of her light, but already a difference of day and
night for this book.

# CONTENTS

# ABOUT THE AUTHOR

**Walter Baets** is Director Graduate Programs at Euromed Marseille – Ecole de Management (F) and distinguished professor Innovation, Information and Knowledge at Nyenrode University, the Netherlands Business School. He has been the director of Notion, the Nyenrode Institute for Knowledge Management and Virtual Education, a competence center sponsored by Achmea, Atos/Origin, Microsoft, Philips and Sara Lee/DE. Today he is responsible for the $E^cKM$ (Euromed center for Knowledge Management), a research center where he continues his work started in Notion. He graduated in econometrics and operations research at the University of Antwerp (Belgium) and did postgraduate studies in Business Administration at Warwick Business School (UK). He was awarded a PhD from the University of Warwick in Industrial and Business Studies. He holds a HDR (Habilitation a la Direction des Recherches) of IAE Aix-en-Provence (University of Aix-Marseille III). After pursuing a career of more than ten years in business, he held positions in the academic world in Belgium, Russia, the Netherlands and Spain, and currently in France. He was particularly active in management development both in Russia and in the Arab world.

Walter Baets (co-)authored or (co-)edited amongst others the following books:
- IT and Organizational Transformation (Wiley, 1998, with Bob Galliers);
- Organizational Learning and Knowledge Technologies in a Dynamic Environment (Kluwer Academic Publishers, 1998);
- A Collection of Essays on Complexity and Management (World Scientific, 1999);
- The Hybrid Business School: Developping knowledge management through management learning (Prentice Hall, 2000, with Gert Van der Linden).
- Wie orde zaait zal chaos oogsten: een vertoog over de lerende mens (Van Gorcum, 2002; 'An essay on complexity, knowledge and learning')
- Corporate Virtual Universities (Kluwer Academic, 2003, with Gert Van der Linden)
- Complexity, learning and organisations: the quantum structure of business (Routledge, 2005)

His research and consulting interests are in complexity, innovation, knowledge management, management learning and the quantumstructure of organisations.

## Principle Bio's

**Marie-Joëlle Browaeys** is Assistant Professor of Cross-Cultural Management and Project Manager in Virtual Education at Nyenrode University. Her appointment includes the development of pedagogical materials for virtual education. She studied first in the Department of Education and Science in Lille (France) and thereafter she graduated (with honours) at the Faculty of Arts, University of Amsterdam (The Netherlands). Her research interests are: culture and complexity, and (e)learning in the business field.

**Sunil Choenni** is Associate Professor Information Systems at Universiteit Nyenrode, and at the computer science department of Universiteit Twente, both in the Netherlands. He holds an MSc in Theoretical Computer Science from Delft University of Technology and a PhD in Database Design from Universiteit Twente. Prior to his position at Nyenrode, he was a principal scientist at the National Aerospace Laboratory (NLR) in the Netherlands.

**Stefan van Diessen** is application researcher for new technologies at Akzo Nobel Car Refinishes and has completed his Masters degree in Management at Nyenrode University, researching knowledge management and knowledge creation ability in Akzo Nobel coatings R&D context. He also holds a MSc in mechanical engineering from Eindhoven University of Technology and has been active in coatings Research throughout his professional career.

**Virginia Dignum** studied Mathematics and Computer Science at both the University of Lisbon and the Free University of Amsterdam. Currently, she works at the Intelligent Systems Group of the Institute of Information and Computing Sciences at the University of Utrecht, where she obtained her PhD. Her professional experience includes consultancy and development of knowledge and information systems. Her research focuses on the role of knowledge in organisations, and the applicability of the agent paradigm to knowledge creation, sharing and representation.

**Machiel Emmering** received a Bachelor's degree in Economics, and a Master's in Business Administration. The contribution in this book is drawn from his current work, based on his Ph.D. (Nyenrode University), dealing with organizational learning. His interests include philosophy and complexity theories, of which cybernetics, cognition, and evolution are the main perspectives for the research.

**Madelon Evers's** PhD research focused on developing practical methods to facilitate collective learning processes in multidisciplinary design teams working in large organizations (Nyenrode University). Madelon did a BA in Literature & Theater at University of Toronto and obtained an MA in Film & New Media studies from the University of Amsterdam. She has worked as a designer and producer in theater, film, TV, and multimedia. She set up an educational design consultancy firm, Human Shareware, in 1995, where she currently works.

**Robin Gommers** obtained a Master Degree in Management at the Nyenrode University. Previously he studied Industrial Engineering and is at this moment working as a business consultant for the PDM-Group. He focuses on change processes within industries in a bio-technological and chemical context.

**Martin Groen** was researcher at Notion on an endowment from Achmea. He graduated in Cognitive Psychology and Artificial Intelligence at the University of Amsterdam. Before starting his research career, he worked as a computer network consultant. In 1998 he started a Masters course in Information Management at the University of Amsterdam. His research interests are in coordination, mental representation and learning. His current research concerns recognition of goals of dialogue partners, more specifically between (potential) customers and representatives from the organisation, preparing for a PhD.

**Saskia Harkema** obtained her PhD at Nyenrode University.  She worked for several years as marketing manager and project manager She has a special interest in intercultural management, after several years' work as consultant in that field, and as a result of her upbringing in South America. She received her Masters in Sociology in 1987 at Universiteit van Tilburg and Amsterdam, a Bachelors degree in Law at the Universiteit van Tilburg in 1987 and a Masters in Business Administration from the University of Bradford in 1998. Her research focuses on innovation and knowledge management, with a special interest in complexity theory. She works on the faculty of the Haagse Hogeschool and the University of Utrecht.

**Hanneke Koopmans** graduated in educational sciences from the Free University of Amsterdam. She has worked for a number of years at NOTION, Nyenrode University, on the topic of workplace learning and self organised learning. She did most of her research on the case of Achmea and worked there in the Management Development group. She is currently finalising her PhD.

**Pieter van Eeden** studied social psychology and philosophical aesthetics at the University of Amsterdam. As knowledge officer for Achmea he was tutor and mentor of a group of PhD researchers, specializing in a variety of knowledge management areas, also at Achmea. Pieter van Eeden is professor at the University of Amsterdam and the HKU Utrecht school of Arts. His professional expertise includes consultancy, marketing research and group decision support systems. Pieter van Eeden is owns a research company, Cadre bv, based in Amsterdam.

**Erwin van Geenen** (1971) received an M.A. (cum laude) in International Relations and Economics from the School of Advanced International Studies (SAIS) of the Johns Hopkins University, Washington, D.C., US, and an M.A. (cum laude) in Cognitive Science from the University of Nijmegen, the Netherlands. He got his PhD from Nyenrode University. He has been affiliated with the Matsushita Institute of Government and Management, Chigasaki, Japan (1995) and the Institute of Southeast Asian Studies (ISEAS) in Singapore (1996). From 1998 to 2000 van Geenen worked at the Dutch Department of Economic Affairs as a policy advisor. Currently he is special advisor to the Board of the University Medical Centre of Utrecht.

**Hans van Leijen** researched the role of organizational learning in business process change and integration. Besides conducting research at Nyenrode, Hans worked for Achmea, a Dutch financial services provider and part of Eureko, as a consultant in business integration projects. Previously he was an IT consultant in the area of knowledge-based systems for risk assessment in the financial services industry. He received his Master's degree in Cognitive Artificial Intelligence from Universiteit Utrecht. He is currently working as consultant for McKinsey.

**Richard Walker** did his PhD at Nyenrode University, the Netherlands, concentrating on the potential of virtual learning. He was sponsored by Microsoft to work as a researcher and course designer within Notion, the Nyenrode Institute for Knowledge Management and Virtual Education. He worked in many educational projects around the world, after obtaining his Masters in History from Oxford University. He is currently undertaking research on virtual learner-centred solutions for competency-based management education at the University of York (UK).

# INTRODUCTION

Over the last few years, both knowledge management and management learning (including e-learning) have received sufficient coverage in publications. I am glad to refer, amongst others, to my own publications with Gert Van der Linden: The Hybrid Business School: developing knowledge management through management learning (Prentice Hall, 2000); and Virtual Corporate Universities: a matrix of knowledge and learning for the new digital dawn (Kluwer Academic, 2003). However, most books/articles are often based on one prevailing focus (be it human resources, IT, strategy, evaluation of intellectual assets), and most of them, if not all, based on a very rational, mechanistic view of knowledge management. Practice, on the other hand, has taught us that knowledge management and learning are highly holistic concepts, difficult to grasp in any particular subfield, emergent, constantly changing. Measurement and rationalisation have lead to a very technology driven development of knowledge management that in practice (in companies) has often failed.

Therefore, there is a need for research and publications embracing that holistic focus on knowledge management, covering a wide range of interesting areas (ranging from learning in the workplace to knowledge infrastructure, via e-learning, knowledge representation, innovation and learning, knowledge culture and learning, knowledge technologies, etc).

With that aim, a number of companies (Philips, SaraLee/DE, Achmea, Atos/Origin and Microsoft) have sponsored a research team, under my direction, for a period of five years, in order to explore new approaches in knowledge management and learning which have practical relevance. The companies shared a common interest: how can we avoid reinventing the wheel every day, and how can we learn faster from past experience in order to avoid repetitive error? The immediate field of action was very often the improvement of innovation management.

The paradigm chosen for these research projects, in order to realise that holistic view required, is the complexity paradigm: dynamic and non-linear systems behaviour. NOTION (The Nyenrode Institute for Knowledge

Management and Virtual Education), and in particular myself, have hosted and tutored these projects. The outcome is a number of new and promising, practically relevant approaches to knowledge management and learning, researched in real life companies. Most of them are not yet researched on at all, and jointly they cover the broad range of knowledge management, as it is seldom dealt with in a knowledge management book. That is the particular contribution of this book. It defines the knowledge management field much more broadly than has been done before, and it immediately gives relevant and workable approaches. Therefore I am happy to be able to make the claim that knowledge management is not just another hype, as some have suggested, but if defined with enough breadth, it is a vision of management that applies to the knowledge based company.

Now that NOTION is about to deliver its lessons, in the form of a number of PhD theses, it is interesting to report the NOTION experience in a book, available on the market. From the outset of this program, the aim was to explore the boundaries of current practice in knowledge management and management learning, mainly from a dynamic systems angle (complexity). NOTION did not have a clean and nicely preset research agenda. Rather, the researchers themselves, in dialogue with the tutor, shaped their own PhD. The least one can say is that the research undertaken was emergent in nature; so is the field of knowledge management. NOTION indeed became an interdisciplinary research group, where theory of different scientific fields is brought together with the perspective of improving business.

In fact, this book suggests an interesting and challenging research agenda for knowledge management in the years to come, without neglecting to deliver usable solutions for real life problems right away.

After an extended introduction and theoretical framework, different researchers contribute to a further deepening of a series of sub themes in knowledge management. Those contributions focus both on the theoretical framework and the practical consequences, and in doing so, suggest many lessons learned which will be of use in practice.

The introductory theory and framework for the different projects is compiled out of a number of my earlier books:

- Bob Galliers and Walter Baets, Information Technology and Organizational Transformation, Wiley , 1998
- Walter Baets, Organizational learning and Knowledge technologies in a dynamic environment, Kluwer Academic, 1998
- Walter Baets, A collection of essays on complexity and management, World Scientific, 1999
- Walter Baets and Gert Van der Linden, The Hybrid Business School: developing knowledge management through management learning, Prentice Hall 2000
- Walter Baets, Wie orde zaait zal chaos oogsten (Dutch version, The one who sows order harvests chaos), Van Gorcum, 2002
- Walter Baets and Gert Van der Linden, Virtual Corporate Universities: a matrix of knowledge and learning for the new digital dawn

*Complexity: an emergent organizational paradigm in the knowledge based economy* gives a general introduction to the theory and paradigm on which this book is based. A logical follow up is *The epistemology of knowledge* in which the necessary epistemological choices are discussed. *The complexity paradigm for a networked economy* is a detailed description of complexity theory. The introductory chapters conclude with *Knowledge Management and Management Learning: what technology still can do*, in which I give an account of what I think is interesting in knowledge management and virtual learning today. It is the somewhat more knowledge technology oriented continuation of the earlier chapters.

Three more chapters have a more general nature, dealing with aspects of knowledge management, rather than with applications. *Supporting technologies for Knowledge Management* (Sunil Choenni, Henk Ernst Blok, and Robert de Laat) deals in detail with the technological side of knowledge management. *Learning and interacting via ICT tools for the benefit of Knowledge Management* (Sunil Choenni, Saskia Harkema, Robin Bakker) reports particularly on the use of agent-based simulations as a visualisation of emergent systems behaviour, for the very simple reason that these technologies are applied in later chapters. Finally, *Seducing, engaging and supporting communities at Achmea* (Virginia Dignum and Pieter van Eeden) gives a first corporate account of how they understand knowledge management.

The second part of the book deals with application domains.

## Part 2: Application domains

A first set of three chapters describes more learning-related projects. *Virtual learner-centred solutions for management education and training* (Richard Walker) investigates the do's and don'ts of virtual learning based on real life cases. This chapter suggests an approach, relevant for corporate universities alike, for developing workable virtual learning applications: applications that support students in their learning. In *A symbiosis of learning and work practice* (Hanneke Koopmans) the often neglected concepts of workplace learning is studied and based on a real life project, suggestions are made how to integrate learning and working for the improvement of both. *Facilitating learning from design* (Madelon Evers) explores the phenomenon of, and suggests a methodologyfor, the use of design teams (for information systems) for group learning. Too often, the knowledge that is created during design gets lost for the company.

*Cultural complexity: a new epistemological perspective* (Marie Joelle Browaeys and Walter Baets) gives a fresh insight into culture and complexity. In general, culture is considered as a static phenomenon and it would be enough to understand the other's culture in order to deal with it. In practice this does not really seem to be reality. Culture (be it national or corporate culture) is an emergent and constructed concept that is highly dynamic and non-linear.

The remaining chapters all deal with a specific aspect of knowledge management. *Dialogues are the bread and butter of the organisation's knowledge exchange* (Martin Groen) investigates the role of language in the creation of possible common ground between company and client. This chapter is highly relevant for people interested in e.g. knowledge creation and management in call centers. It equally gives a fresh insight into the potential (and limitations) of CRM. *The influence of knowledge structures on the usability of knowledge systems* (Erwin van Geenen) attempts to give insight into the qualities required for knowledge systems, in order to improve the usability. It reports on different knowledge representations, both symbolic and sub-symbolic (neural networks). *The role of contextuality in process standardization* (Hans van Leijen) investigates the difficulty in mergers and acquisition of standardizing the different processes. Based on the prime importance of the context, it is suggested that the first step should be to merge the knowledge infrastructures (infrastructure understood as systems, content and context) before embarking on process integration. This chapter opens doors to an improved understanding of the difficulties of BPR.

A last group of three chapters studies the contribution of knowledge management to innovation (management) in companies. *Emergent learning processes in innovation projects* (Saskia Harkema) uses the knowledge and learning model developed in the first chapters of this book and applies it to innovation management. Having redefined innovation as learning, agent based simulations are used in order to illustrate innovation as an emergent learning process, thus suggesting key success and failure factors for innovation. *The dynamics of learning and innovation* (Machiel Emmering) continue that line of thinking but generalise it a bit more. This chapter suggests an adapted vocabulary, or 'context', for innovation to flourish in a company. Suggestions are made on how corporate innovation repositories might be of help in capitalizing faster on learning from innovation projects. *Knowledge Management at Akzo Nobel Car Refinishes R&D – Improving the Knowledge Creation Ability* (Robin Gommers and Stefan van Diessen) is a theoretically-sound case study of the contribution of knowledge management to the improvement of innovative power in a division of Akzo Nobel.

This exceptional range of contributions, all within the same, and explained in detail, paradigm, make this book valuable for both academic and practical use. One the one hand there is the academic, teaching in the field of knowledge management and management learning, in search of a book covering the broad range of aspects that have to do with knowledge management. Though it is not really meant to be a handbook, it could be used as course support material, where the different chapters each cover a relevant area. Alternatively, the book can be used as a second source.

On the other hand, and given that all projects are undertaken in close cooperation with business and therefore are based on a business agenda, the chapters cover all knowledge management applications that matter to business. The book illustrates why and how knowledge management is important for companies. The hype is over but the corporate need is still there. Corporate readers will not only appreciate the wide range of embedded projects covered, they will also gain insight into the how's and why's of the proposed approaches, which makes them transferable to different situations.

Where to go from here?

In the mean time I moved to the South of France where I am currently Director of Graduate Programs at Euromed Marseille – Ecole de Management and coordinator of a research centre: E$^c$KM, the Euromed center for Knowledge Management. The research agenda of this centre has been developed in my "habilitation thesis" (HDR – Habilitation à la direction des recherches; mandatory in order to be allowed to have PhD students in France). The thesis was entitled: « Une Interprétation *Quantique* des Processus Organisationnels d'Innovation » and part of it will be published in 2005 by Routledge under the title « Complexity, learning and organisations: the quantum structure of business ». In that thesis I suggest a somewhat radical rethinking of managerial theory, replacing our strictly causal approach (from cause to effect) by a more synchronic approach (occurring together in time). Chains and hierarchies are replaced by interacting individuals in networks. Behaviour is not managed, but emerges. It really opens the perspective up on different understanding of management, in which the triangule "knowledge, learning and innovation" only becomes more important. There is, of course, too much to summarize here, but it is this theoretical development that has enriched my research agenda for what is currently the EcKM research agenda.

Without being limiting, the topics that are going to get my attention in the decade to come are the following:

- Is there something like a quantum structure existing in management and what would be its structure (what is e.g. the role of consciousness, synchronicity, emergence and morphogenetic fields, etc.)?
- Can we show empiric evidence for the emergent character of management concepts, and in particular for knowledge management and innovation?
- Are Complex Adaptive Systems capable of visualizing emergence and synchronicity?
- Can we improve our understanding of the crucial role that knowledge management, learning and innovation play in a company, and by answering the previous questions, can we make these concepts more

applicable and usable for companies? My research interest was and still is mainly focused on the triangle "knowledge, learning and innovation". I am convinced that the difference in management is made by the adequate understanding and use of this triangle. In my opinion, this importance is only increasing.

I hope I will be able to report you more exciting research findings in the years to come. For the time being, I wish you lots of learning and pleasure with this book.

Other than the sponsors and researchers who have contributed substantially to the success of this book, I like to thank specially Karen Ray and Claude Spano for helping in the preparation of the final version.

Walter Baets
Aubagne, December 24, 2004

# 1.  COMPLEXITY: AN EMERGENT ORGANISATIONAL PARADIGM IN THE KNOWLEDGE BASED ECONOMY

## 1.1  Introduction

A lot has been said and written about knowledge management, probably starting with the proponents of the learning organization on the one hand, and Nonaka's view of knowledge management on the other hand. Increasingly, authors have added the subject to their vocabulary and the more that the 'general management thinkers' have got involved (Leonard-Barton, Drucker, etc.) the more knowledge management has acquired the status of a major buzzword. In the 1999 European Conference on Information Systems (Copenhagen) the 'best research paper award' was given to a paper that argued that knowledge management would be the next hype to forget people (Swan et al., 1999). This choice appeared to me to represent a public act of masochism on behalf of the IS community, given that IS experts, more than any other people, should have a clear idea of why knowledge management is here to stay.

This chapter attempts to provide a broad framework for the subject, highlighting the different aspects (including the human ones) which should be considered when talking about knowledge management. This 'taxonomy in brief' is of course based on a particular paradigm (as any other taxonomy) that is known as the complexity paradigm. Looking through the lenses of complexity theory, we can see why knowledge management is a new and fundamental corporate activity. Complexity theory allows us to understand why knowledge is a corporate asset and why and how it should be managed. The lenses of complexity theory allow us to say that knowledge management is not just another activity of importance for a company.

A number of knowledge management projects, based on this taxonomy, were researched over the last 5 years within Notion (The Nyenrode Institute for Knowledge Management and Virtual Education), a research center fully sponsored by Achmea (second largest Dutch insurance holding; the fifth largest within its European network), Atos/Origin, Philips, Sara Lee/DE and Microsoft. Full details of those research projects can be found in Baets (2004a).

This chapter attempts to present the complete picture of KM, starting with the paradigm, covering the infrastructure and process, with the aim of clarifying the subject of study. Both the corporate and the academic perspectives appear in this paper.

## 1.2     The knowledge era

An important and remarkable evolution in what we still call today the industrial world is that it is no longer industrial. We witness a rapid transition from an industrial society into a knowledge society. The knowledge society is based on the growing importance of knowledge as the so-called fourth production factor. Many products and certainly all services have a high research and development cost, whereas the production cost itself is rather low. Developing and launching a new operating system like Windows costs a huge amount of investment for Microsoft, which makes the first copy very expensive, but any further copies have a very low production cost. Having a number of consultants working for a company is a large investment for a consulting company, so when they are actively working on a project, their marginal cost is close to zero. Having the knowledge base, which means having the consultants available, is expensive. Their real work for a client is relatively cheaper. Even the best example of industrial production in the Western part of the world, which is car manufacturing, became increasingly knowledge based. More than 40% of the cost price of a car is due to research, development and marketing.

We still talk about the industrialized countries, since most of our thinking is still based on concepts of industrial production dating back to the earlier parts of the previous century (the 20th, if not even the end of the 19th century). What we have observed, though, is that increasingly companies get involved in optimizing supply chains and that those supply chains evolve into demand and supply chains. The following step consists of supporting those chains with information technology (IT) in order to increase efficiency. The strange thing that happens next is that a progressive use of IT puts pressure on the existence of the chain itself. The better a chain is integrated based on IT, the more pressure is created which makes the chain explode into a network. Particularly in such circumstances, the 'owner' of the knowledge base manages the process. Network structures evolve around knowledge centers. Companies manage brands and outsource most of the chain itself. Extreme examples of this approach are probably Calvin Klein, Benetton and Nike. Again, knowledge and particularly the capacity to manage, create and share knowledge is becoming the center of the scope of the successful company. This can be translated via brand management, direct marketing to targeted clients, etc. but it is the visual part of the evolution from an industrial market into a knowledge based market. Knowledge becomes yet another attribute of the changing economic reality.

Knowledge in a company takes different forms and, most commonly, one regroups these forms into three categories of knowledge. Tacit knowledge is mainly based on lived experiences while explicit knowledge refers to the rules and procedures that a company follows. Cultural knowledge then is the environment in which the company and the individual (within the company) operate.

Different forms of knowledge are crafted by various different activities. Conversion of knowledge takes place based on the tacit and explicit knowledge that a person possesses or has access to. The creation of knowledge very often takes place during joint work sessions, such as brainstorms, management meetings, etc. Equally important, but more difficult to capture, is knowledge processing via assimilation. Very often, assimilation is based on cultural knowledge as a first input, reinforced with tacit knowledge that quite often collapses with explicit rules and regulations. It seems important to stress, however, that knowledge management is only the 'sufficient' condition. The 'necessary' condition in order to deal with new economic realities is the boundary condition for knowledge management and that is the learning culture of the company. On top of the mere fact that the most interesting knowledge is implicit and therefore 'stored' in people, it is the dynamics of the knowledge creation and sharing activity (for simplicity let us call this 'learning) where the people appear in the picture for a second time.

Above all, knowledge management and learning is an attitude and a way of working with management. It is an overall approach that goes beyond the addition of a number of functional tactics. One could even say that it is a kind of philosophy of management, rather than a science. This process is one of redefining the target of the company from a profit making or share-value increasing entity to a knowledge-creating and sharing unit. The first type of organization has a rather short-term focus, whereas the latter has a more visionary and long-term one.

The aim of the company is no longer purely growth as such, but rather it becomes sustainable development and renewal. Hence, organizations not only need knowledge, they also need the skills and competence to dynamically update and put knowledge into practice. This results in the need for organizations to learn continuously and to look for ongoing improvement in their actions through acquired knowledge. Hence, organizations should embrace the philosophy of learning organizations, the process being organizational learning (Baets, 1998).

A learning organization enables each of its members to continually learn and helps to generate new ideas and thinking. By this process, organizations keep on learning from their own and others' experience, adapt and improve their efficiency towards the achievement of their goal. In a way, learning organizations aim to convert themselves into "knowledge-based" organizations by creating, acquiring and transferring knowledge so as to improve their planning and actions.

In order to build a learning organization, or a corporate learning culture, companies should be skilled at systematic problem solving, learning from their own experience, learning from the experiences of others, processing knowledge quickly and efficiently through the organization and experimenting with new approaches. Developments in information and knowledge technologies make it increasingly possible to achieve these competitive needs and skills.

## 1.3      The complexity paradigm

In the past, when market change slowed down, we got used to thinking in terms of reasonably linear behavior as markets and industries appeared to be more stable or mature. Concretely, people thought they could easily forecast future behavior based on past observations and, in many respects, we developed complex (and sometimes complicated) methods to extrapolate linear trends (Prigogine and Stengers, 1988; Nicolis and Prigogine, 1989). But in reality, markets did not and still do not behave in a predictable way. The future is not a simple extrapolation of the past. A given action can lead to several possible outcomes ("futures"), some of which are disproportionate in size to the action itself. The "whole" is therefore not equal to the sum of the "parts". This contrasting perspective evolved from complexity and chaos theory. Complexity theory challenges traditional management assumptions by embracing the non-linear and dynamic behavior of systems, and by noting that human activity allows for the possibility of emergent behavior (Maturana and Varela, 1984). Emergence can be defined as the overall system behavior that stems from the interaction of many participants - behavior that cannot be predicted or even "envisioned" from the knowledge of what each component of a system does. Organizations, for example, often experience change processes as emergent behavior. Complexity theory also tells corporate executives that beyond a certain point, increased knowledge of complex, dynamic systems does little to improve the ability to extend the horizon of predictability for those systems. No matter how much one knows about the weather, no matter how powerful the computers, specific long-range predictions are not possible. Knowing is important, not predicting, thus there is no certainty (Stewart, 1989; Cohen and Stewart, 1994).

The focus on non-linear behavior of markets collides with the traditional positivist and Cartesian view of the world. That positivist perspective translated in the traditional management literature - the stuff is taught in most MBAs - describes "*the*" world in terms of variables and matrices, and within a certain system of coordinates. Exact and objective numbers are needed in order to create models while simulations can offer a 'correct' picture of what to expect. Particularly business schools have welcomed this 'scientific' way of dealing with management problems as the one which could bring business schools up to the "scientific" level of the hard sciences (mathematics, physics, etc.). It is clear that much of the existing management practice, theory, and "remedies" based on the positivist view are limited by their dependence on several inappropriate assumptions as they don't reflect business and market behavior. Linear and static methods are the ones that are taught in business schools. Therefore, markets have to be linear and static. As we know, they are not (Arthur, 1990).

It seems important to elaborate a little more on positivist thinking as, later on, we want to propose a different paradigm.

A major aspect of positivism is the division between object and subject. This means that the outer world (e.g. an industry) is pre-given, ready to be "truthfully" represented by organizations and individuals. The mind is able to create an inner representation that corresponds to the outer world, be it an object, event or state. Translated to knowledge, positivism considers that knowledge exists independent of the human being that uses it, learns it, transfers it. Knowledge reflects and represents "the world in itself" and can be built up independent of the observer, the "knower". What if the universal knowledge that is transferred is mainly a theoretical framework, a form which is of little use in the non-linear and dynamic markets?

Another premise of positivist thinking is based on a strict belief in (absolute) causality and (environmental) determinism. As there exist clear-cut connections between cause and effect, managerial actions lead to predictable outcomes and, thus, to control. Successful systems are driven by negative feedback processes toward predictable states of adaptation to the environment. The dynamics of success are therefore assumed to be a tendency towards stability, regularity, and predictability. The classic approach to strategy illustrates this reductionism. The complexities of industries are reduced in terms of maturity, continuity and stability so that a single prediction of an organization's future path can be described. As a consequence, the better the environmental analysis according to a number of dimensions, the better the course (strategy) can be defined and implemented (Baets and Van der Linden, 2000, 2003).

My own research over the last years, and currently undertaken in the $E^cKM$, suggests that instead of searching for causality, the concept of synchronicity (being together in time), often referred to as a quantumstructure, allows much more insight in business dynamics (Baets, 2004b). Indeed that quantumstructure is a holistic concept of management, based on interacting "agents". Those networks of agents/people create emergent behavior and knowledge.

Positivism is the prevailing scientific view in the Western world, since it perfectly coincides with the Cartesian view of the world: the over-riding power of man as a fact of nature. Nature gives man the power to master nature, according to laws of nature. In 1903 however, Poincaré, a French mathematician, introduced some doubt in this positivist view. Without really being able to prove, or even to gather evidence, he warned:

"Sometimes small differences in the initial conditions generate very large differences in the final phenomena. A slight error in the former could produce a tremendous error in the latter. Prediction becomes impossible; we have accidental phenomena."

It suggested that with the approaches used, Man was not always able to control his own systems. Hence, there's a limit to the Cartesian view of the world.

It took quite a number of years until, in 1964, Lorenz showed evidence of the phenomenon. Lorenz, an American meteorologist, was interested in weather forecasting. In order to produce forecasts, he built a simple dynamic non-linear model. Though it only consisted of a few equations and a few variables, it showed "strange" behavior. A dynamic model is one where the value in a given period is a function of the value in the previous period. For example, the value of a particular price in a given period is a function of its value in the previous period. Or, the market share for product A in a given period is a function of the market share in the previous period. In other words, most if not all, economic phenomena are dynamic. Such a dynamic process that continuously changes can only be simulated by a step-by-stop procedure of very small increments. It is an iterative process. Once the value of the previous period is calculated, it is used as an input value for the next period, etc.

A computer allowed Lorenz to show what could happen with non-linear dynamic systems. As is known, he observed that very small differences in starting values caused chaotic behavior after a number of iterations. The observed difference became larger than the signal itself. Hence, the predictive value of the model became zero (Stewart, 1989). Lorenz's observation caused a real paradigm shift in sciences. Lorenz showed what Poincaré suggested, namely that non-linear dynamic systems are highly sensitive to initial conditions. Complex adaptive systems are probabilistic rather than deterministic, and factors such as non-linearity can magnify apparently insignificant differences in initial conditions into huge consequences, meaning that the long term outcomes for complex systems are unknowable. Today we know, thanks to the integration of ideas of the two main scientific revolutions of the last century (relativity and quantum mechanics), that another underlying problem, aggravating the complex structure, is the structure of synchronicity in the "business nature".

Translated to management, this advocates that companies and economies need to be structured to encourage an approach that embraces flux and competition in complex and chaotic contexts rather than a rational one. Mainstream approaches popularized in business texts, however, seldom come to grips with non-linear phenomena. Instead, they tend to model phenomena as if they were linear in order to make them tractable and controllable, and tend to model aggregate behavior as if it is produced by individual entities which all exhibit average behavior.

Positive feedback has been brought into the realm of economics by Brian Arthur (Arthur, 1990), who claims that there are really 2 economies, one that functions on the basis of traditional diminishing returns, and one where increasing returns to scale are evident due to positive feedback. Marshall introduced the concept of diminishing returns as early as 1890. This theory was based on industrial production, where one could choose out of many resources and relatively little knowledge was involved in production. Production then seemed to follow the law of diminishing returns, based on negative feedback in the process and this led to a unique (market) equilibrium. Arthur's second economy includes most knowledge industries. In the knowledge economy, companies should focus on adapting, recognizing patterns, and building webs to amplify positive feedback rather than trying to achieve "optimal" performance. A good example is VHS becoming a market standard, without being technically superior. A snowball effect ensued which made VHS the market standard, even though Betamax offered better technology at a comparable price.

Arthur also specified a number of reasons for increasing returns that particularly fits today's economy. Most products, being highly knowledge intensive, with high up-front costs, network effects, and customer relationships, lead to complex behavior. Let us take the example of Windows. The first copy of Windows is quite expensive due to huge research costs. Microsoft experiences a loss on the first generation. The second and following generations cost very little comparatively, but the revenue per product remains the same. Hence, there is a process of increasing returns.

Two more interesting developments have consequences for our argument. Recent neurobiological research, e.g. by Varela (Maturana and Varela, 1984), has revealed the concept of self-organization and the concept that knowledge is not stored, but rather created each time over and again, based on the neural capacity of the brain. Cognition is enacted, which means that cognition only exists in action and interpretation. This concept of enacted cognition goes fundamentally against the prevailing idea that things are outside and the brain is inside the person. The subject can be considered as the special experience of oneself, as a process in terms of truth. By identifying with objects, the individual leaves the opportunity for the objects to "talk". In other words, subject and object meet in interaction, in hybrid structures. Individuals thus become builders of facts in constructing contents of knowledge which relate to events, occurrences and states. Knowledge is concerned with the way one learns to fix the flow of the world in temporal and spatial terms. Consequently, claims of truth are transposed on objects; the subject is "de-subjectivised". There is not such subdivision between the object and the subject. Cognition is produced by an embodied mind, a mind that is part of a body, sensors and an environment (Baets, 1999; Baets and Van der Linden, 2000).

Research in artificial life gave us the insight that instead of reducing the complex world to simple simulation models, which are never correct, one could equally define some simple rules, which then produce complex behavior (Langton, 1989). This is also a form of self-organization, like the flock of birds that flies south. The first bird is not the leader and does not command the flock. Rather, each bird has a simple rule e.g. to stay 20 cm away from its two neighbors. This simple rule allows us to simulate the complex behavior of a flock of birds.

Probabilistic, non-linear dynamic systems are still considered deterministic. That means that such systems follow rules, even if they are difficult to identify and even if the appearance of the simulated phenomenon suggests complete chaos. The same complex system can produce chaotic or orderly behavior at different times. The change between chaos and order cannot be forecast, nor can the moment in which it takes place, either in magnitude or direction. Complexity and chaos refer to the state of a system and not to what we commonly know as complicated, i.e. something that is difficult to do. The latter depends not on the system, but more on the environment and boundary conditions. Perhaps for a handicapped person, driving a car is more complicated than for an able-bodied person. In general, building a house seems more complicated than sewing a suit, but for some other people building a house would be less complicated than sewing a suit. This depends on the boundary conditions for each individual person.

To formalize the findings of complexity theory in a simplified way, we could state three characteristics. First, complex systems are highly dependent on the initial state. A slight change in the starting situation can have dramatic consequences in a later period of time caused by the dynamic and iterative character of the system. Second, one cannot forecast the future based on the past. Based on the irreversibility of time principle (of Prigogine), one can only make one step ahead at a time, scanning carefully the new starting position. Third, the scaling factor of a non-linear system causes the appearance of "strange attractors", a local minimum or maximum around which a system seems to stay for a certain period of time in quasi equilibrium. The number of attractors cannot be forecasted, neither can it be forecasted when they attract the phenomenon.

There are a myriad of insights we gain from complexity theory and its applications in business and markets for knowledge management (Baets, 1998; Baets and Van der Linden, 2000).

The 'irreversibility of time' theorem suggests that there is no best solution. There are "best" principles from which one can learn, but no best solutions or practices that one could copy. There are even no guaranteed solutions that could be used in most circumstances. This fact deems the need for a different way of organizing the process of knowledge creation and knowledge management.

## 1.4    What should be understood by Knowledge Management: the corporate view

Remember that this chapter attempts to present the complete picture of knowledge management, starting from the paradigm, covering the infrastructure and process, with the aim of clarifying the subject of study. Though the corporate and the academic perspectives are at times a little different, they both appear in figure 1.

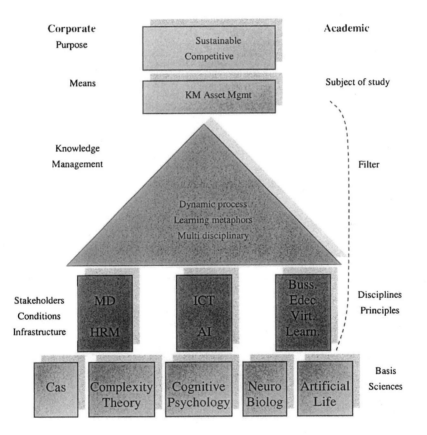

*Figure -1.* A taxonomy of knowledge management

Any managerial concept is based on a particular paradigm and according to the view developed in this paper, the paradigm of complexity (non-linear and dynamic systems behavior) sheds interesting and refreshing light on the nature of knowledge management. Earlier in this chapter we have explained why the complexity paradigm positions knowledge at the center of a knowledge-based company and it does so increasingly with virtual or extended companies.

The left side of the figure shows the corporate logic in understanding knowledge management. The paradigm serves as the glasses through which we look at the corporate purpose (gaining sustainable competitive advantage, or expressed more simply, survival) and what we observe then is the means to achieve the purpose, i.e. asset management. The chosen glasses allow identification of (observation) the way ahead in reaching the goal. The immediate 'next' step is the 'infrastructure' or stakeholders necessary for knowledge management:

Human resources management and management development;
Information and communication technology, in particular artificial intelligence;
Business education and (virtual) learning.

The corporate purpose remains to create sustainable competitive advantage, and the means for realizing that is (and has always been) asset management. However, for knowledge intensive companies this means that knowledge management moves into the picture. A translation (a filter) above and beyond the necessary integration of infrastructure and stakeholders is necessary in order to combine the infrastructure in knowledge management. That filter is a dynamic process, in which the 'learner' should be given responsibility. Pedagogical metaphors give us an insight into this filter process (Baets, 1999).

The prevailing pedagogical metaphor is the transfer metaphor. Knowledge in general and, more specifically, subject matters, are viewed as transferable commodities. A student (a learner) is seen as a vessel positioned alongside a loading dock. 'Knowledge' is poured into the vessel until it is full. Whereas the student is the empty vessel, the teacher is a crane or a forklift. The teacher delivers and places knowledge into the empty vessel. Courses applying the transfer theory would be very much lecture-based, would include talks from leading figures in the relevant fields (the more the better) and would provide students with duplicated course notes. Once the vessel is filled, a 'bill of loading', which is the diploma, certifies the content of the vessel. IT improves the speed of the loading (with high tech cranes). Nobody can guarantee that in the next harbor, the cargo is not taken out of the ship. Monitoring a student means monitoring the process of filling the vessel and sometimes sampling the quality of the contents. This same metaphor became the prevailing one while talking about (virtual) knowledge management approaches (Baets and Van der Linden, 2000; 2003).

However, since knowledge appears to be dynamic and learning non-linear (based on our paradigm), another paradigm is necessary. Here again educational science provides us with a valid illustration. The traveling metaphor is one by which the teacher initiates and guides the students through an unknown terrain that needs to be explored. The student is the explorer and the teacher/tutor is the experienced and expert travelling companion and counselor. The guide not only points out the way, but also provides travelling maps and a compass. The 'teaching methods' (if one can still call them such) which are most used in applying this theory are experiential methods: simulations, projects, exercises with unpredictable outcomes (as in some case studies), discussions and independent learning. In courses applying this theory, monitoring means regularly comparing each other's travelling notes. Experiments have shown that this theory is particularly effective in adult education, since adults are better equipped in order to deal with the increased responsibility that the 'learner' has in this paradigm. One step on from the travelling theory is the growing metaphor. In many respects, this theory does not differ greatly from the previous one. Rather, it is an extension of it, which focuses more on the self-initiative of the student. Subject matters are a set of experiences that each student should incorporate into his/her personality. The aim for the student is to develop his/her personality. This latter paradigm (be it the travelling metaphor or the growing one) perfectly fits complexity theory (our overall paradigm or glasses). It allows us to integrate the infrastructure into asset management. It introduces the rational for work place learning, and the necessary integration of the latter with knowledge management. This makes knowledge management different from and value adding to information management.

## 1.5    Research perspective on Knowledge Management

The combination of infrastructure (with its different stakeholders and/or disciplines) and the learning process (filter) makes knowledge management what it should be. Most existing knowledge management theories either do not get much further than a discussion of means and purposes, or they overstress one of the infrastructural aspects, ignoring the unity and necessity of all the three elements together. In our view, knowledge management, knowledge creation and knowledge sharing (via virtual learning platforms) are integral parts of the same model.

From a research perspective, we consider complexity theory as the basic science(s) involved. In particular the following concepts are of importance for the correct understanding of the paradigm and its consequences for knowledge management:

- Sensitivity of the complex system to initial conditions
- Existence of (many) strange attractors in complex systems
- Irreversibility of time principle (Prigogine)
- Behavior of complex systems far away from equilibrium (Prigogine)
- Learning behavior of systems
- Autopoeisis (Varela)
- Embodied mind (Varela)
- Enacted cognition (Varela)
- Artificial life research and its applications (Langton)
- Law of increasing returns (Arthur)
- Quantumstructure of business

All these aspects need a good explanation and a clear link to managerial consequences is necessary.

As already mentioned earlier, and visualized in figure 1, the disciplines involved in knowledge management are human resources management and management development, ICT and particularly artificial intelligence (AI), and business education, increasingly virtual education. The management development function should be the driver in this knowledge creation, knowledge sharing, learning process, ensuring that each individual receives at the pace that s/he can process. MD should further provide the learning conditions. It is unavoidable that ICT and AI (what I understand as the Complex Adaptive Systems side) are necessary in order to support the knowledge management process (Baets and Venugopal, 1998; Venugopal and Baets, 1995). Building IT platforms, extracting knowledge via AI (the cognitive, neuroscience type of applications) and virtual education are only some of the aspects where IT is of help. Business education, and increasingly this includes virtual education, is responsible for creating some input in the learning process but equally to make some of the extracted knowledge accessible for each individual. Business education in this respect has also to do with the content. The aspect of knowledge sharing is an educational one too. Knowledge management, therefore, needs to successfully integrate disciplines like human resources management, organizational sciences, educational sciences, artificial intelligence and cognitive sciences, etc, implicitly defining a knowledge management research agenda.

It is my firm belief that in the decade to come, we will see a breakthrough in the understanding of the underlying theory justifying the (corporate) necessity for knowledge management, in line with the agenda set out in this chapter. As suggested earlier, the consequence of the concepts developed here and its logical extension is an unavoidable ontological discussion about causality versus synchronicity. In my work (2004b) I call this the quantum structure of business (or in particular, in the reference, of innovation), which provides an integrated and applicable theoretical and conceptual framework in order to understand and consequently manage dynamic processes, knowledge management only being one of them. The first research projects undertaken confirm this potential understanding and its application in business. It is the acceptance of the ontological evidence for synchronicity that drives the research agenda of $E^CKM$.

# 2.    THE EPISTEMOLOGY OF KNOWLEDGE

We often think that philosophers are dealing with philosophical problems. Of course they are. But it is not that simple. In the first place, what are philosophical problems? Are they less existent and real than other problems? Are they of a different nature? As in other social sciences, philosophers thought at a certain moment that in order to be a real philosopher, one should be educated as a philosopher. Hence, are philosophical problems disconnected from reality? In the mean time, philosophy became a discipline in its own right, which has not always been the case in history. Amongst the philosophers, the philosophers of science deal with the conditions under which knowledge can be judged trustworthy. In our daily language, that is what allows us to understand what is right or wrong. Philosophy cannot be seen independent from the aim to discover the final truth, a general understanding of values, and philosophers have oriented themselves towards concepts, rather than to empirical research. Some even pretend that philosophy is searching for knowledge. But many other scientists would doubt that. Both points of view are no doubt correct.

Philosophers of science research something we call epistemologies. An epistemology is a theory, or an attitude about "reality", the sources and limitations of knowledge. It creates a framework that aims to transform intuition into knowledge and in doing so, it creates expressions that are generally true. There is, however, a previous stage, in which the philosophers accept what exists and what is necessary in order to be able to develop a theory. Within the framework of science, we call that ontology: that is, a theory of the things that need to exist, or the conditions that need to be fulfilled, in order for the theory to be proven, to be true. Maybe these definitions are somewhat difficult, but they are also very important for the researcher or the manager who is interested in working with science or comprehension.

Why do we need to be interested in the questions of the philosophers of science, or more generally, why should we be interested in philosophical issues? Because what we accept as true in the beginning has an important impact on what we perceive and on the research for truth and knowledge afterwards. If we believe that the world is the centre of the universe, we are going to research "knowing" that all the planets circle around the earth.

In general, we will even find evidence that confirms our (wrong) hypothesis (what we could call a research hypothesis). Hence, the starting point of our investigation has an important impact on what we can find. If we are searching for something under the light of a lamp, since we can see something, but what we are looking for was lost elsewhere, then we should not be surprised not to find it. Now before we say too fast "that is evident", I would like to draw the reader's attention to the fact that this is precisely what we often do in scientific research.

For instance, we believe that a promotional campaign has an influence on the buying behavior of people, and indeed we find a strong correlation. Other variables that we find less interesting are of course not present in our equations, and therefore cannot show any effect. There is nothing wrong with that if we do not claim that the research "proves" in a scientific (and therefore correct) manner that there would be a positive correlation between campaign and sales results. The only thing one can say is that these results are correct for this particular study, and given the problem as it was defined (in the absence of certain possible variables). It would be a mistake to extrapolate this particular study to a theory that would claim general validity. A researcher researches a specific problem in a scientific way and is afterwards extrapolating it into a general theory. Reducing a problem to something smaller and easier to study is not an error, but then it becomes impossible to draw more general conclusions.

Let us use the metaphor of colored spectacles. If we look at the world through rose-tinted glasses, the world will appear to be rose. That is what we really observe. But of course, it is not reality. A blue pair of glasses would give the idea and also the observation that the world is blue. And that is not correct either. Philosophers of science are interested in the correct representation of the world, but also each manager is in search for a correct representation of the behavior of markets.

The metaphor of the glasses shows that the choice made when starting research determine what we see and find in the research. Each person has, through their education, their schooling and their culture, a vision about how to research and, more widely, about what truth would be.

What are the different views on science and how do they influence our thinking and observation? The last one, the way we observe, is indeed even more important for us. How do philosophical choices have an impact on how to undertake research, what we call the methodological consequences? How do the choices determine the way of observing, for instance, the company or its management processes?

In this chapter we are not going to simply explore philosophy of science. Many books have been published on that subject. Rather, it is important to position oneself in the ideas of the major schools of thought, within a certain social context and with a particular social aim. I would say that it attempts to reinforce the importance of philosophy of science for social systems and, in particular, in order to improve management.

Any person and a manager per se, are developing an image of science that fits the temporal and geographical context. Does it make sense to talk about an "Islamic way of doing research", as some books suggest? The scientists of Medieval times certainly had a different view of science than we have today. Science without any context, as one could say "ins blaue hinein" doesn't make a lot of sense, and in practice is impossible. With a contextual embedding of research we are assuring a kind of thinking, an intellectual reference framework which will allow us to judge the truth value of any new research (or its application). Just as philosophy in general, philosophy of science is embedded in the current sociology of its society and in the history of that same society. The different view of science in Medieval times as compared to today illustrates this clearly. Another illustration is the attitude of the pharmaceutical researcher working for a pharmacy giant like SGM, compared to the researcher working for the WHO. The Ayurvedic medical approach (a classical Indian medical approach), is different in diagnosis, focus (it is holistic) and therapy from what we consider in the Western world as medical treatment. These different starting points cause a different attitude and a different treatment.

Different images of science often remain very under-exposed, or worse still, many people are not even aware of those differences. Therefore it is very difficult to compare different research, since it could have been undertaken within different reference frameworks that might be sometimes radically different.

In this chapter, I would like to give an overview of different philosophical schools that, being within a particular historical framework, generate different images of science: I have labeled that a taxonomy. Within this context, taxonomy is nothing more than an overview of different ideas, but a bit broader than what is often found in literature.

Let us start with an overview of what is known as what we classically consider the philosophy of science. Afterwards, we will take a look into theories that originate somewhat from architecture and the arts and that have gradually entered the area of research methodologies that we often label Post-modern. We will investigate what neurobiologists have researched concerning cognition and the functioning of the mind. A last source of input is the developments in artificial intelligence and their contribution to the understanding of thinking and learning. Working with "learning" artificial intelligence one is rapidly confronted with the fundamentals of what thinking and truth are.

As learning individual, and not limited to researchers, we cannot avoid what I would like to call the dilemma of the researcher. If you have the feeling we go too deeply into academic research, it is enough to replace researcher by "searcher" or even "learner". What is this dilemma of the researcher?

A researcher needs to work in harmony with the environment, the context, such as it is known to the researcher, and such as it appears to be in society. The researcher is part of a socializing process (within a network of peers), within social, intellectual and political traditions, values and norms. In order for the researcher to have his research validated afterwards, s/he has to work within a prevailing context that allows such eventual validation (by his peers). "Validation" is a protected word that already presumes a certain conception of, and choice within, science. Let us for the time being use the word visualization, instead of validation. In order to validate his research, the researcher is confronted with a dilemma that forces him to make choices. This does not need to be wrong, or even very important, provided the researcher is aware. The "pair of glasses" we put on, the choices that we make, will determine what we are able to see and hence what we are going to find as a result of our research.

Let us detail these problematic choices. First of all there is what the researcher accepts as ethical. Is the researcher responsible for the possible (mis)use of the results of his research? As a further consequence, is the researcher responsible for human behavior and human dignity?

Can we only research observable behavior of humans, without considering their emotions? To what extent is what is observed due to the reference framework of the researcher? The political context within which the researcher operates also forces the researcher to make choices. Unfortunately lots of examples exist where mainly totalitarian regimes use "scientific research" in order to justify inhuman behavior or to glorify the system. What role does a researcher want to play and how does this influence his research results?

Another problematic choice is the relationship with the unforeseeable. To what extent are we able to, and do we want to, exclude this from our research? Is this a problem, or rather an opportunity? Finally, the researcher also has budgetary constraints, or time limitations. Resources are limited and choices need to be made.

All these are problematic choices that play a role in research, but also, consequently, in the results of that research. None of the choices are good or bad, but they all have consequences.

Now let us consider the last dilemma. What epistemological choices does the searcher (and not the re-searcher), the learner, make concerning the subject of truth, the observation, the quantitative nature of things, the possibility to generalize. These are all problematic choices in which there is again no good and bad, but certainly all choices have their impact. Certain scientific ideas are typical for a certain time period. What interests us here is the importance of those choices and their consequences for what is good research and the choice of the adapted research methods. Translated into management, we refer here to how we want to consider management processes if we want to improve them. What do we accept as being the best and how can we measure and compare? Next, the question is how to control those processes, how to manage them, and if possible which variables to influence.

## 2.1    What can we learn from the philosophers of science?

The Philosophy of Science is a discipline (that became independent of its object of study, being the practice of science) that is not very old, though philosophers like Plato or Aristotle, for instance, dealt explicitly with science related problems. Philosophy itself is as old as the world, and scientific investigation has always been very close to philosophy in the past. In the beginning, philosophy was positioned as a "proto-science". When other fields became increasingly important, like astronomy or later psychology, the different domains started to shift away. The next step that each of the (sub) domains made was to develop their own scientific tradition. In general, sciences are a product of philosophical practice. It is interesting to explore when the philosophy of science became a separate discipline and the 'why' and 'how' of that. That is what I would like to explore next.

Before the 17th century, say before Descartes (1596-1650) and Galilei Galileo (1564-1642), the Church, or let us say religion more generally, was the seat of science in the world. In certain parts of the world, this is still the case. Science aimed to justify religion. Just remember the struggle that Galileo had to convince the world that the sun was in the center of our galaxy and that the world rotates around the sun. The opposite idea of the world as the center of our galaxy was comfortable for the Church in order to keep its power, or even worse, to justify it. In that period science dealt with what was commonly accepted.

From the 17th century onwards, Descartes launched a rationalism to a degree that was unknown before: "I think, therefore I am". It was the beginning of modern philosophy: thought itself was defined as the subject of philosophy. Science became increasingly interested in experimentation. It might seem strange to the researcher of the 21st century but the researcher in those days was involved and responsible. He took responsibility for the direction of research he was undertaking, of his involvement and all that was not under discussion. It was accepted that the researcher researches based on his values, his beliefs and his hypothesis. This period is identified by what we know today as a typical Newtonian concept: time and space are fixed, known and absolute. Much later, Einstein caused a revolution showing that time and space are relative, hence no absolute truth exists. What exists is a relationship with a subset of the whole world. In those days an important interest in quantitative research developed. Therefore, Cartesian thinking is often referred to as an approach where everything should be measurable. This more rational approach to science was considered as a reaction against a more metaphysical religious thinking. Often we forget that this metaphysical approach was at least holistic, but more by accident than on purpose. Since we could not yet separate correctly, we considered the whole. Cartesian thinking does not reject the existence of God, but does want to give a more profound backing to metaphysical thinking.

If we can take a bit of distance from the religious goals that were behind research in the pre 17$^{th}$ century time period, we observe the contours of a discussion about science that has been going on until today:

On the one hand we have the researchers who consider reality rather as a holistic concept: only within the whole can a part be studied. All depends on everything and hence one cannot deduct simple causal relationships from a larger whole, without doing injustice to that whole. All kinds of observations, that can be highly subjective, are a valuable input for research.

On the other hand we have researchers who feel that this approach is too metaphysical and too vague. They only believe what you can measure "objectively" and from those observations general laws can be deducted. Even if these laws only represent part of reality, they are still more useful, since generally applicable. This last point is of course argued against by the other group. What does it mean "generally applicable" if one only talks about a little part of a more general truth? For this group of researchers, repetition and control of research is crucial.

Holistic researchers do not argue that one could reduce reality in order to study it. Holism also accepts that a whole is constructed out of many smaller parts, but those smaller parts create, via interaction, more than the sum of the separate parts. According to the holistic thinkers, the problem with reductionism occurs when afterwards conclusions are drawn on larger problems than those particularly studied. They argue against drawing conclusions on a whole, based on studies of parts. There is nothing wrong with a detailed study of the stomach. A stomach can indeed hurt a lot. It is certainly possible to find remedies against a stomach that hurts. The problem appears if one wants to draw conclusions concerning the general health of a patient, based only on the research of the stomach. For instance, it is not automatically true that if the stomach is cured, the person will feel better. This still needs to be observed and proven. A reductionist is going to try and cure the stomach by researching the stomach and immediately around it. A holist will research the entire body and even the outside influencing factors, in search for a disequilibrium that would have come up in the body (the body considered as being a whole). A person is more than the correct operations of all its organs.

As already suggested, the relativity theory of Einstein came as a real breakpoint. It became clear that absolute observation did not exist. It equally became very clear that in order to compare different theories, one should use different methods. Moreover, in 1931 Gödel (1906-1978) proved his theorem that opened, without him really wishing it to, a kind of Pandora's box. According to Gödel, no axiomatic system would ever be able to validate or reject all possible hypotheses. In other words, there would always be a hypothesis about which we could say nothing. Hence, independent of the detail of an axiomatic system, it will never be able to give the full truth.

For mathematicians, this was an important theorem. It took a certain while before the theorem became known and "appreciated" by mathematicians. Though Gödel would probably not be considered as a philosopher of science, his discovery also has an impact in that domain.

In the way Gödel proves his theorem, he uses a concept called self-reference to a remarkable degree: an interesting and powerful concept, but also a dangerous one. A bit simplified, the concept says that every system can and has to create its own reference framework, that is used by all elements of the system referring to each other, with the aim that the system operates more optimally, however inside rather closed boundaries. Only if one is inside the system does this self-referential framework make sense. Those that are outside (say, for example, clients) do not understand the system anymore. We could easily make reference here to corporate culture or language, politicians' language, etc.

Around 1920-30 a philosophical movement existed called logical positivism (the Wiener Kreis). Most of the researcher-members worked in the areas of mathematics, physics and the like. For them the credo was that only what was measurable made sense for science. They based their approach on Descartes rationalism and Bacon and Hume's empiricism. Rationality, clarity, measurability and consistence were the key words. This approach went *ligna recta* against the metaphysical controversy of the previous period. The criterion of verification is central for them. What cannot be verified does not exist for science; it is too speculative. The solution is encompassed in the method. Research should be based on axiomatic systems in concrete, and it should use a language as clear as mathematics. Unfortunately, it was Gödel himself, a member of the Wiener Kreis, who proved the limits of this approach.

For them, scientists made the discoveries and philosophers were there to justify those discoveries. For the first time (probably) we seem to observe a clear cut separation between philosophers and scientists. This empiric and positivist approach of science was dominant until the 60s but in fact continued to be mainstream until today. Under pressure of the rise of Nazi Germany, many of those researchers left Austria and Germany in order to settle in the US. Over there they created what is known as analytical philosophy. Research in the US is still very different (more quantitative and positivist) than what we see in Europe. Certainly in the (applied) social sciences, this difference is very remarkable. But fortunately, also in the US, we have known some dissonant voices, such as for example John Dewey (who we deal with later).

Popper (1902-1994) is no doubt the philosopher (of science) who is most often cited. He continued in that positivist and empirical orientation. Nevertheless, Popper developed his theory as a critique on the Wiener Kreis. Critical rationalism (as we call his school of thought) is as crucial for a theory as the attempts that have been made to reject it. The aim of science is to falsify existing knowledge, which allows science to progress. Only deduction is acceptable. Induction is too vague for him and not scientific.

For Popper there exists no context of discovery. Science is a product in itself, and its quality should be guaranteed. Popper's epistemology does not recognize a knowing subject. His epistemology creates or reinforces the subdivision between object and subject that is predominant in most of our scientific work. Science would be something that is outside of the researcher, just as good management would be something that would be outside the manager. Increasingly we see "alternative" research, however, without questioning whether this is based on a different epistemological choice supporting the research in societal problems.

"Until proven to the contrary" is an expression based on Popper's theory. Empirical value of a theory depends on the possibility of falsification. The more you try to falsify a theory, the more it is valid. Every theory is a theory in progress, waiting to be falsified. From the moment when you can falsify a theory you reduce it to a lesser theory (valid in fewer cases). To keep the validity of a theory you cannot do anything other than scale it down more and more. Simple theories, therefore, survive longer. The search for causality is therefore a consequence, rather than a goal in itself. The search for causality, already known in logical positivism, was strongly supported by Popper.

For Popper, scientific discovery went from the known to the unknown. Every researcher must use the same methods, also in the social sciences. But Popper was also self-critical. The idea that society should be predictable was unacceptable to him. Predestination was for Popper a serious limit to freedom and democracy. He intended a democracy which was as much scientific as it was political.

A number of methodological consequences ensued. The mechanism of deduction is the acceptable approach. Everything is contained within a framework of falsification/verification. Something which is falsified cannot be correct. If you have a counter example, the whole theory is reduced to a simpler theory. For the social sciences, that has serious consequences. You start with hypotheses to test which you try later to falsify, but often rather to validate. In practice, however, you first of all do exploratory research and only at the moment when you know what you can validate do you define the hypotheses. In fact, this on-the-ground approach is a constructive approach. The scientific character of research is just as strong as it is supported by a theory.

Then Kuhn introduced his paradigm theory from a historical perspective. He examined existing theories through the lens of the history of science. According to Kuhn, the sciences are part of the historical context. In fact, he said that science can even be an "act": what type of research is more appropriate in the current political context. Research institutes which are close to political power receive larger grants. In his view, it is not the theory itself which makes the difference, but rather social acceptance of the theory. This takes the form of a comparison. Editors decide if a paper is worthy of the label "scientific". A sufficient number of publications in respected journals and you climb the academic ladder.

For him, the context of discovery and that of justification are not far apart. Methodological rules are never obligatory but they remain the choice. A consequence is that in the different sciences, we use different vocabulary. A truth is therefore only a local truth. It is a known phenomenon in sociology that different groups use the same language differently (compare, for example, the Dutch of Dutch people and Flemish people). This also means that this theory supports a growing diversification of the different sciences. This is not favorable to a holistic approach. The mono-disciplinarian does not exist only in teaching, but also in the world of management.

For Kuhn, scientific groups are more important than paradigms; paradigms are too much a "self-fulfilling prophecy". Since they exist, of course they are correct. Outside normal science, as written earlier, you can get to a degeneration of theories, which eventually leads to a revolutionary epoch in science. Finally Lakatos tries to regain the equilibrium a bit between Popper's and Kuhn's theories. For us they do not provide much else. Lakatos is an advocate of "trial and error" approaches, wherein he is more liberal than Popper.

In fact what we learn is that the scientific method, almost by definition, does not really allow innovation in scientific research. This development can only advance in very limited steps and in fact always in the same direction. All research centers adhere to theories of this school of thinking, often without the least dissonant idea. These theories also led to a specific understanding of what is scientific, which we then tried to extend to management and other public functions (law, politics etc). The difficulty therefore is to marry an innovative approach with something which is nevertheless well-founded and rigorous, always keeping the idea of achieving a goal in mind.

In the social sciences in particular, there were vigorous reactions towards logical positivism. There were principally two types of critical thinking. First of all, there is what we can call pragmatism, or symbolic interaction's, known, among others, by John Dewey. The Frankfurt School, along with the likes of Marcuse, was very oriented towards the responsibility of the researcher and was, in fact, rather socialist inspired.

Pragmatism is opposed to logical positivism, especially with regards to the fact that rationalism supposes a strict subdivision between the subject and the object. In practice, rationalism means that a number of independent observers all observe the same thing, independently of their feelings, experiences, etc. This way you can justify the possibility of doing research which has a general value. But you only need to consider two people seeing the same car accident and how they report this. In general, the two stories are very different. People colour their observations with their feelings, their own experiences etc. In fact, a lot of ideas in science and management are based on this subdivision, which in practice does not seem to hold true.

Among the pragmatics, Mead and Dewey played an important role. In classical science, the relationship between cause and effect is explained by understanding, predictions, and trials. Pragmatics is based on the use of a criterion to decide the subject of the truth. Something is good if you can use it for something. A process of change in a company is good, since it makes the employees happy or procedures more efficient. Pragmatics accepts that there is no research independent of values. Do we really think that Organon is going to put the same effort into finding remedies for diseases in poor countries as in rich ones? There are many treatable diseases, where not enough effort is made. The criterion used is often very straightforward.

According to pragmatics, behavior is often based on rules which hold true in a social context, and which are seen as symbols (for example, wealth or class).

Another form of critique is given by the Frankfurt School ( Adorno, Horkheimer, Marcuse, Habermas) but no doubt they take us too far, and are not exactly appropriate to this book. What is important is that the Frankfurt School follows a rather holistic logic. Once we understand someone's point of view, we can better understand their research. Dialogue and communication are much appreciated research methods for this School. An "action researcher", someone who takes part in the process of research and even in the process of change, must explicitly show his position for everyone to understand his remarks and research results. This School recognises conflict as a mode of functioning: in fact we are speaking about conflict between the real world and the world of theories, or systems. For them, integrity is important.

Doubtless, Western Europe is very, even too, focussed on rationalism and positivism. In so being, they deny themselves the power to advance more innovative research. In general, we only look a little further along the path of what has already been researched. We look for the method, therefore the certitude, so we already want to be sure of finding what we are looking for. It is handy if we look where we have already looked since the results are known. The reviews of academic journals confirm it. This mechanism is not a good support for innovative research. Does research look for the path it is already taking? (Making reference here to Antonio Machado's famous poem: Caminate no hay camino, se hace camino al andar). Is it not chaos and the unknown which create the entropy necessary for discovery instead of "re" - search? Then, notably, we come back to the theory of complexity, which will be very instrumental. Academic research unfortunately has a system of auto-reference: with a common jargon to facilitate the debate which is incomprehensible to outsiders. Is that why companies, more and more, organise their own research, instead of leaning on university research centres? The science of management comes back into conflict with the skill of managing.

Often, the scientific approach is only interesting if it can be labelled "independent" and therefore "objective". That way, scientific choice becomes self evident. There are, therefore, two separate worlds: the holistic world we live in; and the rational world we use if we need authority and, therefore, distance. This schism in our society, even in our thinking, is not entirely without danger. How does holistic Man (given that we cannot change) submit to all that? Human beings are looking for a soul and a consciousness of reality, and since they do not find them, they are going to look for them in external factors of daily life. Unfortunately, these are often rather extremist external factors. We see, on the other hand, a movement in quite a few segments of society towards a more holistic approach, for example, in medicine. Western culture is nevertheless too anchored in positivist thinking to be easily able to change that.

How can we break this vicious circle? A system based on giving and obeying orders is in strong contrast to a system based on self-organisation. "Orders" and "organisation" thinking is based on very positivist ideas. Later on we will look at the fact that self-realisation can only be achieved in self-organisation, both at individual and organisational levels. The strength of an organisation remains nevertheless in the hands of individuals. Without individuals, there is no network of agents. This does not at all mean that organisations would be without value, or that organisations, finally, cannot learn. The strength behind all that, by contrast, is the individual with his drive, his engagement, his conviction, etc.

It is interesting, at this stage, to dive into "Post-modern" theories again.

## 2.2    Post-modernism comes in fact from architecture

Post-modernism appeared in the 50s and 60s in reaction to aesthetic modernism. Before the term was already known but was used more in relation to nihilism, in the style of Nietzsche. As a backlash to modernism in art, Post-modernism is an important movement against this modernism. In the 70s we started to see a movement against architectural modernism. In Post-modern literature there are a lot of details and the lack of a general leitmotif running through books. "A La Recherche du Temps Perdu" (Proust) is not really appreciated by Post-modernists. In the Post-modern novel, what are important are the facts (diverse) and the linking of these facts. All of a sudden an action can come and go. The novels are perhaps even realistic. Louis Paul Boon, known for his realist novels, with the through-line of social injustice induced by the economic system, also takes particular interest in coincidence, sundry facts, etc.

Because modernism is well implanted in our society, Post-modernism is seen in quite a few areas of society. From the 80s, philosophers became interested in Post-modernism. It could be said that the beginning, in France, came by way of the poststructuralists. They reacted against rationalism, utopia and the movement by which everything should be based on a scientific approach. Well-known names are Derrida, Foucault, Deleuze and

Lyotard. The last philosopher we see appearing in books about the philosophy of science, however, is Feyerabend.

He said the practice of science is in strong contrast to the theory. Feyerabend spoke almost exclusively about hard sciences. His argument is that all the important scientific discoveries (Einstein, Galileo, etc) could never have been made if the researchers had followed the laws of science. Feyerabend suggests that if we want to find scientific innovation it has to be organised in a non-conventional manner. In fact, one can see the same thing in companies. Those who attack a new market experimentally are those who are still around (for example, in Russia ten years ago). The survivors were those who dared to follow the un-trodden paths instead of sticking to existing theories (about management). By following the rules of the theoretical game you would never manage, for example, to do business in Russia.

According to Feyerabend, it is rather the non-experts who find new developments, often going against what is generally accepted in contemporary science. If science is to make sense, it is, in fact, rather anarchistic. The only principle which allows progress is that "everything goes". Science, therefore, has to discover, to explore, to go against. This does not mean in any case that it is not necessary to be very precise in a scientific approach. The theories which could survive the longest (such as the sun rotating around the earth) did so due to the fact that people continued to think within the existing scientific rules of the time. For the purposes of this book, we can content ourselves with that. Evidently, to understand the modernist/Post-modernist debate better, it is necessary to look harder at those who oppose such theories.

Translated into a methodological approach, we can see here the more constructivist approaches, such as those defended by Le Moigne. The Post-modern theory, or constructivist theory, can be translated into a scientific approach by what I like to call the sciences of design, or the "active" sciences. So research and development in management become the activities to do with rigour, but they must also be useful for the company which commissions them. Rigour means to be accepted in a framework to be defined (for example, the academic world). Useful means that the result must, in fact, deliver something better than what was known before.

A scientific approach in management therefore has the goal of creating useful things. In practice, that takes us back to an approach of building and improving. So we speak about the paradigm of design. We often see the consequences of changes, improvements, etc, in a very precise situation. Often a number of successive cases are resolved in a step-by-step approach.

In parallel with other sciences complementary developments could be observed. Neuro-psychologists develop ideas around the non-existence of the sub-division between an object and a subject. This evidently has consequences in neurobiological developments. The generally accepted rules of neurobiological colonies seem no longer valid. In physics, the theory of complexity is studied, the behavior of dynamic and non-linear systems. Despite the two recent revolutions, relativity and quantum mechanics, the thinking of physics is always for the most part Newtonian. We always accept that time and space will be a given which is known and which one can manipulate. Researchers like Ilya Prigogine developed a completely different approach. In fact, there is a contradiction "in terminus": it is the rational approaches which illustrate the solid foundations of postmodernism.

The discoveries in neurobiology (that were known as radical constructivism), as well as those in physics give an explanation of the fact that the positivist approaches seem a little artificial in social science. If we try to put together all the observations we have, you could get to a new paradigm, which would allow the manager to act in a more responsible fashion with himself and his immediate environment. How and why should we be "learners" in an environment where, manifestly, order leads to chaos?

A paradigm is nothing but a pair of glasses. According to the pair we put on, we see the world through the colour of the glasses. In our case, we want to be conscious what colour the glasses we put on are. This allows us to better understand, relativize and communicate. The problem is that often people are not even conscious of the fact that they are wearing a pair of glasses. The (scientific) culture is not necessarily a known and conscious context.

An extended taxonomy of the theories of the Philosophy of Science applied to management

In summary, I would like to propose an extended taxonomy of the theories of the philosophy of science, applied to management. The table, based

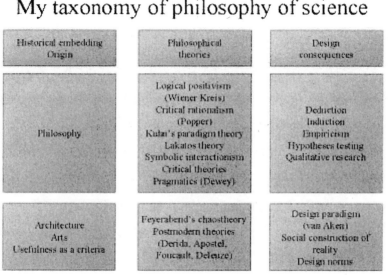

## My taxonomy of philosophy of science

| Historical embedding Origin | Philosophical theories | Design consequences |
|---|---|---|
| Philosophy | Logical positivism (Wiener Kreis) Critical rationalism (Popper) Kuhn's paradigm theory Lakatos theory Symbolic interactionism Critical theories Pragmatics (Dewey) | Deduction Induction Empiricism Hypotheses testing Qualitative research |
| Architecture Arts Usefulness as a criteria | Feyerabend's chaostheory Postmodern theories (Derida, Apostel, Foucault, Deleuze) | Design paradigm (van Aken) Social construction of reality Design norms |

*Figure -2.* My taxomomy of philosophy of science

# My taxonomy of philosophy of science/2

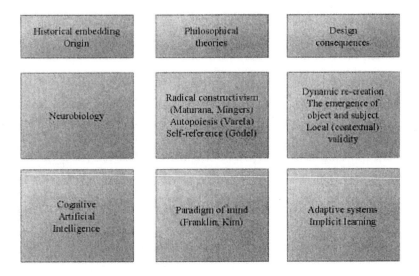

*Figure -3.* My taxomomy of philosophy of science 2

on the previous development, contains some approaches which would not classically be taken up in comparable tables. Perhaps one could call it a multi-disciplinary taxonomy which, in my opinion, would allow us to progress in management research.

The goal is not to proclaim the least validity for this taxonomy. It is nothing more than a representation of the research of the extent of our thinking. I am consciously searching above and beyond what is accepted today.

## 2.3     The widest view: a vision of Man and the holistic world

We have looked at, up until now, a lot of theories thanks to which the reader can perhaps no longer see the wood for the trees. Among other things; they are only a fraction of the ideas which are blossoming in almost all of the sciences and social discussions. In addition, there are numerable religious or esoteric theories, which give the impression of holism, or which do not exist, or have a thousand faces. Is there a common notion of holism? Is there somebody who one day tried to compile all the theories? Perhaps it is evident that one should have all sorts of critiques here. Do not forget that, for me, as long as it progresses things, I am interested.

I willingly make reference here to a concept of Ken Wilber, which is, to my way of thinking, very handy and useable. He visualises something which we could call different dimensions of the image of the holistic world. The figure below gives the compilation in summary of Wilber's concept.

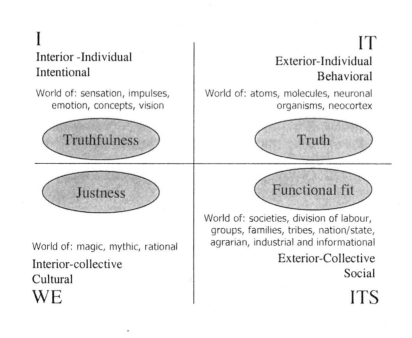

*Figure -4.* Wilber's concept

The quadrants above make reference to the individual level. The quadrants below refer to the collective level. The quadrants on the left have to do with the internalisation of Man (or processes, or things), while the quadrants on the right examine, let us say, the mechanical part (the external). A holistic image is obtained according to Wilber, if all the quadrants receive sufficient attention. He labels these quadrants the 'I' quadrant, the 'we' quadrant, the 'it' quadrant, the 'its' quadrants. All the quadrants have to live to be able to achieve a life, an observation, a research, and whatever other holistic thing.

In the right top quadrant, we study the external phenomena, for example how the brain functions and so we naturally reduce it to very specific parts, like atoms, the classical reductionism. Not completely mistaken, there is a reaction to this partial vision in saying that understanding the functioning of a specific atom does not allow us to understand the functioning of the whole (the consciousness of Man).

What we call, at the heart of science, a global approach, is found in the lower right quadrant; that is nothing more than one of the four dimensions of holism. Here one can think of the systemic approaches (mechanical), of ecological concepts, etc.

If we really want to understand what the brain produces, we can only find that in the left part of the diagram. The brain causes, in Man, emotions, feelings, concepts, etc. and it is those which we use in daily life.

No matter how detailed our understanding of the right part is, it still says nothing about what Man thinks or feels. To get to the dimensions on the left, the classical approaches are insufficient. Communication is the only means to try to understand how people feel and what emotions they go through. In the left part there is also a collective dimension: one could always label it "culture".

That has a rapport with what we accept as a group, the norms and values. So a holistic understanding cannot bypass these internal individual and collective dimensions.

Classical science goes completely in search of the 'truth' (identified top right). More and more we see global approaches of the system in science (systemic): the functional whole. The true notion of Man and his emotions that we call, a little paradoxically, a "flesh and blood" man, while only that does not give us a real understanding of truth and fairness. Here I want particularly to attract attention to the three other quadrants to thus give a more complete understanding than the dominant thinking our western culture allows. My goal is to try a more holistic approach in management research and in the understanding of phenomena.

At the heart of each of the four quadrants, we get once again a natural evolution from physics, via biology, psychology and theology towards mysticism. Translated into the fundamentals, we go from matter, via life, thinking, the soul towards the spirit. This demands a lot more explanation, but there Wilber's book is an absolute must.

While summarising this detailed diagram is not only difficult, it does not give full benefit to this figure either, I would like nevertheless to try. So holism consists of an ensemble of 'I', 'we', 'it' and 'its'. This is quickly recognised in certain metaphors of holism, such as 'Art meets science and spirituality' the "I", "we" and "it" of Wilber. Another saying is that the hands, head and heart lead to holism. This can also be attributed to Wilber.

Though the remainder of this book will primarily introduce the "its" and the "we" quadrant, it remains evident that we cannot avoid asking ourselves the question for the "I" quadrant. Though, arguably, some of the chapters could be positioned in the "it" quadrant, the mainstream of this book aims to go beyond. In fact, the purpose of this book is to give the reader an understanding of knowledge management, and illustrate this with a number of examples, that leads to a more systemic approach of knowledge management. As argued in the previous chapter, the acceptance of holism and complexity (as a paradigm) means that knowledge management does make sense, indeed beyond the hype of the last years. Within this paradigm, knowledge management differs from information management, and really allows a rich understanding and a practical application of knowledge management.

# 3. THE COMPLEXITY PARADIGM FOR A NETWORKED ECONOMY

In previous chapters, we identify why knowledge management continues to be of paramount importance for companies, given that there is always the need to drive change within the context of ever-changing new economic realities. It becomes apparent that managerial complexity not only increases, but also changes. On the one hand, a higher degree of complexity in management and dissipating structures force companies to make fast improvements on a quantitative and qualitative basis. On the other hand, because of swifter change and higher velocity in the world economy, there is often more clarity than ever before. What we observe today, while studying market behaviour, is that we can no longer speak of an objective world where interactions can be described in linear terms, where words have singular meanings, and where prediction and control are paramount.

In the past, we got used to thinking in terms of reasonably linear behaviour as markets and industries appeared to be more stable or mature. This was easily seen when market change moved slower. Concretely, we thought we could easily forecast future behaviour based on past observations and in many respects we developed complex (and sometimes complicated) methods to extrapolate linear trends. But in reality, markets did not, and do not, behave in a linear way. The future is not a simple extrapolation of the past. A given action can lead to several possible outcomes ("futures"), some of which are disproportionate in size to the action itself. The "whole" is therefore not equal to the sum of the "parts". This contrasting perspective evolved from complexity and chaos theory. Complexity theory challenges the traditional management assumptions by embracing the nonlinear and dynamic behavior of systems, and by noting that human activity allows for the possibility of emergent behavior. Emergence can be defined as the overall system behavior that stems from the interaction of many participants - behavior that cannot be predicted or even "envisioned" from the knowledge of what each component of a system does. Organizations, for example, often experience change processes as emergent behavior. Complexity theory also tells corporate executives that beyond a certain point, increased knowledge of complex, dynamic systems does little to improve the ability to extend the horizon of predictability for those systems. No matter how much one knows about the weather, no matter how powerful the computers, specific long-range predictions are not possible.

The focus on nonlinear behavior of markets collides with the traditional positivist and Cartesian view of the world (as described in previous chapter). That positivist perspective translated in the traditional management literature - the stuff that is taught on most MBA programs- describes the world in terms of variables and matrices, and within a certain system of coordinates. Exact and objective numbers are needed in order to create models while simulations can offer a 'correct' picture of what to expect. In particular, business schools have welcomed this 'scientific' way of dealing with management problems as a way to bring business schools up to the "scientific" level of the beta sciences (mathematics, physics, chemistry, etc.). It is clear that much of the existing management practice, theory, and "remedies" based on the positivist view are limited by their dependence on several inappropriate assumptions as they don't reflect business and market behavior. Linear and static methods are the ones that are taught in business schools. Therefore, markets have to be linear and static. As we know, they are not.

It seems important at this point to elaborate a little more on positivist thinking as we want to propose a challenging view on management and management education later on. In order to do that, we take a brief look here at some positivist epistemology. Epistemology is concerned with understanding the origin, nature and validity of knowledge, i.e., the science or theory of (in our case) positivism. These fundamental assumptions built into the epistemological outlook plays a vital role in determining practices with regard to management, organization, and knowledge.

A major aspect of positivism is the division between object and subject. This means that the outer world (e.g. an industry) is pre-given, ready to be "truthfully" represented by organizations and individuals. The mind is able to create an inner representation that corresponds to the outer world, be it an object, event or state. Translated to knowledge, positivism considers that knowledge exists independent of the human being that uses it, learns it, and transfers it. Knowledge reflects and represents "the world in itself" and can be built up independent of the observer, the "knower." This is equally and arguably the basis for most management education today. A student, independent of his/ her background, interest, social environment, ambitions, etc., needs to learn a body of knowledge through courses and is tested on whether that 'objective' knowledge is acquired. Only, the professor who judges is a subject and is involved in the subject matter also. The way one professor teaches is different from the way a colleague teaches and so the content is in fact subject dependent. We call it 'subject matter,' even though we consider it to be an objective set of transferable knowledge. The more companies want to tailor management education to their specific needs based on the pre-knowledge of their employees, the more this positivist object/subject division becomes a problem as it collides with the notion of "universal and objective" knowledge. What if the universal knowledge that is transferred is mainly a theoretical framework, a form which is of little use in the nonlinear and dynamic markets? This would mean management education does not prepare people adequately for the reality of management.

Individualized learning, however, needs an adapted pedagogical approach, which enables dynamic and nonlinear behavior, as is argued in earlier chapters. The successful implementation of the concept of the Hybrid Business School (Baets and Van der Linden, 2000; and summarised in next chapter) is not based on a positivist and reductionist view on management education.

Another premise of positivist thinking is based on a strict belief in (absolute) causality and (environmental) determinism. As clear-cut connections exist between cause and effect, managerial actions lead to predictable outcomes and thus to control. Successful systems are driven by negative feedback processes toward predictable states of adaptation to the environment. The dynamics of success are therefore assumed to be a tendency towards stability, regularity, and predictability. The classic approach to strategy illustrates this reductionism. The complexities of industries are reduced in terms of maturity, continuity and stability so that a single prediction of an organization's future path can be described. As a consequence, the better the environmental analysis according to a number of dimensions, the better the course (strategy) can be defined and implemented.

Positivism is the prevailing scientific view in the Western world, since it coincides perfectly with the Cartesian view of the world. The overriding power of man is a fact of nature. Nature gives man the power to master nature, according to laws of nature. In 1903 however, Poincaré, a French mathematician, introduced some doubt to this positivist view. Without really being able to prove, or even to gather evidence, he warned that "sometimes small differences in the initial conditions generate very large differences in the final phenomena. A slight error in the former could produce a tremendous error in the latter so that prediction becomes impossible; we have accidental phenomena."

It suggested that with the approaches used, man was not always able to control his own systems. Hence, the Cartesian view of the world is limited.

It took quite a number of years until, in 1964, Lorenz showed evidence of the phenomenon. Lorenz, an American meteorologist, was interested in weather forecasting. In order to produce forecasts, he built a simple dynamic nonlinear model. Though it only consisted of a few equations and a few variables, it showed "strange" behavior. A dynamic model is one where the value in a given period is a function of the value in the previous period. For example, the value of a particular price in a given period is a function of its value in the previous period. Or, the market share for product A in a given period is a function of the market share in the previous period. In other words, most if not all, economic phenomena are dynamic. Such a dynamic process that continuously changes can only be simulated by a stepwise procedure of very small increments. It is an iterative process. Once the value of the previous period is calculated, it is used as an input value for the next period, etc.

A computer allowed Lorenz to show what could happen with nonlinear dynamic systems. At a certain moment he interrupted a simulation, and when he returned, he decided not to restart at the end point, but rather a few iterations before. What he observed was remarkable. The new simulation differed increasingly from the one made previously and the differences increased over time. Suddenly, chaos seemed to appear. The observed difference became larger than the signal itself. Hence, the predictive value of the model became zero.

Originally, Lorenz did not understand what happened. He observed that while the computer calculates with a number of decimal positions, the printout shows fewer decimal positions, and therefore the re-simulation starts with a slightly wrong number. This very small difference caused chaotic behavior after a number of iterations. Lorenz's observation caused a real paradigm shift in sciences. Lorenz showed what Poincaré suggested, namely that nonlinear dynamic systems are highly sensitive to initial conditions. Complex adaptive systems are probabilistic rather than deterministic, and factors such as nonlinearity can magnify apparently insignificant differences in initial conditions leading to huge consequences, meaning that the long term outcomes for complex systems are unknowable. Translated to management, this advocates that companies and economies need to be structured to encourage an approach that embraces flux and competition in complex and chaotic contexts rather than rational ones. Mainstream approaches popularized in business texts, however, seldom come to grips with nonlinear phenomena. Instead, they tend to model phenomena as if they were linear in order to make them tractable and controllable, and tend to model aggregate behavior as if it is produced by individual entities which all exhibit average behavior.

Today, we are able to suggest a more in depth insight into the organisational principle that runs management behaviour, i.e. what I labelled a quantum structure. In my "Habilitation" thesis defended in France (Baets, 2004) and elaborated in Baets (2005) a strong theoretical argument is made for a quantum structure as the organisational principal behind management behaviour. In the same publications, a number of examples of research projects are given, that provide first hand evidence of the claimed structure. Some of those examples are also found in the following chapters of this book, however, without the quantum focus. In this book, the focus is, and remains, on innovative use of knowledge management, making it a necessary sustainable investment for companies. However, given its importance for a correct understanding of the role of complexity in a networked economy, a brief introduction is given here.

The concept of synchronicity is introduced, a concept that is already familiar in some other scientific disciplines (like physics, medicine), as an alternative to causality. Synchronicity (occurring together in time as Pauli defines it) appears in those sciences where simultaneous behaviour is an issue. We no longer talk about a causal relationship (from cause to effect) but we talk about coincidence (happening together) that is identified as important, even if we are unable to explain its deeper cause. We talk about synchronicity, if events happen within a particular time frame. Statistical notions or ideas of probability are of a different nature. Probabilities can be calculated using mathematical methods, synchronicity can not.

In other sciences, we can see quantum thinking around energy, information and communication. These theories allow us to talk about causality on a much deeper level, or on a much more detailed level, indeed on a quantum level. The concept of synchronicity appears. This quantum structure is what allows humans to realize what they are able to do: cure yourself from a disease, survive, and innovate in a company. We talk about essential particles on a very detailed level (could it be human qualities?) that are interlinked in solid networks with many other particles (elements; its context) and that interact with each other forming what some call morphogenetic fields that contain knowledge and information. If and when more people in a company are "entrained", their actions will be more successful, let us say within an innovation team. In other words, a richer understanding of knowledge, learning and innovation has to go to a deeper understanding of "entrainment", quantum structures, synchronicity, morphogenetic fields, individual space and self organisation.

This translates into a research agenda for the Euromed Centre for Knowledge Management (E$^c$KM at Euromed Marseille – Ecole de Management in France):

- How can we understand a quantum structure of business and what is the role of synchronicity, networks, interacting agents, morphogenetic fields, etc.?
- Can we create evidence showing, or even proving, the emergent nature of most management processes, in the first place of innovation ?
- Can Complex Adaptive Systems visualize emergence and synchronicity and do they give richer understanding?
- Can we further explore, using these metaphors, the role of knowledge, learning and innovation in companies, in answering the previous questions, but also in improving its immediate application in business?

In my opinion this scientific proposal, as made in my thesis and my publications, already based on early evidence, will further boost the crucial importance that knowledge management has for improved management. This is the focus of this book.

One could ask what this has to do with education. Clearly, knowledge management and learning are only two sides of the same coin (as argued in more detail in the next chapter, as well as in the contributions of Walker and Koopmans). Hence, the answer is quite simple. Human beings behave and think in a nonlinear and dynamic way. Each individual, even from the same region and benefiting from the same pre-education, thinks differently from his or her colleagues. Therefore, one cannot hope that a particular course could suit all students. Furthermore, it is extremely difficult to identify the 'initial condition' of each student. This sensitivity to initial conditions is another reason for investigating new educational paradigms. The old paradigm does not fit the modern world.

Positive feedback has been brought into the realm of economics by Brian Arthur, who claims that there are really two economies, one that functions on the basis of traditional diminishing returns, and one where increasing returns to scale are evident due to positive feedback. Marshall introduced the concept of diminishing returns in 1890. This theory was based on industrial production, where one could choose out of many resources and relatively little knowledge was involved in production. Production then seemed to follow the law of diminishing returns, based on negative feedback in the process and this led to a unique (market) equilibrium. Arthur's second economy includes most knowledge industries. In the knowledge economy, companies should focus on adapting, recognizing patterns, and building webs to amplify positive feedback rather than trying to achieve "optimal" performance. A good example is VHS becoming a market standard, without being technically superior (already described in the first chapter).

Brian Arthur also refers to the American political primaries as another example of this 'positive feedback phenomena.' All presidential candidates make a great effort to gain the very first small yet crucial states, such as New Hampshire. It is not because they deliver a lot of votes, but rather because it is known that the candidate who wins these states will get more campaign funding, more TV time, etc. Those who lose often get into a downward spiral and drop out soon afterwards. American presidents, says Brian Arthur, are not elected by the majority of American citizens, but rather by the minority living in a few small states.

Arthur also specified a number of reasons for increasing returns that particularly fit today's economy. Most products, being highly knowledge intensive, with high up-front costs, network effects, and customer relationships, lead to complex behavior. Let us take again the example of Windows. The first copy of Windows is quite expensive due to huge research costs. Microsoft experiences a loss on the first generation. The second and following generations cost very little comparatively, but the revenue per product remains the same. Hence, there is a process of increasing returns.

Two more interesting developments have consequences for our educational practice. Neurobiological research, e.g. by Varela, has revealed the concept of self-organization and the concept that knowledge is not stored, but rather created each time over and again, based on the neural capacity of the brain. Cognition is enacted, which means that cognition only exists in action and interpretation. This concept of enacted cognition goes fundamentally against the prevailing idea that things are outside and the brain is inside the person. The subject can be considered as the special experience of oneself, as a process in terms of truth. By identifying with objects, the individual leaves the opportunity for the objects to "talk." In other words, subject and object meet in interaction, in hybrid structures. Individuals thus become builders of facts in constructing contents of knowledge which relate to events, occurrences and states. Knowledge is concerned with the way one learns to fix the flow of the world in temporal and spatial terms. Consequently, claims of truth are transposed on objects; the subject is "de-subjectivized." There is no such subdivision between the object and the subject. Cognition is produced by an embodied mind, a mind that is part of a body, sensors and an environment. This issue will reappear in further chapters when we focus on the role of managers, or when we discuss education, and, in particular, assessment issues.

Research in artificial life gave us the insight that instead of reducing the complex world to simple simulation models, which are never correct, one could equally define some simple rules, which then produce complex behavior. This is also a form of self-organization, like the flock of birds that flies south. The first bird is not the leader and does not command the flock. Rather, each bird has a simple rule e.g. to stay 20 cm away from its two neighbors. This simple rule allows us to simulate the complex behavior of a flock of birds.

At this stage let us focus on what is understood as complex behavior. Complex systems behavior is the behavior of nonlinear dynamic systems. We talk about a dynamic system if the value in a given period (say today) depends on the value of the previous period. A nonlinear system is a system in which the evolution of the phenomenon does not take place by adding elements to each period, but rather by multiplying them. Let us take a simple example. Consider water plants on a lake. It is said that in each period, the surface covered by them doubles. That means that each period of time, the surface is multiplied by 2. Over a number of periods t, the surface can be calculated by $2^t$. This is an example of both a dynamic system and a nonlinear system. It is dynamic since the surface covered in period t is a function of the surface covered in the previous period (times 2). It is nonlinear since, in each period, a multiplication takes place and not an addition. This leads to an exponential formula in the end.

Probabilistic, nonlinear dynamic systems are still considered deterministic. That means that such systems follow rules, even if they are difficult to identify and even if the appearance of the simulated phenomenon suggests complete chaos. At different times the same complex system can produce chaotic or orderly behavior. The change between chaos and order cannot be forecast, nor can the moment in which it takes place, either in magnitude or direction. Complexity and chaos refer to the state of a system and not to what we commonly know as complicated, i.e. something that is difficult to do. The latter depends not on the system, but more on the environment and boundary conditions. Perhaps for a handicapped person, driving a car is more complicated than for an able-bodied person. In general, building a house seems more complicated than sewing a suit, but for some other people building a house would be less complicated than sewing a suit. This depends on the boundary conditions for each individual person.

To formalize in a simplified way the findings of complexity theory, we could state three characteristics. First, complex systems are highly dependent on the initial state. A slight change in the starting situation can have dramatic consequences in a later period of time caused by the dynamic and iterative character of the system. Second, one cannot forecast the future based on the past. Based on the irreversibility of time principle, one can only take one step ahead at a time, scanning carefully the new starting position. Third, the scaling factor of a nonlinear system causes the appearance of "strange attractors," a local minimum or maximum around which a system seems to stay for a certain period of time in quasi equilibrium. The number of attractors cannot be forecast, neither can it be forecast when they will attract the phenomenon.

There are myriad insights we gain from complexity theory and its applications in business and markets for management education to better organize the knowledge management contribution around complex markets and behavior. The strength of the capacity of human beings and of groups of people to self-organize forces us to change the focus of education. Instead of being school-centered, education becomes learner-centered. The learner decides, chooses and manages based on what they need for their learning purposes at that particular moment, and in that particular situation, based on the capacity of that particular individual. The concept of enacted cognition invites us to redefine management education towards learning by doing. Project-based education and competency-based education are two focuses that need to be incorporated into the concept of knowledge management. The concept of the embodied mind stresses the necessity to learn within a given context. Management education and knowledge management, certainly if organized by a company itself, should be grounded in the corporate effort in knowledge management. You can only learn efficiently within your own context. Learning and knowledge is not value free; there is no division between object and subject. Management education and knowledge management can only take place within the managerial context, which is integrated and not separated in functional areas.

The 'irreversibility of time' theorem suggests that there is no best solution. There are "best" principles which can be learnt, but no best solutions or practices that can be copied. There are not even any guaranteed solutions that could be used in most circumstances. This fact necessitates a different way of organizing the pedagogical process of learning, once we accept that there are no universal theories in management education.

Recent developments in complexity theory suggest that management education should be based on an integrated, holistic approach and not on a reductionist, rationalist paradigm. Many interesting but ifficult challenges arise when knowledge management becomes a useful tool for companies operating in nonlinear dynamic markets. And essentially, this covers all companies. The concept of the Hybrid Business School that we have developed in an earlier book (Baets and Van der Linden, 2000), depicts the design of a management education and management development approach that supports both companies and managers on an operational level in dynamic and nonlinear markets, with one aim: to improve the knowledge capacity of the companies.

The next chapter summarizes the most important concepts of this hybrid knowledge and learning approach. It is this approach, based on complexity theory that has given rise to the research center NOTION (at Nyenrode University, the Netherlands). The results of this research center are described in the chapters of the second part and all illustrate applications of this new paradigm in knowledge management.

# 4. KNOWLEDGE MANAGEMENT AND MANAGEMENT LEARNING: WHAT COMPUTERS CAN STILL DO[1]

## 4.1 Knowledge and Learning

### 4.1.1 Knowledge and Experience

In the field of cognitive sciences, and even more so in epistemology, a great deal of research and work has been done to attempt to identify and define knowledge. Unfortunately, in management, we do not know what managerial knowledge really is and even though we have a vague feeling for it, there are few definitions of knowledge within a "managerial" context.

Kim suggested that knowledge is a combination of "know-how" and "know-why." Other authors, including Nonaka, identify different types of knowledge, i.e., tacit and explicit knowledge. Explicit knowledge, on the one hand, refers to the formal, systematic language, the rules and procedures that an organization follows. This kind of knowledge can be transferred and therefore can be a subject of education and socialization. Knowledge-based

Systems also work with explicit knowledge. Tacit knowledge, on the other hand, is mainly based on lived experiences and therefore is difficult to identify and to transfer. Deeply rooted in action, commitment and involvement in a specific context, it refers to personal qualities such as cognitive and technical elements inherent to the individual.

Experience is key in acquiring tacit knowledge. An example of tacit knowledge (in business) would be the decision making process of financial market dealers. Based on what they have learned from their past experience, what they read and hear, the "market climate," etc., brokers make buying

[1] This chapter is based on chapters by Baets and Van der Linden, Virtual Corporate Universities : A matrix of knowledge and learning for the new digital dawn, Kluwer Academic, 2003

and selling decisions within a few seconds. We like to call this "instinct" or "fingerspitzengefuhl" but the behavior of individual dealers is different. Each dealer seems to have his own way of dealing based on his experience and his reference framework. It has proven extremely difficult to extract this kind of "knowledge" from dealers but not because they don't want to share it. Rather, it seems extremely difficult for dealers to express their knowledge, or to make tacit knowledge explicit. However, since some dealers are consistently better than others, it would be interesting to understand why they excel, in order to reproduce the principles of "winning" behaviour. Furthermore, if a dealer acquires his experience/knowledge during his stay in a particular bank company, how can this bank keep the acquired knowledge, this intangible asset or human capital, if a dealer leaves the company? Intangibles, as the embodiment of knowledge and ideas, are what drive growth in an information economy. Taken together, intangibles comprise well over half the market value of public companies, and can entail, besides human capital, organizational capital including intellectual property and brands, customer capital, partner capital, and environmental capital.

Many different types of cognitive elements are involved. Those of interest for managerial problems center on "mental models" in which people form working models of the world by creating and manipulating analogies in their minds. Mental models could be described as deeply held images of how the world works. They represent a person's view of the world, including explicit and implicit understanding. Mental models provide the context in which to view and interpret new material and they determine how stored information is relevant to a given situation. There's a clear analogy between how mental models "work" and the way in which the human brain works. The human brain is characterized by a high degree of parallelism. This means that a large number of elements (in this case neurons) are used at the same time alongside each other. A second important characteristic of the human brain is the micro structure of cognition (distributed knowledge) on which it is built. The human brain has no clear equation for what happens in a given situation, but is able to reconstruct solutions and actions quickly and easily, based on this micro structure of knowledge. Consequently, we can assume that knowledge is not sequential (but parallel) and deals with variety (and not with averages).

Based on these definitions and analogies to individual learning, organizational learning is defined as increasing an organization's capacity to take effective action. The emphasis does not lie in reality but rather on perceptions of reality (meanings). It is clear from this description how crucially important context is for learning and knowledge.

The capacity of an organization to take effective action is based on tacit corporate knowledge. The more this corporate knowledge is accessible (which does not necessarily mean explicit) and shared, the easier it becomes to take advantage of it. For management, perceptions of reality become more important than reality itself. Hence the role of corporate mental models becomes extremely important since their ultimate aim is to visualize the shared mental model on any chosen subject. A shared mental model is fundamental to corporate learning, and hence to proactive management. If we want to take this reasoning one step further, we could even consider that it is the manager's role to identify the shared elements or unity within diversity (complexity). This idea introduces the management of corporate (tacit) knowledge as a strategic mission.

The idea of unity within diversity also advocates that organizations are most creative when they operate away from equilibrium, in a region of "creative tension." This involves thinking about the fractal nature of organizational boundaries and the realization that all employees are at some boundary of their organizations, and therefore understand part of their firm's environment. Instead of absorbing complexity, diversity and therefore uncertainty, creative tension gives rise to richness as it embraces advancement and creativity. According to Nonaka, such "creative chaos" may need to be intentionally created by management through an organization, and allow for self-organization processes. If managers are not allowed time for reflection during this time, creative chaos can become "destructive chaos." As a consequence, redundancy should be built into managerial structures and processes.

Despite the variety of definitions, the organizational capability for knowledge creation is gaining momentum in managerial science. Some consider it a potential source of competitive advantage for companies. The organizational competency translating all that information and knowledge into "intelligence," in other words to understand, connect, and exploit those resources in a distinctive competitive way, however, is crucial. Whereas companies were long considered to be a system that "processes" information and/or "solves" problems, we now consider an organization as a knowledge creating system. The dynamic nature, the continuous change, and the discontinuous leaps such a system lives through, are essential. In order to describe a company's pool of knowledge, some authors use the metaphor of a "cognitive map," a written plan in which a person expresses, via blocks and connecting arrows, how a person reasons about a particular subject or how s/he sees "things" fit together. In a similar vein, the term "corporate IQ" is sometimes used while others argue for a more quantitative representation of this "body" and call it a "fusion map." In essence, all describe in one way or the other this portfolio or repository of (tacit and explicit) knowledge.

### 4.1.2    Learning and Mental Models

Learning could then be considered as advancement. It represents an opportunity for individuals to pause, reflect upon and reframe issues and experiences not only from their own insights, but also with reference to interaction with others. Hence, learning is not abstract but contextual: it happens at the appropriate time, in the appropriate dose with the proper experience so that it can be immediately applied. As such, learning can be seen as the process whereby knowledge is created through the transformation of experience. This definition of learning relates to Kim's "know-how" and "know-why." According to this definition, learning takes place in a cycle of four steps. First, something is experienced within a particular context. Second, observations and reflections on that experience are created. Third, abstract concepts and generalizations are formed based on these reflections, and fourth, these ideas on the new situation are tested which, in turn, results in new experiences. These new experiences can then become a first step in a new loop.

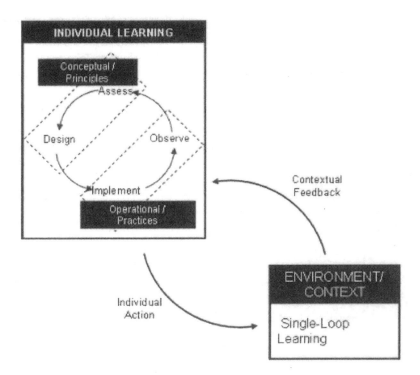

*Figure -5.* Simple model of Individual Learning - the OADI-cycle

The idea of a cyclical learning loop is described in the so-called OADI-cycle (Observe - Assess - Design - Implement).

An easy example of this learning process is to observe how a child "learns" not to put his hand on a hot plate. In many cases, a child cannot be taught not to touch a hot plate. The first time (even if told differently) a child attempts to touch a hot plate. The child observes something that he assesses as heat. He designs, not necessarily deliberately, an action which is probably to take away his hand. Eventually, the child implements that design and takes away his hand. A new observation follows which is assessed as "better." Probably no further design takes place. In the case of the hand having been burned already, the child again observes something different which does not feel very nice. He would (or in the beginning somebody else would) assess it as "burned." A possible design would be to put his hand under cold running water, which he eventually does. The cycle can continue for a number of rounds. Via this process of "learning the hard way," an individual, regardless of age, learns a number of things through experience. Learning is inseparable from "taking action" and it applies knowledge to events. The nature of that knowledge includes not only explicit, but also implicit understanding and meaning that the individual ascribes to events and their purposes. The single-loop process is implemented through individual action, which in turn creates a contextual feedback. Instruction can shorten the learning cycle, but only if the person can make sense of it. This means that the instruction given should fit into the existing reference frame of the person. As a result, instruction without embedding - contextualization - has limited value.

A second stage of individual learning links individual learning with individual mental models. This process is called double loop learning as it includes learning based on contextual impulses as portrayed by the OADI-cycle as well as learning from connecting what is learned from impulses with the individual's mental models.

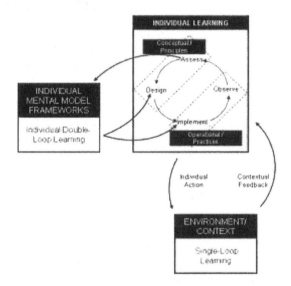

*Figure -6.* Individual Double-Loop Learning

Let us take the illustration of the child again. When a child goes through the above-mentioned "experience" a number of times, he will not do it again. The child does not necessarily know what happens and he does not necessarily understand why he should not touch a hot plate anymore. He has implicitly developed a framework of knowledge that allows him to deal with a new comparable case. He can deal with a new case, without knowing the correct "equations." In some respects it can be argued that this is not a true example of learning, but rather of a human reflex. Probably this is true. However, it indicates clearly how the learning cycle operates in contextual interaction (single-loop learning) and how it leads to the individual mental model (via individual double-loop learning). According to the same principle, the trader "learns" and creates by doing, his own mental model about trading. Any learning experience (courses, or books read) could speed up the process if, and only if, the experiences fit into the existing framework (mental model) of the person. If the gap between the existing mental model and the taught material is too large, very little learning takes place. Teaching is no guarantee for learning: teaching is only one kind of experience that an individual can choose to use for learning purposes and ultimately from which to learn. Experience in the field can be another means or medium of learning. Hence, different people react completely differently to the same learning experience. There is no unique best way of teaching; no unique best way of learning can be identified. Learning remains a free act of individuals.

We will now add a comparable double-loop learning model on an organizational level, in two different ways. Comparable to the single-loop learning in the individual model, each individual action can be part of an organizational action, which in turn causes additional contextual feedback. This is called organizational single-loop learning. Organizational double-loop learning takes place when the individual mental models (images, meanings) are brought together in order to form shared mental models (shared on a corporate or group level), which in turn have an influence on the individual mental models. It is in surfacing and questioning tacit knowledge that it is possible, by a process of "dialoguing," to create shared meanings, which build a sense of identity and purpose with which individuals in organizations can identify. In figure 6, shared mental models are also defined as organizational routines. It will especially be these explicit shared models (the explicit organizational routines) that enable the learning ability of an organization.

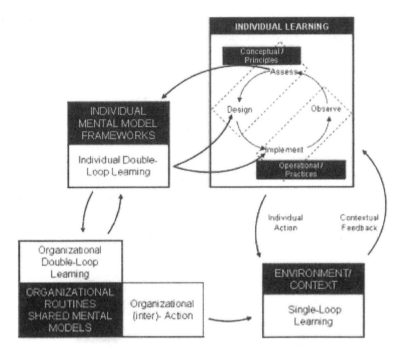

*Figure -7.* Organizational Double-Loop Learning

Organizational double-loop learning can only take place by bringing together individual mental models in a learning space. Individual mental models only get created through individual learning experiences. One particular experience does not have a direct impact, either on the individual mental models or on the shared mental models. In other words, there is no fixed causality between the two. Any change in the shared mental model is caused by individual experiences, which in turn changes the individual mental models and only then would a new shared learning activity be able to change a shared mental model. This does not mean that shared mental models are an addition to individual mental models, or that they are only the addition of a number of individual mental models. On the contrary, any attempt to change a shared mental model has to happen through new experiences at the individual level (even if these experiences can take place in teams or groups). As an individual learns, implying that he fits the new experience into his mental model and produces a different mental model, some changes can occur on the shared level. However, it remains almost impossible to foresee the impact on the shared model of any action on the individual's level, before it comes via the individual mental model into the shared mental model. Therefore, a shared mental model is not a static entity. It should be monitored continuously and that is what we understand as picturing and comparing mental models.

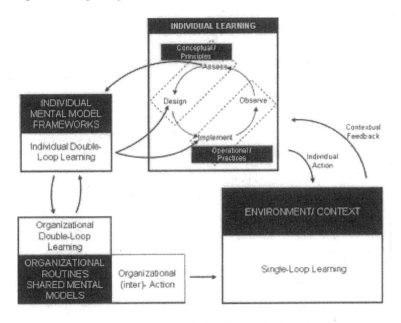

*Figure -8.* An Integrated Model of Organizational Learning

Knowledge management in this sense attempts to visualize mental models with the aim of learning from them and sharing them. As we saw earlier, business is not only faster but also fundamentally different: it moves in a nonlinear and unpredictable fashion. The trouble comes in figuring out how all the forces and elements interact to shape an overall system and determine its often surprising outcomes. As there is no continuity in the flow of (competitive) events, and there is no way to predict the success of products or companies, analytically driven strategies and shaping the organization to meet the needs of the business are obsolete. Without the adequate knowledge base, knowledge management and the organizational capability to continuously capture information, generate new ideas and put knowledge into practice, it is difficult for companies to emerge from the changing economic realities. And information is not just data, knowledge not just codification, but rather the gathering of patterns, the bundling of strategic resources and intellectual technologies and processes to understand, connect and exploit them in a uniquely competitive way. Hence, organizations have to become learning organizations. Besides, the knowledge-creating and learning organization perspectives touch all the assumptions underpinning the organization's structures and processes, and changes the roles, responsibilities, competence and activities of all involved, and especially the roles of managers. Organizational learning magnifies and closes the loop of individual learning within a dynamic corporate and networked setting that allows the learning process inside a company to excel beyond efficiency frontiers. The organization's capabilities, everything from resources, infrastructures and support systems to enabling constraints and core philosophy, will drive that organizational learning. But inherently, we are talking about simple cognitive processes.

The most famous example of how a shared mental model differs from the addition of a number of individual mental models is no doubt the one of the cage of monkeys and the bananas. If one puts twenty monkeys into a cage with a step in the middle and a bunch of bananas on the top, the smartest monkey runs up the steps and takes a banana. This monkey follows its "individual mental model." This story is mainly used as a metaphor, and it is not argued here that monkeys have a mental model. Next, when the monkey takes the banana it starts to rain. Monkeys do not like rain. Then, one monkey is taken out of the cage and replaced. The second smartest monkey runs up the step, and following its mental model takes the banana. It rains again. Allow us to draw your attention to the fact that each monkey individually feels the rain, which gradually influences its mental model in that respect. Again a monkey is replaced. This story continues until the smart monkeys have understood the mechanism. Individually they still like the bananas but they understand the consequences. The least intelligent monkey then tries to take a banana. That monkey has not understood the mechanism yet. Again it pours and we again change a monkey. The new monkey will try and run up the step. All the others, having understood, will not try anymore. But all the monkeys in the cage will also try to stop the new monkey from taking a banana. The new monkey does not understand, but he cannot get to the banana. He follows the shared behavior without understanding. Another twenty replacements will be delivered to a cage full of monkeys that all individually would like to take the banana. As a group they do not do that and none of them knows why. The shared mental model is clearly different from the individual mental models. The change has taken place via continuous new observations and experiences which all the monkeys had individually. None of them has the same number of experiences since they were replaced at different times.

This story illustrates the learning process and also shows that a shared mental model can be completely different from the sum of the individual mental models. Change in a shared mental model only occurs via experiences on an individual level, influencing the individual mental model first. The latter, in turn, will influence the shared mental model. How many times do we recognize this in a corporate environment? "Why do we do it this or that way?" Answer: "It's the way we've always done it." Nobody necessarily knows why and the individual models could well differ from the shared one. Is this what we call "corporate culture"?

If we would like to change corporate culture, we cannot dictate the change process as it is nonlinear and emergent. Actions have to be undertaken in order that all individuals get new experiences. If the atmosphere is positive enough around these new experiences, individuals may - but cannot be forced to - integrate these new positive experiences into their individual mental models, which in turn, eventually, could change the shared model (i.e. the culture). It is a long process, which occurs through individual learning.

Management education can be seen as an important vehicle in developing "emergent" strategies, knowledge management and the organization's capabilities that drive organizational learning. It can help in creating the right conditions for reflective thinking and learning. Referring to figure 7, management education could be situated in the area for single-loop learning. As the figure shows, there is an important role for the context (of which a business school can be part) to give input to the learning process of individuals and groups. However, learning takes place in the double-loop parts and if it did not take place, management education as an input to this process would be a waste of effort.

It is crucial, therefore, that management education and knowledge management be harmonized. They are mutually in need of and reinforce each other. Due to the existence of information technology, both can be easily integrated, resulting in a virtual business school. Technology, however, is only a medium. A context including a pedagogical approach to the corporate learning and knowledge process has still to be provided. Therefore, a virtual business school needs to include these ingredients incrementally in order to be successful. First, an adequate pedagogical approach and an appropriate mix of management education and knowledge management are crucial. Further, the company is required to think about a specific knowledge and learning approach and must have a strong belief and commitment to link management education with knowledge management. Learning and knowledge processes are not static, however, as they are built on information as a dynamic process, working with a dynamic network of human interactions. Lastly, the appropriate information technology has to be used in order to support the educational side, the knowledge side and communication.

After this extensive introduction to knowledge and learning, we should now clearly position the role of virtual education. From a corporate point of view, management education comes into the picture in the single-loop learning cycle, but only to the extent that it fits with the corporate knowledge approach. Management education, and particularly the use of ICT in management education, creates added value if it can be combined with the corporate effort to manage knowledge. Management education can introduce concepts, cases, and activities, but it really becomes interesting if these are taken further in a double-loop learning process via a knowledge approach (or a knowledge network).

Based on IT, the virtual business school is a perfect place for single-loop learning, transfer of contextual knowledge and creation of contextual input for learning. Management education needs to be a stimulus for further in-company learning, further mental model building and further shared mental model building.

### 4.1.3    Some essentials for knowledge management and management learning

- Information is a dynamic process. Knowledge is concerned with the way one learns to fix the flow of the world in temporal and spatial terms;
- Businesses, markets, and organizations change in a discontinuous, nonlinear and dynamic way, allowing for the possibility of emergent and self-organizing behavior. Emergence cannot be predicted or even

"envisioned" from the knowledge of what each component of a system does;
- No single concept of management captures the diversity of roles and activities in which managers are involved;
- The capacity of an organization to take effective action is based on tacit corporate knowledge. Knowledge management attempts to visualize that tacit knowledge to learn from it and share it;
- Managerial competencies better portray the particularities of managerial roles. Managerial competencies are sustained through continuous learning.

We have given some insight into the processes of learning and knowledge transfer. Figure 8 shown again below, demonstrates a schematic and therefore somewhat reduced view on the processes of learning and knowledge management.

At this stage, we would like to take a more technological stance and discuss the information and knowledge technologies that support knowledge management on the one hand and virtual education on the other. While taking this ICT view and attempting to realize and operationalize these processes with the necessary ICT support, we observe a remarkable and interesting overlap.

On a conceptual level, we will not continue to consider knowledge management and virtual education as two separate activities. The left part of figure 9, as argued earlier, describes (tacit) knowledge management. The right part of figure 9 describes virtual education. The overlap of both proves to be the flywheel engine that brings both knowledge management and virtual education to a higher level and closer to the corporate practice, which brings both together and mutually reinforces both knowledge management and virtual education. This construction is what we will call the Hybrid Business School.

The result of this overlap is a textbook example of "1 + 1 = 3" logic. On the knowledge management side, it allows us to deal with tacit knowledge without losing contact with explicit knowledge sharing (virtual education). On the virtual education side it allows us to offer individualized continuous life-long-learning development paths to employees, where the study material is company specific. Education has to be seen as integrated rather than specialized. In other words, our view goes against the common trend of offering more and more specialized courses. We claim that specialization is not in the best interest of companies. Management is the integration of knowledge and skills within a given context. Just as information is meaningless without action, knowledge and skills are powerless without a context. And technology can make education different, rather than more. This approach to virtual education goes far beyond web-based teaching in which Duke University and the University of Phoenix, to name but two, have delivered outstanding programs.

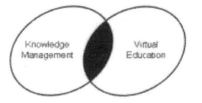

*Figure -9.* The overlap of Knowledge Management and Virtual Education

In this chapter we will further introduce the information and knowledge technologies necessary and available for building the Hybrid Business School: a technology-based approach to integrated (tacit) knowledge management and continuous lifelong learning in companies. The conceptual framework on which we implement technology is shown in figure 10. That figure is schematized to make the goals and/or attributes and processes clearer.

Figure 10 focuses on the information and communication flows and attributes seen in figure 9. All learning is initialized via individual experiences. On the one hand, experiences interact with the individual mental models and thereby create tacit knowledge. On the other hand, experiences interact with contextual knowledge both as input and as products of its interaction. Individual mental models (images) interact with each other in order to generate shared mental models and contribute to the knowledge repository. This latter process is organized using communication platforms. The process of and interaction between experiences, tacit knowledge and knowledge repository, what is called the knowledge management process, has bridges to the contextual knowledge. These bridges attempt to contextualize some of the tacit knowledge with the aim to make it accessible to others. These bridges feed the virtual learning process with some of the individual and corporate tacit knowledge.

The process of dealing with contextualized knowledge and experiences, based on an information and communication platform, is what we call the virtual business school, depicted on the right hand side of figure 10. The process of dealing with experiences, tacit knowledge and the knowledge repository is what we call the "Knowledge Management Approach," depicted on the left-hand side of figure 10. The experiences shared between the two, the contextualization of tacit knowledge and the interaction between explicit knowledge and experiences, all on a continuous and integrated basis, leverage the integration of knowledge management and virtual education. This leverage can only be realized if organized and developed in an adequate information and communication platform, preferably via a learning environment and learning community. Integrating knowledge technologies and learning technologies, in general, use communication technologies, like the Internet, group decision support systems, and the like.

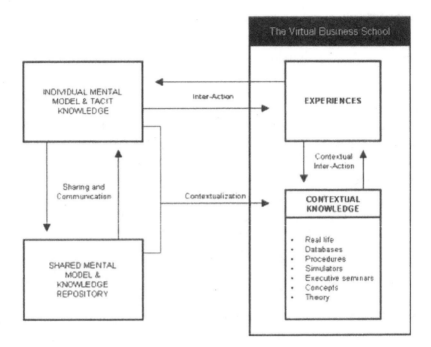

*Figure -10.* A schematic model of knowledge creation and learning

At this point, we would like to briefly introduce the more important knowledge technologies pertaining to the concept of knowledge management and virtual education.

## 4.2     Knowledge Management Technologies

We know that creating a learning/ knowledge-based organization is a simple concept but not an easy task. A new wave of information communication technology (ICT) can be supportive in creating knowledge-based/ learning organizations. New developments in ICT such as Case-Based Reasoning Systems (CBRS), Group Decision Support Systems (GDSS) and Artificial Neural Networks can support some aspects of organizational learning processes and organizational transformation. We can only briefly mention these technologies here.

### 4.2.1    Case-Based Reasoning Systems (CBRS)

CBRS essentially consists of a case library and a software system for retrieving and analyzing the "similar case" and its associated information. The case library has cases covering a broad range of ideas across different industries and business functions. Each case contains a description of the underlying competitive situation, the environmental conditions, management priorities, experience, values that allow a certain strategy to succeed, and moments of learning. A software system helps index each case in such a way that a search yields a modest number of "similar cases." The system can provide a complete explanation of the reasoning that has led to each recommendation. If there is no case that exactly matches the given situation, then it selects the most "similar" case. An adaptation procedure can be encoded in the form of adaptation rules. The result of the case adaptation is a completed solution but it also generates a new case that can be automatically added to the case library.

Exposure to prior cases and experiences, and the steps taken to arrive at a decision, can often be richer and more useful as the system encodes the important learning and thinking that went into the decision. As CBRS can generate details regarding justification for particular decisions and explanations for failures, and it can be a support tool for a learning organization. It can be used as a learning device, but also as an input device for a knowledge base. Companies use this technology as a database of 'best practices.' It makes 'live experiences' accessible to others. What we are looking for are rather 'best principles.' In many respects, a CBRS is a static tool compared to a database. The use of a CBRS, however, as part of the knowledge management cycle as well as the case input of a virtual learning environment, allows us to go beyond the static situation: the process of learning and knowledge building gives rise to developing best principles.

### 4.2.2    Group Decision Support Systems (GDSS)

Participatory management methods are increasingly gaining more interest in the corporate world. Japanese management methods and Dutch management practice have traditionally practiced management by consensus. Consensus management has led to more of a teamwork working environment, such as the creation of committees or work groups where members share their knowledge so as to solve complex and ill-structured problems. In reference to figure 10, participative decision making contributes to the creation of mental models, both individual and shared, out of individual experiences. On the individual level, a GDSS can be used as a tool to help to structure a mental model or a routine, based on lived experiences. On a group level, the act of sharing and exchange allows learning as a group as well, but it also gives further input in the sense that experiences lived by others are used as input data for the creation of an individual's mental model. One can see the immediate application with sharing ideas and therefore in the creation of a group's shared mental model. This process of group learning involves the individual, and is therefore a useful tool for individual learning, but it does not focus solely on individual learning.

Participative strategy formation constitutes a learning process, as the various interest groups within an organization have different perceptions. Some group members may have more knowledge, competence and experience. Group learning occurs as the interaction among members takes place. As one member shares knowledge with the other members in the community, they gain information and knowledge. The contextual feedback instantly adds value for all involved. As each group learns and creates from its new knowledge base, the base itself also evolves. Exponential and nonlinear growth occurs with the value of each sharing group's knowledge base.

Sometimes, participative/ group planning fails due to a lack of proper participation, communication or understanding among the members in the group. Recent developments in information technology have provided systems such as Group Decision Support Systems (GDSS). A Group Decision Support System (GDSS) is a computer-based system consisting of software, hardware, language components, procedures and tools that can support participative strategy formation. There can be many different configurations of a GDSS. These systems are for group planning.

A GDSS enables a group to work interactively using the networked hardware and software to complete the various aspects of the business process. For example, automated brainstorming tools can be used to address questions such as "what should the company do to become a knowledge-based/ learning company in the next five years?" Using the system, group members can generate and evaluate relevant ideas from their individual terminals. The group facilitator can then prioritize the ideas they have generated and can select one for further electronic discussion. Finally, the group can work together using a text editor to formulate a policy statement regarding the goal they have selected.

The capabilities of existing GDSS vary. Essentially, they reduce communication barriers by providing technical features such as the display of ideas, voting, compilation, anonymous input/ interaction, decision modelling, electronic mail and the bulletin board function. Also, they act as group experts by providing advice in selecting and arranging the rules to be applied during the decision making process. The ultimate aim of this technology is to bring people together and facilitate efficient and effective interactive sharing of information among group members.

Today, intranets are replacing GDSS, particularly in the function of a communication device. If the learning is focused on the decision making process, however, GDSS fulfil the purpose better than an intranet.

### 4.2.3    Artificial Neural Networks

Artificial neural networks (ANNs) are tools derived from artificial intelligence (AI). ANNs are also part of a new information-processing paradigm that simulates the human brain. They are very strong tools in pattern finding and structuring, without any prior information. They allow for the structuring of tacit knowledge, without making it explicit, but nevertheless making it accessible. ANNs are vehicles for creating "best principles" out of "best practices." Through learning and developing an epistemology of inquiry, practices can be understood from the level of principles. When a CBRS contains many cases, and a query would generate an excessive number of cases, there needs to be a filter to break them down and summarize the cases. In essence, ANNs are instrumental in creating some tacit knowledge out of stored experiences.

In this section we want to position ANNs as learning tools within the context of Information and Knowledge Technologies (IKTs). ANNS are strong in contributing to the creation of tacit knowledge models, without making tacit knowledge explicit, but with the ability to make that knowledge potentially available for the company (see figure 10). ANNs fit the left (middle part) of figure 10. Though other advanced AI tools could be of help here, the use of ANNs has already shown successes as a knowledge generating tool to support brand-management, to visualize a change management process, or to identify client profiles. The combination of CBRS and ANN is a strong backbone for a knowledge network, particularly in light of the progression to world mass-individualization. Though ANNs lack the ability to give explanation at intermediate stages, integrating them with expert systems can somewhat remove this deficiency and therefore, they can support the learning process.

### 4.2.4    Semantic Search Engines and Link Machines

A recent and interesting development of particular use for knowledge management is what are called Semantic Search Engines. Most knowledge management technologies, including Case Based Reasoning, still need a strict organization of the data and/or cases. The quality of the search procedure relies heavily on the quality of the organization of the data and the labelling of those data. Classical search procedures use predefined labels, related to every specific piece of information. As already argued earlier, however, the problem of knowledge management precisely entails that the user does not always know exactly what he or she is looking for. Furthermore, the user does not always know the organization of the data.

From a user's perspective, the ideal is that one can question a knowledge base in a natural language query, which just means an everyday sentence: "Is there any experience with respect to launching new mortgage products in the last year?"; "My software product XXX does not operate anymore and shows the problems YYY; is there any relevant experience in this company?".

Independent of any structure, the search can be made and launched. Though the information is of course still organized in a particular way, and it could even be possible to access the same knowledge repository in a structured way, in this request the user does not need to worry about that organization.

A semantic search engine uses a kind of an overlay organization, based on keywords that are commonly used together. The search engine scans the texts that are available and that are stored using a format that allows this kind of search. Most commonly, XML is the standard for organizing text files today, increasingly and rapidly replacing HTML. Using some intelligent statistics, keywords are identified. Alternatively, for a company or branch specific database, these keywords could be given to the search engine. What the search engine does next is scan all the text in order to identify which words are often used closely together, for example, in the same sentence. If words are commonly used closely together, the machine presumes that they are semantically linked. Whenever one keyword is requested, the engine will then suggest that there are a number of related keywords.

The search engine creates a semantic network of keywords, which allows translation of any given natural language query in a number of most probably related keywords. Then those keywords can be related to pieces of text where they appear dominantly.

Once those keywords are identified, the texts are codified with the keywords, and the semantic table is made. The system is then ready for both semantic queries and semantic linking.

A minor clarification is necessary before proceeding to the practice. Other than semantic search engines, there are also pure statistical search engines that do not attempt to identify the semantics of a story. They only use observations and numerics on those observations. The most readily available search engines today use statistical search techniques. The following is an example of what they can do. Imagine asking a database for the file of "Gorge." It would probably answer that the file does not exist, but that there is a file on a guy named "George." The search engine has recognized four of the five letters in the correct position and surmises that the letter (in this the case the "e" that is "misspelled") is not of that much importance.

A semantic query is a query according to the examples given above. The system is going to respond with all those texts that come close to having a number of keywords that were either in the request, or that are, via the semantic table, related to words in your request. The idea of distance and proximity in meaning plays an important role here. You would ask for a specific experience with reference to launching a particular kind of business in Poland and the system would answer that it only has cases on Hungary.

The last step in this process, and of paramount importance for knowledge management, is that those semantic proximities are identified through a hypertext link that could be created automatically between semantically related concepts or pieces of text. In practice, that means that one only needs to store the text files in an adequate format (say XML) and that the semantic search and link engine is going to find meaning in the files and create the links between the related concepts. In other words, the semantic search and link machine organizes your information automatically in the most flexible way. In addition, your knowledge repository is then automatically accessible for all, in such a way that helps anyone with his or her search request.

This recent commercially-available technology is extremely promising as a knowledge technology for any company. It is of course, equally important for the Hybrid Business School concept (as developed in the next chapter). The knowledge repository (i.e. the concepts and cases) supporting learning can be organized automatically using semantic search and link machines. It can be updated easily, as it automatically re-organizes whenever a piece of information is deleted or added. Furthermore, it allows 'easy' individualization of a learning lab. For any particular participant of any particular company, a user and company specific learning can be created, by integrating information and best practices of that particular company (and even individual profile). The semantic search and link machine takes care of integrating the specific information into the already existing learning lab. In respect to the creation of corporate virtual universities, this technology is key.

## 4.3     Virtual Learning Technologies

The technology available for building a virtual learning environment is quite similar to that for a knowledge approach. In so far as the knowledge approach and the pedagogical effort reinforce each other, it is clear that the same technologies and technological platforms could be used.

Some technologies, however, are particularly beneficial developing learning environments. The best known examples are Lotus Learning Space (based on a Lotus Notes platform), Docent (a Learning Management System), Saba (an LMS with a particular focus on HR development), Blackboard (which does exactly what it says, replacing the old blackboard for the teacher) and iLearn of Oracle (with integration in the Oracle database technology), to name a few. An adequate learning environment needs to fulfil a minimum set of conditions, and it should at least produce and make available the pedagogical material in the desired pedagogical approach.

The necessary features for a learning environment can be listed as follows:

- A scheduler (agenda) for the learner, which can be managed jointly by the tutor and the student. This schedule acts as a guideline, but it also allows monitoring of both progress and results.

- A media center of resources with hypertext links to:
  Managerial concepts (independent from functional areas);
  Case-studies and applications;
  Managerial skills (or explanations thereof);
  Other resource material
  (The media center should actually include multimedia such as text, pictures, movies, digital videos, etc.)

- An electronic course room for discussions and debating, question and answer sessions, and joint work, which becomes the meeting place of the knowledge-web created around the learning process (communities-of-practice). Here students, practitioners and faculty discuss topics of interest, sharing experiences, and joint work on new cases. On a purely corporate level, the diabetic community mentioned earlier, where patients, medical staff, a pharmaceutical company, and a medical insurance company exchange information and knowledge would be an example of this electronic course room.

- Profiles of students and tutors. Particularly in a virtual environment it is important to distinguish participants and their qualities so as to formulate networks or communities. As can be expected, it is difficult to work over a network with colleagues of whom you have no knowledge or history.

- An assessment manager. The assessment manager has a dual responsibility. In degree-granting courses, it is imperative to measure learning (as a diploma has to be delivered) which he/ she will do. In a personal development path, the assessment manager will work under the framework of the corporate appraisal system, and the overall human resources management strategies and policies.

The Internet (or intranet) can do one or more of the above mentioned tasks. However, integrated software has the greater advantage of promoting the integration of the environment, and the ease of use for both the student and the developer (or tutor). Integrated software takes less start-up time, and users are usually more satisfied. In theory, it is possible for a virtual school to construct its own compatible software, but in practice, this is a difficult and complex undertaking and it often prohibits a virtual school from going beyond some electronic course offerings (web-based education), or creating some discussion forum.

The database of pedagogical material should be linked to relevant web pages, with additional material, or further networks of shared interest. Links can be made between the learning environment and some interesting web sites, e.g. of the companies discussed during cases, or web sites which contain relevant up-to-date study material, taking advantage of the wealth of information on the Internet.

Video-conferencing is also an important and interesting technology. There is still a long way to go until video-conferencing is reliable enough to be optimally used for learning, but it has great potential for the future. Video-telephony, on the other hand, seems to be a very good technological tool, especially for tutoring. Today video-telephony over the Internet is still slow, yet seeing your counterpart does add value to a conversation.

The most probable reason for the low satisfaction and limited success of video conferencing is the dominant pedagogical metaphor, i.e. the transfer metaphor, supporting teaching via video conferencing. Video conferencing attempts to deliver, in the same inefficient way as a sit-in course, to more people in different locations. Video conferencing (or video telephony) for communication and discussion as opposed to one-way broadcasting with some questions (again one-way broadcasting), is not yet widely used or tried. It requires advanced and expensive technology and is still not within easy access to the average student (whether individual or corporate). Multi-point video conferencing requires expensive and cumbersome equipment that, in turn, limits the "time and space" in which courses can be delivered.

As a result, video conferencing is still rarely used. However, this situation promises to change in the near future.

## 4.4     Communication Technologies

To meet the needs of both knowledge management and management learning, an adequate stand-alone ICT environment is necessary, while communication technology is crucial. Figure 10 highlights the importance of communication between all different attributes. Each arrow is only realized by using communication technology. Some technological tools for communication have already been discussed, but we cannot ignore the most popular technological tool, the Internet.

Intranets, based on Internet technology, are widely used in most major companies, mainly as a tool for enhanced communication. The Internet and intranets can also fulfil the role of a communication platform for our purposes, if the pedagogical material necessary for learning has been embedded. Ideally, a good learning platform should contain its own communication facility, or, if the learning platform and the communication facility are separated, they should be integrated by dynamic links (comparable to Internet hypertext links). But one can also easily make an argument for installing communication platform(s) and learning environment(s) independently from one another, which enhances flexibility and inter-operability. There is not one best practice, but rather a few possible ways to proceed. Many companies are developing communication platforms based on Microsoft Exchange or Lotus Notes. Either choice is perfect for most learning environments.

Group Decision Support Systems (GDSS, discussed before) can partly play the same role, however, they are a more restricted communication platform than the Internet.

The same can be said about chat room or bulletin board facilities that some companies may have available. It is not advisable to have a discussion platform and learning materials separated in different software environments. If there are platforms of any kind already available, you should concentrate on the functionality of that discussion forum and compare functionality to ease of use, before taking any decision for new software.

Face-to-face communication cannot to be forgotten. Even in a virtual business school, the sit-in sessions, workshops or seminars are still important parts of the learning process. Certain aspects of a virtual business school, such as competency-driven learning, cannot be achieved in a virtual environment. Face-to-face communication proves to be most efficient and effective. Workshops, though, should concentrate on dialoguing rather than one-way communication.

As we argued previously, the changing economic and management environment supposes that the development of management skills is a crucial factor in the success of today's management. It is not uncommon to find that concepts and cases are more geared towards supporting the knowledge-based side of education, whereas different types of cases, tutorials, project work and other activities are more supportive of competency-based education. Our concept of the Hybrid Business School clearly embraces a balance between skills and knowledge.

## 4.5     The Big Picture

The big picture of an integrated knowledge management and virtual education approach, which is designed for practicing managers, is what we call the Hybrid Business School. The overlap between knowledge management and virtual education, as illustrated in the figure below, helps both act effectively, provided both are adequately supported by information technology. It is this information technology point of view – it could almost be called a technology push view – which allows us to create this "Hybrid Business School leverage" for companies. In this section we will discuss the information technologies necessary to realize both concepts and their overlapping leverage.

In the future, the integrated approach will allow for the availability of individual personal learning plans, or a mass-individualization of management education based on dynamic employee profiles and career path necessities. In the end, the main driver for the Hybrid Business School is the organization and how it deals with managing in the new economy (its philosophy, vision, strategies, managerial roles, alliances, etc.) as discussed in previous chapters. As a result, successful companies of the future will be learning organizations, whose learning aspects will be reflected in its core values, business strategy, training and development, HRD strategies, and HR policies. These elements are the continuous drivers of change and knowledge management, and will constantly update the company's management education offerings, which is where the real added value of the Hybrid Business School lies.

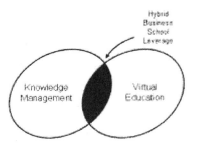

*Figure -11.* The hybrid business school's added value

The knowledge and learning potential of the Hybrid Business School approach is mainly defined by its communication. The existence of the knowledge repository, or of a CBRS, an ANN or electronic pedagogical material is a necessary condition, although not enough. Communication makes knowledge creation and exchange possible. This particular communication paradigm is different from what we traditionally know from most business schools, even from those that experiment with Internet-based courses. Although figure 12 depicts information technology in support of communication, it is the quality and the density of the communication that is the distinctive factor.

The Hybrid Business School is founded on a combination of the travelling and growing paradigms. The travelling metaphor advocates a self-organizing principle. It is the learner who is in charge of his/ her learning process, whereas the teacher takes the role of the experienced and expert leader who guides the students through the exploration of unknown terrain. The teacher/ guide not only points out the way, but also provides navigation tools and techniques. Hence, a more holistic view and the self-organizational character of learning are emphasized. The growing metaphor then brings in the personality development. Rather than creating a body of knowledge, which would define the profession of management like the professional approach it would take, the subject matter is seen as a set of experiences each student should incorporate into his/her personality. As a result, communication makes the crucial difference between the power of the travelling and growing paradigms and the (mainstream) transfer paradigm. A second important difference, at least in practice, is that the transfer paradigm is often organized in functional and specialized courses whereas the travelling and growing metaphors will drive a broader and more integrated point of view.

The practice of each individual Hybrid Business School project will need a different ICT infrastructure, but figure 12 gives the building blocks of such a project. The more a business school or a company can build an infrastructure like the one depicted in figure 12, and fill it with the necessary information, the better it is armed to tackle other Hybrid Business School projects. This infrastructure offers flexibility more than anything else. If a business school can develop pedagogical material and the communication environment around it in order to run a particular degree program, they can easily and swiftly organize, for example, a two-week course in supply chain management for any particular company. The richer the pedagogical base, the more flexibility is created.

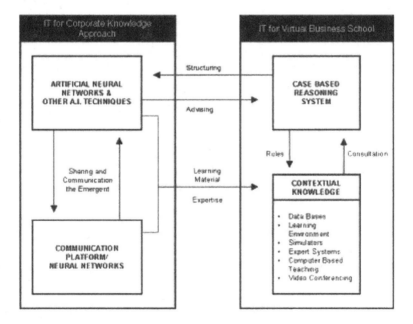

*Figure -12.* Knowledge Technologies for the Virtual Business School

### 4.5.1 Some concluding remarks

- The process of dealing with contextualized knowledge and experiences, based on an information and communication platform, is what we call the Virtual Business School. The process of dealing with experiences, tacit knowledge and the knowledge repository is what we call the "Knowledge Management Approach";

- The overlap of knowledge management and virtual education brings both knowledge management and virtual education to a higher level and closer to the corporate practice. The Hybrid Business School mutually reinforces both knowledge management and virtual education;

- New developments in ICT such as Case-Based Reasoning Systems, Group Decision Support Systems and Artificial Neural Networks can support some aspects of organizational learning processes and organizational transformation;

- The real driver for the Hybrid Business School is the organization and how it deals with managing in the new economy, its philosophy, vision, strategies, managerial roles, alliances, and so on.

# 5. SUPPORTING TECHNOLOGIES FOR KNOWLEDGE MANAGEMENT

Sunil Choenni, Robin Bakker, Henk Ernst Blok, and Robert de Laat

## 5.1 Introduction

Sometimes it seems that the signals that we receive from companies today are contradictory. On the one hand, there is so much data available that we are drowning in data but starving for information. For example, a query about a subject on the World Wide Web often results in hundreds of potentially interesting documents. In general, it is a laborious task to (manually) inspect all these documents. On the other hand, organizations put a lot of effort into actively and systematically preserving the knowledge/experience that is available in their organization, implying that even more and more complex types of data (audio, video, etc) need to be stored.

For a long time, research and development in the field of information systems was devoted to automating routine, often administrative jobs, in an efficient way. The data handled by computer systems in these jobs were well-structured and "true" data, e.g., data with an uncertain character was not an issue. As soon as the automation of these tasks was well understood, research and development in the field of information systems became more ambitious. Currently, research and development evolves in several directions, which are not necessarily divergent. A number of these directions appear to be promising in satisfying the practical need of companies for knowledge management.

In this chapter, we discuss the potentials of information retrieval and data mining for knowledge management. The major goal of knowledge management is to preserve the knowledge/experiences that are available in an organization in an active and systematic way. Furthermore, organizations want to exploit this knowledge/experience to improve its business processes. In order to achieve this goal, a number of steps, which are evenly important, can be distinguished. These are the collection of knowledge/ experiences, codifying knowledge/experiences in a formal system in order to store them in a computer system, the distribution of information/knowledge, and the application of the information/knowledge in business processes. From an (end) user point of view to knowledge management the distribution and application of knowledge/experiences are the most important steps. The focus of this chapter is the distribution of knowledge. We note that the application of the delivered information and knowledge in business processes is beyond the scope of this chapter. In general this is dependent on the business process at hand.

The collection of knowledge/experiences is a typical task of knowledge engineers. In general, a knowledge engineer performs this step by means of literature review, interviews, and protocol analysis. The codification of knowledge/experiences into a formal system is a task of computer specialists. There has always been a trade-off between the simplicity and the expressive power of a formal system. In general, the simpler a formal system is to understand, the less its expressive power is.

The central question that we ask in this chapter is: how can we exploit information retrieval and data mining techniques to supply users of an automated system with interesting and useful information and knowledge, whether or not upon request? We assume that an automated system with data or information is available. We note that although the notions of data, information, and knowledge are subjective, it is widely accepted that a sensible distinction can be made. Data are raw facts obtained from an environment; they do not have a meaning to a user. When data become meaningful to a user, it is called information. This is the case if data is processed, for instance by aggregating similar types of data. The sales figure for beer of a supermarket for example, is just a sequence of numbers. It becomes information if the sales figures of beer are aggregated in order to provide e.g., the annual sales of beer. Information becomes knowledge, according to the authors, if it provides you with new insight in a phenomenon that you did not have before or simply did not expect. To obtain knowledge, often a higher degree of aggregations of different types of data is required. Suppose that the sales figure of diapers is also available, and the aggregation of the sales figures of beer and diapers lead to the conclusion that the sale of diapers is dependent on the sales of beer. This is considered as knowledge, since this conclusion was not expected and leads to new insight, which in turn may lead to a new organization of the items in the supermarket by putting beer and diapers next to each other.

In the field of information retrieval, effort is put into building systems that are capable of handling information needs of a user. Information needs formulated by a user are not exact, as they are traditional (database) applications, but rather vague and incomplete. Often an information need is expressed by a set of keywords. Suppose that we have a system containing a digital library and a user a key word. By means of an interactive session with the user, an information retrieval system attempts to discover what precisely the information need of a user is and to meet this need. The basic concepts and techniques that are used in the processing of information needs of a user will be discussed in this chapter. The basics of another topic that will be covered in this chapter are data mining.

The fields of data mining and information retrieval both aim to meet an information need of a user. The difference between them is the type of information need both fields deal with. An information need expressed in the context of data mining has a higher degree of vagueness and incompleteness than an information need expressed in the context of information retrieval. The goal of data mining is to extract implicit, previously unknown, and potentially useful knowledge from large data sets. The extracted knowledge may support or be used in strategic decision-making. A typical mining question for instance -- in the context of our supermarket example -- is: find me interesting profiles of clients that have not been discovered so far. It should be clear that although we discuss data mining as a knowledge distribution mechanism, it might be considered as a knowledge creation technique as well.

The remainder of this chapter is organized as follows. In Section 2, we give an overview of the basic concepts and techniques in the field of information retrieval. Furthermore, we discuss the relationship between knowledge management and information retrieval in more detail. Section 3 is devoted to the basics of data mining and the relationship with knowledge management. Finally, Section 4 concludes the chapter.

## 5.2    Information Retrieval

The explosive growth of the web has entailed a boost in the development of modern information retrieval systems. Today, the web has become a huge knowledge resource, containing information about many subjects. The challenge the user faces is finding the information he/she needs. Many modern information retrieval systems, like search engines, are designed to facilitate the user in this search for useful information. Compared to the traditional information retrieval systems, modern retrieval systems are designed for ordinary users, i.e., those who are not familiar with the available collection of documents in a system or on the web, the representation of documents, and the use of retrieval operators. This implies that requirements imposed on modern retrieval systems are different from those imposed on traditional systems, like data retrieval systems. In table 1, we list some of the major differences between data and information retrieval systems. As we can see, for data retrieval systems, a question needs to be formulated in a formal query language, which is, in turn, used to search for data that exactly match the question. Therefore, a data retrieval system is capable of giving accurate answers.

*Table -1.* [Differences between data retrieval and information retrieval]

| Aspect | Data retrieval | Information retrieval |
|---|---|---|
| Matching | Exact | Partial & best |
| Model | Deterministic | Probabilistic |
| Query language | Formal | Natural |
| Answers to questions | Exact | Relevant |
| Output sensitivity to errors | No | Yes |

The main requirements for modern information retrieval systems are the following. First, users should be able to express their information need in natural language, e.g., by means of keywords or phrases. Second, the system should rank the output of the system by a degree that expresses the usefulness of each output. The systems should be able to reformulate the user's information need on the basis of new bodies of evidence, e.g. obtained by user feedback. In Section 2.1, we give an overview of the techniques and models to handle these requirements. Then, in Section 2.2, we discuss an application of information retrieval. Finally, in section 2.3, we stress the relationship between information retrieval and knowledge management.

## 5.3 Basics of information retrieval

In a modern information retrieval system, we have on the one hand the contents of an object, e.g., documents, represented in one or another (formal) way, and on the other hand we have an information need mostly represented in natural language. The goal is to find relevant and useful matches between the information need and the contents of the objects represented in the system.

In order to implement these systems, a number of basic processes should be supported by these systems [Crof 93]. In Figure 13, we have depicted these steps as discussed in [Crof 93]. In the figure, squared boxes represent data and ovals represent processes. We assume that we are only dealing with documents and no other type of objects.

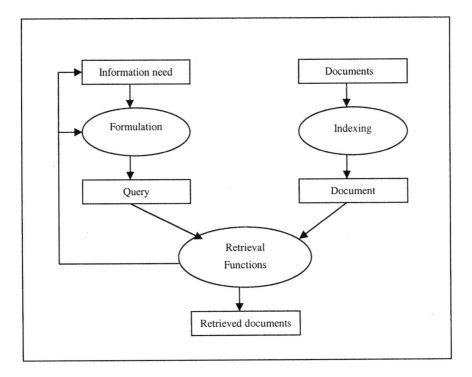

*Figure -13.* basic processes in an information retrieval system

Representing the documents is usually called indexing. The indexing process results in a formal document representation. For example, a document may be represented by a set of words that covers the content of a document or just by the title and abstract and the location where the actual document is stored.

The translation of an information need into a set of queries is called formulation. On the basis of these queries and the document representations, retrieval functions determine the degree of matching between the set of queries and each document. The documents corresponding to the best matches are retrieved and delivered to the user, who in turn may provide feedback on the delivered documents. This feedback is considered as new input in the formulation process, which will lead to a new set of queries, and the matching between these queries and document representations will start again. In this way an interactive session between a user and the system is established, which leads to a better understanding of the information need for the system as well as for the user. In modern information retrieval systems, the formulation process and the retrieval functions are automated. In the following, we discuss the indexing, formulation process and the retrieval functions in more detail.

## 5.3.1    Indexing

There are various ways to represent a document. The two most obvious ways are to represent a document as full text or by a set of keywords (manually) extracted from the text. The advantage of representing a document by the full text is that it is the most complete representation, while the disadvantage is the high computational cost that is associated in processing a query.

The advantage representing a document by a set of keywords is that we have a concise representation of a document. However, the output as a result of a query is in general poor. Therefore, the representation of documents is generally somewhere in between the full text and keywords representation. This in-between representation is partly inspired by Luhn's analysis; the result is depicted in Figure 14. The idea is to select those words as keywords for a document that are able to discriminate against different documents, which means that we ignore the words that appear frequently and the words that appear rarely in documents. On the one hand, this strategy is justified by the fact that words that appear frequently in all documents do not provide significant information. On the other hand, this strategy is justified by the fact that a user almost never uses words in the formulation of their information need that rarely appear in documents. To be more precise, it appeared that the distribution of words in documents and the distribution of words for information need formulations are the same and are distributed according to Zipf law. This means that only 20% of the words in a vocabulary covers 80% of the words in documents and in the formulation of information needs

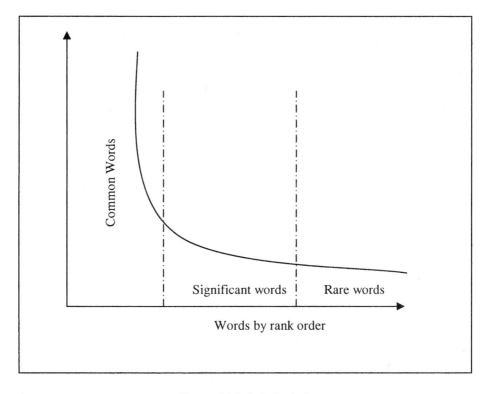

*Figure -14.* Luhn's Analysis

We distinguish a number of phases in generating a document representation. First, the words in a document are identified, i.e., discarding accents, spaces, etc. Next, the high frequency and low frequency words are removed. Then, the words with the same stem are grouped in one class, and possible relationships between classes are established, e.g., synonyms, hierarchical relationships (e.g., an apple is a fruit). This way, each stem becomes an index term. To each index term, a weight is associated expressing the importance of a term. This weight is a product of the so-called **term frequency** (**tf**) and the **inverse document frequency** (**idf**). The term frequency of a term **t** in a document **d,** tf(t,d), is defined as a function of the occurrence of **t** in **d** related to the term with the highest occurrence in **d.** The inverse document frequency of a term **t** is defined as a function of the reciprocal of the number of documents in which term t occurs and the total number of documents in a collection. The weight of a term is used to rank a document on its usefulness as a response to an information need.

### 5.3.2      Formulation

A user's information need is reformulated into a number of queries by an information retrieval system during an interactive session. Such a session is required since a user does not have any detailed knowledge of the collection and the organization of the documents in the system. Therefore, the initial formulation of an information need is a guess to retrieve relevant information. In case of a bad guess, the interactive session is required to eventually formulate an improved set of queries such that the user's information need can be met. A popular strategy to obtain an improved set of queries is to process the feedback of a user. A user is presented with a list of retrieved documents on the basis of the initial formulation of his/her information need. Next, the user is asked to mark the documents that are relevant. On the basis of this feedback a new set of queries is generated containing index terms with an associated weight that are assessed as relevant by the user. A well-known formula to process feedback is that of Rocchio [Roch 71]], in which a term that appears in documents assessed as relevant by a user is of greater significance than a term that appears in documents that are assessed as non-relevant.

### 5.3.3      Retrieval functions

The goal of a retrieval function is to predict which documents are relevant given a set of queries. More formally, a retrieval function takes as input a set of documents **D** and a set of queries **Q**, and assigns to each pair (**d, q | d ∈ D, q ∈ Q**) a real value that expresses the relevance of document **d** for query **q**.

The first retrieval function was the so-called Boolean retrieval function. In this case a keyword represented a set of documents. For example, the keyword "knowledge management" corresponds to the set of documents that are indexed by this keyword. The operators AND and OR are used to extend and to reduce a set of documents respectively. For example, a query including the keywords "knowledge management AND information retrieval" will retrieve a subset of the documents that are indexed by "knowledge management", while a query including the keywords "knowledge management OR information retrieval" will retrieve a superset of the documents that are indexed by "knowledge management". The major drawback of the Boolean retrieval function is that it either retrieves a document or not; it does not have the capability to rank documents. For example, a document that is not indexed by knowledge management but deals with information retrieval will not be retrieved as a response to the query "knowledge management AND information retrieval", while it might be an interesting document for a user.

One of the first functions that was able to rank a set of retrieved documents is the so-called vector space model. Index representations and queries are considered as vectors. Let $\vec{d} = \{d_1, d_2, d_3, ..., d_m\}$ be an index representation of a document **d**, in which each $d_i$ is associated with a keyword *i*. For example, $d_i$ takes the value 1 if the *i*-th keyword occurs in **d** and 0 otherwise. And if a query **q** is a similar vector $\vec{q} = \{q_1, q_2, q_3, ..., q_m\}$ with regard to the same keywords, then the ranking of documents is determined by a similarity measure, which is defined as the cosine of the angle between the two vectors $\vec{d}$ and $\vec{q}$, that is

$$sim(\vec{d}, \vec{q}) = \cos \Theta = \frac{\sum_{i=1}^{m} d_i \cdot q_i}{\sqrt{\sum_{i=1}^{m} (d_i)^2} \cdot \sqrt{\sum_{i=1}^{m} (q_i)^2}}.$$

We note that the inner product $\sum_{i=1}^{m} d_i \cdot q_i$ expresses the number of shared keywords between a document d and a query q. To illustrate the implications of this function, we have depicted it for m=2 in figure 15. The smaller the angle between $\vec{d}$ and $\vec{q}$, the larger the cosine and the similarity between them. The major disadvantage is that it is not clear how to determine the values for the vectors $\vec{d}$ and $\vec{q}$.

Many efforts can be found in the literature that attempt to include the weight of a term in these vectors. However this appears to be a tough problem.

The second class of functions that are used to rank documents are the probability functions, which use Bayes' rule as underpinning. In these type of functions, the estimate of the probability (P) that a given document d is relevant, expressed as P(r|d) is the central issue. According to Bayes' rule,

$$P(r \mid d) = \frac{P(d \mid r).P(r)}{P(d)},$$

in which P(r) is the prior probability of observing a relevant document, P(d), the probability of retrieving a document d, irrespective of whether it is relevant or not, and P(d | r) is the probability of retrieving d, given the fact that it is a relevant document. The probability value of P(r | d) is, amongst others, used to rank documents. In general, it is not easy to estimate the probability P(d | r), which depends in turn on the index representation of d. For a more detailed discussion, we refer to [Fuhr 92, BaRi 99]. The probability values for P(r) and P(d) are easier to determine. Suppose we have a collection consisting of 1000 documents, and 100 of these documents are indexed, amongst others, by the keyword "knowledge management". Suppose that we know beforehand that only 10 documents are relevant to a query that contains the key word "knowledge management." Then, P(d) = 1/1000 and P(r) = 10/1000.

In most of the retrieval functions, the weighting of terms is of importance in implementing these functions. Therefore, research in terms of weighting algorithms is an active part of research. The effectiveness of information retrieval systems is determined by the so-called precision and recall measures. Precision is defined as the number of relevant documents among those that are actually retrieved, and recall is defined as the number of retrieved documents that are indeed relevant. In other words, let A be the set of relevant documents and B the set of retrieved documents. Then, the precision and recall can be computed by $|A \cap B| / |B|$ and $|A \cap B| / |A|$. Today, the average recall and precision values of IR systems are both about 40%.

### 5.3.4 Applications of information retrieval

In the past it was impossible for multinationals to store, and more importantly, retrieve information about all activities carried out by its employees. Even now, it is a time-consuming task to find someone within a company who carried out a specific task before and is able to provide information about this task. Many different types of organizations face this problem. For example, in the research field questions may arise like: did someone already investigate the possibility of a synthetic elbow? And if so, what did he/she do and can I take advantage of that? In a banking environment, if you receive a request to supply a credit for building a skyscraper, you would like to find people and/or documents within your company that might help you evaluate the request. This are typical types of problems where information retrieval systems may contribute to the solution. Other types of problems that companies face are that employees working on the same project have a different frame of reference. To speed up a common understanding, it might be useful to tailor information such that it fits to the frame of reference of an employee.

Information retrieval systems based on variants of Boolean, vector space, and probabilistic retrieval functions are able to solve the above-mentioned problems partially. A promising direction for obtaining an overall solution for these problems is to incorporate semantics into the retrieval functions. The idea is to capture the meaning of a concept within a given context, since the meaning of the same concept can be different in different contexts. For example the following search strings "Gates founding Microsoft" and "Closing the gates in front of the house" both use the word gates, but they have a totally different meaning. Based on other concepts around the word "gates", using semantics, we are able to recognize which meaning of gates a user is referring to. This is a significant step forward in comparison to retrieval functions discussed so far. Implicitly, all appearances of gates will come up, no matter what the meaning is in the discussed retrieval functions. This may cause the user to have to search within the given answers.

To find out the semantics of a concept, information retrieval systems may combine and exploit a number of language tools and properties. For example, the application of lexicons on a string can be exploited. Advantages can also be taken from the structure of a document and the syntax (and morphology) of a sentence. Heuristics can be used in determining the semantics of a concept, especially if the application domain is well understood. An ontology is an important tool to map related concept to each other, e.g., "red " is an instance of the class color. The appearance of dates and time series can also be exploited for semantics purposes. For example 'Three days after September 11, two men were arrested'. It is important to recognize these language constructions in order to provide answers to questions like: 'what happened after the 11th of September?'

Modern information retrieval systems, such as Cyntelix, contain robust semantics engines in order to determine the meaning of a given concept within its context. The goal of a semantic engine is to take advantage of the above-mentioned tools.

In the development of information retrieval applications, a number of steps can be distinguished. In figure 15, these steps are depicted.

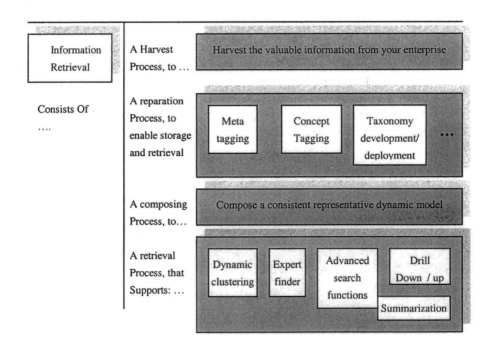

*Figure -15.* Steps in an information retrieval process

If we take a closer look at the processes that have to be supported we can distinguish between the following.

Harvesting. In the harvest process, we collect the valuable information from our enterprise. Old information should not be published and/or disturb the retrieval process. Regarding information that is not digitally available, the decision has to be made what information should be scanned and published. If we take a closer look at the technical implementation of this layer, we can conclude the following:

Information retrieval can be implemented "on top of" existing systems, retrieving and combining information from multiple sources. However, this implies flexibility in the connectivity of this layer. A large number of file formats have to be supported, or, if not supported, it should be possible to add a converter/fetcher within a limited period of time. For example Cyntelix can support all office applications (xls, doc, ppt, PDF, Lotus notes, DXF, DWG, MP3, Exchange, ODBC, html, and many others).

Preparation. The next step is necessary in order to enable an optimized storage model, and to provide the end-user with an intuitive and well performing retrieval environment. In current document management implementation, we see that many of the tasks that need to be performed in this step are done manually. This introduces inconsistency, error, and poor meta data, and concept tagging capabilities. To prevent the end-user (retriever) from being bothered with the way information is stored, it is important to perform an (semi-) automatic preparation step. This preparation step can be a combination of:

- *Meta tagging*; extracting meta information from a document, e.g. MS Word saves author information in a meta field that can be retrieved from the file.
- *Concept tagging*; a document is based on a number of concepts, and focuses on a specific domain. This information can be retrieved from a document by language tools as explained above.
- *Information extraction*; some types of documents contain patterns that can be recognized and used in the retrieval step. For instance an order always has an order date, order number etc. These can be retrieved using pattern-matching technologies.
- *Categorization*; in order to support the use of categorical searches, new documents should be categorized based on the concept tagging information, and eventually based on a (trained) taxonomy.
- *Taxonomy development*; To support the categorization step, taxonomies have to be supported, loaded, but also automatically learned based on a set of documents.
- *Storage preparation*; To achieve a well performing information retrieval, the incoming information has to be transformed in a model that is storagable and optimized for the end-user retrieval functionality.

Cyntelix contains several autonomous engines to support all the preparation steps described above. It also contains a learning based categorization tool, where taxonomies can be deployed, but also learned automatically and semi automatically.

Storage. As outlined in the figure above, the information stored in the retrieval system must be a consistent representative model of the source information, optimized for retrieval. In the Cyntelix environment, only relevant information (needed for end-user functionality), including the important tags, is stored in combination with a link to the original document. If the retriever requests the full document, it is retrieved from its source.

Retrieval. The last step in the process is the retrieval step. This is the most visible step in the whole process for the end-user. Users only see and interact with this part of an information retrieval system. The user can be provided with a lot of end-user functionality like:

- Dynamic clustering of documents (clustering the available documents, in combination with current search directions of the end-user).
- Expert finder functionality; based on available information from multiple sources, (e.g. employee curriculum, employee e-mail, written documents etc.) it is possible to find the expert within an organization for a given domain.
- Advanced search functionalities, such as providing users with alternatives, interactive dialogs, etc. Based on the available information and the search/query the end-user performs, the end-user can be supported in finding the right information.
- Drilling down on concepts; since the information retrieval system contains a lot of concepts and relations between concepts, it is possible to support drilling down or up (e.g. Clicking on the concept pets, will provide the end-user with a list of pets like dog, cat, fish etc.; clicking on dog, will provide the end-user with a list of dogs, etc.).
- Summarization; it is very time-consuming for an end-user to study documents and determine whether they are relevant. Using summarization techniques it is possible to generate dynamic summarizations of documents, and even to customize these (e.g. summarize a given document and come up with all relevant paragraphs, or pieces of text concerning given topics). This reduces the end-user's retrieval time drastically.

Cyntelix contains very advanced retrieval functionality and capabilities in composing dynamic summarizations. In information retrieval, the more advanced the underlying techniques are, the more advanced and intuitive the end-user functionality is.

As we have seen in the previous paragraphs, we do not want to bother end-users with the way information is stored. Additionally, to be able to easily implement information retrieval software in or on top of existing systems, it is important that the retrieval environment is flexible regarding end-user functionality. This can be achieved in several ways, like J2EE implementation, component based development, or, as implemented within Cyntelix, using an open query language in combination with XML.

### 5.3.5    Information retrieval as supporting technology

Information retrieval is one of the cornerstones of knowledge management. Development in this field attempts to deal with the subjective perception of information of individual users. An adequate handling of subjective perceptions is crucial in knowledge management, since different users may have different associations with the same set of data or information. Therefore, development in the field of information retrieval may give a boost to the feasibility of computerized knowledge management systems.

## 5.4    Data Mining

The implementation of data mining applications in for-profit as well as in not-for-profit organizations has seen a recent surge. These organizations have realized that their databases may contain knowledge that could improve the quality of decisions taken in the present or the future. Conventional data analysis tools are inadequate to extract this knowledge, while manually extracting it is a time-consuming and tedious process at best. Therefore, there is a practical need to (partially) automate this process. Data mining contributes to fulfilling this need by combining techniques from different fields, such as database technology, machine learning, statistics, and artificial intelligence.

Within the scope of knowledge management, data mining is an interesting technology, since knowledge evolves over time and therefore the knowledge base of an organization needs to be updated. Some knowledge may be very useful today but might become obsolete in the future. For example, if we want to open a store to sell CDs, some knowledge about different potential locations of the store is desired. But if it becomes common in the future to sell CDs via the Internet, knowledge about the potential location of a store is no longer needed.

In Section 3.1, we discuss the basics of data mining and provide an overview of data mining techniques. In Section 3.2, we discuss how to develop data mining applications successfully. Finally, in section 3.3, we discuss the relationship between knowledge management and data mining in more detail.

### 5.4.1 Basics of data mining

The field of data mining has been developed in a rather ad hoc way, sometimes using vague concepts. Many informal definitions can be found in the popular press about data mining, such as the search for knowledge, patterns, regularities and so on. But let us take a closer look at what is formally happening in data mining.

Data mining algorithms induce models from large databases, which contain observations from the real world. The goal of inducing a model is to provide insight into a phenomenon of interest that is part of the real world. This insight may help in understanding the phenomenon, or it may help to predict the outcome of similar phenomena. Although data mining algorithms induce models from a large set of observations from real-life, this does not necessarily mean that these models are correct. The explanation for this fact is that an induction process is not truth preserving. Popper illustrates this with the following example. Suppose we have a database that records data about swans. In this database, the color of all swans appears to be white. Under the closed world assumption, the conclusion "all swans are white" is correct, but this might not be true in the real world. The fact that we have observed only white swans (until now in the real world) does not mean that all swans are indeed white. It is possible that there are black swans, but we have not observed them yet, and therefore they are not recorded in our database. This implies that a model obtained by data mining should be tested on its validity and to what extent it deviates from the real world. This can be done by comparing simulation results to real-life results. In figure 16, the formal data mining process is depicted.

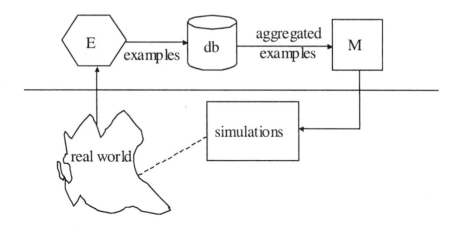

*Figure -16.* Sketch of a data mining process

Since statistical techniques also induce models from large data sets, it often raised the question what is the fundamental difference between statistics and data mining. Although it is very hard to point out exactly what the fundamental difference is, it is easy to list a number of major differences between them, which justify the separate identity of data mining.

Firstly, statistical techniques require that a model/hypothesis is given beforehand, and then that the data is used to test the model in order to accept or reject it. Data mining algorithms use the data to come up with (useful) models for a user. Although the number of models that can be induced from a set of data is enormous and grows exponentially with the size of a database, data mining algorithms are currently able to handle this complexity due to the arithmetical power of contemporary computers.

Secondly, data mining algorithms use data from different databases, which complicates the induction of models. Often these databases have noisy and contradictory data. Furthermore, decisive attributes essential for the mining process might be missing simply because databases are set up and maintained for other reasons than mining. In statistics, data is collected for the purpose of testing hypotheses, and therefore, the focus is on the collection of relevant and useful data.

Thirdly, statistical packages are very efficient in handling numerical data but very poor in handling other types of data, such as categorical ones. Codifying other types of data into numerical values before using statistical techniques may lead to biased results in some cases. Suppose we have a database that records the city people live in (a typical categorical attribute). Suppose that we code Amsterdam as 1 and The Hague as 3. Then, the application of many numerical operators, which is the strength of statistical packages, will lead to confusion, e.g., it is unclear how to interpret the meaning of 1+3 in this case.

Over the past years many algorithms have been developed and implemented for data mining tasks by both the research and the business community. A question that is raised by many users is: "What mining algorithm do I need for the problem at hand?" A categorization of the mining algorithms is a first step towards answering this question. Currently, we may distinguish three categories of algorithms, namely: classification and clustering algorithms, algorithms for association rules, and algorithms focused on mining time series databases. Classification and clustering algorithms aim to distribute object/tuples into a number of classes on the basis of common properties. Algorithms for association rules focus on the search of frequently occurring patterns in a database. Mining algorithms for time series databases search for common patterns embedded in a database of sequences of events. Since the classification and clustering algorithms are used most extensively, we briefly discuss these types of algorithms.

### 5.4.1.1    Association rules

The field of association rules has been inspired by databases that store items purchased by a customer as a transaction [AgIS 93, FPSU 99]. A planning department may be interested in finding associations between sets of items. An example of such an association may be that 90% of the customers that purchase diapers also purchase beer. This might be a good reason to place these two items close to each other to provide the customer with better service.

For reasons of convenience, we model a supermarket database as a relation **basket** ($i_1, i_2, i_3, ..., i_k$), in which $i_j, 1 \le j \le k,$ is a binary attribute that records whether an item has been sold or not. Note that a tuple in the database corresponds to a shopping basket at the counter.

Let $I$ be the sets of all items, $X, Y \subseteq I,$, and $s(X)$ the percentage of baskets containing all items in $X$. Then, $X \rightarrow Y$ is an association rule with

$$\text{regard to } t_1 \text{ and } t_2 \text{ iff } s(XY) \geq t_1 \text{ and } \frac{s(XY)}{s(X)} \geq t_2, \text{ in which } Y \not\subset X.$$

The latter equation expresses the confidence in a rule, while the former equation guarantees that item sets should have a minimum size, and therefore a minimum support.

The problem is to find all rules that have minimum support and confidence greater than the defined threshold values $t_1$ and $t_2$. In general, two steps are distinguished in solving this problem. In step 1, all item sets that have minimum support are selected. And in step 2, for each item set $X$ found in step 1 and any $Z \subset X$, all rules that have minimum confidence are generated.

Suppose that we have the following four transactions: $T_1 = \{a, b, c\}$, $T_2 = \{a, b, d\}$, $T_3 = \{a, d, e\}$, and $T_4 = \{a, b, d\}$. Let the minimum support and minimum confidence be 0.7 and 0.9 respectively. Then, the following item sets meet the minimum support: $s(\{a\}) = 1$, $s(\{b\}) = 0.75$, $s(\{d\}) = 0.75$, $s(\{a,b\}) = 0.75$, and $s(\{a,d\}) = 0.75$. The valid association rules are: $b \rightarrow a$ and $d \rightarrow a$, both with confidence 1.0. Note that $a \rightarrow b$ is not valid, since

$$\frac{s(\{a,b\})}{s(\{a\})} = \frac{0.75}{1} < 0.9$$

Having obtained the item sets that meet the minimum support, step 2 is straightforward. The solution for step 1 is harder. A simple solution for step 1 is to form all item sets and obtain their support in one pass over the data. However, this solution is computationally unfeasible, since the number of item sets grows exponentially with the number of items. The challenge is to minimize the complexity and the number of passes over the database. A large number of papers in the literature report on various types of solutions for this problem, exploiting mathematical properties as well as domain knowledge.

### 5.4.1.2    Classification

As noted before, classification aims to distribute the tuples of a database into a number of classes, predefined or not. In general, if the classes are not pre-defined, the term clustering is used. In the remainder of this section, we restrict ourselves to the case that the classes are pre-defined.

Currently, the most popular classification techniques are based on decision trees, while evolutionary techniques are gaining considerable attention. Classical techniques, such as regression, kernel density methods, etc. are still appropriate for many data mining tasks. Due to space limits, we briefly characterize decision trees and two evolutionary techniques namely, genetic algorithms and neural networks. Our characterization is based on the following: the assumptions on which a technique is based, the quality of the solution produced by a technique, and the "complexity" of a technique. Such a characterization can be made for classical techniques as well.

Decision trees. This type of algorithm picks an attribute as root, and splits it into all possible values, resulting in a tree with depth 2. If all corresponding tuples to a leaf are in the same class C, label that leaf with C. As long as leafs are unlabeled: choose a new attribute and expand the tree by splitting it into all possible values again. This process terminates when all leaves have been labeled.

Algorithms based on decision trees differ in the way a choice is made for an attribute that will be split. The results of decision trees are easily interpreted and are useful as long as the trees are not too large. In general, large trees have a higher misclassification rate than small ones. There are techniques to determine the right size for a tree.

The most expensive operation is the splitting of an attribute on attribute values and the classification of all objects according to these values. Furthermore, a tree grows exponentially with the number of attributes.

Genetic algorithms. Genetic algorithms start with an initial population. Traditionally, an individual/object in the population is represented as a string of bits. The quality of each individual is computed, called the fitness of an individual. On the basis of these qualities, a selection of individuals is made. Some of the selected individuals undergo a minor modification, called mutation. For some pairs of selected individuals a random point is selected, and the sub strings behind this random point are exchanged, called cross-over. The selected individuals, whether or not modified, form a new generation and the same procedure is repeated with the new generation until some defined criterion is met.

Genetic algorithms have been successfully applied in a wide variety of applications. In some cases, it is proven that it converges to a local optimum. In other cases, experiments show that convergence occurs. We note that in order to apply genetic algorithms a representation of a population and a quality measure should be defined. The most expensive operation is the computation of the fitness function. A genetic algorithm searches different (small) parts of a search space. The complexity is linear with the number of individuals in a population and the number of generations that should be investigated.

Neural networks. A neural network is a function that maps input patterns to output patterns. It consists of nodes and connections between nodes. Nodes are organized in layers, one input layer, a number of hidden layers, and an output layer. A node in layer i is connected with all nodes in layer I +1. The connections are labeled with a weight. The input nodes receive binary values from their environment. The other nodes compute a function from their weighted input and propagate the result. The function looks as follows:

$$V_j = g(\sum_k w_{j,k} \cdot V_k)$$

in which $V_j$ denotes the value of node $j$, $w_{j,k}$ the weight of the connection between node $j$ and node $k$, and $g$ is a function. The output of the network strongly depends on the function $g$.

To make the network learn the correct function, we let it adjust the weights using a set of input-output pairs. A simple idea for an adjustment scheme is: if a network gives a wrong answer, the weights are adjusted proportionally to their contribution to the wrong answers.

A neural network should contain at least one hidden layer to approximate continuous functions. In general setting the proper parameter, including number of nodes, hidden layers, etc., for a neural network values is a difficult task. The computation of the values that should be propagated is the most expensive operation. Furthermore, once a neural network is established, the complexity is linear with the input. The number of connections also grows linear with the addition of a node in a layer.

### 5.4.2    Applications of data mining

Applications of data mining technology can currently be found in a wide variety of business fields. Airline companies analyze historical reservation data in order to get a better profile of their customers. In the field of marketing, data mining technologies are used to decide which customers to send an advertisement to and which not to send to. Retailers analyze historical supply and demand data to detect trends that help in planning sales promotions and optimizing their purchasing. Supermarkets are looking for associations between items that improve the organization of the items in their shops. Data that pertain to the performance of large complex systems are analyzed to detect abnormal behavior. Insurance companies use data mining algorithms to discriminate between "good" and "bad" clients. And the list of data mining applications is actually still growing.

Data mining is in fact a step in a larger process, the so-called Knowledge Discovery in Databases (KKD) process. We roughly distinguish the following steps in the KDD process.

- A so-called mining question should be formulated. This question should specify the kind of information one is looking for. In general, a mining question is formulated together with domain experts.
- Then, the data that may be used in order to answer the mining question should be selected, enriched, cleaned, and integrated, i.e., constructing a data warehouse. Since intelligence gathering is an important activity in many applications, data enrichment is a key factor in building data warehouses successfully.
- A mining algorithm has to be selected / developed that will search the data warehouse for appropriate answer to the mining question.
- Finally, the answers of the search process should be presented in such a way that domain experts are able to understand and evaluate these answers.

We note that these four steps are defined as Knowledge Discovery in Databases (KDD) [FPSU 99] and should be iteratively applied. In general, data mining is a highly interactive process. In practice, users start with a rough idea of the information that might be interesting. During the mining session the user more explicitly specifies, based on, among others, the mining results obtained so far, which information should be searched for.

### 5.4.3    The relationship between data mining and KM

Data mining may be considered as one of the driving forces behind knowledge management, since it focuses on the search of strategic knowledge for the user, although the notion of knowledge has a limited definition. Therefore, data mining systems will continue to be a part of computerized knowledge systems.

## 5.5    Conclusions

There is currently a practical need to use the knowledge that is (implicitly) available in organizations to improve core business processes. Therefore, organizations are interested in preserving their knowledge and experiences in an active and systematic way in computer systems. In this chapter, we focused on knowledge management from an end user point of view. We discussed the technologies that are of importance in trying to meet the information need of the end user. We expect that information retrieval and data mining are major supporting technologies for knowledge management. The difference between data mining and information retrieval lies in the type of information need that is handled by each type of technology. In general, data mining is capable of handling an information need that has a higher degree of vagueness and incompleteness than information retrieval.

# 6. LEARNING AND INTERACTION VIA ICT TOOLS FOR THE BENEFIT OF KNOWLEDGE MANAGEMENT

Sunil Choenni, Saskia Harkema and Robin Bakker

## 6.1 Introduction

Currently, the field of knowledge management receives a lot of attention from the business as well as the academic community. From an academic point of view the field of knowledge management raises many challenging research questions. In companies, the growing importance of knowledge management emphasizes the strategic value of knowledge. Depending on the what view is taken, scholars have come up with different definitions of knowledge management, each stressing certain aspects of knowledge management. Swan gives a comprehensive definition of knowledge management. He argues that knowledge management can be regarded from two distinct perspectives, a cognitive model and a community model. In the first, knowledge is conceived as being captured and codified from individuals, packaged, transmitted, and processed through the use of ICT, and subsequently disseminated and used by other individuals in new contexts. The second perspective focuses on social interaction and negotiation, and emphasizes the idea of supporting interaction and collaboration in order to manage knowledge. In this model, knowledge is regarded as socially constructed through interaction within communities of practice. Knowledge is considered to be situated and contextualized. Since it is dependent on the exact situation and context, knowledge is not static, but dynamic, changing with every different situation and context under the influence of interaction. This implies that knowledge management should not only focus on merely managing knowledge, but also in creating a proper environment that stimulates interaction and fosters learning. In the field of knowledge management, both individuals and machines are considered to be learners. Although these two types of learners are completely different, their point in common is that ICT may act as a supporting tool to contribute to the learning process. In machine learning, researchers try to simulate various learning aspects of human beings in computers, e.g., neural networks, modeling of agents, and so on. To *support* the learning of human beings, the capabilities of computers are exploited as a learning tool. In this paper, we focus on learning as a vehicle for knowledge management. We discuss the potential of machine learning for knowledge management, and how ICT tools may support the learning of individuals.

The field of machine learning is primarily interested in including learning capabilities in information systems. Many techniques in machine learning are inspired by the learning process and problem solving behavior of human beings. Those aspects of the learning process and problem solving behavior that are well-understood can be built in information systems successfully. At present, researchers attempt to model dynamic business processes in a so-called agent framework. A computer agent is regarded as an entity that controls its own actions, behaves autonomously and has the power to achieve one's goals. Human agency refers to the mediating factor between structure and individual. Agenthood exists at the individual and collective level. Each level has a behavioural and a cognitive component. Autonomy refers to the fact that an agent is capable of operating independently. Building on his or her cognitive structure an agent is able to engage in a variety of cognitive processes, one of which is learning. Computer agents are aware and interact with their local environment through simple internal rules for decision-making, movement and action. In this paper we report on the opportunities and limitations of the agency framework.

The field of e-learning studies is primarily interested in how ICT technology may be exploited to support the learning process of individuals. Today, a large amount of advanced tools are available that might, at first glance, be helpful for the learner. However, it appears that not all the tools are equally appreciated by the learners. We discuss the requirements that tools according to us should meet in order to be helpful and useful for human beings. We note that results in the field of machine learning feed the development of helpful and useful tools to speed up and support the learning process of individuals.

After an analysis of several learning aspects our overall conclusion is that learning as a vehicle for KM supported by ICT tools, is feasible and may be exploited by the business community. For some aspects of learning we argue that there is hardly sufficient technological support, and therefore, the implementation of these aspects might fail, or only restricted versions of these aspects can be implemented.

## 6.2     Learning as a vehicle for Knowledge Management

It has been pointed out that companies want to learn from their own (past) experiences and to be able to further enhance that experience with best principles and lessons learned from other companies. In these companies, knowledge management focuses on the relationship between knowledge and learning within a company. In [Raelin], it is argued that learning should merge theory with practice, knowledge with experience. This approach differs from conventional learning in that it involves a conscious reflection on actual experience. Practitioners build theory as they consciously reflect on challenges of their practice; reiteratively engage in problem posing, data gathering, action, evaluation, and reflection; and then share the knowledge produced with others in practice. Knowledge creation within the company is depicted by the process of transforming experiences, which can be regarded as implicit knowledge, into shared knowledge that is explicit, especially through spirals of ongoing interaction between individuals, work teams, and organizations. It is widely recognized that ICT may support this process of learning.

The field of e-learning studies how to create a proper e-learning environment that may contribute to merging theory with practice and knowledge with experience (for more detail see also the chapter by Walker). Although we do not have a widely accepted definition for e-learning, an e-learning environment may be described by a number of desired requirements. An example of such a requirement is that an e-learning environment should focus on the needs of the learner, given his or her practical experience. To meet such a requirement implies that e-learning tools should be equipped with personalisation modules. Such a module should take into account a learner's prior knowledge, experiences, and preferences. This means that a personal model is a dynamic model that frequently needs to be updated on the basis of newly collected information. For example, suppose that a learner is interested in learning about databases and formulated in a search the keywords database and performance. Actually different learners may have different interpretations and association with these words. Suppose that a document retrieval system selected a number of documents that are apparently relevant for these keywords and return them to the learner. The learner has the possibility to give feedback about the returned documents. Suppose now that the learner rated the documents that discuss the performance of relational databases as relevant, while the documents discussing the performance of network databases is less appreciated. Then, a personalization model for this learner should be updated according to this knowledge/ preference. An architecture that supports such a scenario is given in figure 16, which consists of different components.

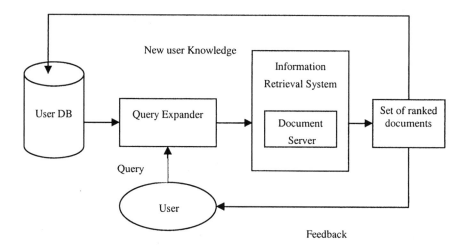

*Figure -17.* New user knowledge

An important component in the architecture is the Information Retrieval System which closely co-operates with the other components. The document server contains the documents that are available in an environment. The information retrieval techniques can be used to select the documents that meet a set of terms, called a query. These documents can be ranked according to a measure that expresses to what extent a user might be interested in a document.

The user database records a learner's knowledge and interests over time. If a user poses a query, the query expander enlarges this query with additional terms based on the knowledge available in the user database. The information retrieval system retrieves and ranks the documents that meet the terms in the expanded query. These results are presented to the learner, who is asked to provide feedback on the ranked documents. From this feedback, we search for previously unknown knowledge about the learner and store this knowledge in the user database.

Suppose that a learner is interested in performance aspects of relational databases, and he/she types in the keywords "performance" and "database". Then, the query expander consults the user database to find out whether the learner's query can be augmented by additional terms. Suppose that in the user database it is recorded that the learner's interest is relational database, and then the query expander expands the user query with the term "relational". The retrieval system searches for the documents that satisfy the terms {" relational", "database", "performance"} or a subset of these terms. These documents are ranked according to how interesting they are and presented to the learner. Suppose that the learner gives feedback, e.g., by means of re-ranking the documents, and we can derive from this feedback that he is interested in the term "index selection" , then this term is stored in the user database for the learner.

It should be clear that expertise and results from different disciplines should be combined in order to design and implement a personalisation module. The field of machine learning is especially interesting in this respect, since machine learning attempts to simulate relevant aspects of the learning process of human beings. The insights obtained from these simulations are used to develop tools that hopefully accelerate the learning process of human learners. In the next section we elaborate on this field.

Another requirement that is posed to an e-learning environment is that it should offer the learners more than one learning method, e.g, a combination of a virtual classroom, collaborative tools, self-paced instruction, etc. Actually this requirement implies that mutual interaction between learners is required. Through the years many tools have come out on the market that supports interaction. In section 4, an overview of these tools is presented.

## 6.3    Machine learning

Previously we discussed that machine learning refers to the fact that researchers try to *simulate* various learning aspects of human beings via computer modeling. Some examples of ways in which this is done are neural networks, genetic algorithms (both briefly discussed in previous chapter), and modeling of agents. We will briefly review some of these options in the next section.

Prior to the simulation of human-like aspects of learning via computers, a social phenomenon has to be identified that is perceived as being problematic in a company. This problem subsequently has to be represented in a conceptual model, which in a graphic form reveals the variables that play a role, the relationship between the variables, and the intricate interconnectedness between variables. It should be emphasized that these models do not represent a linear causality but that the causality is circular – everything is connected with each other. In these non-linear and dynamic models learning plays a crucial role: that is the reason why operationalisation of these models is difficult. Computer scientists have developed computer models that represent the way our brain works and in so doing they have created possibilities to simulate and explore how human beings learn and what the effect of learning is in a specific situation. We will, in the first instance, focus on neural networks.

Artificial neural networks basically form a metaphor for the way human brains work and as such they can be regarded as computer models of how our brain processes information and learns. McCulloh & Pitts were among the first to develop models of neural networks. Contrary to conventional computers which use an algorithmic approach, neural networks process information in a similar way to our brain. Baets describes the process that takes place in our brain as follows: *"When a neuron receives a certain stimuli and when the sum of received stimuli reaches a certain threshold value, it will react and transmit the stimuli to adjacent neurons. Knowledge is not stored somewhere in the network, rather, the network is activated each time a question is asked or an action needs to be processed....Knowledge is created over and again each time, using possibly different neurons. Each neuron is a very simple processor. Only in the densely connected network do they deliver the human performance we all know"*. The way in which these connected networks of neurons emerge, namely by reinforcing the connection between neurons, is relevant in this case. The network is composed of a large number of interconnected processing elements, which work in parallel to solve a specific problem. Neural networks learn by example; they cannot be programmed to perform a specific task or solve a problem. So learning is crucial in the development of networks which are aimed at problem-solving. These networks develop under the influence of interaction and it cannot be foreseen beforehand what the network will look like, since this is a learning process which depends on many factors. This emphasizes the dynamic and non-linear character of learning and the fact that humans learn in this way and not in a linear way.

Genetic algorithms work somewhat differently. Genetic algorithms were developed by Holland in the 60's and 70's of the last century and are grounded in Darwin's evolutionary theory. In evolutionary theory, organizations are compared to living organisms. Three principles play an important role in the evolution and survival of organism: variation, selection and reproduction. For their survival, organizations depend on their ability to acquire adequate resources – as biological organisms do. The principle of variation refers to the fact that members of a population vary in characteristics that convey relevant significance. The principle of heredity and reproduction suggests that the characteristics of individual entities are copied – i.e. reproduced – over time through certain mechanisms of which selection is a very important one. The principle of selection implies that when entities interact with each other, the characteristics of some entities may be better suited to survive and contribute to the growth of the whole population. Selection is an important mechanism in this process, since those entities that are able to adapt better to the environment have a larger chance of surviving. Evolution explained in this way is an adaptive learning process.

Company routines can be used as an example to explain how such a process works. Routines are then regarded as the genetic material of an organization. The rules that underlie these routines are then comparable to the genes of an organization. Variety is brought into the system, for instance, by means of changes in the external environment or by the changes within the organization. The measure of success in evolutionary terms is determined by the extent to which adaptation has taken place and the survival and continuity of an organism – the organization - has been secured. Adaptation is determined by fitness criteria, which in turn will determine which genes will survive – i.e. which routines are viable and which are not. Learning is crucial in this process, since organisms adapt by learning.

Both in the case of neural networks and genetic algorithms we observe how human behavior is reproduced and represented in computer modeling to support organizations in their learning process. Another possibility to simulate learning processes is via agent-based simulations. These simulations are not necessarily aimed at solving a specific problem, but are meant to explore what the behavior of human beings is if they are represented as a complex adaptive system. Harkema has done extensive research on this subject in the domain of innovation and she has demonstrated that learning is an emergent process that is subject to self-regulatory forces.

Agent-based models draw on ideas of the complexity paradigm and complex adaptive systems theory. The theory of CAS teaches us that instead of viewing organizations as machines, we should consider viewing organizations as complex adaptive systems. The theory of CAS was developed by a number of scholars gathered together in the Santa Fe Institute in the USA, which has come to be considered as the cradle of complexity theory (see earlier chapters). Complexity theory is an umbrella term for a number of theories that all fall under the same denominator and of which CAS theory is one. A characteristic for a CAS is the *dynamic* and *non-linear* character of processes in addition to phenomena like emergence and self-organization. CAS theory tears at the fundments of the predominant paradigm inside many companies, which draws an analogy between organizations and machines. The machine metaphor of organizations becomes manifest in the way organizations deal with structure, people and processes; the three main pillars upon which a company rests. But also in the way they deal with knowledge management.

Whereas the machine metaphor rests on the assumption that reality can be broken up in parts – the reason why structure, people and processes are viewed as distinct processes and knowledge is regarded as a "thing" that can be extracted from someone's brain– CAS theory is based on a holistic view of reality. This implies that instead of viewing social reality as compartmentalized, social phenomena are approached from a multi-layered perspective. The interconnection of elements is one of the premises which lies at the basis of a CAS. Holland, for instance, defines a complex system as one made up of many parts which are interconnected with each other. The interconnection between the elements that compose a system leads to the earlier described processes of emergence and self-organization. Emergence refers to the fact that the phenomena which one can discern at systems level develop bottom-up in a process of self-organization, whereby the emergent phenomena are not merely a sum of individual behaviors at the micro-level.

As one can observe, this is contrary to the main premise upon which traditional academic research rests, but it is also contrary to how many organizations operate. Whereas the machine metaphor rests on neo-classical economic theory, and the equilibrium state of systems which can be achieved by matching demand and supply; CAS theory assumes that adaptability is the main parameter and learning the main indicator to determine the adaptability of an organization.

Agent based simulation can be used to represent an organization or a community of practice as a CAS. Extensive research within a multi-national manufacturer of fast moving consumer goods revealed that when an innovation project is modeled as a CAS, emergence and self-organization occur. In order to build such a model a number of steps have to be taken into account. According to Lewin the heart of a CAS is formed by agents. She distinguishes the following steps to build a model:

- Who are the agents and what are their schemata?
- How are the agents connected? How do these connections change over time?
- What payoff functions do these agents pay attention to? What kind of tradeoffs are they willing to make among different types of pay-off?
- How do the actions of one agent affect the payoffs of others?
- How does the system evolve under the influence of changes within the system?

We saw that agents can represent a variety of entities: individuals, teams, managers, customers, and an organisation. Agents, in principle, are the decision-makers within an organization or project. Each agent's behaviour is dictated by a schema, a cognitive structure that determines what action an agent takes given his/her perception of reality. Cognitive schemata are the mental models of people and can be defined as mental representations of reality in terms of norms, values, principles, rules and models.

All the agents together form a population – a community. Populations are of importance because they form a source of possibilities to learn from, and they are part of the environment wherein agents operate. It is the *variety* of agents that causes the complex behaviour in a CAS. The behaviour is based on the different strategies of individual agents. The strategy is basically a conditional action pattern that indicates what to do in which circumstances. These may be shared among a group of people, or they may be highly personalized and individualistic as mentioned previously. In principle, the strategy of an agent is intended to improve the agent's overall condition, in the sense that an agent is driven by individual motives which are offset against what a company wants and expects.

As for the process underlying the behaviour of agents, CAS theory assumes that living systems operate best in the transition phase between chaos and order – this transition phase is called *"the edge of chaos"*. It is in this transition phase that self-organization may occur. This idea of the edge of chaos assumes that people do not strive to reach equilibrium, but that they are continuously adapting and learning. The order that is hence formed is merely temporary and continuously changes under the influence of the interaction between the agents. Attractors play a role in this process. Attractors are strange phenomenon that can best be described as "something that attracts" – within a system it is a force that draws phenomena or events into a certain direction. Attractors become manifest in for instance the cohesion within a group - people all go in one direction or they agree on something. Attractors play a role in the development of a temporary order; they emerge and disappear with the same ease. Henceforth the structures that develop are dissipative. Prigogine speaks about *"dissipative structures"* that evolve within complex systems – structures that emerge and dissolve in order to re-emerge in a new appearance in a bottom-up process. *"Dissipative structures"* refer to the emergence of new structural arrangements from the interplay between a system and its environment, or between the agents within a system and the context wherein they are embedded.

In a recent article Bonabeau illustrates how a better understanding of emergent phenomena using agent-based simulations, can help employers improve incentive programs, predict changes to corporate culture and monitor operational risk.

## 6.4     ICT tools to support learning of human beings

In the context of knowledge management within an organization, ICT tools should not only be able to simulate human learning and interaction, but also *support* social interaction and individual learning. In this section we will discuss how this may be achieved and to what extent this is currently possible.

Supporting individual learning with ICT tools is often called e-learning. There are three main properties an e-learning tool should support:

1. It should focus on the needs of the learner, given his or her background;
2. Consequently, it should support a personalized learning process, giving the learner the option to choose his or her own learning pathway;
3. It should offer several learning methods (e.g. a virtual classroom, collaborative tools, self-paced instruction, etc.).

The current state of technological development does not allow these properties to be fully supported by ICT tools. In particular, the personalization of tools (a consequence of properties 1 and 2) is not yet completely possible.

Given the increasingly global nature of firms, the role of ICT in supporting interaction will become more and more important, since meeting face-to-face is often remains impossible. Many tools that support interaction exist, for instance e-mail, instant messaging, video conferencing, discussion boards, file sharing, etc. Often these tools are not thought of as supporting knowledge management, but from the community model perspective, as described in this chapter, they are very important. First, these tools play a role in individual learning (see property 3 of an e-learning tool above). Secondly, individual learning needs to be shared within the organization in order to increase shared knowledge. Thirdly, through interaction, a community of practice is created in which the exchange of knowledge is made easier because of shared routines, words, tools, ways of doing things, stories, gestures, symbols, actions and concepts. In other words, there is a recursive effect in that interaction facilitates interaction.

In conclusion, we can state that ICT tools are particularly useful in supporting interaction within an organization. This will help both individual learning as well as organizational learning. Other tools to support individual learning need to be developed further before they reach their full potential.

## 6.5    Conclusions

From this chapter it is learned that social interaction and learning are important aspects of knowledge management. We have discussed how ICT can support these aspects through e-learning and communication tools. A well designed e-learning tool should incorporate a personalisation module that returns only the information to the user that is relevant for him / her. Currently personalisation is not possible to the extent that we would like. The field of machine learning offers a possible solution by simulating the learning behaviour of a user. By following a user's learning through machine learning, we can anticipate what type of information a user expects when asking the system a question.

There are currently many ICT tools that support communication and, although these tools are being further developed, they are already quite mature. We therefore feel that ICT tools can be useful in supporting this aspect of knowledge management. Overall, our conclusion is that ICT tools are capable of supporting most, but not all, of the aspects of knowledge management that follow from the second perspective of knowledge management in Swan's definition.

# 7. SEDUCING, ENGAGING AND SUPPORTING COMMUNITIES AT ACHMEA[2]

Virginia Dignum and Pieter van Eeden

## 7.1    1. Introduction

Communities of Practice (CoP) are groups of people who come together to share and to learn from one another, face-to-face and virtually. They are held together by a common interest in a certain area, and are driven by the desire and need to share problems, achievements, insights, tools and best practices. CoP members deepen their knowledge by interacting on an ongoing basis, and will, over time, develop a set of shared practices (Wenger et al., 2002), (APQC, 2001). Although CoPs are not new and have existed in a variety of forms probably since the beginning of mankind, only recently have organizations discovered the potential of CoPs to the sustainable advantage of business practice, the realization of strategic objectives and improvement of organizational performance. As organizations grow in size, geographical scope, and complexity, it is increasingly apparent that sponsorship and support of communities of practice can improve organizational performance (Lesser, Storck, 2001). CoPs have the following characteristics. They:

- stimulate interaction
- decrease the learning curve of new employees
- provide a forum for members to help each other solve everyday problems
- develop and disseminate best practices, guidelines and procedures
- respond more rapidly to customer needs and inquiries
- reduce rework and prevent 'reinvention of the wheel'
- create new ideas for products and services

---

[2] Achmea is a large Dutch Insurance Holding

It is commonly agreed that CoPs have the potential to overcome the inherent problems of a slow-moving traditional hierarchy in a fast-moving virtual economy, the ability to handle unstructured problems and to share knowledge outside the traditional structural boundaries, and that CoPs provide adequate means for developing and maintaining long-term organizational memories. However, problems can arise due to the voluntary participation of its members, and CoPs are not always targeted to the collection and transfer of knowledge. This means that an approach to the creation and management of CoPs must combine the positive knowledge-sharing capabilities of CoPs with manageable task solving capabilities and an orientation to business processes.

In this chapter we describe why CoPs are important to Achmea and how Achmea nurtures and organizes CoPs within the organization. The chapter is organized as follows: In the next section we will introduce the current status of CoP developments at Achmea. In section 3, the SES model used and developed at Achmea to create CoPs is introduced. In section 4 we use an example CoP to demonstrate the method and in section 5 we present a model to support collaboration in distributed communities. Finally, in section 6 we present our conclusions and discuss areas for further research.

## 7.2    Communities of Practice at Achmea

Achmea, one of the top 3 insurance groups in the Netherlands, originates from the merger of a large number of companies, and is active in the financial services, insurance, security and health care fields. Achmea aims at a flexible, innovative and personal response to the requirements of customers. Since 2001 the central theme of the mission is summarized in the slogan 'Achmea unburdens', the realization of which has large consequences for the structure and processes of the organization. Achmea aims at a position of sustainable adaptability and advantage in its environment, which requires an innovative and flexible approach to customers and their needs and plans, and therefore a better management of knowledge and expertise in the organization (Drucker, 1995).

However, the current organizational structure, based on business unit independence, is not always conducive for the realization of synergy. An environment that encourages and facilitates the development of networks of people, is one of the ways to achieve the objectives above (Davenport, Prusac, 1998). In our opinion, communities must be developed in a participatory way, involving members and stakeholders. On the other hand, communities should contribute to the realization of the strategic priorities of the company, what leads to a need for the explicit specification and monitoring of targets and objectives of a CoP. Even though CoPs are of great value for Achmea and Achmea is very keen on the creation of communities, experience shows that forcing the creation of communities top-down does not work if the target group does not already have any common interests, activities and objectives (Gongla, Rizzuto, 2001). The bottom line is that support of communities must focus on building social capital (including trust, norms, reciprocity, identity) as this provides a continuous basis for sustainable advantage and innovation.

CoP literature distinguishes between two types of communities: **self-organized** and **sponsored** (cf. Nickols, 2000). Self-organizing CoPs are created bottom-up, by the members, as a way to watch over and organize their own interests. Owing to their voluntary nature, they are fragile (as control attempts can result in their disappearance), but extremely adaptable and evolve according to members' interests. Sponsored communities are supported and initiated by the management, and are expected to produce measurable results that benefit the company. The internal structure of a sponsored CoP must, however, be decided by the members. An important aspect to keep in mind when dealing with sponsored communities is that *"a CoP reflects the members' understanding of what is important. ...Even when a community's action conforms to an external mandate, it is the community – and not the mandate – that produces the practice"* (Wenger, 1998).

In order to combine the advantages of both types, Achmea identifies groups - active in areas essential for the core business - that exhibit some of the characteristics of self-organization and then actively sponsor their activities. The process of matching community goals and interests to organizational strategic aims can only succeed if community members are convinced of the possible targets and organizational benefits of community activities and if they are active and explicitly involved in the formation of the CoP. When self-organizing communities become sponsored communities with clear targets and outward-directed activities, the need arises for the CoP to develop a clear profile of themselves as a group. That is, the community develops an identity of its own, centered around its achievements and targets. The development of an own identity is therefore an important means of connection within a group and provides an adequate interface for communication with the outside world.

## 7.3    The SES Model for community facilitation

The above sections make clear that CoPs are of great importance for Achmea due to their potential to contribute to synergy across business units. Several CoPs have been initiated or are currently under development. These projects confirm that the motivation of the management and the employees, as well as the choice of infrastructure for collaboration, communication and information are crucial for the success of CoPs.

The **SES (Seduce, Engage, Support) Model** was developed at AKN (Achmea Knowledge Net) to facilitate CoPs across the organization. SES is a participatory method and borrows ideas from community-centered development (Preece, 2000) in the sense that the characteristics and needs of the community members are leading and prior to any decisions concerning technology and social structure. The aim of SES is to combine lessons learned, success stories and collective experiences, skills and tools from previous projects, in a way that is easily identified and understood by the organization. In this section the SES model is first introduced in a generic way, and then each of its components is explained in more detail. One main contribution of the method is its simplicity and adaptability to the needs of different groups.

The SES model identifies four groups of actors involved in the activity and development of a community:

- **Initiators**: the individuals who realize that the organization can benefit from the nurturing and encouragement of such a group and take the lead in the creation of the CoP.
- **Members**: The people that participate in the CoP, and whose mutual concerns, interests and activities form the body of the community (Talbott, 1995).
- **Stakeholders**: the group who can affect or be affected by the results and policies of the CoP (Vidgen, 1997).

- **Organization**: The corporate context in which the CoP exists. Within this group, decision makers play a special role and are often referred to explicitly in the model.

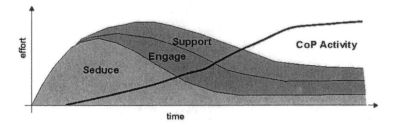

*Figure -18.* The activity phases of the SES model

After the initial awareness, the development of CoPs evolves along three main phases. During the first phase, **seduction**, the context and aims of a CoP are identified and described, potential members are made aware of their connections and common interests or objectives, and the community is advertised in the organization. The aim of the second phase, **engagement**, is to design a community that is as closely related as possible to the requirements and wishes of the members and whose tasks and targets are well embedded in the strategic priorities of the organization. The third phase, **support**, is geared to the consolidation and continued evolution of the CoP. Figure 18 gives an overview of the development phases throughout the life of a CoP.

## 7.3.1     Seduce

The aim of the Seduce phase is to create a feeling of anticipation about the CoP in both its potential members and in the organization as a whole. This phase also aims at the clarification of the context and objectives for the CoP. One of the first activities in the Seduce phase must therefore be the identification of the target groups: initiators, stakeholders, members, organization. The activities of the Seduce phase are described in table 1.

*Table -2* **Activities during the Seduce phase of CoP development**

| Target group | Activities | Aims | Tools |
|---|---|---|---|
| **Initiators** | - contact members and stakeholders | - guide CoP development<br>- describe CoP purpose, aims, members | brainstorm |
| **Stakeholders** | - Interviews<br>- Organize group discussions | - Clarify CoP purpose<br>- Define CoP targets<br>- Make context explicit | Acceleration Room[3]<br>Questionnaires |
| **Members** | - Organize meetings<br>- Form pilot group | - Introduce CoP concept<br>- Increase awareness<br>- Develop trust<br>- Identify common interests | Acceleration Room[2]<br>Mood boards[4] |
| **Organization** | - Elicitation of members<br>- Publicity campaign | - Show added value of CoP<br>- Attract new members<br>- Secure support | Intranet<br>Newsletters |

Although the order of activities is not fixed, and indeed Seduce activities will continue well into the CoP lifecycle in order to keep the excitement and

---

[3] The Acceleration Room is a software tool that allows the rapid inventory of characteristics and aims of an issue (in this case the CoP) and helps create common focus.

[4] Mood boards are visual support tools (posters) and they are used to express the look and feel characteristics of a certain object. They are effective tools to share individual concerns and support the discovery of the identity of a group.

involvement of members and stakeholders alive, it is advisable to start this phase with activities directed to the stakeholders. In this way, their objectives, concerns and targets for the community which form the basis for the participation of members, are identified and agreed upon at an early stage. However, in the development of any community, the members and their view on the organization and content of the CoP are central. The process of re-accessing and consolidating CoP aims and activities is dynamic and must be a constant part of the community lifecycle.

In the later stages of development of a CoP, seduce activities are geared at the publicity and distribution of results and actions, so that the support for the groups is maintained and funding secured. The generation of quick wins at an early development stage is therefore crucial. The successes of one CoP are a great boost for other CoPs and for groups which are considering the creation of CoPs.

## 7.3.2     Engage

This step of development of CoPs is geared to the involvement of all target groups in the further shaping of the CoP. The aims of the Engage phase for each of the target group are summarized in table 2.

*Table -3.* Activities during the Engage phase of CoP development

| Target group | Activities | Aims |
|---|---|---|
| **Members** | - Interviews of pilot group<br>- Group synopsis sessions<br>- Identification of requirements and functionality | - insure involvement<br>- enable group's identification<br>- link CoP to member objectives<br>- Identify functionality requirements |
| **Stakeholders** | - Group synopsis sessions<br>- Group discussions | - Agree on targets and processes<br>- Appoint champion |

| Target group | Activities | Aims |
|---|---|---|
| | | - Identify functionality requirements |
| **Organization(Decision-makers)** | - Make CoP objectives explicit<br>- Identify strategic priorities | - Match CoP aims to strategic priorities |

In our experience, identity is the key issue for individual participation in a group. This means both the development of a group identity, as well as the assurance that individual objectives and concerns are incorporated in the objectives of the CoP. People need to get a clear, positive answer to the question, "what's in it for me", in order to adopt the CoP as their own. Therefore the assurance that individual objectives and concerns are incorporated in the objectives of the CoP must be part of the development of the CoP, which is achieved using group synopsis methods. The focus of the Seduce phase towards CoP members is to involve them from the very beginning of the development of the CoP and make sure that personal requirements and desires are incorporated in the functionality and targets of the CoP. For the engagement of stakeholders and organizational decision-makers, activities are twofold: (1) appointing a champion to assure the bridge between the CoP and the organization, and (2), defining a clear and explicit link between the targets of the CoP and the strategic objectives of the organization which helps clarify the benefits of the CoP towards decision-makers, and ensures their support.

The engagement process is a continuous one, to be worked on throughout the lifecycle of the community. An important issue is how knowledge sharing evolves within CoPs, through the continuous motivation of people, the creation of trust and overcoming individual objections (Gurteen, 1999). Furthermore, measurable characteristics of the CoP and reward/sanction systems for participation are specified during the engage phase.

## 7.3.3     Support

Once a CoP has been identified, and participants and stakeholders are engaged in its formation, active support for the CoP is fundamental for its continued success. By support we mean the facilitation of community activities in terms of infrastructure, funding, social structure and monitoring.

**Infrastructure**. Infrastructure support includes (1) the creation and facilitation of time and space for CoP activities, so that members are enabled to participate in community life and meet others, and, (2) the availability of a technical infrastructure to back up CoP targets and activities. The existence of adequate information and collaboration support systems is an important aspect, but not a self-sufficing one. In our approach, we concentrate on the formation of the community, and are only starting the development of ICT after its requirements and functionality are agreed upon and shared by the group which is going to use it. Furthermore, support systems must fit with the specific characteristics of the CoP. We have developed a conceptual framework (described in section 5) that meets this requirement.

**Funding**. Like most things in life, a well functioning community will need funds to back up its activities. Meetings, training and the implementation of a sound infrastructure are crucial. In order to secure funding, the activities related to the engagement of stakeholders and organization as described above are of great importance. The community itself contributes to the continuation of these engagements both by being accountable and reporting on the usage of funds, as well as by maintaining an explicit link of its activity to strategy and goals of organization. When the targets and expectations of a CoP are well set and realistic, their achievement will have positive consequences for company revenues and therefore justify the funding of the CoP.

**Social structure**. The activity and achievements of CoPs are much influenced by their social organization. Therefore, the design of a social structure for the CoP must go beyond the identification of members, and their requirements and preferences, to include the specification of the social structures (roles and communal behavior norms) and interactions between actors (de Moor, 1999). The enactment of social roles results often in the success or failure of a community. This is especially so for the role of a CoP leader or facilitator, and special care must be taken when appointing a leader.

**Monitoring**. Finally, the support of a CoP should include the specification and realization of processes that monitor the activity of the CoP. Monitoring activities check how well the CoP is meeting its targets, whether members are satisfied with CoP activities, and provides a way for change and continuous adaptation to a changing environment. Monitoring will also ensure the engagement of stakeholders and of corporate management. Monitoring objectives and tools are community specific and should be agreed upon by its members.

# 7.4    KennisNet: an example CoP

In this section, we apply the SES model to the development of the "KennisNet" CoP. KennisNet brings together non-life insurance developers and actuaries working in different business units. KennisNet was one of the first communities created at Achmea and lessons learned from its development process contributed greatly to the development of SES. Initiators for this CoP were members of the Knowledge Center Non-Life who realized that knowledge was not being optimally used because people working in different units did not know each other and were re-inventing the wheel and using external consultants on issues that could be supported by colleagues in other units. In the next subsections we briefly describe the three steps of the model. In particular, we describe the support phase, which required special attention due to the distributed character of KennisNet.

## 7.4.1    Seduce

Early in the process it was clear that potential members should be made aware and enthusiastic for the community. The initiators visited most groups, initiated email discussions and organized workshops geared to the potential members in order to

- make them aware of the activities of related groups in other units,
- whenever possible, get people to meet each other,
- show the added-value of collaboration, and,
- create a feeling of community among the group.

It must be noted that, at the time, the need to include stakeholders and organizational decision makers in the Seduce process was not well understood. The development of KennisNet therefore occurred mainly outside the view of management, which has resulted in a need for constant reassurance and explanation of the needs and results of the CoP. Since then, the Seduce phase was improved to actively and explicitly involve stakeholders and decision makers in the development of communities.

### 7.4.2     Engage

Once the idea of KennisNet was well known to the members and its purpose known in general terms, a group incorporating representatives of each unit was established with the objective to formulate the objectives, structure and activities of the CoP. Members of this steering group would report back to their unit colleagues and bring their input into the steering group. Special attention was given to the development of a common classification for knowledge on the non-life insurance field.

Furthermore, a quick meeting for all members was organized well at the beginning of the development process, which helped the formation of community identity and set the tone for the quarterly workshops that would become part of the KennisNet structure.

### 7.4.3     Support

At an early stage it was decided that, besides activities and processes to help people get in contact and collaborate across business units, KennisNet would need to implement a repository to collect and distribute knowledge sources to its members. A main reason for this repository was to keep a memory of organizational knowledge on the non-life field (Achmea is the largest car insurer in the Netherlands, and one of the biggest home and disasters insurers) to be used asynchronously and to be kept for future use.

The structure of KennisNet combines face-to-face contacts between members of the group, formalized as quarterly workshops, with an intranet-based knowledge sharing server. An intranet-based knowledge repository was implemented based on the existing technical infrastructure, a Lotus Notes network. The functionality of Lotus Notes is used to support direct access to contents, as well as publishing and browsing of knowledge items. The repository of KennisNet, inspired by work on knowledge repositories and organizational memories (cf. Domingue, Motta, 1999), allows for the implementation of facilities for the discussion and broadcast of questions and requests.

As part of the monitoring activities that make up the support phase, a user satisfaction survey was conducted by researchers of the University of Twente after the system was running for one year. The two main conclusions from this survey are:

- the face-to-face structure is well appreciated and its value is clear
- the added value and potential of the knowledge server is not always clear to the users and the server is hardly used.

The main reason for this lack of use, as pointed out in the survey, is that users need a more personal means of interaction to make them comfortable exchanging knowledge. The survey also indicates that knowledge owners prefer to share their expertise within a controllable, trusted group under conditions negotiated for the specific situation and partners.

Other recent studies also show that success of knowledge sharing is dependent on the level of trust and dependency between community members and on the kind of culture holding in the society (Ali et al., 2002). That is, users wish to keep the decision about sharing knowledge in their own hands, and want to be able to decide on a case-by-case basis whether an exchange is interesting to them or not, which is also explained by the need for reciprocity in knowledge exchange (Ahuja, Carley, 1998). Technology can facilitate knowledge sharing, but it is trust that enables it. That is, people will agree to share their knowledge with others if they feel that they will gain something from the exchange. Therefore, the support system of KennisNet was extended to handle negotiation and the realization of exchange agreements. In the next section, we describe how knowledge sharing was improved in the KennisNet CoP and how technology was used in this process.

## 7.5    Collaboration in Distributed Communities

Due to the distributed nature of KennisNet, and of many other communities active and envisioned at Achmea, community support must rely for a large part on virtual, internet based, systems. Nurturing communities is hard enough when the members are in a single location with good connectivity and increase considerably when the members are spread around different locations, possibly in different areas and with different languages and cultures. Members of distributed communities are not always aware of each other's capabilities and often they will discuss their business problems with a direct colleague just because he/she happens to be conveniently close and not because he/she is the best person to consult with. Links between members of distributed CoPs can be strengthened by webs of communication technologies. Moreover, in distributed groups, although the common goal binding the members is long-term, contacts and relationships may be relatively fluid with members entering and exiting as their task needs evolve. In this scenario, collaboration will need to be based on concrete, explicit commitments making clear what each partner is supposed to contribute and expects from the others.

Agent technology is particularly well suitable to model collaboration management systems due to the autonomous, pro- and reactive character of agents. Furthermore, agent concepts can lead to advanced functionality of KM systems (e.g. personalization of knowledge presentation and matching knowledge supply and demand), and the rich representational capabilities of agents as modelling entities allow faithful and effective treatment of complex organizational processes (van Elst et al., 2003). In our opinion, one of the main contributions of agent-based modelling of KM environments is that it provides a basis for the incorporation of individual initiative and collaboration into formal organizational processes. That is, a system does not need to be completely designed and fixed a priori but it is developed as a set of components and interaction processes that can be adjusted to the needs and requirements of the specific participants. We have developed a conceptual agent society framework, the OperA model, based on this principle of interaction between individual initiative and organizational structure. Due to space limitations we cannot describe OperA here but refer the reader to (Weigand et al., 2003).

Based on the survey results concerning the use of the repository and the user requirements for knowledge sharing, an extension to the KennisNet based on the OperA framework was proposed. The Knowledge Market is characterized by informal relationships between independent partners, interested in collaborating in a win-win way. A more detailed description of the Knowledge Market can be found in (Dignum, 2003). The Knowledge Market (depicted in figure 19) aims to support people exchanging knowledge with each other, in a way that preserves the knowledge, rewards the knowledge owner and reaches the knowledge seeker in a just-in-time, just-enough basis. Knowledge Market adds the following functionality to KennisNet:

- Possibility to share knowledge that is not available in the knowledge repository
- Support for coalition formation (in order to develop new solutions when knowledge is not available)
- Support for direct exchange between parties where the negotiation of exchange conditions happens on a case-to-case basis.

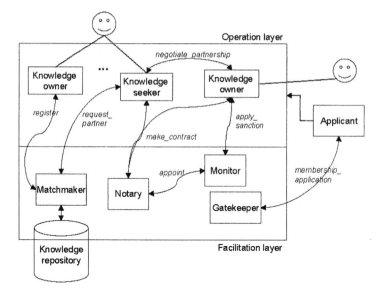

*Figure -19.* The social structure of Knowledge Market

People seeking collaboration through the Knowledge Market initiate a personal agent that acts as their avatar in the system. Several knowledge seeker and knowledge owner agents are typically active at any moment, and each user can own more than one agent simultaneously. This agent uses the preferences and conditions specified by the user to find appropriate partners and negotiate exchange terms. Depending on the specific task, the personal agent will take either the role of knowledge seeker or knowledge owner. Requirements concerning privacy, secrecy and competitiveness between brands and departments that influence the channels and possibilities of sharing are also described in the specification of the personal assistants.

Knowledge seekers and knowledge owners must first apply to enter the society. If this application is successful, the agent proceeds to the 'observing' scene. In this scene the agent is not active in any knowledge exchange but can access the repository, follow newsgroups, etc. Both seeker or owner agents can initiate an exchange by respectively announcing a need or a skill. The matchmaker agent helps seekers and owners to find the best match for their needs. Once seeker and owner are put in contact with each other, they will negotiate the terms of their exchange. If successful, such an exchange contract is registered with the notary agent, who appoints a monitor agent to check the interaction between seeker and owner. These contracts are used for the automatic monitoring of exchange and describe the activity of the community. Exchange contracts make interaction explicit and enforce reciprocity of actions. Furthermore contracts can be checked to verify society activity.

The following example illustrates a contract between two members. In this fictional example, Anne will provide Bob with a report about competition prices, on the condition that Bob will give her comments on the report (which can help her prepare an upcoming presentation) and eventually share with her his new pricing concept for car insurance. This contract is generated during the 'Negotiate partnership' scene and registered in the 'Register partnership' scene. In this scene, the notary agent will assign a monitor agent to check the fulfilment of the contract between Anne and Bob. Monitoring can be a very simple activity, where status is checked when a deadline is reached. However, we have chosen to use an agent as monitor because monitors can take a more active role, reminding parties of approaching deadlines or by suggesting possible actions when sanctions occur. Informally, the clauses of this example contract are described in figure 20.

| Interaction Contract: '*ID*' | |
| --- | --- |
| **Parties** | Anne (A), Bob (B) |
| **Clauses** | |
| 1. | OBLIGED A TO receive(B, report-concurrent-prices) BEFORE *next-week* |
| 2. | IF received(B, report-concurrent-prices) THEN OBLIGED B TO<br>( receive(A, comment-report-concurrent-prices)  BEFORE *3-days*<br>AND receive(A, concept-pricing) BEFORE *1-month* ) |
| 3. | IF delayed(B, concept-pricing) THEN OBLIGED B TO inform(A, delayed(concept-pricing) ) |

*Figure -20.* Collaboration contract example

The Knowledge Market system enables personalized interactions in a structured organizational setting, and is therefore suitable to the requirements of the members of the KennisNet Schade CoP. Due to space limitations, we cannot describe here how roles, interactions and contracts are specified but refer the reader to (Dignum, Dignum, 2003).

## 7.6    Conclusions

Most KM management efforts attempt to document and share information, ideas and insights so that they can be managed, organized and shared. However, methods to leverage tacit knowledge often do more harm than good (McDermott, 2000). CoPs are an answer to this problem by providing the means for people to interact and to access each others' expertise and insights directly. In this paper we presented ongoing work on the development of sponsored communities of practice at Achmea. The development process is based on the empowerment of communities, and stresses the role of the participants. Our work resulted in the development of the SES method which is also presented in this paper. The SES model focuses on the critical factors to develop communities, by seducing and engaging individuals and management, and by identifying and providing the means to support CoP activities. The model is now being applied to the creation of several CoPs (as illustrated using the KennisNet Cop) and best-practice on its use is being gathered. Experience with the method and its application to different CoPs is being used to fine tune and adapt the different steps.

Many communities at Achmea are spread across business units, which have special requirements on the support of distributed groups. Therefore, CoP support can be best assisted by an agent-based architecture, OperA, to model interaction in communities. Further research will focus on the analysis of the results of application of the SES method to the development of several CoPs and its further refinement. We are further working on the development of a prototype for the OperA Model.

Although, so far, the SES method has only been applied within one organization, the communities involved are fairly diverse, and we are confident that the method is generic enough to be applied in other organizational settings and we are currently seeking external application domains for SES.

# 8. VIRTUAL LEARNER-CENTRED SOLUTIONS FOR MANAGEMENT EDUCATION AND TRAINING

Richard Walker

## 8.1 Introduction

This chapter looks at the contribution of e-learning to management education and training. Over recent years, strong claims have been made regarding the value of computer mediated learning to management education and the support that this delivery medium offers to individual learning. E-learning has become a key buzzword in management training – a cornerstone of knowledge management practices within the workplace. On-line learning has been heralded as a solution provider for "just-in-time", "just-enough" training. It remains unclear, though, how virtual tools may be leveraged effectively to support individual learning. In this chapter we present a critical appraisal of e-learning, considering how computer technologies may be used in combination with face-to-face training methods.

We consider three different e-learning models, assessing their contribution to learner-centred instruction within a range of management degree programmes at Nyenrode University. We round off this chapter by identifying a number of instructional issues and responsibilities, which are intended to guide the way we combine e-learning with face-to-face methods to support effective learner-centred instruction.

## 8.2 The case for e-learning: revolutionising management education and training

Technology-supported innovation in course design has been advocated by a number of authorities as a necessary and progressive step forward in the way we deliver business education (Albrecht & Sack, 2000; Ives & Jarvenpaa, 1996; Lenzner & Johnson, 1997). Its importance is recognised as a means of preparing students for computer usage in their prospective workplaces and enhance their learning (Chong, 1997), as well as to deliver competitive advantage to business schools, transforming educational processes (Ives & Jarvenpaa, 1996; Leidner & Jarvenpaa, 1995).

Computer-mediated learning offers management trainers and educators the opportunity to transform pedagogical practices, shifting instruction from the physical to the virtual classroom (Hiltz, 1994). It challenges the traditional notion of instruction as being contingent on a physical and social context - i.e. a classroom setting. We may go a step further though and argue that the shift in the pedagogical environment also presents opportunities for new types of learning. Most classrooms are designed with the assumption that there will be a one-to-many transmission of information from instructor to students. The shift to a virtual classroom offers the potential to establish new patterns of instructor and student interaction and accordingly, different teaching and learning roles and practices (Becker & Ravitz, 1999; Jaffee, 2002; Leidner & Jarvenpaa, 1995; Ravitz, 1997).

Theorists such as Paquette (1998) argue that the "virtual campus" offers new opportunities for learning, which are compatible with constructivist pedagogical goals:

"A learning system proposes a constructivist pedagogy by bringing forward the learner's pro-activity in building his own knowledge, by taking into account his characteristics and by helping him integrate available information, within a context and usage, that is to say by helping him transform information into knowledge."

"A learning system offers the different actors various ways of accessing and processing information, such as software environments available for research and communication, for process-related advice, for collaboration among learners as well as among learners and other actors who facilitate the learning process." (Paquette,1998; p.22)

In line with this thinking, Schank (2001) has highlighted the possibility of using the computer to revolutionise traditional classroom courses, by using its ability to create simulations in the subject domains that students are trying to master. In this way, computers may support an interactive learning process that responds to students' actions.

Shoffner et al. (2000) indeed claim that technology also assists in many social aspects of learning, complementing class-based experiences by supporting student-centred learning, co-operative learning, and self-regulated learning, as well as components of motivation, including attention, relevance, confidence, and satisfaction.

## 8.3      Management education and e-learning

The case for the introduction of computer-mediated learning to management education appears compelling, based on the theoretical insights we have discussed. Yet in spite of the claims and support for new modes of instruction, progress has been quite limited in the field of management education. There has only been a preliminary level of research on the impact of technology on course design and delivery (Arbaugh, 2000; Dumont, 1996; Frand & Broesamle, 1996; Morissey, 1997; Romme, 2003; Salmon, 2000). Indeed, in recent years there have been calls for more research to be conducted on the most appropriate uses of the Internet for management education (Alavi & Leidner, 2001; Arbaugh, 2000; Arbaugh & Duray, 2002; Ellram & Easton, 1999; Freeman & Capper, 2000).

A few universities have experimented with virtual classroom courses for business or information systems courses, notably New York University and Pennsylvania State University. The University of Phoenix indeed offers a complete business program interactively on-line. On a less ambitious scale, we have seen a number of universities and business schools experimenting with computer mediated communication systems (CMC) [5], as a means by

---

[5] CMC systems include all forms of communication that occur over a network of computers. Nixon and Salmon (1996) state that CMC systems enable individuals and groups of people to carry on "conversations" and "discussions" based on the typed word, over computer

which collaborative learning can be introduced to management courses, either distance or campus based. For example, UK institutions such as Henley Management Centre and Lancaster University have replaced part of the face-to-face content of their management programs with CMC based activity. The UK Open University has also played a major role in experimenting with CMC applications and their impact on the learning process. An attempt has been made to use this medium as a means to develop "conversational" rather than "instructional" interaction between faculty and students (Salmon, 2000).

CMC technology has been selected to support on-going discussion between instructors and students – allowing each to express their viewpoints. It has been used either as a supplement to classroom teaching (an added extra, to support social contact and interaction out-of-class), or as a central part of the delivery and assessment framework for courses. However, research findings regarding the added value of using this technology for teaching and learning have been quite mixed.

According to Leidner and Jarvenpaa (1995), the impact of these initiatives has been to automate and facilitate information flows between an instructor and students or among students. Such automation efforts have often led to efficiency and effectiveness gains, increasing teacher / student interaction (Hiltz 1995; Schutte, 1997), but they have not led to fundamental changes in learning and teaching. Instead, in many instances, computers and communication technologies have replaced or augmented blackboards and chalk for instructors and paper and pencils for students. The emphasis has therefore been placed on the use of technology for "e-teaching", rather than for learning purposes.

Alavi et al. (1997) argue for a new approach to learning and instruction:

"The integration of information technology into management education is by no means trivial, and it is not simply a matter of providing computer access and training to faculty and students. Effective use and integration of computers into classrooms requires a departure from

---

networks. CMC may include electronic mail, computer conferencing, computer bulletin boards, facsimile, teletex and videotex, voice messaging and desktop videoconferencing.

traditional interaction modes so that a technology-mediated learning environment becomes pedagogically effective and even superior to alternative modes of learning and instruction" (Alavi et al., 1997).

The challenge therefore remains to develop learning pathways that complement the technology and provide a new approach to management training and education – an alternative to traditional classroom teaching. Computer technology should be leveraged in such a way that it transforms the instructional process, promoting "a fundamental paradigm shift in the way that students learn" (Baets & Van der Linden, 2000). Part of this approach to instruction should include some focus on the needs and interests of the learner.

## 8.4     Towards a learner-centred application of e-learning tools

The work of Leidner and Jarvenpaa (1995) is insightful in this respect, helping us to rethink our approach to education technology and its relevance for instructional purposes.

Leidner and Jarvenpaa define the relationship between technology and learning according to two process dimensions:

- Control of the pace and content of learning
- The purpose of instruction (knowledge dissemination and knowledge creation)

They argue that learner-centred education can only be delivered with technologies that place much of the control of the content and pace of learning in the hands of students, not the instructor. The purpose of using instructional technology should move away from knowledge dissemination towards knowledge creation. The instructor should no longer be the primary creator of the knowledge. Instead, students become a very important part of the knowledge creation process, with the instructor serving as a mediator rather than a dictator of the learning process.

According to their vision, technologies that give students the control of the pace and rhythm of learning are the only appropriate tools to support constructive and collaborative learning – which lie at the heart of the knowledge-building process. They hold the key to conceptual learning and higher-order thinking, facilitating student access to information to improve the availability or reality of learning materials. In their opinion, virtual learning environments (VLEs) represent an appropriate form of technology which can support learner-centred outcomes.

We may define VLEs as learning management software systems that synthesize the functionality of computer-mediated communications software (e-mail, bulletin boards, newsgroups etc.) and on-line methods of delivering course materials (e.g. the WWW). They can be designed to accommodate a wide range of learning styles and goals, to encourage collaborative and resource-based learning and to allow sharing and re-use of resources (Britain & Liber, 1999). Piccoli et al. (2001) indeed claim that VLEs provide high levels of student control, support participant contact and interaction throughout the learning process, and provide an opportunity to restructure the learning experience in ways not feasible with other instructional tools such as computer aided instruction software.

With these recommendations as a guide, we have developed a prototype virtual learning environment at Nyenrode University. This was used to explore the contribution of virtual tools to learner-centred management education and training.

## 8.5     Applying learner-centred principles to the development of a virtual learning environment

In support of learner-centred pedagogical principles, we have designed a virtual learning environment based on a *Whizzdom* platform[6] (see Figure 21 below), which aims to give students pace and control of the learning process. The platform incorporates the latest Microsoft Web-Technology,

---

[6] See www.whizzdom.nl for further details

allowing for scalability and performance. It represents a flexible, open architecture that supports integration with other enterprise systems.

The learner is positioned at the centre of the system and can freely communicate with instructors or peers through collaborative tools such as e-mail, threaded discussion groups (via bulletin boards), chat boxes (for synchronous communication) and synchronous document-sharing (via NetMeeting). Students may interact with the system by saving links to assignments / hypertext pages (via bookmark options), making annotations to pages and uploading documents to the database. The information resources contained within the system are fully searchable via a keyword search engine. The platform combines these e-learning tools with administrative functions, including a space for the entry of personal grades, self-assessment tests and results, reports on the learning of individual users, as well as course assignments and notes from course instructors. In our estimation, the *Whizzdom* platform therefore offers more to users than learning management systems such as *Docent*[7] and *Blackboard*[8], which support administrative functions, but not the learning functions that are required for this research investigation.

---

[7] See http://www.docent.com/ for further details
[8] See http://www.blackboard.com/ for further details

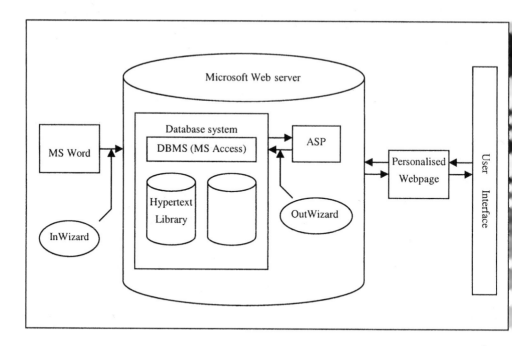

*Figure -21.* The architecture of the Whizzdom learning environment

## 8.6    Experimentation with the *Whizzdom* learning environment

For the experimental phase of our research, we adapted the *Whizzdom* environment to support three different e-learning models. Our intention was to observe students using a range of virtual tools and information resources during their studies at Nyenrode University. We experimented with six courses, selected at random from the International Modular MBA, International MBA and MSc management programmes, as well as the PDCO accountancy programme, encompassing both part-time and full-time study trajectories. For the part-time courses, the classes were comprised of middle managers combining study activities with their full-time job responsibilities. The full-time courses were followed by students who had at least three years management experience. In both study trajectories, participants were requested to follow a *hybrid* or mixed mode learning approach, combining virtual learning with traditional class-based learning methods. The e-learning models reflected a range of tools, which were intended to support individual knowledge-building and collaborative learning activities – in line with the learner-centred principles we have identified.

Jonassen's (1996) classification of "Mindtools" was helpful in guiding us in the tool selection process for each model. In Model 1 we introduced conversation tools to support a simple discourse approach for student learning. These tools were intended to be used by students to support work-based discussion and collaborative discussion for the off-campus phase of their learning. Models 2 & 3 were based on a combination of conversation and knowledge construction tools to support the processes of discussion and knowledge building between students. The e-learning models and experimental courses are summarised in Table 1 below:

*Table -4.* E-learning models for the course experiments

| Model 1 | Model 2 | Model 3 |
|---|---|---|
| **Group-based discussion** | **Knowledge-sharing and discussion** | **Knowledge acquisition, communication and discussion** |
| *Tools supporting collaborative learning for individuals working within study groups. Students used a combination of bulletin boards and chat boxes to complete group-based discussion activities.* | *Tools supporting knowledge sharing via the uploading of group / individual work to the environment. Students used group & plenary bulletin boards to post feedback and discuss assignments / course issues. Documents were uploaded via a digital archive.* | *Tools supporting knowledge acquisition, knowledge-building and collaborative discussion activities. Students used a virtual library of management concepts, group and plenary bulletin boards, NetMeeting tools and digital archive.* |
| ***Management Information Systems IMMBA 1999-2000*** (part-time programme) | ***International Money & Finance MSc & IMBA 2001-2002*** (full-time programmes) | ***Management Information Systems IMMBA 2000-2001*** (part-time programme) |
| Work-based discussion and collaboration activities | Group-based research assignments | Work-based discussion, collaboration & knowledge-building activities |
| | **Business Ethics IMBA 2001-2002** (full-time programme) | **Information Management PDCO 2001** (part-time programme) |
| | Case-based discussion on ethical dilemmas | Work-based discussion, collaboration & knowledge-building activities |

## 8.7      Research approach

We selected an exploratory case study design (Robson, 1993; Yin, 1993) in order to research the experiences of the participants following the six experimental courses. The study aimed at revealing student attitudes towards the hybrid delivery methods (virtual and class-based learning modes). The investigation also considered the contribution of the virtual learning environment (e-learning model and tools) to student learning - to what extent the tools and resources added value to their learning experiences.

Student learning and assessment of the preparatory phase of the course was recorded using a combination of questionnaire and interview techniques. A pre-course questionnaire was designed to gauge student expectations towards the hybrid course design. Through the use of a post-course questionnaire, we aimed to revisit student attitudes to the course design and pedagogical approach. Responses were measured using a five-point Likert-type scale, adapted from Hiltz's (1994) instrument designed to evaluate the effectiveness of an online course. In addition to these instruments, selected students were interviewed at different intervals during the course, in order to provide further detailed feedback on their learning experiences.

As with all research the study results from this course have certain limitations. The courses focused on small class populations (approximately 30 students per course), with no control group included in the analysis. Scope for the measurement of the effectiveness of the hybrid course design approach was therefore quite limited. Consequently we may offer only general observations on the learning outcomes for this course. Indeed, the research for this experimental course should be viewed as a pilot study, offering a first step in the examination of student responses to a learner-centred course design using virtual courseware.

## 8.8    Summary of the findings from the course experiments

The feedback from the experimental courses highlighted a number of strengths for the e-learning tools, relevant to the performance of the learner-centred activities. Students differed though, in terms of their appraisal of these strengths. In particular, we observed a difference in perception between full-time students and the managers following the part-time courses over the contribution of the tools to their learning. These differences may be attributed to the contrasting learning conditions and contexts which part-time and full-time students faced.

For the part-time courses, (based on e-learning **Models 1** and **3**), managers saw value in using the *Whizzdom* environment to conduct ideas sharing and reciprocal teaching in their off-campus learning. The asynchronous communication tools facilitated the exchange of information between peers, both on a pair and group-based basis. The tools facilitated the exchange of work-based practices off-campus, introducing participants to different contexts. Students were thus able to broaden their learning, applying the theoretical concepts of the courses to different organisational environments. There was a clear pay-off for the class-based learning, with participants able to engage in discussions on work-based practices at a deeper level, due to their familiarity with a range of organisational contexts.

Full-time students (**Model 2**) valued the e-learning tools in a different way. The tools were used as a stimulus for follow-up discussion, conducted on a face-to-face basis. By showcasing individual opinions and assignments, the *Whizzdom* environment presented participants with a global view of the class-based learning. The environment represented a supplementary learning resource, which was used by students to review the work of other participants and follow up virtual feedback with face-to-face discussion. The environment also served to extend the scope for discussion and increase the number of participants who were active in these discussions.

Common to all the experimental courses though were the technical barriers which limited the adoption of the tools. Participants were largely unfamiliar with the technical requirements related to the installation and use of the e-learning software. The learning curve was far too great for the majority of IT novices, particularly with regard to the use of NetMeeting and the synchronous communication tools, which were introduced in **Model 3**. The time investment needed to master these tools and use them effectively led students to opt for simple applications, in this way avoiding the conduct of interactive discussions on-line. The high technical threshold for adoption acted as a barrier for students across the courses and e-learning models that we observed. Consequently pair and group discussion was conducted through traditional media such as e-mail and the telephone, with the *Whizzdom* environment failing to serve as a location for interactive discussion. The feedback from students indeed suggests that IT novices require considerable preparation and guidance in order to use these communication tools effectively.

## 8.9     Lessons learned from the course experiments

Reviewing the evidence from the experimental courses, there appears to be no automatic link between the introduction of hybrid study methods and the adoption of active learning strategies by managers. The combination of virtual and class-based methods by itself does not appear to motivate individuals to take control over their own learning – or to actively engage learners in knowledge building and experience sharing. In spite of the positive expectations which participants recorded in the pre-course questionnaires towards the hybrid study methods, the level of adoption of these tools[9] and the appreciation of the combined study methods was quite low. Indeed the adopter segment - those participants active in using the tools to support their learning - amounted to only a third of participants in the

---

[9] Reflected through the recorded levels of activity and interaction between students on-line.

classes which we observed. We may view these outcomes as contrary to the Technology Acceptance Model (TAM) (Davis, 1989; Davis et al., 1989), in which positive attitudes are purported to reflect a predisposition to the use of computers. The opposite effect was observed in this investigation, with the positive pre-course expectations of students (as recorded in the pre-course questionnaires) not translating into adoption of the tools by participants in the experimental courses.

Indeed, participants cited a number of reasons for the low level of adoption of the virtual tools and engagement in active learning. Students identified the poor technical performance of the tools they were using as an obstacle to self-directed learning, along with the lack of orientation on how to use these tools to support active learning strategies. Participants also highlighted the task-tool relationship in the courses as being quite weak, with the use of virtual tools not deemed to be essential to the performance of the study activities. The hybrid design, from this perspective, appeared to be quite artificial, with instructional methods not aligned closely enough to the targeted study activities in each course. Finally, students commented on the time investment that was necessary to master the tools and combine their class-based learning with on-line interaction with peers. For part-time students, the competing pressures of work responsibilities and other courses restricted the time they had available for discovery-based learning. Indeed, students following the 1999-2000 MIS course remarked that these pressures complicated the experience-sharing process and the co-ordination of group activities on-line. Consequently, students focused on the minimum requirements to complete the coursework and study tasks, rather than using the tools in the way they were intended, to support knowledge acquisition and knowledge building. In summary, we may conclude that the learning conditions and instructional design of the experimental courses presented obstacles to the adoption of learner-centred study methods.

However, it would be wrong to discount altogether the potential of hybrid study methods to support learner-centred outcomes and complementary knowledge-building processes. Based on the evidence from the experimental courses, we may indeed point to some positive outcomes. As we have already noted in the evaluation of the e-learning tools, managers following the part-time courses were able to recognise some advantages in combining traditional course activities with virtual tasks. MIS participants from both courses (1999-2000; 2000-2001) appreciated the introduction of communication tools in the preparatory phase of learning, viewing them as valuable in supporting the exchange of ideas and work experiences off-campus. Participants in the 1999-2000 MIS course and accountants from the Information Management course commented on the contribution of the tools in supporting the delivery of feedback on individual assignments. The virtual course environment therefore played an important role in fostering discussion and reflective thinking between adopters outside the classroom - a trend which theorists such as Dede (1990) and Harasim (1990) have observed in their own studies of virtual learning. The presentation of information resources, study activities and communication tools within integrated learning environments for the IM course and 2000-2001 MIS course also offered participants flexibility and convenience in their learning. In spite of the difficulties in co-ordinating group-based collaborative activities on-line, participants recognised the advantages of time and place independence, permitting them to log on and complete individual study activities at a time of their choosing. Managers were therefore presented with an element of control over the location and timing of their learning – with virtual tools enabling them to conduct both knowledge acquisition and knowledge building tasks off-campus.

Full-time students also recognised the contribution that virtual tools could make to their learning – and the advantages of combining class-based and virtual learning methods for campus-based courses. Adopters in both the IMF and Business Ethics courses highlighted the advantages of the bulletin boards in extending ideas sharing and discussion outside the classroom – helping participants to share mental models. The asynchronous communication tools also contributed to knowledge sharing and knowledge building processes by supporting an increase in the number of participants who were active in these discussions - a finding consistent with previous studies of virtual learning in management education (e.g. Bailey & Cotlar, 1994; Berger, 1999). The tools also supported the delivery of a broad range of perspectives on individual / group assignments. The exchange of on-line opinions served in some cases as a stimulus for follow-up face-to-face discussions, in which participants engaged in further ideas and experience sharing. Indeed, the feedback that students delivered to each other through the virtual discussion medium, served to encourage students to review their own assumptions and presentation of their written assignments – introducing a reflective loop to their learning. This was apparent in both the Business Ethics and IMF courses. These outcomes highlight the scope for learner-centred instruction, and the compatibility of class-based and virtual study methods in the conduct of student learning on campus.

The evidence from the experimental courses therefore indicates the potential of hybrid delivery methods to support student-centred learning. The virtual tools helped managers to reflect on their individual experiences at work and leverage their tacit knowledge in knowledge sharing and knowledge building tasks. However, the mixed reception of these methods by participants suggests that the learning conditions and instructional responsibilities need to be managed carefully by trainers / learning managers. In the final part of this chapter, we therefore sum up the instructional responsibilities, which appear to be central to the effective delivery of a hybrid course.

## 8.10    Instructional issues related to the design and delivery of hybrid learning

Comparing the feedback from the experimental courses, we observed a number of issues, which students identified as being important to their learning and central to effective knowledge building and sharing. Indeed, based on this feedback we may propose a framework of responsibilities, which appear significant to the design and delivery of a hybrid course. We focus here on the actions of the learning manager or trainer, how the presentation of virtual tools to students may influence adoption patterns. This involves a discussion on the presentation of the instructional setting to participants and its management by the trainer. The instructional setting is an all-inclusive term, covering the presentation of the hybrid course design, study methods and learning environment to individuals. Our framework of instructional responsibilities also focuses on the management of the learning process – the actions by which the trainer facilitates individual learning from the early stages, right through to the end of the cycle.

We acknowledge, though, that any general conclusions on the effectiveness of instructional design must involve a level of empirical testing – a task for future research. We would also need to take account of a variety of variables specific to each individual, focusing on issues such as learning experiences / preferences in learning style and their bearing on the reception of hybrid design and delivery methods. The evidence from this exploratory research investigation suggests that these variables will have an influence on individual attitudes towards the hybrid delivery methods. The responsibilities of the trainer therefore represent only one dimension to the learning process.

The instructional responsibilities which we have identified may be grouped into the following categories. The categories represent five distinct phases in the design and delivery of a hybrid learning pathway:

**Preparation of the hybrid learning pathway** (design phase) – establishing the pedagogical process – aligning the pedagogical objectives with the delivery methods. Integrating the virtual and class-based components within one learning design. Developing a suitable assessment ) policy, which matches the new learning approach (pedagogical)

**Socialising learners** (start of the learning pathway) – preparing managers to conduct their learning on-line: (attitudinal; technical; learning variables)

**Supporting on-line participation** (early stages) – supporting virtual knowledge-sharing (technical, pedagogical and learning variables)

**Sustaining on-line interaction** (later stages) – supporting individuals in their on-line activities – knowledge sharing and knowledge building (technical; pedagogical; motivational variables)

**Summing up the learning outcomes** (end of the learning trajectory) – identifying the lessons learned – emphasising the link between the virtual and class-based phases of the learning (pedagogical and learning variables)

**Preparation of the hybrid learning pathway** (design phase)
In this design phase, the instructor should establish the pedagogical vision for the learning trajectory, identifying the objectives and targeted learning behaviour. These decisions should then determine the choice of study activities and selection of e-learning tools which will be used in the learning design. The alignment of the tools with the tasks and learning objectives is of particular importance. Critics in the experimental courses commented on the "artificiality" of the interaction

on-line - that the medium of virtual communication was not really essential for the coursework and the targeted learning processes. This suggests that the design of the experimental courses could have been improved on – particularly the learning activities, in order to align them more closely with the use of the asynchronous communication tools. From a user's perspective, the effectiveness of the tools and the virtual approach appear related to their "fitness for purpose" – their alignment with the targeted learning processes (Chee, 2002; Collis, 1995; Leidner & Jarvenpaa, 1995).

**Socialising learners** (start of the learning pathway)
In this opening phase of the course, the instructor should focus on the effective presentation of the new study methods and tools to managers. The instructor's positive attitude towards the technology in the IMF course appeared to motivate students, unlike the Business Ethics course, where the opposite effect appeared to take place. The evidence suggests that the instructor's presentation methods and teaching style will influence attitudes within the class towards the learning tools – a finding consistent with previous studies (Webster & Hackley, 1997). A common remark from the experimental courses was that participants received only a limited orientation from the instructor on the e-learning study methods to be used. Based on the interview feedback, respondents highlighted a range of factors, which indicated that they were not properly prepared to embrace e-learning methods. Here we refer to affective issues such as the reasons for adopting a new way of learning, the rationale for a new course design using e-learning and its introduction so late within the study programme. Participants also highlighted motivational issues, pointing to the fact that there was no direct encouragement to use the site or interact on-line, when they could exchange ideas face-to-face. They were not triggered to conduct their learning in this way. Parallels can be made here with IS research literature, which has highlighted the influence of social norms and e / affect on IT adoption (e.g. Triandis, 1971).

We also observed a technical barrier to the adoption of the virtual tools. Some participants encountered problems with the log-in process when attempting to access the site. This finding suggests that new users need time to familiarise themselves with the virtual tools. In particular, we refer here to first-time users (IT novices), who require the space to develop the technical skills to function effectively on-line – a conclusion drawn from other studies of virtual learning (e.g. Hara & Kling, 2000; Mason, 1998; Renzi & Klobas, 2000). The evidence from the courses suggests that user-friendliness and accessibility for computer tools are important determinants of learning effectiveness, particularly IT novices' affective reaction to virtual learning – a finding replicated in previous studies of on-line learning (Hiltz 1993; Webster & Hackley, 1997). Other participants appeared to lack the requisite learning skills and competence to work effectively on-line. They appeared unaware of how to get the best out of the forum as a communication medium – to relate their postings to other comments on-line and build a discussion thread. This finding concurs with the research of Salmon (2000) and Knoll and Jarvenpaa (1995), who have argued that users need time at the beginning of a course to learn how to work collaboratively on-line, before tackling content-related activities. Turoff (1989) has indeed argued for users to receive a grounding in the 'Netiquette' of communication and expression on-line, prior to starting virtual learning activities. Turoff sets out a four-stage competency model, focusing on key skills such as learning system mechanics; learning how to communicate; learning how to work electronically within a group; and learning how to adapt and develop the system to maximise utility.

Beyond these motivational and technical concerns, the evidence from the experimental courses suggests that managers need to generate a common sense of purpose in order to work collaboratively on-line. This sense of shared purpose is difficult to achieve when managers are accustomed to traditional study methods. Indeed, as the results from the Business Ethics course demonstrated, even when participants are familiar with the technical concerns related to on-line collaboration, there is no automatic trend towards adoption of virtual learning methods. Users need time to recognise virtual learning environments as spaces for ideas and information sharing. Jarvenpaa et al. (1998) emphasise the need for students to build new social relationships and trust for on-line learning. The sense of "common ground" (Preece, 2000) or shared purpose also requires a collective commitment from participants to invest time and effort in this way of learning. Levin et al. (1990) describe this dynamic as a shared sense of responsibility to the on-line group – a key factor in the successful functioning of a network community. Evidence from the experimental courses suggests that this might be easier to establish at the beginning of the programme of study, rather than at a later stage for one specific course. Renzi and Klobas (2002) have demonstrated how this might be achieved by organising face-to-face activities prior to starting virtual activities, which help students to develop skills for participation and engage in community building. They also argue for the inclusion of community building activities among the initial online course exercises.


### Supporting on-line participation (early stages)

Based on the feedback from the experimental courses, it appears that participants require a degree of guidance and support in the early stages of an on-line learning experience. Participants highlighted the continuing need for technical support to help solve problems related to the uploading of case reports to the site or simply accessing the site. They also looked for guidance on how to express themselves on-line. Participants noted that the course instructor could elicit contributions by pushing students to respond to comments within the on-line forum. He could also play a pro-active role – modelling targeted learning behaviour on-line (e.g. by posting new discussion themes; responding / referring to postings on-line – integrating student responses etc.) There is indeed an extensive list of studies advocating intervention by course instructors along these lines - i.e. a 'managed' process of teaching and learning, establishing study norms for on-line learning; e.g. Collis (1996); Renzi & Klobas (2002); Salmon & Giles (1995). Levin et al., (1990) have suggested a number of instructional models suitable for virtual learning, such as "teletask forces" and "teleapprenticeships", which guide novices in the performance of online tasks.


### (d) Sustaining on-line interaction (later stages)

In the later stages of the experimental courses, students participated more confidently on-line. The visibility of the instructor on-line appeared to be less important, a finding consistent with previous studies of virtual courses (e.g. Nixon & Salmon, 1995). However we observed that the course instructor still needed to remain vigilant, monitoring the learning processes on-line, ensuring that the interest of students in the course was maintained. For instance, students from both IMF courses remarked on the lack of significant 'pull' factors to use the virtual environment and e-learning tools. Individuals noted that they would have been more interested in visiting the site if there had been new articles and resources included on the site, which could add value to their learning. This finding is consistent with published research on high-ability students, who are believed to benefit from 'pull-based' learning (Bovy, 1981). Respondents also noted that there was no extrinsic reward or recognition for active participation on-line – i.e. discussing and responding to the comments of others, referring to these comments when completing the feedback obligations. The assessment policy was directed towards evaluation comments, which could be delivered on a 'one-shot' basis. A change in assessment policy might have stimulated greater on-line interaction between students. Aligning the assessment policy with targeted learning behaviour is therefore important in this respect, in encouraging students to participate on-line. This appears to limit the scope for opting out, motivating students to meet the participation requirements for the course.

### (e) Summing up the learning outcomes (end of the learning trajectory)

Participants agreed that there should be a significant concluding phase to hybrid study trajectories. They expected the instructor to identify the key outcomes of the class-based and virtual learning, tying together the loose ends of the learning experience. This was found to be important in two respects; the summing-up process would help to present a coherent learning experience to participants, whilst emphasizing the complementary nature of the virtual and class-based learning processes. In this way the final class sessions could reinforce the lessons learned from the virtual phase of the course. Outstanding issues from these assignments could be dealt with in the final class sessions, with the trainer or educator providing feedback on the research and collaborative learning activities. Students would therefore complete the course with a clear understanding of the learning outcomes and the relationship between the virtual and class-based learning processes.

The instructional framework for hybrid learning represents the key finding from our research investigation. We present these results as a preliminary pedagogical framework for management trainers and course designers. Empirical tests are still required though to verify the significance of the variables we have identified.

The evidence from the experimental courses indeed appears promising – suggesting that virtual tools may serve to support managers in knowledge sharing and knowledge creation tasks, bringing together individual mental models within one learning space. Knowledge management and management education may therefore be combined using virtual technology. Matching the technology with the correct learning approach is central, though, to the success of the hybrid design and delivery methods.

We intend to conduct tests in future course design experiments within the Nyenrode management programmes.

# 9. A SYMBIOSIS OF LEARNING AND WORK-PRACTICE

Hanneke Koopmans

## 9.1 Increased attention for learning

Knowledge is shifting to a more central position in our society. The traditional economy, based on capital, raw materials and labor, is changing in a system where knowledge has more value: the knowledge economy. It is 'an economy where the acquisition of knowledge offers more value than the traditional production factors such as capital, raw materials and labor' (Kessels and Keursten, 2001). This shift, caused by increasing globalization in constant innovation of products and services, has significant consequences for our society and the meaning of learning within this society.

## 9.2 Consequences for organizations and individuals

The possibility to learn and produce new knowledge is essential for the 'survival' of an organization (Senge, 1990; Nonaka, 1994). "We can find the economic and productive strength of a modern enterprise faster in intellectual and service oriented abilities than in assets, such as land, buildings and machinery (Quinn, 1992)". The value of most products and services is strongly dependent on the appropriate way in which technological knowledge, product design, market approach, insights into needs and wishes of the consumers and innovation is developed. These are all knowledge based, non-tacit issues (Nonaka and Takuechi, 1995).

For an organization, flexibility and dealing with change are important (Pakkert, Kuijpers and Mulder, 1999). Therefore they must be able to apply and use knowledge. The goal of education and training is to increase skills or knowledge in order to raise the value of individuals for an organization. On the other hand it seems difficult to apply this knowledge acquired via training in daily work practice. How can organizations stimulate this applicability of what is learned?

In this chapter, the focus is on the professional for which learning and change are key factors of daily importance. The professional in our research is seen as a prototype of a knowledge worker (Van der Krogt, 1995).

Kwakman defines professionals in two ways. First it is someone who is working in a well defined profession, for example a lawyer or a doctor. His or her job has certain specific characteristics. The second definition starts from the characteristics of the profession, and not from the profession as a whole, as in the previous category. The tasks of the profession are service oriented and complex; an example of such a profession is a manager or HR-advisor. By complex we mean that have to deal with many non-routine problems which require unique solutions; it does not necessarily refer to the concept of dynamic and non-linear behavior (complicated would probably be a better alternative). The work is also complex, because goals are not always clear, which makes judgment of performance difficult.

In this chapter (and our research) we are interested in this second group of professionals. We consider employees (of an insurance company), professionals with a complex task which requires a high level of knowledge and skills (Kwakman, 2000). Professionals are expected to be able to acquire the necessary knowledge and skills independently and continuously, so that they can deal with unexpected problems. Many organizations consider professionals responsible for their own career development. They expect them to develop in line with the organizational goals without necessarily giving them lots of support.

Kwakman observes two more changes that highly influence the work of professionals (2001). First of all there is the changing structure of the population of customers; employees must be able to deal with the increasing diversity of the population. The second important change is the increased control at work. Ever increasing efficiency is required and the focus is on output and results. Bolhuis and Simons (1999) add that functions are changing and will continue to change, with higher demands on analytical and problem solving skills and on flexibility.

From the professional's point of view it is productive to further develop, not only because the organization requires it, but mainly in the interest of their own career. Work becomes like continuous learning. 'Routine and reproductive labor are being replaced by knowledge work; work that needs to combine and interpret information in order to solve new problems, in cooperation with others, and that occurs daily" (Kessels & Keursten, 2001). This work shows many similarities with learning processes.

## 9.3     Integration of learning and work

Work becomes increasingly close to learning, employees receive more responsibility and skills as 'problem solving' and 'analyzing' are becoming more important. That is why, in the past, more attention was given to the integration of learning and work (Kessels & Keursten, 2001). Employers today have more attention for work-learning integration because they need new knowledge. It seems logical that the employee, who receives more responsibility, can now create his own learning. Another party that is interested in the integration of work and learning is the training department.

A couple of interesting issues emerged. The first question is related to the way in which work and learning are integrated exactly. Where does learning start and where does it stop, and where does working start? Or can they not be separated and are they already intertwined almost by definition? And if they are intertwined, what does that mean in practice? Is there a way to stimulate learning at work, without interfering with work itself too much. And what are the consequences if we do so? In this chapter we are looking for answers to these questions.

Different authors researched learning at the workplace. They show that the workplace is a rich learning environment, in which the development of the professional largely takes place. Poell studied the way actors, for example employees, managers and consultants, arranged their learning projects in order to learn and improve their work (1998). He established a tension between the relevance of the learning project for work and for the development of the employee. Four different strategies can be identified: individual representation, direct representation, continuous adaptation and professional innovation. The use of one of these strategies is dependent on the specification of the work and on how much other actors are able to impose their strategy on others.

Poell explicitly mentions that employees, in the case of the organization of their learning, are often not taken seriously. Learning is mainly approached from the manager's perspective, which results in a functional approach to learning (1998).

Onstenk investigated learning abilities in working situations. He distinguished elements that are of influence on learning in the workplace (1997). He calls this the 'learning potential' of the working situation: "the possibility that in a working situation certain learning processes occur" (1997). He distinguishes the following elements; individual skills, learning opportunities in the workplace, learning motivation and training possibilities offered in the workplace.

Relevant for this research is the learning offer in the workplace and he mentions the following aspects:

The content of the work and the characteristics of the function: learning from the job itself;

The social environment: learning from the people you work with;

The information environment: learning from the available information at the workplace.

"Most of the things people should know or can know in order to reach a good performance, they don't learn in professional education or training, but during work itself. This is especially the case for the implicit and situated aspects of adequate professional performance" (Onstenk, 2000). Apparently the work environment is identified as a rich learning environment. How can this learning environment be best used?

## 9.4    Adult learning

In general managers and educators design education and training in organizations. The participants, or the "learners", usually have little to say about their learning. Little is taken into account about their wishes and needs. Usually the manager decides what the course is about, after which the educator or trainer designs the course. This is surprising when taking the life- and learning history of every adult learner into account.

Knowles identified and coined the label 'adult learner' in the early fifties (1953). He developed some core principles. This field of study was called 'andragogy', the theory of adult learning. Based on his core principles more effective learning processes could be designed. The principles were originally aimed at educators. They were developed based on the characteristics of the adult learner who was, according to him, naturally curious and willing to develop himself (1953).

After Knowles and his core principles an ' Andragogy in Practice Model' was developed, that was applicable in different domains of adult learning (Holton, Swanson, Naquin, 2001; Knowles, Holton & Swanson, 1998). The model consists of three dimensions: aims and guidelines for learning; individual and situational differences; and core principles of adult learners.

These core principles entail six aspects:

1. The learner should know the why, what and how of the learning.
2. The self-concept of the learner is autonomous and self-directed.
3. The previous experiences of the learner form a source, which is based on mental models.
4. The learner is willing to learn when the training is related to real life and when there is a developing task.
5. The orientation of a problem is centered on a clear problem statement and it is context bound.
6. The motivation to learn is intrinsic and personal results are of importance.

These principles can hardly be observed in the current learning of adults.

Poell gives as a reason the functionalist focus with which in-company training is usually constructed. The aim of learning is regarded to be functional for work and is considered to be a tool of management (1998). A rich work environment creates good learning possibilities and is supposed to be a good learning environment.

## 9.5　Integration of learning and working

Working is similar to learning in that employees have more responsibilities, and skills like 'problem solving' and 'analysis' are becoming increasingly important. That is why, lately, integration of learning and working has received more attention (Kessels & Keursten, 2001).

In a study held in different organizations, about the influence of technology on learning, Zuboff concludes: "learning is not something that takes time from productive work, but learning is the core of productive work" (1988).
Employers pay attention to learning these days because of the need for knowledge.

First of all the question arises of how exactly this integration of learning and work takes place. Where does learning begin and where does it stop and of course where does work start? Are these two separated or intertwined? And if they are intertwined, what can we do with that? Is there a way to stimulate learning at work? What are the consequences of such a choice? This research tries to find an answer to some of these questions.

## 9.6　Research Approach

We selected an exploratory case study design (Yin, 1993) in order to research the experiences of the participants during learning trajectories integrated with work. The study aimed at revealing employees' abilities to create and follow learning trajectories. The investigation also considered the support that an organization can offer to employees who are willing to learn, and more specifically how they can support their employees.

Participants in this research cooperated voluntarily. They were between 25 and 35 years old and were professionals in a large Insurance Holding. Professionals need to be understood as follows: "employees with complex tasks which acquire high levels of skills and knowledge" (Kwakman, 2001).

They all worked at different Business Units of this Dutch financial services organization.

The research, and therefore the learning trajectories, took place over a period of three months. They were integrated with work and follow up took place every month using semi-structured interviews and short questionnaires. All together, we did three types of interviews. The first was about the employees' views and experience with learning at the workplace. In the second interview they designed their learning trajectory. In the third and last interview we evaluated the course of the trajectory. We followed seventeen employees in the first phase of the research. After analyzing the data we improved our approach and followed ten different employees in their learning trajectories.

The study results from such an exploratory constructivist research have certain limits, as is the case with all research. The field of stimulating learning at the workplace, with close integration to work, was explored with small groups of employees. The employees were between 25 and 35 years of age. This means that most of them only had a couple of years of work experience. In general the chances are high that they experience more learning situations than employees with more experience. Another issue is the amount of time that was spent by the participants on the learning trajectory. This "work" load was deliberately kept as low as possible. It is estimated that participants spend an average of eight hours over a period of three months. Insights have developed on the possibility to stimulate this intriguing form of learning, as well as on the ability of professionals to create and follow their learning trajectory.

## 9.7    Summary of the findings from the learning trajectories

Two main questions were asked in this research:

1. How do professionals organize their learning at the workplace?
2. Can we stimulate learning at the workplace with learning trajectories?

In most organizations there is an assumption that professionals do not have a particular opinion about their own learning. In some courses trainers ask the employees about their learning goals. However they are seldom asked to specify the learning path.

In this research both questions were asked:
- What do you want to learn?
- How do you want to learn this?

Most professionals had an opinion about what they wanted to learn and they were able to come up with a concrete and clear answer to this question. Some had an idea about what they wanted to learn, but they had not formulated it in concrete and clear terms yet. Others had no idea of a topic they wanted to learn about. During the interview the researcher and the participant constructed the topic together.

The level of ability to define a learning goal varied as well. Some were specific and clear on their own and some were more vague. Some did not find it necessary to define a learning goal.

The actions were also created at different levels. Most of them had an idea about how they should come to the learning goal. During the interview the actions became more concrete or were being imagined. The findings show that professionals are able to decide upon a topic, learning goal and learning activities. Of course, this requires some knowledge in these areas. Based on this we can conclude that professionals do indeed have some insight into their learning process and are able to transform this into learning plans.

The topics employees chose to work on varied a lot. The variation was almost as large as the number of participants. Despite the variation, we constructed a certain list of topics employees chose.

The topics employees wanted to learn about were:
- Communication skills, they wanted to improve their communication or their ability to be assertive.
- Specific skills for the function, e.g. learning how to win a case.
- Career issues, e.g. what requirements their next job should have.
- Social skills, like how to improve a persuasion style.
- Improving their professionalism, to develop a certain vision on their role in the organization.
- Specific knowledge, like what the rules are for a certain insurance package.

- Planning skills, e.g. how to work within a certain budget.
- Knowledge or insights into why one's own advice was not followed.

All these topics were closely related to the work and tasks of the employees. They were also of direct interest to him or her. The topics mentioned can be found in courses but usually only as a part of a course, never as a general objective of the course. This means that the learning needs of these employees were quite limited, personal and specific.

Although every professional was able to create some parts of their learning trajectory, the ability to construct their learning varied. Some were very well able to specify what they wanted to learn and how they wanted to reach their goal. For others this was more difficult. In conversation we constructed the learning trajectory. But their choices were always leading.

Learning goals that were defined based on the learning topics are quite similar. The reason for first asking about learning topics and later about learning goals are twofold. First of all, when you start making a learning plan, no matter how large or small, it is difficult to immediately define a concrete, specific and clear learning goal. Therefore we started by talking about the topic an employee wanted to learn about and explored that issue. When the topic was clear we continued with clarifying a learning goal.

For learning goals, employees chose:
- To increase communication skills
- To acquire knowledge and insight
- Finish a certain project or task
- Pass on knowledge
- Clarify career issues
- Improve social skills
- Increase planning skills.
- Some did not define a learning goal

As we already mentioned these learning goals are quite similar with the topics raised above.

To reach the learning goals professionals choose the following learning activities.
- Improve communication: pay more attention to how to present new tasks and to non-verbal behavior.

- Extent/intensify networks: find new contacts in the organization, or talk to certain people more often.
- Experiment: try something new.
- Prepare: take the time to prepare one-self.
- Evaluate: think about what you did.
- Acquire knowledge/information or insight: search specific items of knowledge/information or insights.
- Develop general skills: learn how to finish a case successfully.

These actions are small and can easily be performed during work. Most of these actions are daily activities and part of one's job. Because of the size of these activities a good integration with work is possible. They do not take a lot of time, but together, and with a certain aim, they can generate learning.

The success of the learning trajectories differed a lot. The way people followed their trajectories varied a lot as well. Not everyone executed the same amount of actions or experiences. Moreover, the integration of learning and work was not good with every trajectory. For example, someone wanted to learn how to maintain her position and beliefs in a powerful discussion. The problem was that this did not happen very often. This in turn could also be an explanation why she was not very good at it.

Another trajectory was overtaken by the workload. Someone wanted to develop a vision of her role in the organization. Her learning activities were mostly conversations with others to gain more insight into her role and the expectations of others. She had to develop a certain plan, for which it was necessary to talk to many people in the organization. This all happened so fast that work went faster then her learning trajectory.

The learning trajectories that were successful were the following:
- The learning goals concerned a problem that was directly related with the function.
- The problem was of importance for better performance on the job.
- Regularly, a couple of times a week, situations occurred which allowed the employee to work on the problem.
- The problem touched upon 50% of the work.
- The problem was broad enough for different solutions to be worked on.

- The problem was clear at the start, further clarification was not necessary.
- The employees were highly motivated to solve the problem; they carried out all their learning activities and more.
- The employees were willing to seriously experiment and take risks, for example taking the risk of positive or negative reactions.
- The employees were competent in learning at the workplace, in the way that they were able to explain what they did and why they did certain things.

The attitude of the employee and especially his or her motivation was crucial for learning. Besides this a good integration with work was important as well.

In the first interview we asked the participants what they considered to be obstacles to learning in the workplace. They gave the following answers: capacity problems (in terms of work or time); lack of own initiative; too few people on the team; manager; function; small budget; private circumstances; and other departments.

The participants considered the following aspects to be a support for learning at the workplace: colleagues, manager, new business, own ambition, being open minded for new things, the learning trajectory, education, presentations, internet, intranet and a mentor.

Most employees mentioned consciousness as one of the main learning results. They became more conscious of what they wanted to learn and the process of learning itself. That led to results.

## 9.8    Lessons learned

How can your organization stimulate learning in the workplace? The first and most important question you need to answer is: what needs to be learned? What is the learning question? Learning in the workplace is not the right solution for every learning question. But if you want your employees to develop their expertise or to improve their work, or if *you* want to improve your work, then there are two options.

We tested in this research the first question: how can we improve workplace learning and how can we help the employee to take more responsibility in his own learning? Given that the research took place within a relatively stable environment, the guidelines developed for this form of learning will most probably only hold for this kind of environment. However, we can consider most companies as this kind of relatively stable environment. In what follows, we describe a procedure and its related questions which could be successfully followed in cases where workplace learning could be an issue.

- Choose a learning goal that is closely related to your work and that is connected with different tasks, which means there are often opportunities for you to "work on" or to learn.
- The learning goal is connected with approximately 50% of your tasks.
- There are multiple small solutions for the problem studied, which lead to solving the problem.
- Take the time to clarify your problem.
- Take the time to think about the ways you already explored in order to solve the problem and which ones did not work.
- It is important that you are working in a relatively stable environment, which implies that the learning goal and your learning sources are relatively stable.
- You need to be motivated in order to finish the trajectory successfully. There should be a clear intention to work on your problem.
- Be prepared and willing to experiment. Experimenting means taking risks.
- Formulate clear and concrete actions and consider how these actions contribute to your learning goal.

**Preparation of the learning trajectory**
Set a time for yourself, for how long you want to work on this issue, (e.g. three months). Find someone nearby in your network, to support you with this learning trajectory. This could be a coach, or someone from the organization, but not from the same department. Consider at what point you want to evaluate and how you want to evaluate. Is it:
- after every learning experience?
- after a week?
- after two weeks?

- once a month?
  How do you want to evaluate?
- on paper, for yourself?
- on paper, via e-mail, to another person?
- by chat?
- on the phone?
- in a conversation (this is probably the easiest one)?
- any combination?

Keep in mind that evaluation is crucial for the success of a learning trajectory.

The length of the period you choose to work on your problem differs for every problem or issue. Make sure that the evaluation moments are not too far away from your learning experience.

It is advisable to make a trajectory with someone else. This always gives a second view on your learning and therefore offers another source for learning in itself. If you are going to include someone else in your learning, clarify the above mentioned points.

In order to become more conscious of how you learn at the workplace at this moment (before the experiment), ask yourself the following questions.
- What do I learn from in my work?
- From whom do I learn?
- What is my learning really about?
- Do I take initiatives to learn, and if so, how do I do that exactly?
- What, in my environment, stimulates learning (maybe other colleagues)?
- What supports my learning?
- What impedes my learning?
- How do I know whether I have learned something?
- Is it important that my learning is visible to others, and if so, why?
- How would I describe learning at the workplace?

### Learning sources

What learning sources do you have at your workplace? Those are the sources where you can get knowledge, others' experiences, advice, support, etc. The goal of this questioning is to become conscious of the mechanisms of getting the things you need for your job. Based on this inventory, you can get an idea of where to get the necessary input for your learning trajectory.

But also it questions whether you have the right sources to learn what you want.

Make an individual network, and clarify the following;
- <u>Who</u> do you speak to? You can mention names or functions, or types of departments.
- <u>What</u> do you speak about? Is it knowledge or expertise, or is it about the organization, personal issues? And what do you do in those contacts? Do you: check, get feedback, evaluate, ask questions, discuss experiences, prepare?

Afterwards, make an inventory gaining insight in your organized and less organized meetings. A meeting can be with many people but equally only with two. Ask the same questions as mentioned above with the individual network.

Then identify the written sources you use for your learning, mentioning the following:
- What is the source (internet, literature)?
- What is the information about?

Design of the learning trajectory
- Now you are ready to design your own learning trajectory. Answer the following questions and keep your preparation in mind, especially follow the guidelines:
- What kind of problem or issue do you choose? Take some time to think this over. You can discuss this with your manager in order to get his or her view, or you can choose something that came up during your annual evaluation meeting.
- Think about your motivation? This is very important for a successful trajectory.
- What did you learn about dealing with your problem and what have you tried already? What worked and what did not and why?
- Where do you want to be by the end of your learning? Formulate a concrete learning goal in active terms. Think about the feasibility of your trajectory.
- How can you reach your learning goal, what actions can you come up with? Make your actions very concrete and plan them. Realize how your actions lead to your learning goal.

- What is the goal of every specific action? Why do you do it?

The design of the learning trajectory on paper contains a problem or issue to learn about, actions, and of course, a learning goal.

*Mid-way point evaluation*
Evaluate the planned moments. Answer the following questions:
1. What actions did you do?
2. How did it go? What happened? (answer for every action)
3. What did you learn? (answer for every action)
4. Did anything else occur unexpectedly that was related to your problem?
5. What happened?
6. What did you learn?
7. Is your learning goal coming any closer?
8. Would you like to adjust your design?

   - Do you want to adjust your problem or issue, is it still adequate?
   - Do you want to come up with new actions, or do you want to repeat actions?
   - Would you like to adjust your learning goal?

Repeat the above evaluation for as long as your learning trajectory goes.

**Final evaluation**
Start with the first six questions of the half-term evaluation and proceed with:
1. Did you reach the learning goal?
2. Why did you, or did you not, reach your learning goal?
3. What else did you learn from this trajectory, besides your learning goal?

Then follow a couple of questions about the way you created your own learning trajectory:
1. Was the learning period correct, or did it need to be longer or shorter?
2. Were the moments of evaluation well chosen, or did you need to evaluate more or less often?
3. What factors impeded your learning?
4. What factors supported your learning?
5. How would you describe your learning in the workplace now?

When you are going to work with this learning trajectory, formulate the learning goal and the actions specifically and concretely. This enhances the chance that the actions will be actually undertaken.


## 9.9    Conclusions


Learning in the workplace is something that already takes place and very often we are not really aware of it. Furthermore we know that 80 % of what is learned during action is remembered, whereas it is commonly accepted that only 20 % is remembered with "just in case" learning. Unfortunately, many companies today see workplace learning not (yet) as a valuable aspect of knowledge management, or at least they do not act upon it.

In this chapter we gave insight into how workplace learning can be practically organized for employees (and for managers themselves). In the research project that formed the basis of this chapter, the participants were able to choose what they wanted to learn. This choice appeared to be crucial for their motivation. The combination of workplace learning and retention rate is most probably related to this observation.

Workplace learning is not an alternative to knowledge management, but rather a composing part, or a complement. As argued in the conceptual chapters, knowledge management and learning go hand in hand and are in fact two sides of the same coin. Particularly workplace learning could be a good reinforcement of a more structured knowledge management approach.

It is sure that much more practical experience should be researched before clear-cut opinions and solutions are suggested. This research, however, gives the company in question valuable insights and practical guidelines.

# 10. FACILITATING LEARNING FROM DESIGN

Madelon Evers

## 10.1 Introduction

This chapter suggests that a key to the successful design of knowledge management systems lies in an organization's choice of design methodology. Design methodology influences the way people gather and interpret knowledge to make design decisions. A learning perspective on design suggests that organizations should develop methodologies that facilitate design teams to learn from multidisciplinary design processes, with a view to improving collective design skills in an organization over time. I describe a new 'Design and Learning Methodology' (DLM), developed to facilitate learning from design by integrating principles of "human-centered design" described by Gill (1996) and Earthy (1998), with "action learning" theories developed by Zuber-Skeritt (1997), Marquardt and Revans (1999) and Garvin (2000). Exploratory action research to apply a conceptual model of the DLM took place in 12 multidisciplinary design projects over three years. I describe the basic research issues, objectives, and settings, summarize the main results, and explain the DLM model. I discuss the relevance of the research and make suggestions for using the DLM in organizations.

## 10.2 Research issues

### 10.2.1 Issue 1: Failure of technical systems design

Over the last few years, organizations have increased investment in the design of knowledge management systems (KPMG, 2000; Megens, 2001; Forrester 2003). In service-oriented companies, knowledge management systems (KMS) are created out of a need to optimize or restructure interrelated, dynamic business processes, offer communication channels for co-located groups, and manage transactions with clients (Davenport, 1993). The design and implementation of a KMS is a complex process: design must meet the evolving needs of users, develop intelligent ways to share knowledge, accommodate changes in business strategy and markets, and keep up with developments in technology (Evers, 2000). For years, the literature has reported high failure rates in technical systems projects, despite investments of up to 12% of annual budgets in design (see for example Heygate, 1993; Willcocks and Griffiths, 1994; Lei, 1994; Standish, 1995; Battles et al., 1996; Glass, 1998; Cooper, 1999; Laudon & Laudon, 2000; Forrester, 2003).

## 10.2.2    Issue 2: Failure of design methodology

Design methodology consists of ways of thinking and acting by which designers analyze and understand design problems and processes (Ishizaki, 2003). It is a strategic framework to manage a multi-layered process to move from design problems to solutions specification to implementation of a technical system.

Research shows that the process by which systems are developed influences the way design teams gather and interpret multiple types of knowledge required to make design decisions (Rosenbrock, 1989; Buchanan, 1991; Dorst, 1997). In many large organizations, technology-driven design methodology tends to prevail in design projects (Laudon and Laudon, 2000). Techno-centric approaches focus on technology, paying less attention to social and strategic requirements that impact on systems acceptance and use in organizations (Olsen et. al., 1994; Stowell, 1995; Gill, 1996; Norman, 1998). A techno-centric design methodology gives little priority to the exploration of non-technical issues through interaction with non-technical stakeholders, as their involvement in design decisions is an efficiency-related cost (Wilson et al., 1996). To control design decisions, engineers tend to avoid working with people outside their specialized domain (Cooper, 1999; Armstrong, 2000). As a result of using techno-centric design methodology, however, engineers create a lack of awareness of fundamental contextual problems that can result in inappropriate systems designs and cause the system to be rejected by the very same organization that invested to develop it (Beyer and Holtzblatt, 1998).

### 10.2.3    Issue 3: Learning from design

I argue that techno-centric design methodology has another, equally fundamental, impact on design projects. This impact is on the ability of all stakeholders in design – technical and non-technical -- to develop collective, design-related knowledge and skills to improve design outcomes from project to project, and across disciplines. Research by McNeice Filler (2001) reveals that managers, analyzing their own project failures, find that 86% of failures are not due to time, capacity, budget or technology, but are related directly to a lack of collective competence in design teams. This includes teams' lack of ability to define clear objectives (17%), to develop insight into the scope of a project (17%), to manage communication processes (20%), and to manage design processes effectively (32%). I contend that design methodologies in use in organizations today fail because they do not 'facilitate' stakeholders to develop these much-needed, collective design skills from multidisciplinary processes.

'Facilitation' is a process of intervening in work processes, usually carried out by skilled mediators who create conditions for teams to reflect on products, processes and learning outcomes from work (Schwarz, 1994). Facilitation of design-related competence development is important for a number of reasons. First of all, requirements change as a project evolves (Bourgeon, 2002), so stakeholders from different disciplines need to shoot at many moving targets at once. To do this, they need to become aware of all the dimensions of a shared design problem, and develop collective knowledge to tackle these dimensions effectively. The more multifaceted a design problem is, the more likely solutions will fail if there is inadequate knowledge integration across an organization (Rothwell,1992). In the face of this complexity, there is nothing for people to do but "learn a way through the design process" (Van Langen, 2001). Collective learning occurs when team-based knowledge is actively shared and reapplied across an organization (Dixon, 1999). However, collective learning does not occur automatically if teams are left to their own devices (Homan, 2001). Developing collective learning skills involves dealing with many external and internal factors that block peoples' ability to learn effectively as a team (Walz et. al., 1993; Gieskes, 2001). Facilitation of collective learning could support stakeholders to learn beyond their own knowledge domains, to make this learning explicit to others, and to find ways to develop collective skills for use in further design projects.

### 10.2.4    Issues for facilitating learning from design

In order to facilitate collective learning from multidisciplinary design, an understanding is needed of what facilitation entails. I see facilitation as an ongoing process of support, by skilled mediators, to help MDTs (Multi Disciplinary Teams) to become aware of what is happening *now* in the context of their organization, to critically *question* what they assume is the 'best' solution at any one time, to *readjust* decisions as a result of trying to understand what is *not yet known* about a problem, and to actively develop *new ways* to tackle more dimensions of the problem based on expertise built up collectively over time. Facilitation of learning from design should be geared towards what Malholtra (1999) calls adaptation to "permanent white-waters", which means that stakeholders in an organization must be given the support to learn to continuously re-examine "their alignment with the dynamically changing external reality".

By engaging in multidisciplinary design, specific types of collective competence can be developed within and between teams, which are not just related to the content or context of a specific design problem, but which expand inter-team skills in dealing with the design process itself. The development of these process management skills can also be facilitated, so that MDTs can make this knowledge explicit and share their expertise from one project to the next, with a view to improving design skills in the organization over time. Facilitators can also act as mediators to ensure that collaboration processes between departments, stakeholders and individuals inside and outside an organization are managed properly and that commitment to sharing knowledge between MDTs is sustained. Facilitation of collective learning can assist MDTs to take time to meet and share experiences, and to evaluate and find solutions for processes that are described by Cooper (1999) and Armstrong (2001) as particularly problematic, including processes such as collaboration, relationship management, expectations management, customer management, knowledge management, and strategic and organizational change related to design.

## 10.3    Research objectives

In practice, few organizations currently appear to use techniques to systematically facilitate collective learning from multidisciplinary design processes, as a core principle of design methodology. In theory, researchers and consultants have, since the 1980s, developed design approaches that are based on participatory, collaborative and multidisciplinary design processes (Bekker and Long, 1998). Currently, however, there is no formal design methodology that describes practical methods to actually facilitate *collective learning* from multidisciplinary design processes, considering learning as an explicit outcome of design. I have therefore developed a new Design and Learning Methodology (DLM), which aims to help organizations to improve the collective design skills of MDTs over time.

## 10.4    Preliminary conceptual model

I sought to apply and iterate a preliminary conceptual model for research, illustrated in Figure 22 below.

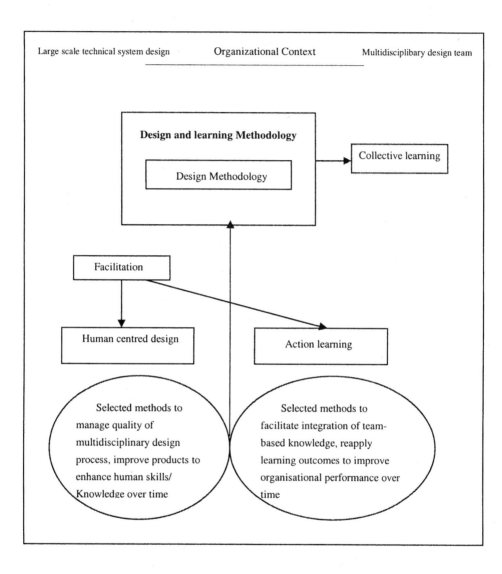

*Figure -22.* preliminary conceptual model for research

## 10.5     Research settings and activities

I carried out action research to develop the DLM over three years in two main settings. The first setting consisted of four knowledge management and e-learning systems design projects in different business units of the European financial services group Achmea Holding NV, in the Netherlands. The second setting involved eight multidisciplinary design teams engaged in design projects during production training at SAE Technology College in the Netherlands. SAE is a commercial institute certifying engineers and multimedia producers. Trainees develop websites on commission from the media marketplace or for their employers.

Action research allows the researcher to be full participants in a research process (Barton Cunningham, 1993). At the same time, it involves participants in the research to generate, collect and interpret empirical data, with which the research can then develop meta-level, academic theory (Eden and Huxam, 1999). To develop theory in practice, and to facilitate change at the same time, I used designed action research interventions in the manner illustrated in Figure 23 below.

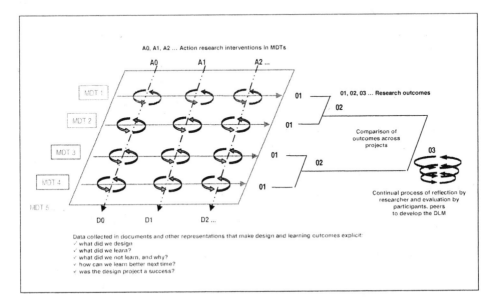

*Figure -23.* action research interventions

In a series of action research interventions (A), I collaborated with MDTs to analyze and apply the proposed combination of action learning and human-centered design methods, and to test the feasibility of this framework for facilitating collective learning from their design projects. This process produced a number of 'design documents' (D) which recorded collective learning outcomes (O1) as well as the normal technical systems design outcomes from various phases of design (see Table 1). Collective learning outcomes were then evaluated in the course of multiple design meetings involving the whole MDT and their managers. Outcomes per MDT were then compared by the researcher, in order to assess criteria for facilitation (O2) and to produce an adjusted model of the DLM (O3). This model was reviewed in workshops involving professional peers from the Dutch Action Learning Association, who conduct action learning facilitation in other business processes in other organizations in the Netherlands, as well as with academic peers in the fields of design and organizational development (Evers, 2001, 2002 and 2003).

## 10.6    Main results

### Outcome 1: Varied achievement of collective learning

Through action research interventions over longer periods of time, I looked for indications of whether collective learning was considered to have been achieved (or not) as a result of using the DLM. From the perspective of MDTs and managers involved in the projects, the achievement of collective learning was very dependent on the kind of collaboration process they had managed to sustain together. For example, in the business setting, after a number of months into the design project, we evaluated the status of collective learning in MDT 1. Responses were collected through a Group Decision Support System, involving the whole MDT to answer pre-prepared questions simultaneously, typing data into locally networked computers and displaying results for the whole team to review. I cite some answers regarding their experiences with collective learning below (translated from Dutch):

*MDT member 1: just because we are spreading information around now does not mean we are really communicating.*

*MDT member 2: communication is a time investment; no one is doing anything with what we communicate right now outside the project.*

*MDT member 3: there is not enough commitment to communication outside this project, and no one cares what you communicate, really.*

*MDT member 4: instead of saying what we learned, we should be using our lessons learned to signal problems in the organization.*

*MDT member 5: you get a good idea of what is going on with your learning when you still don't know who you should inform, and who decides what to do with it?*

*MDT member 6: we should be able to force communication about these things with management, they don't do anything with what we propose to them, everyone is isolated.*

*MDT member 7: if the pressure at work goes up any more I will start to consider sharing knowledge as something outside my core tasks. I need more time, I don't have enough time to do what I have to do everyday and still 'network' all the time to learn from others.*

Near the middle of a three-year design project involving MDTs, participants were involved in an evaluation session, to discuss whether they had achieved any collective learning during design. Their answers were, again, mixed. I quote (from Dutch):

*MDT member 1: the time pressure in meetings is too intense for us to keep really learning from each other. Agendas for the meetings we had up to now limited us, actually, to formulate new thoughts about a core aspect.*

*MDT member 2: it took too long from one meeting to the next for us to share learning in the short term. I want to get something out of this in the long term, but it's a double thing for me, what does this learning mean for me in the short term?*

*MDT member 3: the question is what do these sessions actually give us? How important are the outcomes for our managers? We share everything with them but how is that going to help us? What are we going to do with all of this?*

*MDT member 4: we recognize now that we all have the same problems, but we also know that we do not all have the answer.*

*MDT member 5: the main gain from the sessions is a group feeling that we really learn from meeting face to face. But how are we going to hold on to this when we go virtual again? What do we do with our knowledge when we have to confront each other and have a big discussion when we are not together?*

*MDT member 6: we still didn't really take enough time to confront each other and have a deeper look at what was going on.*

*MDT member 7: I still don't know what the new knowledge is that we have when it comes to changing our behavior. Together.*

*MDT member 8: We want to learn from each other, that much I think we know by now, but still, how?*

As a participant-researcher, I concluded from these evaluations that the achievement of collective learning from multidisciplinary design processes is not something that can be defined as a 'fait accompli' or 'end point' corresponding to the end of a design project. MDTs did reflect on what they had learned collectively, but tended to tie the perceptions of an achievement of collective learning itself to conditional, other, future, unresolved and problematic factors in the organization or team.

Many MDT members remained confused or skeptical about the concept of 'collective learning', asking what their MDT could actually do with any new knowledge gained from other people they do not normally work with for a further project. Most MDTs expected management to take action on knowledge shared between them; MDTs expected increased commitment from managers to pick up on what they had learned and to make the collective learning go forward in the organization. There was a certain passivity in teams which may have resulted from facilitation or the way in which managers influenced perceptions of the value and purpose of the MDT's knowledge. Managers were also consistently rated by MDT members as taking insufficient action to share their (managerial) knowledge with the MDT.

### Outcome 2: Establishing criteria for facilitation

I collected evaluations about the process of facilitation during each design project. Based on an analysis of these evaluations, I summarized and formulated a number of specific criteria for facilitation that can be perceived as important for the DLM. The basic facilitation criteria are:

1. facilitation should invest time to help teams get used to shifting focus from work content to reflection on (learning) content. This shift or 'double' focus can cause some confusion in MDTs at the beginning of a design process.
2. facilitation of reflection on learning should always take place within the actual design meeting, with the group present, rather than after a session.

Leaving reflection or review for later often caused evaluations to be forgotten, incomplete, completed only by one individual from the MDT, or not carried out consistently across a project.
3. facilitation activities should be explained and visible to management, and committed to by management, before launching into the actual facilitation process during a design project. This is a challenge, as many activities are chosen as the process goes along, and depend on how the MDT responds to facilitation.

**Outcome 3: Iterated model of the DLM**

Four basic activities were considered important, for the DLM to be able to support learning during multidisciplinary design processes. These activities are: participation, evaluation, negotiation, and creativity. These activities were integrated into the DLM, resulting in a new version of the model (see Figure 24 below).

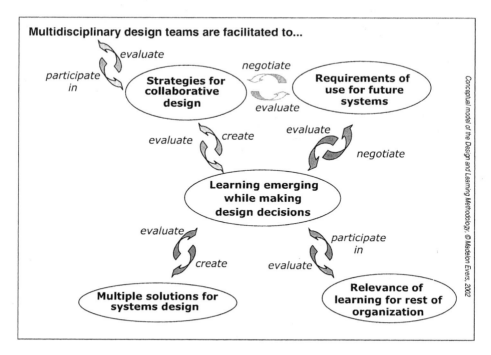

*Figure -24.* New model of the DLM

In the new model, the activities that participants in the research considered important for the DLM can be described in the following manner:

## 10.7    Participation

The DLM assumes that it is possible to achieve meaningful participation of a wide range of stakeholders in tackling complex design problems, in order to enrich design-related knowledge with non-technical experience that can ground design decisions in the organizational and social context. In order to achieve this, facilitators should ensure that at least four different disciplines (technical and non-technical) should work together at any time during design meetings. Also facilitation should aim to create conditions in which stakeholders can participate in on-going discussions with different groups inside and outside an MDT, share these discussions as broadly as possible, for example through workshops, meetings, and a virtual forum or 'community of practice' online. Participation is significantly hampered by changes in management and delays in decision making to allow various stakeholders to join an MDT, for example due to departmental differences or capacity problems of sub-units to let employees off 'core production' to engage in design. A facilitator should try to influence decision-makers to include more non-technical employees in design projects; a role which a technical project leader often cannot or will not take on themselves due to their positions and goals in the organization.

## 10.8    Evaluation

The DLM assumes that the task of multidisciplinary design is not just to build a KMS as quickly as possible using a single technical solution, but to seek multiple solutions to many of the problems impacting both design and learning in an organization. This requires MDTs to evaluate multiple strategic, market, social, cultural, and technological perspectives that affect their design decisions. Action learning facilitation is essential, to train MDTs to think in a more strategic and team-based manner. Facilitation of evaluation processes ensures that MDTs will actually take the time to reflect on the content of their own design decisions, to discover the problems with what they have done, to plan better actions based on what they have learned from this reflection, and to evaluate why certain problems are as yet unresolved in the context of their organization.

## 10.9    Negotiation

The DLM suggests that facilitators create space and time for MDTs to negotiate constructively about their collective design decisions. Negotiation gives stakeholders a chance to discover the way others think and work, what the reasoning is behind design decisions, and how to deal with certain power configurations that may affect decision-making and implementation processes in further phases of design. Negotiation requires the development of debating skills and insight into group influence in MDTs. Facilitators can support teams to engage in a systematic and deliberate confrontation of beliefs, intentions and assumptions that may be held implicitly, and create conditions for comparison with other stakeholders inside or outside an organization. The facilitator must ensure that design debates are not restricted to technical issues, but are focused on expanding negotiation to design process issues and to collective learning issues on an ongoing basis.

## 10.10    Creativity

MDTs must share different types of knowledge in a structured way in order to make effective design decisions. In order to solve complex problems for which there is not a known answer, however, MDTs also need to become more creative. There are hundreds of creative thinking tools that facilitators can use to encourage creativity in team-based design processes, such as scenario-based design, mood boards or 180 degree thinking. A scenario is a description of activities in narrative form, describing alternative views of a common problem situation. A mood board is a rapid visual sketch or collage that expresses the main feelings and images that people have in their minds when thinking about a problem situation. 180 degree thinking is an activity where a team takes an idea or suggestion and plays with it, flipping it around to come up with an opposite idea or suggestion, in order to discover other solutions.

## 10.11    Suggestions for using the DLM in practice

The following is a summary of suggestions for use of the DLM to facilitate collective learning from multidisciplinary design practices in organizations.
1. The first step to implementing the DLM is to reserve a few minutes of each design meeting to consciously reflect on team learning outcomes from each day's multidisciplinary design process. 'Quick wins' can be gained for organizations using the DLM simply by facilitating MDTs to engage consistently in collaborative evaluation of learning outcomes, during daily design practice. Reflection on both design and learning should take place in one design session, not extraneously.
2. Facilitation of reflection on learning from design should be carried out by skilled mediators experienced in the management of collaborative engineering processes and/or in action learning coaching. In our projects, many facilitators worked with consultants or coaches, in 'duos'. They acted as mentors to each other when their backgrounds were in a limited or specialised domain.

3. MDTs must be clearly supported by their managers to take concerted and sustained action to share design-related knowledge through presentations or workshops to others in the organisation. The DLM is suited to helping MDTs tackle complex design problems during large-scale technical systems projects such as the design of a KMS. The DLM is therefore an alternative to the prevailing techo-centric design methodologies.
4. Organizations should bear in mind that the DLM is not meant to achieve quick solutions for design problems. The DLM focuses on achieving collective learning *from* design. The DLM complements ongoing programmes to support people to learn in teams, and can be used in combination with other design methodologies, but with the realization that the DLM facilitation process demands real investment of time and space for participation, evaluation, negotiation and creativity enhancement activities with and between MDTs, with a vision to develop design-related knowledge across design projects.

## 10.12     Relevance to business and academia

### 10.12.1   Organisational relevance

The problem of achieving collective learning is rooted in an organisational paradox described by Cooper (1999), in which technical systems designers struggle to balance two contradictory needs. On the one hand, the need to design a system efficiently, and on the other hand, the need to have enough time and space to understand design problems to tackle them effectively. This efficiency-effectiveness paradox raises the question of how to develop a design methodology that facilitates qualitatively high levels of learning from design, but in an efficient way. This paradox presents a significant challenge, as can be seen from the results above, and from the fact that the use of methods to facilitate learning from design during design projects is still far from common, let alone accepted as an explicit strategy in large-scale technical systems design projects in organizations. The development of the DLM is directly relevant to organizations, as the research struggles with this paradox and seeks methods that can achieve some kind of response to this paradox from the basis of real practice in MDTs, rather than from a purely theoretical formulation of methodology.

### 10.12.2   Academic relevance

This research tackles two aspects that are relatively new to research in the engineering and human-computer interaction studies (HCI) fields. Firstly, I focus on multidisciplinary design; research into the nature of multidisciplinary design teams is just getting off the ground (Lloyd and Christiaans, 2001). Secondly, I take a *learning perspective* on design methodological development, seeking to embed practical methods for facilitating five levels of learning within one design process. This research also aims to fill a specific gap in engineering and design research. Although many researchers have observed over the last 30 years that designers are not very successful at solving complex design problems, there has been little theory developed on *the relationship between collective design competence* and the ability to solve complex design problems effectively. Although some recent studies describe the phenomenon of learning in multidisciplinary design teams (for example, Bucciarelli, 2003; Adams et al., 2003), the studies tend to focus on individual learning, not on design in relation to collective learning or organisational learning. Other studies discuss the link between multidisciplinary design processes and learning processes (Steiner, et al., 2001; Lawson et al., 2003), but these studies do not develop a design methodology that describes practical methods to actually facilitate action learning during multidisciplinary design. Finally, most design theories remain theoretical, rarely being applied in real organisational contexts, and developed instead in short periods of time in quasi-experimental settings, using student groups (Sole and Edmondson, 2002). By contrast, this research was carried out in real-world settings, involving professional MDTs, through action research carried out over a longer period of time (from January 2000 to November 2003).

## 10.13   Summary

The main contribution of this research is:
- An expansion of formal design methodology to integrate human-centered design with action learning and facilitation principles;

- A description of challenges facing facilitation of learning from design based on empirical action research;
- Description of action research interventions to develop design methodology from practice;
- An applied and iterated conceptual model of the Design and Learning Methodology

# 11. CULTURAL COMPLEXITY: A NEW EPISTEMOLOGICAL PERSPECTIVE[10]

Marie-Joëlle Browaeys, Walter Baets

"Complexity is a problem construct rather than a solution provider" (Morin,1990,p.10)

## 11.1 Introduction

Complexity is defined by its sources, its principles and its objective. This is what the newspaper *Le Monde* (2003), wrote in a review of the book by the sociologist

Réda Benkirane [1]: *La complexité, vertiges et promesses.* This author presents a series of interviews with scientists of various disciplines - such as Prigogine, Varela, Morin, Steels, Kauffman -, all using the concept of complexity, a multidisciplinary idea that refuses to parcel out fundamental problems. This epistemological approach [2] bringing together different disciplines, was already announced by Bachelard (1934, p.11) in the *Le nouvel esprit scientifique.* He foresees an epistemology that will express the "character of a non-Cartesian epistemology", which he qualifies as being "the real innovation of the contemporary scientific spirit".

Culture is a complex process. This process is not in harmony with traditional ways – based on the Cartesian epistemology - of the management

---

[10] This chapter has been published before in The Learning Organisation - Volume 10, Number 6, 2003, pp. 332-339 - MCB UP Limited, ISSN 0969-6474 and is reprinted here with the authorization of MCB Ltd.

of organizations which is too simplistic to be satisfactory. What is the place of culture in the organisation?

Research on organizational culture shows the necessity of taking cultural references into account when tackling management problems. Referring to Thévenet (1999,p.10), the culture assists the organization in dealing with management problems: "In all of our field studies, we never saw a firm interested in the culture itself, but focus on culture always had the aim of solving actual problems, related to strategy, take-over, mobility of employees, re-organization, thus, to communication. Culture is just a tool to better deal with these problems".

But what does cultural complexity mean? According to Sackmann (1997,p.2) the concept of cultural complexity "encompasses both ideas: simultaneously existing multiple cultures that may contribute to a homogenous, differentiated, and/or fragmented cultural context". Hence, the cultural complexity perspective suggests that culture in organizational settings is much more complex, pluralistic, diverse, contradictory, or inherently "paradoxical" than it appears at first sight.

Many others also show the importance of the concept of culture in organizations. In their critical review of literature on organizational learning, Wang & Ahmed (2003,p.11) noticed that "there is a strong emphasis on the cultural perspective of the learning organization." In addition, there is a need for a new epistemology as was made clear by Søderberg & Holden (2002). They state that the learning organization "becomes the knowledge-creating organization, a new kind of communicating entity ... that requires new forms of intercultural communication know-how" and that "[t]he key engine of learning is the multicultural team"( Søderberg & Holden, 2002, p.110). Therefore we need to understand and use another epistemology that "will allow for new concepts to describe and analyse the cultural complexity in different business settings."(Søderberg & Holden, 2002, p.112).

## 11.2     The problem of "culture" in (learning) organizations

In the world in general, one of the topics most often approached currently, is that of globalization. The researchers of any discipline are led to pose questions such as that posed by Benkirane (2003, p.216) to Kauffman:

"This globalization or universalization, can be regarded as a holistic process [3], in other words like a process which is truly universal, general, which takes into consideration the various dimensions - social, cultural, ecological, and why not spiritual – of human societies? "

In his answer, Kauffman believes that there will be a combination of globalization and decentralization. He also foresees an increase in diversity: "we will invent diversity more quickly than we will make it homogeneous" (Benkirane, p.217).

### *What does globalization mean for an organization?*

Berthoin-Antal (1998) answers that globalization depends on the degree of globalization of each company and the experience which it has been able to acquire. This comprises both the globalization phase of the company – multi-domestic, international, multinational, transnational - and the functions related to international responsibilities. Ruigkok & Wagner (2003, p.72) add to this the international disposition of firms' top management teams and give as examples the members' educational and professional experience in foreign countries, the breadth of nationalities on board, the top management teams' cultural heterogeneity.

In summary, we can say that it is now beyond doubt that the process of globalization is a reality and that it is still progressing at high speed. The same is true for the increase in cultural diversity in domestic and international companies where people from different cultural backgrounds work more and more together. (Browaeys, 2000, p.13). The globalization of companies would be related to the diversity which would in turn be related to the internationalization of the organizations.

### *What problems underlie the process of internationalization?*

According to a survey by Adler (1991) the heterogeneity of the cultural background of the members of these kind of organizations is seen on the one hand as a potential source of problems, but on the other hand as a possible advantage for the organization. Within organizations operating in an international environment, both partners and collaborators will be brought into intercultural situations that need to be turned into an advantage to prevent the failure of the strategy of internationalization. (Browaeys,2000). According to Harzing & Sorge (2003, p.191), internationalization strategy refers "to the way multinationals fashion relations between headquarters, subsidiaries and the diverse markets and institutional contexts in which they operate". Based on this statement we conducted interviews in several companies which revealed that managers may have very different perceptions of the notion "international context". We asked the following question: "What does 'being international' represent for you?"

Below is a selection of their answers to the question:

"For a company, to be "international" does not necessarily mean that it has to have foreign managers. International thinking is independent of the question of nationality. In my opinion, to be international is a question firstly of mentality: nationality has nothing to do with it. Secondly it is useless, not necessary, to have too many nationalities at the top" (Dutch Executive Board).

"One of the best things to do in building an international culture in a company is to have managers with international experience outside their countries" (Dutch Corporate HRM).

"Being international is also to accept differences, and to build upon differences. And to benefit from differences" (French Corporate Managing Director).

"The essential solution lies in having international people (not just an international veneer) at the Head Quarters who are sensitive to what is going on in the operating companies" (Belgian Technical Director).

"My active involvement in the recruiting of my management team is a crucial factor. I consciously apply my insight into the cultural 'make-up' of the candidates for managerial positions, and carefully assessed the cultural requirement of the positions to be filled" (French Managing Director).

"A large organisation has to set its international orientation up step by step. One can be Dutch in the first place and make place for other cultures having common a strategy and objectives. Results have to be reached, but how you do that cannot be identical, for example, in France and Italy. Thus, you have to be international to manage the cultural and market differences with a single vision. You have to recognise the value of all internal partners regardless of their origin" (Italian HRM Director).

### How to interpret these examples?

These examples show how difficult it is to formulate the ideal profile of the international manager. It is no more the person who has work experience abroad than the one who followed cross-cultural management workshops. Moreover, since the people interviewed created their own 'subjective reality' (Schumacher 1997, p110), there is a discrepancy between perceptions and reality. Koenig (1994, p.83) points out that the complexity and the ambiguity of the real world give room to interpretations which may be not only different, but also contradictory.

However, just these subjective representations that the managers have about what 'being international' means, shows you how they see reality. These representations are based on the natural knowledge that an individual acquires during his history. According to Genelot (1998, pp.110-11) our relationship with reality, our acts, things we build and direct have no other source than our subjective representations. He adds that, "if we thus build the complex reality from our internal representations, it is crucial for better directing our future that we understand how our representations build up , how our "system of representations works (Le Moigne)" (Genelot, 1998). A system which is composed of three elements: the paradigm, the context and the objective.

## 11.3     A new perspective on cultural complexity?

The debate on the external culture (national cultural context) and internal culture (organisational culture) of a company causes antagonism between the researchers in the field of intercultural management. Referring to the article by Meschi and Roger (1994, p.198):

The idea has been widespread that organizational culture moderates or erases the influence of national culture. It assumed that employees working for the same organization even if they are from different countries are more similar than different (Adler 1991,p.46).

On the contrary, others affirm that national culture is predominant compared with organizational culture (Hofstede,1980; Laurent, 1983; d'Iribarne, 1986)".

### *What does culture mean?*

You can never use the word 'culture' without being obliged to launch into multiple definitions which only serve to oppose them even more! And what if this term had only one meaning? Would culture, irrespective of whether it is aesthetic, philosophical, national, organisational or managerial, not only be a form of individual or collective representation? Genelot (1998, p.195) stresses that "men are products of their culture: their representations, their visions of what is good and what is wrong, their behaviour at work, their concepts of organizations are the fruit of the representations carried by their ancestors". Can one thus state that a change of culture would only be a change in representations?

### *How to approach the cultural problematic of organizations?*

To first of all make the choice which paradigm among the paradigms - in the sense given to them by Edgar Morin (1990), 'des principes *supralogiques* d'organisation de la pensée' ('*Metalogical* principles to organise our thinking') - is the essential epistemological condition for any research. This does not mean to imply a complete adhesion with the selected paradigm. He adds that a paradigm is made up by a certain type of extremely strong logical relation between the main concepts, the key concepts, the key principles (p.79). For Thévenet (1999, pp.52-3) the relevance of paradigmatic approaches to organizations is to bring about a contrasted and subtle approach of reality through various frames of reference.

According to Wunenburger (1990, p.16) "the natural sciences as well as the social sciences have given up the ideal of epistemological unity which would permit to illuminate the totality of reality by a single and universal reason ". Indeed, Prigogine (2000, p.11, cited in Granier, 2001, p.207) points out the distinction which was made between the social sciences which include "the unforeseeable, the qualitative, the possible, the uncertainty" and the physical sciences - "the certainty and the temporal reversibility". The concept of "uncertainty" could be an example of bringing sciences together, as stated by Lissack (1999, p.119): "Both complexity science and organization science have a common problem they wish to address : uncertainty".

Complexity thinking is presented in the form of a new paradigm born both from the development and the limits of contemporary sciences. And we think that the paradigm of complexity seems more appropriate for studying culture in organizations, since it is not unaware of interference and interaction between human beings and their organizational environment. "We can indeed fear that constructions which are either monistic or dualistic, analytical or synthetic, taxinomic or dialectical will in most cases only lead to exaggerate or underestimate the differences" (Wunenberger 1990, p.11). Morin (1986, p.232) adds that complexity thinking is an approach which helps "to deal with interdependence, multidimensionality and paradox". This approach goes perfectly with the definition of the concept given by Sackmann on the cultural complexity quoted in the introduction. Morin insists on the fact that complexity is not only the problem of the subject but also that of the method used to acquire knowledge about this subject. Therefore, he proposes a method which requires "the formation, reformulation and full employment of a way of thinking which is at the same time dialogical, recursive and hologrammic". It is these basic principles which we will develop below.

## 11.4    What is complexity thinking?

The concepts of complexity thinking are different from a positivistic epistemology. As stated by Bachelard (1934, p.139) "There always comes a moment when one does not find it beneficial any more to seek the new on the traces of the old, where the scientific spirit can progress only while creating new methods". Moreover, the complexity approach brings closer the scientific and philosophical disciplines and becomes one transdisciplinary discipline since it refuses the "parcelling out of the fundamental problems between the disciplines" (*Le Monde, 2003*).

In his interview with Benkirane (2003, pp.23-6), Morin recalls the two organizing principles of thinking defined in his work, *La Méthode*, notably, "a principle of simplicity and a principle of complexity". The first separates the objects of knowledge from their context whereas the other principle, even if it distinguishes the objects, interconnects them. For Morin, complexity is a way of thinking which includes concepts such as uncertainty "because there cannot be total and absolute knowledge", contradiction "forms of antagonisms between concepts", and also applies to "men and society". Rather, "complexity is not the opposite of simplifying, it integrates this one". (Morin & Le Moigne 1999, p.256).

In their study of complexity literature, Richardson & Cillers (2001, p.8) mentioned that a number of schools of thought are developing and that they differ substantially. Besides the strong and the soft complexity science there is a school which is called "complexity thinking". "It involves a shift in philosophical attitude that might well put off practicing managers ...". According to this school, if one assumes that organizations are indeed complex systems, a fundamental shift in the way sense is made of our surroundings is necessary. (Baets, 1998, 2003)

### The concept of complexity

Genelot (1998) sees in complexity a "major challenge of our time". He defines the term complexity while not limiting it to only this aspect, as: "what escapes us, what we have difficulty with to understand and to control" (Genelot, 1998, p.41). He tries to give a definition of the concept of complexity by using a descriptive approach of the characteristics. He distinguishes three levels of complexity, "the one which emerges from reality with its procession of the unforeseen, of the dubious, of the instable", followed by a second level of complexity, "the one of knowledge, that of the way we represent our reality and from which we work out our reactions" and finally the last level consisting of "the feed-back of our representations on reality" (Genelot, 1998, p.70)

### The notion of complexity

Le Moigne (1995) stresses systemic modelling: "a complex system is, by definition, a system which one holds for irreducible to a finite model, whatever the complexity and sophistication of this model, whatever its size, the number of its components, intensity of their interactions... The abstract notion of complexity implies that of unforeseeable factors, of plausible emergence, of new elements and intrinsic properties which one holds for complex" (Le Moigne, 1995, p.3). Further on, he concludes that "to understand and thus to give significance to a complex system, one must model it to build his intelligibility (comprehension)".

### Complexity thinking

Morin (1990) brings with his "Paradigm of complexity" the conceptual framework to the complexity thinking. Traditional thinking is too simplistic to be satisfactory, as he explains; its ambition is limited to the control of reality, whereas that of complexity thinking is "to account for the articulations between the disciplinary fields". He defines complexity thinking as another way of thinking which does not seek to complicate but to open thinking towards other conceptual fields and to progress towards the comprehension of the complex. To understand complexity it is to know how to accept ambiguity, contradiction, the inaccuracy of the concepts and the phenomena and to accept the unexplainable (Morin, 1990, p.50). For him, if, in the first place, complexity seems to belong to the quantitative, it does not, however, only comprise quantities of units and of interactions; in a certain way it always has something to do with likelihood. One cannot reduce complexity to uncertainty, complexity "is uncertainty within richly organized systems" (Morin, 1990, p.49). One can conclude with Morin and Le Moigne (1999, p.261) that "complexity thinking is thinking which at the same time seeks to distinguish (but not to separate) and to connect".

## 11.5 Complexity thinking and its principles

To grasp the paradigm of complexity better, Morin (1990, pp.98-101) proposes three guiding principles which can help when thinking about complexity: the dialogic principle, the hologrammic principle; and the principle of recursivity:

1. The dialogic principle offers the opportunity to maintain duality (e.g. between subject and object or agency and structure) while at the same time transcending that duality and creating a unity of the whole.
2. The principle of recursivity, in which causes are simultaneously effects. Individuals create society which in turn creates the individuals. This is a recursive process, and as such this breaks with the idea of linearity and a causal linear relationship between input and output underlying traditional organizational thinking.
3. The hologrammic principle which goes beyond reductionism, that only sees the parts, and holism, that only sees the whole. Holons or whole/parts are entities that are both wholes and parts of ever greater wholes, simultaneously and at all times.

Larrasquet (1999, p.453), claims the paradigm of complexity, affirming that "complexity thinking requires to regard the problems of reference as fabrics of dynamic relations complex, bathing in the recursivity, the fractality, and the dialogy". These problems are not for him more of the network type than of the vertical type. He does not regard these terms as being able "to be used to qualify exclusive forms of organization, (hierarchical system, system network…) ".

Morin (1990, p.176) explains the term 'dialogic' in *Science avec conscience,* by saying "that two logics, two principles are unified without the duality being lost in this unity." He takes the example of the man who is "at the same time completely biological and completely cultural".

Morin joins the dialogic principle to the hologrammic principle, since in a certain way the totality of the genetic information of the individual is in each cell, but says that also "the society as a whole is present in our minds via the culture which trained and informed us" (Morin, 1990, p.177). The third principle of complexity stated by Morin, the principle of recursivity, is for him also linked to the hologrammic principle. He stresses that this principle is the basis even of self-organization: "the recursive organization is the organization of which the effects and the products are necessary to its own causation and its own production."(Morin, 1990, p.69)

Le Moigne (1990, p.105) identifies principles which he regards as the bases of constructivist epistemologies. We will retain the "principle of representability", which means the principle of the experiment of reality since it refers to our subject. Referring to the work of Von Glasersfeld in *The construction of Knowledge* in 1987, knowledge reflects "the organization of our representations of a world constituted by our experiments (our models of the world)". This means that we will recognize our models, not as representations of reality but because they agree with our experience of reality.

In search of the fundamental principle of the organization, Larrasquet (1999, p. 453) proposes a "holistic complex approach" that respects two logics, which he names the 'holon' of the organization: "it means the fundamental dialogic unit of two inseparable principles for comprehending and constructing an organization". Wunenberger (1990, p.17) adds that "the holon becomes thus a kind of new configuration of objects which as well challenges the analytical intelligence of the parts as the synthetic intelligence of amalgamated totalities".

Larrasquet (1999, p.458) sees in organization the dialogy between "identity and distinctiveness". Self-referencing is only conceivable in relation with others, there is no autonomy or conscience without relation to others. That does not make sense. According to him, to give sense, to make sense in the company, it is "a phenomenon which rests on two dimensions, a collective social dimension, and an individual dimension, which means a dimension of distinctiveness, opening, on the one hand, then a dimension of identity, particular closing on the other hand. These two levels are dialogically non-dissociable "

## 11.6   What does complexity thinking mean for the cultural problematic in organizations?

By applying the concepts and principles of complexity thinking to organizations, we can offer a new way of thinking about culture in a globalizing business world, and a link between individual, culture and organizations:

- The dialogic principle - which permits the association of contradictory notions to conceive the same complex phenomenon – highlights the relationship between individual and company. This is one of the principles guiding the cognitive process of complexity thinking. «Thus, the distinction of the individuals and their potentialities, is accompanied by a conjunction, setting in synergy of these elements with another logic, that of the company of which they form part » (Genelot 1998,p.138).
- The principle of recursivity is a concept of self-production and self-organization. Thus, individuals produce the organization by their interactions, but simultaneously, the organization produces the culture of the individuals. "The specific culture of a company concerns this recursive process: prior to the people who arrive in the company, the culture works them, and these people become in their turn carrying this culture". (Genelot 1998, p.77)
- In the hologrammic principle – in which not only the parts are present in the totality, but also the totality in the parts - *we* can see that the organization is present in all individual members, throughout its culture and norms.

Finally, the fundamental principle of the company – 'sensmaking' - applied to the culture: We saw with Genelot (1998, p.204) that our representations condition our future and that the cultural construction of the company happens by the expression of this future. Insofar as the company wants to imagine its culture, to affirm its values, it must associate with all the people who make it up, "because what is significant in the complex universe of the company, it is that each one is carrying the whole, in the image of a hologram". This implication, this engagement of people by favouring intelligence, creativity, Larrasquet (1999, p.505) sees as a way of opening to them the possibility of building sense.

However, Morin, in his interview with Benkirane (2003, p.27), says "the principles of the complexity thinking cannot dictate a knowledge program to you, they can just dictate a strategy". The strategy remains the keyword, because only strategy makes it possible to advance in the doubt and it can be modified as progress is made in the investigation. This word 'strategy' is taken up again by Larrasquet (1999, p.289) who does not see any more the practical interest for the organization of a "general strategy made in advance ". To apply the principles of complexity thinking remains the work of the researcher who adopts a strategy, "it means a guide in the uncertainty", adapted to his objective and not to "a universal method ". (Morin & Le Moigne 1999, p.203)

## 11.7     Conclusion

In this contribution we have proposed another epistemology to approach the cultural complexity of international organizations through the complexity thinking paradigm. First, we have argued, along with Morin & Le Moigne (1999,p.266), that "complexity thinking is not reduced to either science or philosophy, but allows their communication by operating the shuttle between the two". Second, we have outlined the concepts and principles which form the framework of this paradigm, and we have given some examples in applying them. We are convinced that further research on these issues related to the culture of organizations using this theoretical approach will be useful to learn about the cultural complexity of the globalization of the business world.

In this paper an attempt has been made to discuss the conditions for organizational learning, rather than the process itself. The paradigm of complexity thinking *"la pensée complexe"* is very instrumental for this improved understanding.

Notes

[1] Consultant for international organizations

[2] In Anglo-Saxon countries, the word epistemology is a philosophical term designating "theory of knowledge", whereas in France it means "philosophy of science". ( Dortier, 1998, p.433)

[3] Holism: (G.Holos=Total). Term invented in 1926 by S.C. Smuts to designate a tendency by the universe to build units forming a whole and of increasing complication. (*Nouveau vocabulaire philosophique*, Armand Colin, 1966)

# 12. DIALOGUES ARE THE BREAD AND BUTTER OF THE ORGANIZATION'S KNOWLEDGE EXCHANGE

Martin Groen

Access to *long-term needs and values* of customers and prospective customers is a crucial asset for organizations (e.g., Hoffman Ponder, 2001). An insight into long-term needs and values is needed by organizations to enable them to develop products or services that address these long-term needs and values. Long-term needs and values are supposed to reflect stable attributes of purchasing habits of the customer over time. Organizations want to appeal to the needs and values to ensure that consumers understand and can relate to their offering – rationally or emotionally, which is generally assumed to be an incentive to purchase the offered product or service. They need to be *long-term* needs and values to enable the organization to establish a sustainable source of income and engage in lasting relationships with their stakeholders. Notice that the assumption here is that (the people within) organizations strive to achieve continued existence of the organization as a unity in the long run.

Organizations invest a lot of money in an attempt to determine what the long-term needs and values of their (potential) customers are. Investments are made in, for instance, data warehouses to search for patterns or trends in transaction databases, focus groups to see how people respond to certain changed offerings, and questionnaires to collect opinions about a market offering of a random sample of (potential) customers. For example, in 2001 the accumulated expenditure on market research executed by third parties for the French market in total was € 858.2 million and € 1,652 million for the UK market (Euromonitor, Market Research: Market Size section, ¶ 1, 2001).

It pays to look behind the façade of business activities such as the ones mentioned in the previous paragraph and other activities such as management information systems, knowledge management and customer relationship management. While doing that we find that they all seem to be attempts to answer a common and longstanding problem for, and within, organizations:

How to capture, store and disseminate important information about specific relevant entities within the organization and its environment that are required or needed for e.g. sound decision making by managers?

Let's call this type of information 'steering information'. We will discuss three current activities of organizations where this observation is salient: management information systems, customer relationship management and knowledge management.

## 12.1     Management information systems

Ciborra (1993) pointed out, after collating a large body of ethnographic data in a large number of organizations, that this 'steering information' is primarily exchanged at the coffee corners and water coolers of organizations, interspersed with bouts of small talk. This is a disconcerting finding with respect to how we usually structure organizations and management information systems. The default organization type can be described as hierarchical, with a president or a board of directors at the top who are reported to by a number of "lower-level" managers. The managerial decisions that these "larger-level" employees need to make, for example strategic decisions, are based and informed by, amongst other information sources, the information that is reported in the management reports prepared by the "lower-level" employees. As it turns out, according to Ciborra (1993), the information that is exchanged via this vertical route – that is, in a direction from subordinate management level or lower to superior employees at the directors level – is by definition tainted by the career goals of the manager, or other reasons for augmenting the content of the management report, such as saving face. On the other hand, at the horizontal level – a bit of a misleading term, since it refers to everything that does not fall under the previous vertical information exchange – these career considerations, as Ciborra (1993) argues, do not seem to distort the information exchange too much. Therefore, information exchanged at the horizontal level is considered more relevant, or closer to what actually happened, than reports that are produced at the vertical information exchange in, for example, the boardrooms.

This observation has implications for management information systems as well. These systems are designed to facilitate the hierarchical and vertical information exchange that we described in the previous paragraph. When the information that is delivered at the input side of these systems is unreliable, what must we make of the eventual result at the managerial cockpits (as they are sometimes called) in the boardrooms?

Another observation due to Ciborra (1993), related to the previous one, is that these hierarchical information exchange structures and, consequently, management information systems, all seem to rely on the implicit assumption that the goals of the organisation coincide with the goals of the employees of the organisation. This is often not the case, as we saw in the discussion with regard to the vertical information exchange and with the use of management information systems. People often have very different reasons to be in, or to leave for that matter, an organization, and these goals are not necessarily identical to the goals of the organization. For instance, an ambitious young employee might consider the management position that she was offered a nice intermediate position for her next relevant position in her career, whereas the organization is investing money to develop her management skills in management development programs, preparing her for a long-term top position in the organizational ranks.

Baets (1998) identifies a number of problems with current practices in organizations with respect to management information systems. He argues that management information systems are "still, to a large extent, technology-driven." This potentially leads to the situation where investments in technology might be more inspired by technological possibility than organizational necessity. An additional problem, which is related to the previous one, is that it has been established (Baets, 1998) that aspects of business strategy are insufficiently integrated in the context of management information systems. A source for this neglect has been identified in the lack of agreement within organizations on the market potential of the organization itself and aspects of the market in which the organization operates (Baets, 1994, as cited in Baets, 1998).

## 12.2    Knowledge management

Probably the most cited book within the scholarly topic of knowledge management is that of Davenport & Prusak (1998). They define knowledge as a manageable asset of organizations that is composed of:

"...a fluid mix of framed experience, values, contextual information, and expert insight that provides a framework for evaluating and incorporating new experiences and information. [...] It originates and is applied in the mind of knowers. [...] In organizations, it often becomes embedded not only in documents or repositories but also in organizational routines, processes, practices, and norms."

This definition, which is quite a common definition in the field of knowledge management studies, must be a disappointment for managers. When they want to initiate activities to capture and disseminate the knowledge that is available to some employees and not others, they need to select or steer what they think it does within contexts that are of relevance to the organization. So, they do not need to know what knowledge *is*, they need to know what knowledge *does*. Knowing how to keep a customer is more important, than knowing that you kept a customer, while not having a clue how you managed to do that. To make knowledge management work, or better, organizations successful we need to know what employees do to successfully deploy their knowledge and try to capture and disseminate those methods or tricks.

## 12.3    Customer relationship management

When we ask marketing practitioners to determine how they would describe customer relationship management (CRM) they tell us that, in essence, CRM started for nostalgic reasons. Let's call this position the shopkeeper's perspective.

With the shopkeeper we refer to the neighborhood grocery shop owner, who somehow knew when there were new people coming to live in the neighborhood, when people went away for a while and when the new baby was due of the lady from three doors up the street. But how did this shopkeeper manage to do all that? Most likely, the shopkeeper remembered the gist of conversations and used that gist together with the specific groceries that were bought as an organizing principle for remembering this information. CRM is, basically, about the same issues as the task that the neighborhood shopkeeper saw himself presented with, but on a larger scale with more customers at the same time. All made possible with the promises of modern information technology.

However, some problems with CRM in practice can be observed:
- It appears to be hard to disseminate (and identify, for that matter) the relevant information about customers within organizations.
- The huge amount of conversations on a daily basis within organizations leads to a loss of perspective on the gist of the dialogues.
- The possible absence of the principal participant in the dialogue leads to fragmentation of the gist of the dialogues.

This line-up of these three current activities of organizations, that is, management information exchange, knowledge management and customer relationship management, is aimed at illustrating that determining what is organizationally relevant information, and consequently how to capture and disseminate that information is not a straightforward matter. Where management information systems, via human structures or via computational means, struggle with how to get the relevant steering information to the boardrooms, knowledge management is trying to benefit from the enormous amounts of knowledge that appear to go untapped in employees working in organizations, and, lastly, customer relationship management is getting to grips with how to get this steering information and apply it when commencing, maintaining or discontinuing a relationship with a customer. Although, these different activities appear dissimilar they share a commonality: how to benefit from relevant information in management decisions at every level of the organization.

This is a considerable wide field of problems with a common core, as should by now be clear from the above exposition. Here we want to focus on the use of relevant steering information in an activity which is, without doubt, the most important activity of organizations: interacting with the customer.

With the current research we want to propose a structural mechanism for organizations to collect information about the long-term needs and values of customers. This mechanism will be developed in the course of carrying out research into labelling and recognizing the larger purposes customers have when they are engaged in dialogues with representatives of organizations[11]. In the next three sections we will elaborate on the specifics of larger purposes and their relationship with customers' long-term needs and values. After that we will explain what we might do with the results of applying the mechanism in day-to-day business practice and what it does to an organization's ability to orient towards the needs and values of customers.

## 12.4     Larger purposes and long-term needs and values

When we want to know about the larger purposes a customer might have with a dialogue that he is having with a representative of the organization, we are actually asking a psychological question: what factors drove this individual to have this conversation here and now with this organization? When this question is formulated like this it is far too abstract and should not be answered too lightly. How can we reliably answer this question without resorting to measuring instruments that are ill founded? To approach this problem we need to go to the basics of the social mechanism of conversations in order to determine what it is that we are actually measuring by developing the definitions of the primitives involved.

The social mechanism that we want to discuss is projected by the discourse participants to enable them to realise certain goals they have. We propose to subdivide these goals in *task-oriented* goals[12] and *social-affective* goals, since these two types of goals serve different needs. In the next subsection we will elaborate on the task-oriented goals people have when they are engaging in conversations. In the consecutive subsection we will treat social-affective goals that conversationalists want to realise.

---

[11] Note that this basic mechanism of the exchange of larger purposes in discourse is applicable to all human-to-human dialogues, not only customers to sales personnel.
[12] In this chapter I will use the terms purpose and goal interchangeably for purposes of style.

## 12.5    Task-oriented larger purposes

When a person decides that he needs to turn to an organization to provide him with a certain product or service, he makes this decision based on a perception of a need or motivated by a value. This leads to the person making, for instance, a shortlist of organizations that he intends to contact to enquire about the needed product or service. When sufficient product or service information is collected, he makes a decision to buy the product or service from a selected organization, selected by some criteria. What we see at work here are the effects of the realization of a hierarchy of goals where action taken to fulfil the super-ordinate goals leads to action to establish subordinate goals, which in turn leads to action to accomplish subordinate goals of these subordinate goals, and so on. The more we get to the top of the hierarchy the more intimate and relevant the goal will be for the person, the more we go down the hierarchy the more 'mundane' the goals become. From the point of view of organizations, with their aim to come to grips with the long-term needs and values of customers, the top-most goals are the most relevant as well.

As an example of a hierarchy of task-related and social-affective goals consider the following example: Alan wants to have a successful career that will provide him with status and at the same time will lead to the full use of his talents, and a nice income as well. To achieve this kind of high-level hierarchical goal he decides that he needs to switch jobs. Alan finds a position in a company which is sixty kilometres away from his home. Therefore he decides that he needs a comfortable car that expresses his newfound status to his peers and whoever happens to be around, and takes him back and forth to his new employer. He buys the car and realises he needs insurance for the risk of damages and accidents to the car. That is why he creates a shortlist of three financial services organizations where he wants to enquire about the offerings they have with respect to the type of car he has, the conditions and the premium they ask for. He talks to three representatives of the respective organizations and remembers that the representative of the second organization was a cheerful, service-minded person who took time to explain all the details of the conditions of the insurance. After comparing the three offerings he decides to select the one that he remembered had the best conditions, which happened to be the offering from the second financial-services organization. Alan has the expectation that one day when he might need to use the services of the organization, the best place to be served seems to be the organization where they appeared to be the most service-minded. He trusts them more to deliver the service that he will need.

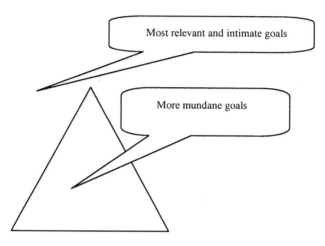

*Figure -25.* Hierarchy of goals and their relative importance to the owner of these goals

The effects of the actions to realize these goals permeate the actual observable conversational behaviour. Not only can the effects be seen of the 'mundane' goals exerting their transient influence on a turn-by-turn, contribution-by-contribution basis (see also for example Sacks, 1995), but also the effects of the more relevant, more intimate goals can be observed. All the layers of the aforementioned hierarchy of goals are all executed at the same time during the course of the dialogue. Within the confines of this research we are interested in the effects of the more intimate, relevant goals, since these are the goals that flow from the long-term needs and values of the customer. When organizations pay attention to these goals they will then be better prepared to retain the customer and embark on a lasting relationship with their valued customers.

## 12.6     Social-affective larger purposes

People cannot help but being social (compare Tuomela, 2000). Within dialogues we tend to want to realize the social and affective goals we might have with our dialogue partner as well. Normally, or rather by *convention* (Lewis, 1969), we want to be polite and give the other the respect that he deserves until proven otherwise. Also, we want to make the encounter as pleasant as possible to make sure that our goals are fulfilled. These social and affective larger purposes, in other words, *lubricate* the workings of the dialogical mechanism.

But another important function of these social and affective larger purposes is that they also extend their influence beyond the current dialogue. They make it possible for the conversationalists to build a relationship or strengthen the quality of their relationship or change it otherwise. When an organization wants to retain its customers we need information about the social and affective larger purposes to enhance the ability of (the people in) the organization to increase retention of the customers, and build lasting relationships with customers. Obviously, relationships are supposed to extend the current dialogue as well.

In the previous two sections we have set out two types of larger purposes: task-oriented larger purposes and social-affective larger purposes and their association with the long-term needs and values of customers. We have explained that organizations need to address both types of dialogical goals of customers to establish and maintain lasting relationships. In the next section we will explain our suggestion of what we do when in dialogue to enable our discourse partners to recognise our larger purposes and therefore, in the end, our long-term needs and values.

## 12.7     Indicating and recognising larger purposes

Speakers (regarded as a turn -by-turn role of each of the discourse partners) indicate to their addressees that an important stretch of discourse will be presented. The reason that they present such a signal is twofold:

1. The stretch of discourse that follows the signal has certain relevance for the speaker. In fact it is one of the goals, albeit task-oriented or social-affective oriented, that they want to see established.
2. They want to prepare or alert the addressee that they should pay more attention to the upcoming stretch of discourse since it bears this high relevance to them.

The addressee presents his acceptance of the signal in many ways, for instance with continuers like yes, ok or hmmhmm; with a re-phrase of the focal stretch of discourse as perceived by the addressee; with non-vocal signals like nodding or gesturing and so forth. By presenting an acceptance signal the addressee is indicating that he has recognised the signal presented by the speaker and accepts the contribution of the speaker. Notice that these are all presentations and acceptances as perceived by the speaker and the addressee. There is no mention of any truth claim here, just what the conversationalists seem to decide will do for current purposes (compare Clark's Principle of Joint Closure (Clark, 1996, p. 226)).

Notice that the speaker has presented a signal in order to be recognized as such, as signalling something relevant, by the addressee. The addressee presents his recognition of the signal by the conventional signals as set out in the previous paragraph. This does not mean that the addressee has understood the utterance. This is a next step in the conversational process (and understanding processes in general) and will have to be dealt with by the conversationalists in the upcoming discourse. This process is called *grounding* (Clark & Brennan, 1991; Clark, 1996) and will not be treated here.

These signals alert the addressee to an upcoming important stretch of discourse. In other words, the signals can be used to predict that a certain important stretch of discourse will be presented. The speaker presents the signals to enhance the possibility that the relevant stretch of discourse will be recognised as being relevant to the speaker and treated likewise by the addressee. The speaker therefore intends, with the presentation of the signal, that the addressee recognizes that he needs to give special attention to the stretch of discourse that follows the presentation of the signal. Notice that the speaker communicates a social-affective goal with the signal as well as a task-oriented goal: the speaker seems to find it important that the addressee knows about a goal relevant to him which in effect will reveal something about the speaker's task-oriented and more intimate social-affective goals. It will also enhance the odds that the goal of the speaker will be accomplished as such.

Due to the hierarchical nature of goals in the determination of human goal-oriented behavior we assume that the goals that the speaker wants to satisfy here and now with a specific dialogue is, amongst others, the result of the working of super-ordinate goals and, eventually, the top-most goal. Organizations want to appeal to the larger order goals to make sure that they fulfil the long-term goals of their customers. When an organization structurally collects information about these larger purposes then they will enable themselves to address these long-term goals of their customers and serve any long-term future needs the customers might have.

In the current circumstances in most organizations long-term needs and values can only be approached by approximation, as they are based on abstractions inferred from market research and applied to the organization's body of customers. When information is structurally collected as we have set out here then it is possible to attain a closer fit between the long-term needs and values of the customer. Notice that we do not ask the customers here what their long-term needs and values are; we propose to gather them from the goals they express during their conversations with representatives of the organization. In doing this, we prevent the known problems with interpretations, answering questions according to social conventions and the like.

To summarize, speakers present signals to indicate the upcoming presence of their larger purposes. Larger purposes flow from the long-term needs and values of people. The signals predict that a larger purpose will be presented. Collecting larger purposes enables an organization to gain insight into the long-term needs and values of customers. Armed with this information organizations will be able to adapt their products and services to the needs and values of the customers that they want to service. With this ability they enhance the likelihood that the customers will continue their relationship with the organization.

## 12.8    Harvesting the fruits: Applying larger purposes to sales conversations in call centres

So far, we have elaborated on long-term needs and values and the way they are expressed when customers present them when they are engaged in discourse with representatives of the organization. We have proposed that when organizations pay attention to these larger purposes structurally then they are better able and prepared to continue the relationship with their customers and prolong the chances of survival of the organization. It is therefore of crucial importance to organizations to find a way to structurally deal with the task-related and social-affective purposes of their customers. When they accomplish this they will no longer be too dependent on the coming and going of successful sales personnel and will be better able to deliver the high quality service that they wish to provide.

Unfortunately, it is not an easy task to pay due attention to the purposes of all the customers. For example, in *one* of the business units of an Insurance company the amount of commercial telephone calls amounts to 1.3 million on a yearly basis. Sales personnel working by telephone talk to many different people every day, which makes it hard to remember, let alone register in a system, what has been discussed and what the gist of the conversation was. Chances that the customer will talk to the same sales advisor are quite low as well, since people might have a day off or might move to a different position in or outside the current organization. In this situation it is likely that the customer will have to explain some parts of, or all of, his "story" to the sales representative to ensure that he gets the best offering possible and bring the current dialogue partner up to date about the current status of the relationship between the customer and the organization. The experience of the quality of the relationship by the customer might decrease considerably because of that (Keursten & Bolte, 2003).

It is common in organizations to store information about customers in computerized registration systems. Most of this information concerns the products or services they have bought. Often information produced by market research organizations, for instance concerning spending patterns of people in the same area as where the customer lives, augments this information. These kinds of information systems can be classified as transactional information systems since they store only the information regarding the transactions that have been executed with the customer up until now or any future transactions that might arise because of the fact that the customer has been categorized as belonging to a specific group (market segment as they are often called) based on some inferred shared property. No information about the relationship besides the transactions seems to be stored.

When we want to mimic the one-to-one conversation between a customer and a salesperson in a large-scale call centre with many call center personnel serving many customers, we need to incorporate this relational information as well, as that seems to be the bread and butter of the sales talk. (Compare Keursten & Bolte, 2003).

With this research we want to add information about the long-term needs and values of customers as they perceive and formulate it themselves. After a proper registration of this information and some time it will be possible to categorize the customers based on their own perception of their long-term needs and values. This might be a relatively cheap and accurate aggregation of customers based on their long-term needs and values. It might prove to be easier to sell the products when the sales representative is more aware of the long-term needs and values *and* it enables the organization to give input to a prolonged relationship with the customer, for instance using the information about larger purposes from aggregates of customers with similar larger purposes might improve the effect of marketing activities.

Having a long-term relationship with customers seems to be fruitful. For example, Reichheld (cited in Winer (2001)) has shown that a slight increase (5) % in retention of customers leads to a positive influence of 84% on the net present value delivered by customers. Reichheld (1993) also claims that a 5 % "increase in customer retention lowers costs per [insurance] policy by 18%."

In what we have revealed so far we have made an assumption concerning the association between the beneficial effect of having available information about the larger purposes of customers, assuming that they flow from the long-term needs and values of customers, and an improvement in the effect of sales conversations of call-centre personnel with customers. We have devised an experiment to test this assumption.

Next to this experiment we have also devised three experiments where we attempt to determine what dialogical elements people use when they are presenting or recognising, as respectively speakers or addressees, larger purposes. When we know what those dialogical elements are, then we might be able to predict that a larger purpose is about to be presented in an ongoing dialogue[13]. Even better, judging from specific signals of larger purposes we can determine whether we are about to hear a task-oriented larger purpose or a social-affective larger purpose. These experiments serve a scientific purpose *and* an applied purpose. From an applied point of view, with the results of these experiments we are able to improve on the computational model we have built of the recognition process of larger purposes leading to a software tool that automatically infers larger purposes from what customers say. We also want to compare three groups of employees with different levels of expertise in a call centre to see whether increasing experience in this line of work also leads to an increase in the proficiency and efficacy of recognition of the larger purposes of customers. From a psychological point of view we will be able to understand and predict human conversational behavior better. Before we show the results of the experiments we will introduce the computational model.

## 12.9     The computational model

A computational model is a hypothetical imitation that serves as an existential explanation of the phenomenon that is imitated by the model implemented in a computer program. As is clear from this definition we use the computational model as an exploratory device to construct a number of hypotheses about the phenomenon under study, which is the basic social and cognitive mechanism of exchanging larger purposes in conversation in a commercial setting. In other words, to make a computer program work some operationalizational choices have to be made. These operationalizations are, in effect, hypotheses that can be empirically tested. You are forced to be very specific about the details of the psychological model when you want to imitate it with a computational model. This is a big gain that can be accomplished by using computational models.

---

[13] Given that the available speech recognition technology is in a more mature state than it is now.

But this effort to compose a computer program can also serve as a prototype for an eventual software tool that will assist representatives of organizations when they are engaged in dialogue. Since we are investigating basic mechanisms of dialogue here, the findings of this research can be generalized to other types of dialogues as well. Due to the immature state of current (2003) voice recognition software, the processing has to be done off-line.

The computational model has been programmed in Prolog and aims to imitate the "processing steps" human beings go through when they infer larger purposes from the contributions of their discourse partners. In table 5 the algorithm is specified. The "business-at-hand"-thesaurus has been established in a pilot study where we gathered the product- or service-related terms that are used in the daily business of financial services organizations.

*Table -5* Computational model of presentation of larger purposes by discourse partners through dialogue

1. Read utterance.
2. If utterance not equal to stop condition
   a. Match words in utterances to "business-at-hand"-thesaurus.
   b. Pop utterances that match to "business-at-hand"-file, remove utterance from file.
   c. Check utterance not equal to stop condition.
3. If utterance equals stop condition place file pointer at start of file and proceed to next step.
4. If utterance not equal to stop condition
   a. Match words in utterances to back-channels thesaurus.
   b. Pop utterances that match to "business-at-hand"-file, remove utterance from file.
   c. Check utterance not equal to stop condition.
5. If utterance equals stop condition place file pointer at start of file and proceed to next step.
6. If utterance not equal to stop condition
   a. Select utterances that begin with larger purpose marker (so, well or but, or in Dutch: dus, nou of maar) and copy utterance to larger purpose file.
   b. Check utterance not equal to stop condition.

If utterance equals stop condition exit and present file with utterances containing larger purposes to user.

## 12.10   Experiments

In this section we introduce four experiments that we have devised to test some of the hypotheses that follow from our proposal thus far.

### 12.10.1 The effect of presenting larger purpose information of customers on sales dialogues

As said, larger purposes are presented in a conversation to inform the addressees about the goals the speaker has with this particular conversation or the relationship between the discourse partners in general. The larger purposes can be of a task-oriented kind, where the purposes are intended to be understood as having a particular position in a hierarchy of goals. Or they can be of a social-affective kind, where they "locally" lubricate the course of the current dialogue, and "globally" aim to maintain the relationship between the discourse participants.

The hypothesis that we want to test with this experiment is: Does presenting utterances containing (hints to) larger purposes to sales personnel in a call-centre of a financial services organization have a beneficial effect on the resulting sales?

The context of this research is the outbound call centre of a large financial services company in the Netherlands. Customers are called there on a daily basis as a response to the completed and returned questionnaires of those customers. The questionnaires consisted of questions concerning the financial products these customers have and the way they want to be approached by the financial services organization. In the first conversation the customers are asked whether the organization can provide them with any products or services that they have indicated they need or have bought elsewhere. This type of conversation mostly comes in series of two, three or more instants since the customers often have to be called back to see whether they have any additional enquiries regarding the offering of the organization.

We created three groups for the experiment. The first experimental group received the transcript and the spreadsheet with the utterances that contain (a hint to) one or more larger purposes; the second experimental group received only the transcript. Both experimental groups received group-specific instructions detailing what to do with the information supplied. We made sure that they would receive either just the transcript, or the transcript plus the spreadsheet with the larger purpose utterances (with the respective instructions), before the onset of the second conversation. The control group did not receive any interventions. In all three groups we taped all conversations that followed the receipt of the questionnaire. We analyzed only the first and second conversation in the series. We collected 180 phone calls on tape, giving the following table:

Table -6. The three experimental groups as we created them in the experiment where we aimed to measure the effect of presenting customers' larger purposes to sales personnel on an increase in sales numbers

| Groups | Phone call 1 | Intervention | Phone call 2 |
|---|---|---|---|
| 1. Experimental group 1 | T0 taped and registered | Supplying transcript plus information concerning larger purpose of the customer they are (going to) call(ing) plus instruction what to do with this information. | T1 taped and registered |
| 2. Experimental group 2 | T0 taped and registered | Supplying transcript plus instruction what to do with it. | T1 taped and registered |
| 3. Control group | T0 taped and registered | No intervention | T1 taped and registered |
| 3. Control group | T0 taped and registered | No intervention | T1 taped and registered |

The taped telephone conversations were transcribed in Microsoft Excel spreadsheets. Then the transcripts from experimental group 1 were analysed with the computational model. No additional modifications were made to the results of this analysis. The results of these analyses were handed to the participants depending on the experimental group they were assigned to. The consecutive telephone conversation was also taped by the participant and returned to the experimenter, who transcribed this second conversation as well. All transcriptions were stored to be used at a later stage to gather the sales figures based on the customer identification numbers. All personal information of either customers or sales personnel was anonymous. Alongside the testing of the hypothesis, we also tested the effectiveness of the computational model as a sales support tool.

### 12.10.2  Inventory of entry and exit markers of larger purposes

As explained before, we suggest that people use specific signals to indicate that they are about to present a larger purpose. In a pilot study we counted the frequency of discourse markers in a large corpus of 10,000 e-mail messages. Discourse markers (e.g. Schiffrin, 1987, Schourup, 1999) are, according to Byron & Heeman (1997): "… a linguistic device that speakers use at the beginning of a contribution to signal its relationship to the current discourse state. For instance, discourse markers can be used to mark changes in the global discourse structure, as exemplified by 'by the way' to mark the start of a digression and 'anyway' to mark the return from one." So there are two important aspects of discourse markers:
1. They are lexical items that belong to a specific function category.
2. They tend to occur at the start of a contribution.

To our knowledge "start of a contribution" has not been specified further so we define it as the first four words of the contribution that has a discourse marker at the beginning of it. We chose to use discourse markers due to the aspect of the concept that it signifies a digression of the course of the dialogue, the course being the activities that need to be done to establish a local (that is local to this dialogue) goal.

We found that the words so, well and but (dus, nou and maar in Dutch respectively) were the discourse markers that were used most often in our pilot study. Therefore we used them as our hypothetical larger purpose markers.

Every contribution to a dialogue consists of a presentation phase, in which the speaker presents his contribution, and an acceptance phase, in which an addressee overtly or covertly presents that he accepts or rejects the contribution. The start of a contribution where a larger purpose is presented in an utterance is therefore called the entry larger purpose marker and the contribution with which the addressee indicates acceptance or rejection of the contribution is called the exit marker.

We handed the transcripts to thirty people and asked them to judge three dialogues with regard to three items:
1. To what extent did the dialogue partners establish their task-oriented goals?
2. To what extent did the dialogue partners establish their social-affective goals?
3. To what extent would the judge consider this conversation a complete conversation?

In a fourth question we asked them to indicate on the transcripts which parts of the transcript they used to answer the previous three items. We asked them specifically to indicate the start and finish of these stretches.

Preliminary results indicate that the participants tend to use the larger purpose entry markers that we have proposed. Additionally, the participants tended to use the same exit larger purpose marker. So far, this seems to corroborate our expectations.

### 12.10.3   Manipulation of larger purpose digressions in discourse

This third experiment is aimed at establishing whether the entry and exit larger purpose markers from our previous experiment do indeed have the role that we propose, as directly associated with the larger purposes they indicate. In other words, are the larger purpose markers that we have found really larger purpose markers or just markers of discursive digressions from the main line of the course of the conversation?

The design of the experiment will be the same as the previous experiment. No data is available yet.

### 12.10.4    Comparison of dialogues where both participants have larger purposes and where one of the participants does not have a larger purpose

With this experiment we want to establish what role larger purposes play in dialogues. We expect that they have an orienting function for the discourse partners. Larger purposes enable them to adapt their contributions to assist in establishing these larger purposes, like a ship adapts its course to a lighthouse. Consequently, when one of the discourse partners does not have larger purposes it will render the other participant confused, since the latter cannot orient his next contributions to the larger purposes of his dialogue partner.

The design of the experiment will be the same as the previous experiment. No data is available yet.

## 12.11    Conclusions

With this research we expect to find that providing information concerning the larger purposes of customers to sales personnel has a positive effect on the eventual number
of sold items. Additionally, we expect that the provision of task-oriented and social-affective larger purpose information of customers to sales personnel will enhance the quality of the relationship with the customer leading to enduring relationships as can be judged by larger retention rates and a larger deep-sell (that is, more products or services sold per customer) and up-sell (that is, more aspects of each product or service sold to each customer).

Due to the effort that we have made to establish what the signals are that people conventionally use to indicate their larger purpose we are now able to predict a type of larger purpose, social-affective or task-oriented, based on the presentation of such a signal. These larger purpose entry markers function as an early warning system making it possible to heighten the awareness of sales personnel to raw material that can be exploited to enhance the quality of the customer relationship and retain the customer.

Additionally, in training programs sales personnel can be made aware of these conventional markers of larger purposes making them more responsive to the manifest or latent goals of the customer and, in the end, making them more emphatic.

Lastly, using the information about larger purposes from aggregates of customers with similar larger purposes might improve the effectiveness of marketing activities.

# 13. THE INFLUENCE OF KNOWLEDGE STRUCTURES ON THE USABILITY OF KNOWLEDGE SYSTEMS

Erwin W. van Geenen

## 13.1 Introduction

Knowledge engineering is the discipline of building knowledge systems such as expert systems, data mining systems, and decision-support systems. These systems are considered to deliver increased quality of decision-making, faster decision-making, and increased productivity (Martin et al., 1996). There is, however, extensive evidence to suggest that knowledge systems often fail to deliver their projected advantages (Alberdi et al., 2001; Green et al., 1991; Morgan et al., 1996; Cunningham et al., 1998). An important reason is that many knowledge systems are difficult to learn and complicated to operate. They have low user comfort and are prone to be rejected by frustrated users. Problems such as these are referred to as usability problems. Usability is a widespread term which has been defined by the International Organization for Standardization (ISO) and the International Electrotechnical Commission (IEC) in different standards. ISO 9241-11 (1998) defines usability as the extent to which a product can be used by specified users to achieve specified goals with effectiveness, efficiency and satisfaction in a specified context of use.

A common reason why many knowledge systems face usability problems is the failure in system development to incorporate sufficient knowledge of the cognition of domain experts and system users (Alberdi et al, 2001; Alberdi and Logie, 1998, Coiera, 1994). Domain experts are people who provide the knowledge system with specialist knowledge in order to enable the system to perform its task. System users are people who apply a knowledge system during the execution of their professional tasks. The lack of cognitive aspects in knowledge systems has boosted research in the field of cognitive task analysis. Cognitive task analysis is a family of methods with which a researcher can elicit the cognitive processes that underlie observable task performance (Jonassen et al., 1999). The analysis can play – and in fact has played – an important role in the development of more usable software systems (e.g. Egan et al., 1990; Gray et al., 1993; Edworthy and Stanton, 1995; St Amant and Riedl, 2001).

Cognitive task analysis typically focuses on eliciting concepts such as working processes, problem solving strategies, and perceptual cues to improve the usability of systems. The analysis has virtually not been concerned with the elicitation of the knowledge structures which are used by domain experts and system users during the execution of their tasks (DuBois and Shalin, 1995; Hall et al., 1995; Williams and Kotnur, 1993; Benysh et al., 1993; Williams et al., 1998). A knowledge structure could be conceived of as the form in which the content of knowledge is represented (Leddo and Cohen, 1989). Only recently researchers have argued that cognitive task analysis should elicit the knowledge structures that are involved in a task (Chipman et al., 2000; DuBois and Shalin, 2000).

We suspect the usability of knowledge systems to improve if cognitive task analysis would elicit the knowledge structures used by domain experts and system users. The improvement would be the result of a better knowledge acquisition process and user-interface design as part of the development process of knowledge systems. Both aspects will be discussed.

Knowledge acquisition refers to the process of systematically gathering and structuring domain knowledge and transforming it into a computer formalism (Cooke, 1994). Knowledge acquisition has long been emphasized as a pivotal process associated with the development of expert systems (Hayes-Roth, 1983; McGraw and Harbison-Briggs, 1989; Luger and Stubblefield, 1992). More recently, researchers have stressed the importance of knowledge acquisition for the development of other knowledge systems as well (Langley and Simon 1995; Fayyad et al., 1996; Witten and Frank 2000; Kohavi and Provost 2001).

Knowledge acquisition is generally considered as the bottleneck of knowledge system development (Cooke, 1994). The term indicates that the major problem in the development of knowledge systems is to gain expert knowledge in a usable form. Experts are often forced to describe their knowledge in a form which is imposed by the system and does not correspond to the forms they use themselves to describe their expertise. Consider, as an example, rule-based expert systems. The knowledge base of such systems consists of (numerous) 'if-then' rules which have the computational advantage that they are fairly easy to implement into a computer. However, experts sometimes find it exceptionally difficult to articulate their expertise in if-then rules. (Markman, 1999). Cheng et al. (2001, p. 461) put it like this:

*"The forms of representation used in knowledge acquisition are typically tied closely to the computational representations used in knowledge systems, such as logic and production rules. However, such formalisms may be unfamiliar to domain experts, and of a form wholly unlike the representations experts actually use to understand their domains. Using representations for knowledge acquisition that are normally used by the experts may be an effective way to overcome the knowledge acquisition bottleneck."*

User-interface design refers to the process of designing the way an information system presents information to and interacts with the system users. Nowadays, graphical user interfaces (GUI's), also known as visual display terminals (VDT), have become the norm. They encompass the use of *inter alia* windows, a pointing device such as a mouse, menus, buttons, selection lists, and check boxes. Most implementation environments provide a standard set of GUI-based facilities.

Over the last ten years a comprehensive range of international standards to support the development of usable user interfaces has been published (Bevan, 2001). The standards can be used to specify the appearance and behavior of user interfaces (ISO 14915, IEC 61997, ISO/IEC 11581, ISO/IEC 18021, and ISO/IEC 10741), the design of user interfaces (ISO 9241), and the criteria for the evaluation of user interfaces (ISO/IEC 9126). The standards provide principles, requirements, guidelines, and recommendations which incorporate many findings of cognitive task analysis. None of the standards, however, make explicit reference to the cognitive knowledge structures of system users. In fact, the entire body of scientific literature on user-interface design is scarcely concerned with the knowledge structures that system users adopt when working with a system. We found only one reference relating usable interfaces to the cognitive knowledge structures of system users:

"The best way to make a system user-friendly is to base [the user interface] on the work processes and knowledge structures of the system users."
(McGraw, 1994, p. 90).

Notwithstanding the very limited explicit references to system users' cognitive knowledge structures, there are many implicit and related links. Consider as an example one of the prime principles of user-interface design which is described in various standards:

"Users should not be forced to adapt to an interface because it is convenient to implement. The interface should use the terms and concepts which are familiar to the anticipated class of users." Sommerville (1995, p. 263)

The principle is consistent with Cheng et al. (2001) who argue that a software system should not impose structure on the experts during knowledge acquisition. Extending their argument to user-interface design, one may argue that the interface should not only use the terms and concepts which are familiar to the anticipated class of users, but should also adopt the knowledge structures that are used by this class. A few prudent studies have been published which adopt this notion. Patel et al. (1998) and Vora et al. (1994) have attempted to structure computer interfaces to one specific knowledge structure (i.e. semantic networks).

Our research aims to investigate whether knowledge structures affect the usability of knowledge systems. The research question of our inquiry is: *what is the influence of knowledge structures on the usability of knowledge systems?* Our hypothesis is that using cognitive knowledge structures of domain experts and system users in the development process of knowledge systems leads to relatively usable systems, while incorporating non-cognitive knowledge structures yields systems with a relatively poor usability.

## 13.2    Our empirical research

We have conducted our research in the domain of underwriting for private health insurance. Underwriting involves the assessment of an applicant for private health insurance on two aspects. Firstly, whether or not an applicant meets the statutory eligibility criteria for private insurance (technical underwriting) is assessed. Secondly, the medical costs and risks that are associated with the applicant are assessed (medical underwriting). Basically, the result of the underwriting process is a decision whether an applicant is accepted or rejected for private insurance. The domain experts and system users in the field of underwriting are medical doctors and medical underwriters. We conducted our research at a large health insurer in the Netherlands.

We have delimited the implementation of our research in a number of ways. First, we have focused on two usability dimensions, i.e. user satisfaction and effectiveness. Secondly, we have developed knowledge systems which are capable of conducting the risk assessment part of the medical underwriting process of one particular disease, i.e. diabetes mellitus. Thirdly, we have restricted our research to three different types of knowledge structures. Firstly, we have incorporated some of the cognitive knowledge structures which are used by medical doctors and medical underwriters.[14] Secondly, we have used a knowledge structure which is based on Bayes' classification rule. Thirdly, we have included a neural knowledge structure in the form of an artificial neural network (ANN). The knowledge structures were implemented into three distinct "expert" systems. Observe that the first two knowledge structures are referred to as symbolic structures while an ANN is also known as a sub-symbolic knowledge structure.[15]

It is important to observe that we have adopted a human knowledge modeling approach. This means that the systems model the expert knowledge of the medical doctors and the medical underwriters. As part of the development process of the three systems –which will be referred to as

---

14 The structures had been elicited by means of Cognitive Structure Analysis, or CSA for short. CSA constitutes the (only) knowledge elicitation method which is capable of eliciting cognitive knowledge structures. CSA was originally put forward by Leddo and Cohen (1989). As part of our research we have further developed the method and tested its validity.

15 The interested reader is referred to Luger and Stubblefield (1998) for a detailed description of the differences between symbolic and sub-symbolic knowledge representations.

the cognitive system, the Bayesian system, and the ANN – we have examined the consistency among the medical doctors and the medical underwriters. Once the three knowledge systems had been developed, we tested the user satisfaction of the systems by means of the Software Usability Measurement Inventory, or SUMI for short (Kirakowski, 1996). SUMI is, to our knowledge, the only commercially available questionnaire for the assessment of user satisfaction of software which has been developed, validated, and standardized on an international basis. SUMI is also mentioned in the ISO 9241 standard as a recognized method of testing user satisfaction. Medical doctors and medical underwriters were required to process 20 real-life application forms (which involved diabetes mellitus) by using the three systems. After they had processed the forms by using a system, they were asked to fill out the SUMI questionnaire. The results showed that the user satisfaction of the cognitive system is higher than the user satisfaction of the other systems. The results were statistically significant.

Then the effectiveness of the three knowledge systems was tested. We constructed a random sample of 1,324 diabetes mellitus patients who had either been accepted or rejected for private company insurance. If they had been rejected, they had been accepted for government insurance (which is administered by private insurers and bears no risks to them). The sample members had been insured between 1 January 2000 and 1 January 2003, and ranged in age between 1 and 64 years.[16] The total net medical costs of the sample members had been collected from the databases. Analysis of the dataset indicated that about 9% of the sample members generated net medical costs which exceed € 15,000. They were classified as outliers. Further analysis showed that the net medical costs of 5 outliers were not associated with diabetes mellitus. They were removed from the sample in order to prevent a distortion effect.17 This resulted in a sample of 1,319 diabetes mellitus patients. The net medical cost of each sample member was related to the premium income in order to calculate the profitability of the patient. The three systems processed the application forms of the sample members. The decision of every system with respect to each application

---

[16] From the age of 65, people are automatically offered government insurance in the Netherlands. This means that health insurance underwriting is conducted for people between 0 and 64 years (birth and adoption are the only two exceptions to this rule).

[17] Recall that the expert systems were confined to the underwriting of diabetes mellitus patients.

form was compared to the profitability of the sample member. The results showed that the three systems yield unprofitable decisions. The net loss of the cognitive system was about equal to the net loss of the ANN and amounted to approximately € -114,000 and € -85,000 respectively. The net loss of the Bayesian system was significantly higher and amounted to about € -1,800,000.

## 13.3     Conclusions and implications

We will discuss the conclusions and the implications of our research with respect to the central question and the application domain of our research.

### 13.3.1     Conclusions and implications regarding the research question

Three conclusions can be drawn on the basis of our research:
1. the incorporation of symbolic cognitive knowledge structures into the development process of knowledge systems yields a higher user satisfaction of knowledge systems than the incorporation of symbolic or sub-symbolic non-cognitive knowledge structures.
2. the incorporation of symbolic cognitive knowledge structures into the development process of knowledge systems yields a higher effectiveness of knowledge systems than the incorporation of symbolic non-cognitive knowledge structures.
3. the incorporation of symbolic cognitive knowledge structures into the development process of knowledge systems yields knowledge systems which are more or less equally effective to knowledge systems which have incorporated sub-symbolic non-cognitive knowledge structures.[18]

The conclusions give rise to a number of implications with respect to cognitive task analysis. First, we noted in the introduction that only recently

---

[18] It is obvious that this conclusion should be understood within the constraints and limitations of our research. For example, we have focused on one type of knowledge system and we have conducted our research in one application domain.

researchers in the field of cognitive task analysis have focused their attention on the cognitive knowledge structures that are involved in a task. An important implication of our research is that the wider cognitive task analysis research community should support the efforts to "identify the abstract nature of the knowledge involved in a task, that is, the type of knowledge representations that need to be used." (Chipman, et al., 2000, p. 7). Indeed, our research has shown that cognitive knowledge structures play a role in the development of knowledge systems with a sound user satisfaction.

A second implication – which is related to the previous one – is that our findings give reason to believe that cognitive knowledge structures also play an important role in other domains. Consider, as an example, the domains of training and education. Textbooks and manuals often contain a combination of text, graphs, diagrams, and formulas to explain a single subject matter. The content of the subject matter is identical but the form in which the content is presented differs. Training and learning may very well be facilitated if we know which (combinations of) knowledge structures are optimal to describe the content of the explanation. In addition, the knowledge structures used by experts and novices may be compared and used to guide the training and teaching efforts towards expert level.

Thirdly, Chipman et al. (2000) correctly observe that the identification of knowledge structures is not explicit in the literature. Hitherto, cognitive structure analysis seems to be the only elicitation method which explicitly aims to elicit the knowledge structures and content in a specific domain. We have tested and validated the method and it appears to be a convincing approach. Cognitive structure analysis should therefore receive the attention it deserves from the cognitive task analysis community.

The conclusions also give rise to a number of implications with respect to knowledge engineering methodologies. The first implication is that knowledge engineering methodologies should accommodate the incorporation of cognitive knowledge structures in the development process of knowledge systems in order to develop knowledge systems with a high user satisfaction. In other words, cognitive knowledge systems should become the norm in knowledge engineering from the viewpoint of a high user satisfaction. In order to develop such systems, the results of cognitive task analysis should systematically be incorporated into modern knowledge engineering methodologies.[19]

The second implication of our research for knowledge engineering methodologies is concerned with improving the effectiveness of knowledge systems. Our research has shown that the effectiveness of the three knowledge systems was unsatisfactory. This result is grounded on the expert knowledge which has been modeled into the systems (i.e. human knowledge modeling approach) and clearly demonstrates the limitations of human expertise. The unsatisfactory effectiveness constitutes a rebuttal to the observation by Schreiber et al. (2000, p. 16) that "the most important reference point is the human side: the real-world situation that knowledge engineering addresses by studying experts, users, and their behavior at the workplace [..]." The observation is true only from the viewpoint of user satisfaction but it is not *necessarily* true that humans are the most important reference point with respect to developing effective knowledge systems.

Especially in application domains with large databases, one could complement human knowledge modeling with quantitative data analyses (which we refer to as the database knowledge modeling approach). One might think of techniques in the field of data mining to model these data. Recall that data mining is concerned with developing algorithms that are capable of discovering patterns in data. The field is part of the wider discipline of knowledge discovery in databases (KDD) which encompasses the overall process of finding and interpreting patterns in data (Fayyad et al., 1996). This process is interactive with domain experts and includes a number of iterative steps, such as developing an understanding of the application domain, using prior expert knowledge to identify the important concepts and relationships, creating a target data set, data cleaning and preprocessing, data reduction, data mining, interpreting the mined patterns, and consolidating the discovered knowledge (Brachman and Anand, 1996). Knowledge engineering methodologies should attempt to use the techniques from the field of KDD to attain effective knowledge systems. This implication, together with the one described in the previous paragraph, is summarized in Figure 26.

---

[19] Admittedly, modern knowledge engineering methodologies do not predominantly focus anymore on issues such as computational efficiency and expressiveness. Yet it is striking that the term 'cognition' is found only once in the index of the CommonKADS methodology, i.e. in relation to the cognitive bias which is typical for human expertise.

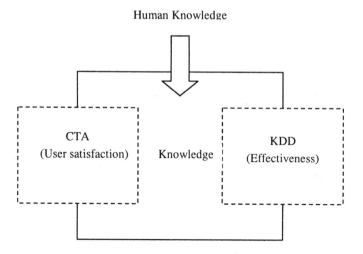

*Figure -26.* Implications of our research for knowledge engineering methodologies.

The central rectangle in the figure represents the field of knowledge engineering. The dotted rectangles represent the fields of cognitive task analysis (CTA) and knowledge discovery in databases (KDD) respectively. The partial overlap of the two dotted rectangles with the central rectangle represents the need for current knowledge engineering methodologies to incorporate parts of the fields of CTA and KDD. The use of the practical spin-offs of CTA will result in knowledge systems with a high user satisfaction. The adoption of KDD implies that knowledge engineering should not solely rely on human knowledge modeling to develop effective systems (represented by the upper arrow). Instead, if there are sufficient data in the application domain, human knowledge modeling must be complemented with database knowledge modeling (represented by the lower arrow) in order to improve the effectiveness of the systems.

There is a third implication of our research for knowledge engineering methodologies. We have distinguished between the human knowledge modeling and the database knowledge modeling approach, but we have also discussed the distinction between the symbolic and the sub-symbolic knowledge modeling approach.[20] Knowledge engineering methodologies have, almost without exception, adopted the symbolic approach. There are only a few references that have incorporated sub-symbolic modeling efforts into a knowledge engineering project. Yet neural computing research has developed into a mature discipline itself, and applications can be found in many domains for a wide range of problems (see Tarassenko, 1998 and Bishop, 1995 for overviews). Knowledge engineering methodologies should acknowledge the sub-symbolic approach and, as a guide to the knowledge engineers who work as practitioners, provide the criteria to select the approach which is best suited to the engineering project under consideration. We believe that the most important selection criteria include the characteristics of the problem and the application domain, and the time and cost constraints which delimit the engineering project. We will discuss the applicability of the two modeling approaches in light of these criteria.

The symbolic knowledge modeling approach is required if there are only scarce cases available regarding the problem. The approach must also be adopted in case the underlying reasoning process of a knowledge system must be made explicit. More specifically, we argue that symbolic cognitive systems should become the norm with respect to the usability dimension of 'user satisfaction'. The argument is based on the conclusion of our research that the incorporation of symbolic cognitive knowledge structures of domain and experts and system users results in higher user satisfaction than the incorporation of symbolic non-cognitive knowledge structures. We do *not* argue that, in the symbolic approach, cognitive knowledge systems should necessarily become the norm with respect to the usability dimension of 'effectiveness'. Although in our research the (symbolic) cognitive system outperformed the (symbolic) Bayesian system, we may very well imagine

---

[20] Similar to the database knowledge modeling approach, the sub-symbolic knowledge modeling approach is capable of identifying patterns in large datasets. Note, however, that the sub-symbolic knowledge modeling approach is not identical to the database knowledge modeling approach. Database knowledge modeling may also encompass symbolic approaches, while the sub-symbolic approach may also be used within the human knowledge modeling approach (as has been done in our research: a neural network has been trained on the classification judgments of domain experts).

that in other domains and for other tasks, a symbolic non-cognitive system is more effective than a cognitive system. Indeed, many symbolic non-cognitive knowledge systems that have been engineered by the 'hard AI' community have outperformed the systems of the 'soft AI' community on the dimension of 'effectiveness'.

Let us now discuss the criteria which determine the use of the *non*-symbolic approach and aim to answer the question when cognitive knowledge systems should be preferred over neural networks and vice versa. If we face an application domain and a problem which meets the requirements of the symbolic knowledge modeling approach (described above), then cognitive knowledge systems should be preferred over neural networks. Indeed, it is still very difficult to extract and make explicit the knowledge that is contained in the weights of neural networks[21], and neural networks require large amounts of data for training. On the other hand, there are also characteristics of application domains and problems that foster the use of neural networks instead of symbolic cognitive systems. Tarassenko (1998) lists three main requirements to use neural networks. Firstly, it should not be possible to explicitly describe the solution to a problem. Secondly, there should be some evidence that an input-output mapping exists between a set of inputs and a set of corresponding outputs. Thirdly, there should be a large amount of data available to train the network. It is evident that in cases where the first criterion applies, cognitive knowledge systems should not (in fact cannot) be used by the very nature of their explicit characterization.

But how about problems and application domains which meet the other two characteristics? Such problems render the use of both sub-symbolic and symbolic modeling approaches possible. We argue that in those cases the pros and cons of each approach must be weighed with reference to the whole engineering project under consideration. The important advantages of cognitive systems are their high user satisfaction and their ability to store and explain knowledge. There are also disadvantages associated with these symbolic systems. The development and the maintenance of symbolic systems are labor intensive and therefore expensive. They are brittle to

---

[21] Symbolic knowledge extraction from neural networks is currently an active research area (see, for example, Corbett-Clark and Tarrassenko, 1997; Setiono, 1997) but has not yet delivered its promises.

required changes and they cannot handle noisy and missing data well. Neural networks, on the other hand, have poor user satisfaction and do not guarantee a good performance. Yet they are cheaper to build and to maintain, and their performance is robust for noisy, inconsistent, and missing data. The relative importance of the pros and cons in light of the entire business case should ultimately determine whether a symbolic cognitive system or a neural network could best be developed.

### 13.3.2    Conclusions and implications regarding the application domain

Three conclusions can be drawn on the basis of our research:
1. there is considerable inconsistency in the underwriting decisions among the medical doctors and the medical underwriters.
2. the underwriting policy for diabetes mellitus is not profitable and should be adjusted.
3. an expert system for health insurance underwriting can be developed such that the system attains a good user satisfaction. An *effective* expert system for health insurance underwriting, however, is not easily attained by adopting a human knowledge modeling approach.

Our research has several implications for health insurers. Perhaps the most important implication is that health insurers, endowed with large databases, should adopt database knowledge modeling. With respect to the underwriting business process, the adoption of a KDD program may be used to formulate and to evaluate the profitability of the underwriting protocols[22]. There are, however, other business processes which may benefit from database knowledge modeling. For example, a KDD program that focuses on the classification of insured on the basis of diseases, claims data, and medical consumption may be used *inter alia* for procurement and disease management. A program that aims to predict the profitability of customer groups may tailor the marketing strategy of health insurers.

---

[22] Recall that we have found that the underwriting protocol for diabetes mellitus generates a loss and should therefore be adjusted. It may very well be true that the underwriting protocols for other diseases also generate losses.

Secondly, health insurers should answer the question whether they want to develop an expert system for health insurance underwriting. An important aspect that should be taken into account by Dutch insurers is the introduction of the 'basic insurance' scheme which the government aims to implement in 2005. The 'basic insurance' scheme abolishes the distinction in the Dutch health insurance system between sickness fund insurance and private insurance (private company insurance and government insurance), and introduces an insurance package which is more or less similar to the current sickness fund coverage. People are allowed to take out private health insurance for medical costs which are not covered under the 'basic insurance' scheme. Lastly, the new scheme imposes a mandatory acceptance of applicants to health insurers. This means that underwriting cannot be conducted anymore. We argue that health insurers should take two aspects into account with respect to the new scheme. Firstly, the coverage of the 'basic insurance' scheme is less than the coverage of current private health insurance policies offered by insurers. One may expect that the currently privately insured people (about 33% of the Dutch population) will take out additional private company health insurance in order to sustain their health insurance coverage. Insurers are allowed to sustain underwriting for these private insurance policies, and this could be conducted by an expert system. Secondly, an expert system which is hooked up to KDD may provide key insights into the customer base of health insurers. Knowledge of one's customer base will become even more critical than now as insurers are bound to accept *any* applicant. For example, claims data and actuary provisions may become more volatile, while the required procurement of health care may get more difficult to predict.

In case a health insurance company decides to develop an expert system for underwriting, a number of recommendations can be formulated. Firstly, symbolic knowledge modeling should be adopted to develop the system. This implication follows directly from the requirement imposed by law on health insurers to explain the reasons which underlie the underwriting decisions taken. Secondly, we can be more specific about the kind of symbolic system that should be developed. In order to optimize the user satisfaction of the system we recommend the development of a cognitive expert system. Thirdly, human knowledge modeling should be complemented with database knowledge modeling in order to guarantee the effectiveness of the system.

It is obvious that the high levels of inconsistency among medical doctors and underwriters are tackled if an expert system for underwriting is implemented. There are, however, other cheaper means to alleviate the inconsistencies. One may formulate underwriting protocols per disease and disorder on the basis of KDD. The protocols should be tailored to the different user groups (medical doctors, medical underwriters with a medical background, and administratively trained underwriters). This means that the protocols must incorporate the knowledge structures and the knowledge content that are associated with the different user groups. Once the protocols have been formulated they should be integrated in the business process such that they are actually used at the underwriting departments. This could be done, for example, by using the protocols for training during peer review sessions. They could also be placed on the server at the underwriting departments as reference material.

# 14. THE ROLE OF CONTEXTUALITY IN PROCESS STANDARDIZATION

Hans van Leijen

## 14.1 Introduction

### 14.1.1 Process standardization

In recent years, organizations have been rationalizing their business processes. The eighties' decentralization fashion, and the nineties' merger mania, have led to large conglomerates of service providers, who are now seeking an optimal and low-risk exploitation of the potential for operational synergy. This is not just for commercial companies; governmental institutions are also *re*centralizing. For one, they are trying to gain more control over execution of policies by concentrating the activities executing those policies; secondly, they are trying to increase efficiency by standardizing processes and information systems.

A closely related development can be characterized as *professionalization*. Organizations believe that processes can be executed in a more professional, disciplined manner, and the workforce is slowly cured of the "not invented here"-syndrome, more and more willing to *not* invent things themselves, but instead, to efficiently adopt them from some other party. This "art of imitation" has been stimulated by the knowledge management phenomenon. In that field, the popular "best practice" concept was stipulated: a way of working that has originated from some practice, not as a consequence of a design effort, but as an outcome of experiential learning. A best practice should be *spread*, which boils down to standardization, doing things just one way (the best way). The difficulty of implementing best practices is adapting them to local circumstances, something that is sometimes overlooked, but more often done too much, leading to incapacitated best practices and lack of adequate change. Knowing what *is* the special circumstance, and what influence that should have on the best practice, if problematic.

Doing things the best way is hard, even if that way is known. Implementing best practices is often easier done by a specialized partner. This has made *outsourcing* popular. Justification of the decision to outsource often appeals to the notion of the *core competence of the firm*. Theoreticians and practitioners alike seem to think that each firm has its own, uniquely identifiable core competence, and that it is advantageous to outsource all else. Yet, identifying this core is not easy and not evident. Nike, as a well-known example, has outsourced almost everything except the competence to identify and contract popular top athletes for promotion of their products. And many insurers these days outsource the only process that directly creates value for their customers: claims handling.

These changes are strongly influenced by the history and current state of information technology. Many organizations dug themselves deeply into tailor-made information systems in the seventies and eighties. After a merger, one of the thorniest issues is often which application portfolio to choose; this issue is so thorny because, on the one hand, the choice of application portfolio often influences choices of product portfolio and process architecture, and on the other hand, the strategy of mixing and matching the best components of each application portfolio has turned out not to be feasible (Veltman, 2002).

IT creates possibilities for new process structure because it lowers the cost of coordination. An important phenomenon is the rise of "commercial off-the-shelf" (COTS) software for business process support. Examples are enterprise resource planning and customer relationship management packages. Creating tailor-made software turns out to be too expensive and risky, in spite of object orientation and other advances in software engineering. The idea that it might be smarter to adapt the processes of an organization to a piece of standard software into which the supplier has built the best practices of the industry, was unthinkable in the eighties but is common in the twenty-first century.

A modern kind of business integration is *shared services*: pairing operational synergy with commercial diversity, by disentangling transaction processing "factories" from originally integrated companies. This creates a matrix organization of customer-oriented marketing and sales departments, and product-oriented administration and processing departments (Swagerman and van Steenis, 1998).

Shared services is about the mutual adaptation of value proposition and core competence: it is about combining and merging competencies of separate business units in such a way that the resulting competence is enhanced while the differentiation in value propositions that the business units originally offered remains intact. This applies to some extent to business integration in general.

The common denominator in the developments described is standardization on a certain way of working, due to either information technology usage, business integration after a merger, or simply the wish to settle for an internal or external standard. This implies a decrease in the specificity of a process with respect to the value proposition that that process supports. It requires a process of disentanglement, in which it is discovered how the current way of working is interwoven with its context, the thing that makes the proposition unique and competitive, and subsequently adaptation of non-standardized parts of the process to standardized pieces. In other words: a struggle to maintain uniqueness amidst standardization. If not properly orchestrated, this struggle can be costly and yield a sub-optimal outcome.

It can be asked how it is possible that organizations do away with their contextually developed ways of working, without losing their competitive advantage. Apparently, either core competence has nothing to do with ways of working, or competitive advantage has nothing to do with core competence. Both conclusions are unsatisfactory. A few authors have researched this question. Porter and Biggelkow (2001) hypothesize that competitive advantage is in specific combinations of features that are successful only in a very particular context. Cotteleer and Frei (2003) do not investigate this question directly, but they do pose the question of where packaged software evolution comes from: from a vendor who "knows what's best", or customers whose needs "drive development". Perhaps surprisingly, their conclusion is that evolution comes from vendors, mostly. If organizations do wise to adapt their operations to best practices and standard software, and if those practices are developed by global parties, then what constitutes core competence?

Part of the resolution of this paradox might be in the distinction between *exploration* and *exploitation* (see Nooteboom, 1999). It might be that the above phenomena of synergy realization, shared services, standardization, and so on, are all instances of exploitation: ways of exchanging best practice among a group of activities. Exploration would then correspond with diversification: experimentation, spin-offs, doing new things on a smaller, experimental scale. According to this view, centralization and decentralization waves trade turns with each other in order to develop the organization by creating new experiences, new ways of doing things (decentralization) and spreading them via best practice transfer (centralization).

Rather than answering these questions at the business strategy level, we will try to shed more light on what it is that makes processes contextual, because in practice, organizations have more trouble implementing best practices than choosing them.

This research seeks to contribute to insight into the cognitive dynamics of organizations, to support business process transformation and change management. Cognitive dynamics is a rather new concept, originated from the organizational learning field and from more traditional fields like managerial cognition and cognitive psychology. Cognitive dynamics refers to the evolution of concepts, shared mental models, of participants in an organization. Seen from this angle, change management can be understood as management of a process of knowledge conversion.

Cognitive dynamics is applied to the domain of process standardization, and limited to the process aspect of organizations: the structure of activities in an organization. There is a consensus in the scientific community that there is a lack of integration and theory-building concerning implementation of change in business processes. There is a discrepancy between, on the hand, the "engineering perspective", suggesting that processes can be *redesigned*, and on the other hand, the problematic character of changing organizations. It is a well-known fact that company mergers usually take much longer than expected and never achieve the synergies hoped for (Bakker and Helmink, 2000). The cognitive perspective might help bridge this theoretical gap between "design-ability" and "change-ability".

In integration and standardization efforts, differences between local processes have to be done away with. In many cases, this increases efficiency, and, by replacing differences with "best practices", effectiveness and quality are increased as well. Many of those differences have only historical significance. However, when local differences in process structure support a unique commercial proposition, eradication of those differences might damage competitiveness. This is a oft-heard internal argument against change. To be able to make good decisions with respect to taking away differences, it is useful to obtain more insight into why differences between similar processes exist. It is also interesting to see how the effort needed for adequate change depends on the context specificity of a process.

Whereas most existing literature, especially in the economics and strategy field, attempts to explain the motives behind synergy, mergers and standardization, we take contemporary organizations' lust for standardization largely as a given. Instead, we seek to describe what stumbling blocks are likely to turn up, and how to deal with those wisely. Organizations differ substantially in their ability to integrate acquisitions effectively (Nadler and Limpert, 1992). Yet, recent research demonstrates convincingly that this integration capability is something that can be learned simply by writing up experiences with integration and disseminating this knowledge (Zollo and Singh, 2003). We aim to contribute to this learning by offering more insight into what happens to the knowledge embedded in the organization when it undergoes standardization.

### 14.1.2   Conceptual model

Here, we describe the concept of the knowledge structure, or meaning system, underlying a business process. Knowledge structure is the whole of symbol systems, categories, causal relationships, and routines that the ensemble of people and machines uses to serve stakeholders' interests. The idea of a business process, a structured set of activities, is a crude abstraction of this.

The basic object of our study is an organization, for which we employ an agent-based model (Weigand, 2003): each agent knows a set of interventions, or *affordances*, that he, she or it uses to achieve certain goals. To relate interventions to goals, agents employ knowledge, understood here as: information about cause-effect relationships between entities in the world. Knowledge of agents is overlapping: they have knowledge about each others' knowledge; it is this *shared knowledge* that enables them to coordinate their actions (Grant, 1996). The stakeholders of the organization (investors, customers, employees) have certain interests, and it is in the interest of each agent to help guard stakeholders' interests. Organizations are embedded inside each other; the largest kind of organization is society as a whole.

An organization, at each level, imposes norms upon its constituents, to ensure coordinated action in the best interests of the whole. An organization's goal in general is to engage in, and then fulfil, mutually beneficial relationships with partners and customers. Fulfilling relationships generally amounts to appropriately responding to events. Such an event usually originates from a customer having some wish. Events happen to the organization semi-randomly; they can be triggered and influenced, for example by marketing actions. Appropriate response amounts to planning effective actions by exploiting the collective knowledge of the agents.

Usually, the event represents some instability, a disturbance from a stable, certain state. For example, a prospective customer calls in to inquire about a product. This leads to a period of uncertainty, in which the customer might or might not agree to buy, and in which multiple future states of the world have to be constructed and evaluated. Hopefully, this leads to a new situation in which the prospect has become a satisfied customer; certainty in the longer run has been restored. Thus, a business process can often be seen to be a regulatory process that seeks to correct instabilities (Regev et al., 2003). This account of business processes derives from cybernetics, as pointed out by Vidgen (1998).

*Knowledge*, or competence, consists of three things: ontology or a set of categories; causal relationships between entities that can be described in terms of the ontology; and routines, repetitive sequences of actions that have proven effective in the past. To possess a competence, an agent must know its ontology, be able to recognize and categorize events in terms of it, know useful causal relationships, and know routines to take appropriate action. Various authors have proposed concepts and measures to characterize knowledge-intensiveness. Eppler et al. (1999) distinguish *complexity* and *knowledge-intensiveness*, and name properties of each; Zack (2001) divides it into complexity, uncertainty, ambiguity, and equivocality.

Routines, or *scripts*, emerge from repeated planning using causal relationships; they speed up application of knowledge, but also cause inflexibility, because the causal relationships on the basis of which routines were once conceived, might not be valid anymore, or might simply be forgotten. In psychology, this process is called *compilation* (Gioia and Poole, 1984). An amount of embedded knowledge can be characterized on a scale with flexible, goal-directed, and context-sensitive on the one extreme, versus efficient, fast, accurate, but inflexible, insensitive to local circumstances and goals, on the other hand. Information systems lie on the second extreme; they contain little explicit causal knowledge and consist of highly compiled, "frozen" knowledge.

Routines and knowledge work on sets of information that are expressed in terms of its ontology. This information is stored in information systems, document collections, on paper, and in people's minds. Together, they are often called *organizational memory* (van Stijn and Wensley, 2001).

A knowledge source performs physical or informational actions. Informational actions can be: registering information, aggregating it, deciding on the basis of it. In the administrative organizations we are discussing, physical actions hardly occur. Yet, some informational actions can be *instrumental* if they change their social environment, for example, if they lead some outside party to perform a physical action or to agree to some obligation. In this sense, instrumentality of action is relative to the abstraction level at which you are looking at an organization or a part of it. Instrumentality is only a matter of degree. However, any informational action will, sooner or later, lead to some physical action that brings some agent closer to his or her goal. This model of process knowledge has been elaborated in Van Leijen and Baets (2003).

Knowledge is highly contextual. Categories are developed in a local context, and their names and meanings are socially negotiated. Even if, at a higher level of abstraction, the goals of two similar processes are identical, their embedding in the meaning system of the individuals executing them might differ in a multitude of small details. Some of these details derive from differences and are related to the context in which a process is embedded; others have resulted from more or less coincidental circumstances in the past. In general, we will call this *contextuality*.

The concept of contextuality might be judged by some to be ill-defined; how can a concept be defined as having "difference in spite of superficial similarity"? In practice, however, the concept is readily identifiable. When an organization strives for standardization of processes that superficially seem equivalent, individuals in the organization intuitively feel that it might be harder than expected because of a multitude of seemingly unimportant details. Nevertheless, they often cannot explain or summarize what these details are. As an operational definition, we propose this phenomenon as contextuality. Contextuality strongly resembles Szulanski's (1996) concept of *stickiness*, but is a bit more ambitious in that it suggests a reason for knowledge to be sticky: bits of knowledge are strongly dependent on their context of usage.

### 14.1.3    Research problem and questions

Some of the literature relevant to this domain is prescriptive at a low level of abstraction, high in practical content, but poor in theory, such as Bakker and Helmink (2000). Other literature provides prescriptions drawn from empirical research, but often at a high level of abstraction, hard to apply unambiguously in particular situations; examples are Nadler et al. (1992), Robey et al. (2002). Many of the case studies are descriptive at a very low, hard to generalize level of abstraction, like Halverson et al. (2003), or Patriotta (2002). What we particularly value, is work that is rich in theoretical explanation, rich in empirical content, and yet offers concepts that are readily recognizable and applicable in particular situations. In our opinion, examples of this "sweet spot" are Kock et al. (1997), where the role of knowledge exchange in business processes is studied empirically, and Szulanski and Jensen (2001), where knowledge transfer between business units is studied, and which offers the *un*intuitive, practically relevant insight that knowledge should *not* be adapted to local circumstances, but should be taken at face value and implemented meticulously.

While there is ample management and information systems literature on how to redesign processes, little of that deals with implementation other than via theory-poor step plans and phase models. Traditionally, BPR has been approached from two angles (Dietz, 1996). The top-down, "strategic" approach from the management literature tries to improve certain performance measures by offering step plans and guidelines. The bottom-up, "technical" approach from the information systems field, on the other hand, offers modeling formalisms to represent and analyze existing and future processes. A growing number of authors have started to develop a middle ground between top-down and bottom-up process reengineering by systematically gathering, integrating and evaluating redesign principles and heuristics (Reijers, 2002; Kock and Murphy, 2001). These principles and heuristics give good hints regarding where to look for improvements in business processes, but are ambivalent about *what it is* that is being redesigned. A business process is not just a structured set of activities that can be expressed exhaustively in a graphical formalism, for if it was, reengineering would then be a purely analytical exercise.

The issue of implementation, of "getting there from here", is often neglected in scientific literature, because it is regarded a matter of "simple execution". Yet, while the management literature offers many methods for strategy formation and for finding and planning process improvements, research shows that it is not so much the strategy chosen or the method used that matters, but more importantly, the quality with which that strategy is implemented (Nohria et al., 2003). In implementation, things go awry.

Much of the literature on change management deals with emotional, political, and motivational issues. These are important, but they cannot be the only elements to be managed; the primary aspect to be managed in an implementation process is ultimately the cognitive structures of humans and machines, as we have argued. As Szulanski (1996) has convincingly demonstrated, the purely cognitive difficulties in knowledge transfer are separately identifiable and can be even more problematic than the traditional concept of resistance to change, and thus warrant special attention in scientific research. The organization science literature offers a lot of theory about the human, social aspects of change, but not about the human, cognitive aspect of change: how change affects patterns of work and their embeddedness in human knowledge. It offers few useful abstractions on the complexity of these patterns.

Our research goal is to offer insight into the way business processes are rooted in the contextual knowledge patterns of the individuals that execute them. We wish to substantiate concepts like shared and individual knowledge, variety, and complexity, at a level of abstraction at which they become observable and useful. Our research problem is to explain the contextual nature of business processes and what makes them unique and hard to standardize, on the basis of features of their knowledge structure. In the following sections we will search for answers to the following questions.

1. What is contextuality: how are similar processes different in subtle ways? How does contextuality evolve?
2. What effect does contextuality have on standardization efforts? Is it problematic, does it have to be "overthrown"?
3. What effect does standardization have on contextuality? How is knowledge structure affected by it?
- Aside from these main questions, we have some secondary questions:
- *What is the role of standardization in spreading knowledge? Is (contextual) knowledge destroyed by standardization, or is valuable knowledge preserved and spread by decontextualizing it?*
- *How is knowledge disentangled, decontextualized, and transferred to a new context?*

## 14.2    Empirical research

### 14.2.1    Choice of method

The questions we have identified are exploratory in nature. There has been little empirical research as yet. Therefore, we have conducted a study for the purpose of theory-building, using the grounded theory approach (Richardson, 1996): multiple cases are analyzed one by one, while the conceptual model is refined continuously. Cases are chosen to explore the breadth of the problem; the extremes of the spectrum of situations that the new theory is proposed to cover are represented in the cases. The research is "uncritical" in that it seeks to detect relevant variables and candidates for relationships between them, rather than proving those relationships. Identification of hypotheses is also a goal of the research.

To "seed" the grounded theory approach, a focus group session has been used to reflect on, and elaborate, an initial set of distinctions. This is actually the opposite of the way focus groups are normally used in scientific research, namely as validation of exploratory research. Reasons for this choice are quite opportunistic: for purposes unrelated to this research, a group support system session was scheduled, the agenda and structure of which was under the control of the researcher. A group support system is a very useful instrument for quickly and unobtrusively collecting feedback from an arbitrarily large number of people.

## 14.3    Research object and approach

For the focus group part of this research, eight business consultants were invited to participate. They were all members of a team of internal business consultants of the parent company. The participants had worked in various synergy projects within and outside of this company. They all had considerable experience in business process analysis and redesign. A group support system was used to pose questions and collect feedback (Dennis et al., 2002). Within the GroupSystems application (a commercial product), the BrainStorm tool was used, and settings chosen to allow participants to see each others' entries. Anonymity was not used, because there were no conflicts of interest between the participants, and the purpose of the session was idea exchange.

Participants were asked to call into memory six projects team members had recently undertaken, and that they were all familiar with because of direct or indirect involvement. Then the following statement was made:

Differences in process structure can be due to the following reasons:
1. commercial propositions
2. differences in task decomposition and ordering of process steps
3. lack of organizational simplification in the past.

The three categories are not mutually exclusive (a difference can be a member of more than one category), but they were only meant to trigger thinking in different directions. Participants were allowed to come up with other kinds of differences. After some clarification of this statement, the following question was asked:

Can you give concrete examples of the three mentioned differences in process structure?

The BrainStorm tool was used to offer participants three sheets, each labeled with one of the three categories. After 20 minutes of typing and informal talking, 48 entries resulted. After filtering these for irrelevant remarks (mostly about resistance to change) and duplicates, 18 distinct examples remained. These were then further categorized and used for setting up the interview protocol for the exploratory part of the research.

For the exploratory part, seven standardization efforts were examined. All seven took place inside one Dutch financial services conglomerate (see below). Because of the exploratory nature of our research question and the grounded theory approach chosen to elaborate it, the projects were chosen to reflect the breadth of the domain under study. The criterium for including such an effort was that there had to have been a goal of either economy of scale, or standardization proper, because both those goals are assumed to require decontextualization. In each of the projects, a number of *local processes* play a role that is homogeneous in some sense; we will call this the *reference group* of each of its members. Furthermore, in each case some *reference process* can be discerned, a goal state in which each of the local processes has either been absorbed into some concentrated process, or at least conforms to a set of homogeneity requirements represented in the reference process.

There were a number of characteristics that the projects did *not* share. The size varied from quite small (some twenty employees affected and little financial investment) to very large (hundreds of employees affected, large investments in, amongst others, new IT systems). The domain varied from primary to secondary business processes, from private clients to business clients and from banking to health care brokering. More interestingly, projects differed in the role that standardization played and the extent to which it was central to the effort.

Projects were examined by conducting either one or two interviews. Before each interview, project documentation was supplied to the researcher by the respondent for preparation. After the interview, more documentation was collected and studied to resolve any lack of clarity. Respondents were typically the most knowledgable people involved in the project, and were either line managers, project managers or consultants.

## 14.4     Results

In this section, we will describe the findings that we got from the interviews. Following the grounded theory approach, findings have been categorized into "themes" which are described in approximate causal order, with themes higher up explaining themes further down in the description. We start off with a description of the seven cases examined (section 14.5). We will then describe features of the environment of a business process that explain its contextual features (section 14.6). These have been synthesized partly from the focus group and elaborated upon, or confirmed by the interviews. Then, we will describe in detail various kinds of contextuality with their relationships to the environmental features that partly determine them, and the consequences they have for standardization efforts (section 14.7). In section 14.8, we will describe how we have found business processes to evolve over time, to be able to explain the behavior of processes before, during, and after standardization efforts. In section 14.9, the effect of standardization on the knowledge structure of business processes is described from a *design* perspective. In the final section (14.10), this will be done from an *implementation* perspective.

## 14.5     Description of cases

The parent company of the seven standardization efforts examined is a result of the nineties merger mania, and consists of a number of business units and a strategic controller holding company. It manifests itself in the consumer and commercial marketplace of insurance using a number of distinct brands. Internally, the company has been in the process of realizing economies of scale by concentrating activities for many years. Business units still largely correspond with brands one-on-one, but more and more inter-linkings are coming into existence, blurring the lines between organizational units. All seven efforts are part of this ongoing consolidation process, which is not planned or managed explicitly as a change program, but rather is encouraged and partly controlled by top management.

As written before, in each effort, two or more *local processes* can be discerned as well as a *reference process*. In most cases, the reference process absorbs only part of the original activities of local processes, leaving context-specific activities dispersed. This implies that some boundary has to be established at which work is handed on from a local to the concentrated process. We will call this boundary the *divide* (internally, it is usually called "the split", or in Dutch, "de knip").

We will now shortly describe the seven cases, for later reference.

1. *Human Resources Center* is a supporting department in the process of being established, and will handle administrative HR processes such as payment of salaries and staffing. At the time, local department of each brand and department handled HR tasks. Although local departments share a common information system, the way this system was used differed substantially across departments. Standardization is an unavoidable by-product of concentrating these activities.

2. *Document Services* is a supporting department that handles paper output for numerous departments in primary activities. Document Services was established in 1999 and has grown since then, extending their services to "absorb" output processes from client departments one by one. Before Document Services, departments would print their own output, such as fill-in forms and benefits statements, and mail them out. This is, or was, often done manually. Document Services brings much more automation and scale to this process, and requires client departments to disentangle output activities from their normal workflow and adapt it to Document Services' way of working. Interestingly, Document Services deals with many different local processes and views them in an abstract way, focusing just on the output aspect.

3. *Mortgages Center* is a back-office and mid-office for handling mortgages. The parent company offers mortgages under three brands, that, prior to establishing the mortgages center, used to do their own underwriting and administrative handling. In a first phase, back-office activities were concentrated from 1999 to 2001. In the current phase, which is still ongoing, mid-office activities are concentrated as well.

4. *Retirement funds* is a large business unit that sells all kinds of pensions; directly to individuals, via employee benefits programs and by offering administrative services to public pension funds. Composed in 1997 from three brands, internally it still consists of three highly separate entities that correspond to product types, called *interest line*, *unit-linked*, and *administration*. This business unit has established a Six Sigma program to increase efficiency, shorten throughput time and improve quality of service. Six Sigma (Linderman et al., 2003) is a process and quality improvement methodology, aimed at measurement and variance reduction. Although standardization was not a goal here, it is a crucial

element in any Six Sigma effort since variation is reduced by collecting best practices and transferring them.

5. *Property Insurance Underwriting* is a department that does underwriting for consumer property and casualty insurance as well as policy administration. It has been established towards the end of 2002 as the result of merging two underwriting departments. Because both departments are large and mature organizations, and because the IT systems used are expensive to replace or integrate, the two departments have not merged operationally but do try to absorb each others best practices.

6. *Care Brokering* is a department that acts as an intermediary for health care insurance clients who are put in a waiting queue by their local care provider. It tries to find treatment capacity for such clients elsewhere in the Netherlands or abroad. Care Brokering has been the result of merging two such departments from two different brands. Also, Care Brokering has undergone a period of growth and maturation amidst an unstable legislative environment. During this maturation period, Care Brokering has taken over some activities from departments they collaborate with.

7. *Care Procurement Policies* is a department that advises so-called expert groups who are responsible for procuring care for health care insurance clients. Each expert group has its own specialty, such as dental care, hospital care, and so on. The Procurement Policies Department tries to standardize and professionalize these procurement processes so as to improve quality and put pressure on care providers for lowering their prices.

Below, we will discuss the "themes" that emerged from the data. Some of these were part of the initial conceptual model, whereas others surfaced as relevant indicators or problematic phenomena pertaining to knowledge structure.

## 14.6    Environmental features influencing contextuality

A business process evolves in its own, more or less unique, environment that imposes requirements and changes on it. This leads to idiosyncratic evolutionary paths, resulting in more or less unique features for each process within its reference group. In order to be able to explain standardization difficulty on the basis of degree of idiosyncracy, we wish to understand how these locally different features depend on their context of operation. From the 18 distinct examples resulting from the focus group, we synthesized the following preliminary account.

In general, contextual features are valuable to some extent depending on the strategic or competitive position the local process is trying to occupy. Features that are solely the effect of idiosyncratic evolutionary paths, and not dependent on strategic position or unique environmental requirements, are here classified as "historic complexity". On the other hand, features that *are* valuable in their local context will henceforth be called "strategic contextuality". A feature being historic or strategic thus depends not just on its nature, but also on its embedding. We will first describe some characteristics of competitive position from the perspective of knowledge structure, and then we describe some kinds of contextual features, and how they relate to competitive position. Also, for each kind of feature we will describe its adverse effect on standardization efforts. We discern three "exogenous" characteristics that influence kind and value of idiosyncrasies.

- *Product features* are the most obvious reason for local differences in business processes. Although the product diversity is generally quite low in the financial services domain, these features do have consequences. Product features are also taken to include features of the sales approach, such as the way discounts are offered.
- *Value discipline* refers to the familiar competitive strategy choices of *customer intimacy*, *product leadership* and *operational excellence*. The choice of value discipline has effects on many process design decisions.
- *Customer binding* is the extent to which customers are "tied" to the organization. For example in commercial markets, corporate customers usually take on longer-lasting relationships than in consumer markets, where customers are much less loyal. Customer binding has an effect on the way information and knowledge is exchanged between customer and organization.
- *Size,* in terms of the number of employees or the amount of business involved, has an effect on the size of work groups and their extent of specialization in subtasks.
- *Asynchronicities in process innovation cycles.* Investments in process innovations in the past have usually not been in parallel across all local processes. Due to fast-changing technological possibilities and the effects on ways of working thereof, processes are likely to differ substantially with respect to their extent and quality of information technology usage.

- *Complexity reduction efforts, or the lack thereof.* Innovation of product or process often leads to additional complexity, especially in times of economic growth, when internal operations are considered to be less important than commercial success. Organizations differ in the extent to which they invest in simplifying their operations.

These dimensions are clearly not orthogonal, as a high customer binding will often (but not always) correspond with a customer intimacy value discipline, and operational excellence often corresponds with high levels of automation and more frequent process innovation. Yet, the dimensions do distinctly explain different kinds of contextual process features. Next, we enumerate these kinds of contextuality and relate them to these dimensions.

## 14.7 Kinds of contextuality with their origins and consequences

Below, we describe kinds of idiosyncratic features of local processes, describe their origins or how they depend on their environment, and lastly, what adverse consequences they have on standardization efforts.

### 14.7.1 Process boundaries and activity groupings

Grouping of activities, or allocation of activities to organizational units, can vary according to at least two dimensions. For one, a higher importance that is attached to an activity can lead to that activity being more closely tied to a primary process. In the *Human Resources Center* case, administration of courses taken by personnel was assigned to middle management in one local process. That particular business unit had a clear customer intimacy positioning, and highly trained personnel was comparatively highly important. In other local processes, course administration was left to the local human resources department. Because the human resources support system to be introduced assumed course administration to be centralized, this alternative grouping of activities was an obstacle to change, especially as having course administration handled by individual middle managers introduced yet more idiosyncrasy to the procedures and information structures used.

In the *mortgage center* case, the allocation of handling life insurance policies coupled to mortgages varied; in one local process, it was assigned to the mortgage handling process itself, whereas in others, it was assigned to a dedicated life insurance process. This allocation depends on the relative level of product leadership of life insurance vs. mortgages: a business unit that is an expert in mortgages would rather concentrate on the mortgage rather than a relative byproduct. Conversely, another business unit aspired to product leadership in neither mortgages nor life insurance; their strategic positioning was to focus on cross selling by having mortgages and life insurance handled closely together.

In *Property Insurance Underwriting*, another issue led to variation of grouping. Because one of the two underwriting departments was the largest processor of mail-in coupons and required specialized scanning software for this purpose, other internal departments outsourced their mail handling to them.

Variation in activity groupings brings with it alternate entanglement patterns between activities, and more difficulty controlling the change process, as the interests of change participants differs and the required change efforts will differ. The decision to assign a particular process step to one or the other group, other than for the abovementioned reasons, seems to be quite arbitrary and hard to explain, even for insiders.

### 14.7.2    Sequencing of activities: order of information exchange, branching and the locus of decision making knowledge

Every exchange of value between customer and organization starts out with exchange of information. Especially in financial services, the customer has to be supplied with good advice and eligibility, while the organization has to be supplied with information about the customer's situation and risk profile. But also more in general, customer and organization are likely to engage in "conversation for clarification" (Weigand et al., 2003) in order to be able to mutually judge the appropriateness of the envisioned relationship.

It turns out that the order in which such information exchange activities are undertaken depends on the amount of "customer binding", that is, the chances of a customer breaking off the sales process and choosing another provider. If that chance is high, a provider will try to maximize their sales effort, but minimize their efforts on up-front fulfillment of the sale before the customer has made a final decision. On the other hand, if the chance of customer loss is low, the provider might do some up-front fulfillment work even if the sale is not yet final, if doing this up-front work is more efficient. Besides the efficiency issue, in the first case, the provider does not want to "burden" the customer with having to supply detailed information. Rather, exchange of details is deferred until after the final sales decision.

In the mortgage center case, there was a marked difference between business units that sold via intermediaries vs. business units that sold directly (direct writers). With the former, customer binding is higher as the customer visits the intermediary personally; this means the customer already has a higher commitment to this particular intermediary. While filling in the request for proposal, the intermediary can easily assist the customer with filling in intricate details like the execution value of the property. This way, the company receives a complete request in one turn. By contrast, in the direct writer case, customers employ a "scattershot" strategy by seeking proposals from multiple providers simultaneously. Moreover, customers are much more quickly scared off by having to supply details. Therefore, the proposal phase is more light weight; obtaining detailed information and performing expensive checks (like checking customer credentials) are deferred. This also means the hit rate distribution is more uniform across the chain of sales activities. In the former case, when a request for proposal comes in, the chances of a successful sale are 80%; in the latter, that chance is only 40%, and customers run a much higher chance of defecting or being rejected later on in the process, because less information and knowledge has been exchanged up-front. This sales channel difference thus has a large effect on the sequencing of workflow.

Customer binding is related to, but not identical with, customer intimacy. In the insurance business, direct writers can be said to be more "customer intimate" than companies that sell their products via intermediaries, because the direct writers have direct contact with their customers. In practice, this translates into higher investments in customer relationship management technology, and a bigger emphasis on cross-selling. Intermediary companies more often have a product leadership focus towards the end consumer. However, they do have a customer intimacy focus toward their intermediaries. In any case, although direct writers are more intimate with their customers, as explained above they have lower customer binding.

More in general, when there is a less intensive contact between two partners, and fewer opportunities for knowledge exchange, or when the knowledge employed is less stable and less uniformly shared, then success or failure will be more uncertain and more distributed along the process chain. A business process usually has a number of branching points. Most branching points have a nature of success vs. failure. The amount of resources spent in each phase of handling a case reflects the relative "skewness" or "uniformness" of the distribution of outcomes at each branching point: resources are spent to increase chances of success, while resources are saved if success is uncertain and spending them can be deferred. Uniformness of an outcome distribution refers to lack of decision making knowledge; thus, bundling such knowledge, and locating it earlier in the process chain (detecting and judging more distinctions up-front) leads to more sharply skewed outcome distributions, for good or for bad.

A special case of this is the knock-out principle, employed in BPR and also in software engineering. The knock-out principle states that if there is a chance of failure, it is more efficient to fail as soon as possible by doing tests with a higher chance of failure first. In the *Retirement funds* case, it was reported that some idiosyncrasy was due to employees having personal preferences as to the order of their activities, and in some cases, the knock-out principle helped speed up the process.

Differences in sequencing can lead to harder decisions on whether to assign activities to local or to central processes. In the mortgage case, the direct writer business unit wanted more control over the sales process than the intermediary business unit, leading to less standardization across sales channels.

### 14.7.3     Horizontal segmentation of activities, and specialization

An obvious source of differences between comparable business processes is the way activities are split up in tasks and distributed over work groups. In general, the bigger an organization becomes, the larger the number of work groups and task split-ups. This principle is tempered somewhat by heightened awareness of the relative advantages and disadvantages of specialization, and counter movements towards more generic work such as team-based work, empowerment, and striving for a "single point of customer contact". Extent of segmentation depends not just on size, but also on the education and experience level of personnel; more experienced and well-educated personnel can handle more tasks on their own, requiring less segmentation. Segmentation of activity chains is often negatively associated with bureaucracy, as it brings with it higher levels of formalization. Yet, ever since the first writings in the field of economy by Adam Smith, specialization has been seen as a fundamental source of prosperity. There is a trade-off between the virtues of specialization against the inflexibilities it brings along.

Perhaps surprisingly, differences in the extent of segmentation across local processes were almost non-existent in all seven cases, and were consequently not judged to be problematic (but see "vertical segmentation" below). This might be explained by a finding that human prejudice regarding bureaucracy can lead to misperceptions of the extent of segmentation. In the *property underwriting* case, one of the two departments was multiple times larger than the other. The larger department was perceived by most as being *bureaucratic, rigid, geared for volume*, and *not transparent*. Yet, the newly appointed manager of the merged department, originating from the smaller, had to conclude after some time that the extent of segmentation was the same for the two, at least regarding their core processes.

### 14.7.4    Vertical segmentation of activities: handling exceptional cases

As explained in section 14.1.2, a business process can be characterized by the set of situations that it can respond to. Some of those situations will likely be "easy" or "standard", whereas others are "complex", or "exceptional". The word *exception* itself suggests that handling those situations will be hard to standardize, and findings confirm this. The way exceptional cases are handled differs substantially across local processes, and is almost invariably deemed problematic. Being able to effectively deal with the exceptional, whether by extending the standard process to handle it, by isolating it, or by abandoning exceptional activities altogether, is an important success factor for standardization efforts.

Consensus among respondents was that exceptions should not exist. Exceptions lead to longer and less predictable throughput time and lead to uncontrolled growth of activities around them. In the *mortgage center* case, one business unit had weekly meetings to discuss exceptional cases. Usually, the exceptionality lay only in a higher or harder to assess risk. Abundant discussion probably served more to distribute responsibility for the decision to take a risk, than it really served to more precisely assess that risk.

Something which is especially problematic about exceptions is that it is hard to decide up-front that a case *is* exceptional. In line with the observations about the ordering of activities described earlier, a company will usually *assume* a case is standard, in order not to bother the customer with questions that are probably irrelevant to the case in hand, such as "*is the property you want to mortgage in a foreign country?*". When a case is deemed exceptional later on in the process, it has to be handed off to a more experienced employee or a more specialized department, often leading to double work. Still later on in the process, the case will have to be handed *back* to the original handler. If we could decide earlier that the case is exceptional, it could be handled by a specialized employee in its entirety instead of being split across employees.

In the *retirement funds* case, the struggle between standard and exceptional handling was a central theme. Because of a history of demanding, large-size customers (employers, pension funds), client specific regulations had been agreed upon that resulted in specialized teams per customer and unwieldy extensions to information systems. Deciding on exceptionality of a case was problematic. Whenever a batch of some 100 cases had to undergo some standard process, the possibility that there might be one or two exceptions among them would often lead to the whole batch undergoing special treatment, if at that point in time it was not clear which were the ones being exceptional.

One of the measures to solve these problems was to equip the *work preparation* process, which examines incoming mail and assigns tasks to teams, with decision trees to better match complexity of a case with its appropriate treatment. A "work preparer" will judge a case on the basis of the distinctions that the decision tree prescribes, and assigns the work team and employee (junior or senior) that the decision tree recommends. An issue in the design of these trees was how much handling to put into the tree, and consequently into the preparation process, vs. leaving work for the primary process itself. It was important to choose indicators that were easy to check yet gave a good indication of difficulty level. Put another way, knowledge residing with experienced people in the middle of the process was formalized and transferred to an earlier point in the process.

In the *document services* case, keeping exceptions out of the main process was necessary to obtain economies of scale. This led client departments to withhold subsets of cases with special properties from the document services department, handling them manually. In the *property underwriting* case, there was no difference in exception handling across the two local processes. Exceptions did not exist; or if they did, were resolved by informal consultation of colleagues.

Obviously, extensive exception handling is associated more with product leadership and customer intimacy value disciplines than with operational excellence; also, excessive exception handling is the result of weak leadership and immaturity of process management. For example, the property underwriting department, being strategically essential to the parent company, was managed tightly and had grown very mature; both local processes therefore had the same very low level of exception handling.

Excessive exception handling has a strongly adverse impact on standardization efforts, because each exception type warrants deviations from standard handling. The problem of reengineering exception handling is aggravated by knowledge asymmetry between management and specialists: because exceptions are hard to explain, and specialists often derive their *raison d'être* from them, management can be easily left in the dark about the possibilities for reducing them. In general, it seems that having a clear policy on exceptions is helpful. For example, *document services* left them to their clients for handling, while property underwriting did not allow them to become explicit in the work flow. Pensions, being hampered by a history of allowing complexity to pile up, installed a special program (Six Sigma) and special tools (decision trees) to assess, reduce and handle exceptions. In multiple cases (*pensions*, *mortgages*), it was expressed that the ability to accurately assess difficulty level of a case was important but challenging.

### 14.7.5    Rework, prudence and foresight

Local processes differed in the extent to which they were able to prevent problems, but not very much. Given our contention that knowledge consists fundamentally of cause-effect relationships, one of the hypotheses this research started out with was that differences in performance across local processes would primarily depend on the extent to which a group of people had the collective ability to predict behavior of the system they were part of. Yet differences in this category were only found in three cases.

In the *document services* case, some client departments were much better able to keep errors out of the output information flow than others. Some of them would "toss the specifications over the wall", only to discover errors in the generated output, while others would scrutinize specifications beforehand. Document services try to detect this attitude to help correct it. This error prone-ness often results from the presence of an ignorant "middle man" in the work flow. In one case, a client department routinely collects output information from five separate information systems, but the department doing the collecting has insufficient knowledge about the reliability of those information sources.

In the *retirement funds* case, preventing errors is one of the main goals of the Six Sigma program. Because of the high complexity of the product offered, and because of the old and inflexible applications portfolio, many errors result from having to do information intensive work manually, for example, making typos in copied monetary amounts. A special category of errors is the misuse of templates and examples. For instance, letters would often be typed manually for client A and then adapted for client B, without replacing all occurrences of A by B, or otherwise without appropriate or complete adaptation. There was a similar problem with failed re-use of knowledge. Whenever a document template, thoughtfully contributed by a colleague for re-use by the team, was accidentally garbled by one colleague (likely because of the absence of an adequate content management system), the remaining colleagues would lose trust in this particular template, even if the error was later discovered and the template restored.

The findings say little about the dependence of foresight on context. It can be reasonably assumed that guarding against rework is associated more with operational excellence and product leadership than with customer intimacy.

In summary, although evidence was found that processes of rework and forethought differ in their error prevention capability, the findings indicate that this is no problem for standardization. Perhaps the opposite is true: whenever one process is better able to prevent problems, this capability can be copied by others, which makes the standardization effort worthwhile.

### 14.7.6    Verification and inspection, authorization, employee autonomy

These issues have a lot in common with rework and foresight, because checks are often done to guard correctness. However, an additional dimension of inspection and autonomy is the prevention of fraud by employees. Local processes differed substantially in the way they implemented checks and the level of autonomy that employees enjoyed.

Respondents felt that too many resources were allocated to verification activities. Some teams in the *pensions* case would have its output (generated by the document services department) returned to it to physically check all of it, although it was too late for any corrections. Also, many checks were not effective enough; errors would get through. The Six Sigma program tried to implement Poke Yoke, the Japanese quality principle that states you should try to organize work in such a way that common errors are impossible. One particularly effective verification procedure was to compare an altered amount to a particular amount given by the system, and verifying that the change was not more than 10%. This example suggests that the variables that influence a check's appropriateness are sensitivity, specificity, cost, and effectiveness, or, the ability to act cost-effectively on a negative outcome.

In the *pensions* case, verification and inspection was high in level and highly formalized. This was caused by the high task complexity and the poor IT architecture. Whether or not to verify a case depended on its difficulty level, having values low, medium or high. Cases that required determination of a monetary amount, were classified as medium by default. Although the decision to verify was formalized, the procedure was not. Verification could be implemented by "four eyes", by a dedicated employee, or by a quality team. This varied by team size, distribution of competencies within a team, and trust relationships.

Also, the way verification and authorization was implemented differed. In general, business units that had workflow systems also had much more elaborate authorization structures and procedures. Business units that did not have modern technology relied more on "human" techniques such as the four eyes principle. In the *mortgage center* case, at the most advanced business unit, the information system was explicitly regarded as "the second pair of eyes". As such, the use of workflow technology has a dual influence on the level of autonomy, or the reliance of employees on their superiors for decision making: on the one hand, by offering decision support it allows employees to make decisions on their own; on the other hand, by offering authorization functionality, authorization procedures are more formal and more strictly adhered to.

Apart from technology usage, level and implementation of verification and autonomy depend on department size. A finding from the *human resources* case was that in small departments, results are verified by collegial interaction, whereas in larger departments, people are more afraid to open themselves up to scrutiny, necessitating formal procedures. The consequences of verification and inspection implementation on standardization efforts are unclear; it seems they have a lot to do with exception handling and have the same, problematic consequences.

### 14.7.7    Level of standardization, formalization, and documentation of processes

One of the hypotheses given in par. 14.1.3 was that standardization would be easier when existing processes were highly standardized, formalized and well-described. Here, standardized means that employees have a uniform way of working; formalization means ways of working are strict and discrete, often supported by conceptual structures such as decision trees or sanctioned by information technology, and documentation means simply that working instructions are kept and maintained in a designated place. Although local processes differed substantially along this dimension, this was seen as a problem only by some.

Standardization is an issue not just between business units, but also on the level of individual employees. Where possible, people are bound to develop their personal preferences. This can become problematic when certain norms are at play that can be manipulated by employees in the interests of a client, or more generally, to increase chances of commercial success. An example from the *mortgage center* case was how to handle client requests for alteration of a quote, after the interest rate had increased. Some employees would retain the old rate in the quote, even if alteration would grant the company the right to dismiss the quoted rate and replace it with the current, higher, rate.

People can choose to follow locally preferred *norms*, but they can also locally develop *representations*, or information structures. As described above, proliferation of locally developed process knowledge hidden in spreadsheet files was problematic in most projects examined. These files are highly specific for the work situation of a small group of people or even one particular individual, and often implement functionality that no standard package or custom application offers. Particularly problematic is the fact that they often make implicit, undocumented assumptions about their context, rendering them useless and even unreliable in a wider context.

Another problem of local, individual work preferences is that they necessitate verification and inspection procedures. Evidently, if the *process* quality is not guaranteed, we have to guarantee the *outcome* quality. In the *document services* case, it was observed that shortcomings in the IT systems of a client department required manual information processing, which in turn, via personal differences, led to the client department requesting that the physical output be sent back to them for additional inspection.

Formalization refers to the use of standardized information structures to guide work. The decision trees from the *pensions* case are one example; checklists are another. In general, level of formalization is strongly dependent on the level of IT usage, and in particular on the use of workflow systems. But apart from this dependence, some interesting observations can be made. Also in the *pensions* case, the respondent indicated that in general, people do not like being forced to follow checklists. Nevertheless, checklist usage did have a positive impact on process quality, but with a catch. In a particular process, an employee would receive a file, covered with a list of tasks to be checked. Some of them would be completely filled in, others completely empty, and yet others filled in half-way through. It turned out that files with their checklist filled in either completely or not at all, were equally quick to further process; files with their checklist filled in only half-way, were slowest. The explanation lies in the fact that in the first category, the employee would assume his colleague had performed all tasks required because he had checked all the items in the list; in the second category, the employee simply trusted his colleague for his seniority. The third category, however, was problematic; a checklist filled in only half-way is an ambiguous signal, triggering re-inspection of the whole file. The lesson to be learnt is obvious: either use formal structures consistently, or do not use them at all, but guard the trustworthiness of their content.

With regard to process documentation, there seems to be a love-hate relationship between employees and process descriptions. In the *pensions* business unit, there was a separate administrative organization department that maintained process descriptions. Employees would go there to request modifications. Yet, those descriptions were under-used. Employees tend to request inclusion of handling of exceptional situations, but the administrative organization employees resent this, claiming that is not "procedural knowledge". Moreover, when such a situation is included in the process description, it often turns out later that the actions it prescribes are not always valid given the conditions that it requires. In all, it is hard to determine what to regard as "procedural" knowledge vs. "task" or "domain" knowledge, and if that line is pushed, completeness or correctness often suffers.

The *property underwriting* case is exceptional in this category, as it is in most others as well: in the two local underwriting departments, every step has been documented, and uniformity of behavior across employees is regularly inspected. This is caused by the high maturity of process management in this department.

Process documentation is deemed not very relevant for standardization efforts. For one, their contents are often outdated. But more importantly, it is considered best practice to do redesign in a participative fashion, inviting employees to express their knowledge interactively.

This finding does not refute the hypothesis that process explicitness is helpful to standardization, but merely that the existence of up-to-date process documentation is a bad proxy for the level of understanding of, and insight into and overview of, the process that personnel and management have. In the *document services* example, the respondent indicated that a if client department does not do sufficient process analysis and does not have adequate understanding of their process often leads to over-ambition and under-implementation, and to pendulum-swinging between concentration and dispersion of output activities.

The findings do not tell us much about the contextual dependence of standardization, formalization and documentation, other than that they are heavily influenced by extent and quality of IT usage, and by the size of a department.

The consequences of local differences in standardization, formalization, and documentation for standardization efforts are similar to those of differences in IT systems, but with two additions. For one, local *norms* will likely command discussion and consensus building during the redesign phase, and changing them will stir up resistance. Second, local *representations* will significantly impede the implementation phase, because their meaning and their range of applicability is often not well understood by anyone.

## 14.8 Adaptive evolution of knowledge structure

Whenever the environment in which a business process operates imposes a changing requirement or an opportunity for improvement upon it, the process will absorb this feature and change its behaviors accordingly. A new behavior will firstly be implemented in a flexible, ad hoc fashion, both to be able to experiment with different ways of dealing with it, and because new requirements tend to be unstable, subject to further change. Rigorous, efficient implementation will therefore be too expensive until stability sets in and effective process knowledge has been built up. This experimentation was first described by Nonaka (1994) and then elaborated upon by Nooteboom (1996) from the perspective of organizational cognition.

New behaviors will start out having their own, flexibly implemented process, which will then be migrated as much as possible to efficient standard processes. This process of *compilation* requires explicitation (Nonaka, 1994) of knowledge that had hitherto been personal and tacit, using soft categories.

This evolution is most explicitly seen in the *property underwriting* case. One of the efforts undertaken there was to transfer more situations in the fire and theft line from a complex, flexible process to a standard process. They did this by imitating the way the motor insurance line was implemented. In this way, they used a template in the sense of (Szulanski, 2001). Motor insurance is a much bigger business, enabling higher investments in IT systems. Knowledge from this business line could thus be better exploited by transferring it to the fire and theft line.

Stabilization of the environment, enabling compilation of process knowledge, is not always beyond the organization's control. In the *care brokering* case, stabilization was achieved by building trust relationships with select care providers in foreign countries, signing contracts for those treatments that the respective care provider had ample capacity for. The fact that those relationships were stable and formalized enabled the care brokering department to formalize and standardize the process of brokering care for the subsets of situations that required exactly those treatments. This in turn enabled the brokering department to take over the approval decision for foreign treatment of these subsets from the Foreign Claims department, thus achieving its goal of controlling customer service quality independently from other departments.

Whenever a set of new situations is added to a standard process, that process will increase in complexity because it now has to respond to more variety. This was most explicitly seen in the case of *Document Services*, as they had to absorb client departments' output processes one by one. In their own words, a "generic framework" emerged, into which new clients can now be "hung up" much quicker and more reliably than they could before. This generic framework is a "progressing insight", that partly consists of deep knowledge of the possibilities of the technologies used, and partly of "checks and arrangements" to prevent problems experienced in the past. This is much alike the Banc One case described in Szulanski (2000).

### 14.8.1    Choice of archetype and its effect on process representations

One other kind of contextuality came up during the period in which the interviews were conducted, but not as a part of the investigated efforts per se. It is the choice of archetype for the representations behind a business process. From psychology, it is well-known that people use *prototypes*, specific instances of broad categories, and classify other instances by assessing their similarity to the prototype. For example, it is quite hard to precisely define what a table is and what it is not. Rather, objects have some degree of *table-ness*. People use a particular instance of a table, for example, a simple wooden kitchen table, to judge the table-ness of other objects. It is well-known that small children learn concepts by first overgeneralizing specific instances. For example, they use the word *dog* to refer to cats, dogs, and cows alike. It would be too difficult for a small child to first learn the abstract concept of *mammal*, and refine it later into lower species. Rather, the first dog encountered is taken as the *exemplar*, serving as a prototype for assessing the nature of animals encountered later.

Representational systems evolve by adapting the prototypes used in them. If adaptations become too complicated, small paradigm shifts are necessary. For example, a cat might be classified as a *small dog* at first, but this categorization bogs down when encountering chihuahuas. Only then do we develop new categories, for example introducing the categories of *cat*, *canine*, *carnivore*, and *herbivore* to properly relate and differentiate cats, dogs, and cows.

Representations in business processes evolve like this, around archetypes or metaphors that are adapted until adaptation is no longer feasible. Because this source of contextuality was discovered late in the process, we have not been able to identify it in the projects examined, but it is not hard to find examples. One person in the financial services company was involved in a project for merging investment portfolios. Financial services companies collect money from their customers in a number of ways: by collecting insurance premiums for example, or by offering savings accounts. As long as this money remains with the company it should invest it effectively and wisely. The company had decided that investment portfolios of the different business units should be merged to increase economies of scale, lower transaction costs, and pool investment expertise. The returns from investing this pool of money would then be relayed back to the individual business units, so they could establish their profit & loss statement.

The respondent explained that modern financial services companies are inhabited by two kinds of people: *bankers* and *insurers*. Whereas banking and insurance used to be completely separated disciplines, with separate cultures and legislation, in the last two decades they have drawn closer to each other. This leads to more integrated products for consumers and efficiencies of scale. However, *bankers* and *insurers* sometimes struggle to cope with the differences between their archetypes.

The project team was staffed largely with *bankers*. Investment management is a banker's core business. For a banker, the basic idea of investment management is about combining as many financial resources as possible, and then investing them as effectively as possible. As an afterthought, the investment returns have to be relayed back to the individual investors according to some reasonably fair principle. For an insurer, however, the core business is to cover risk. The basic idea is to collect premiums from as many parties as possible, and price risks high enough to always be able to refund a client's damages. As an afterthought, it is smart to invest those premiums to increase profits, but with the constraint that enough cash has to be available for paying claims at all times.

Late in the project, it was discovered that the model that was designed for pooling money and dividing the returns, was inadequate for insurance premium money. The law requires that for each type of insurance portfolio (like property, fire, health), its provisions (cash and investments that are reserved for covering damages produced by the portfolio) have to be adequate *and identifiable*. For a banker, this requirement defeats the purpose of pooling resources. The model that the *bankers* had come up with was geared for maximum pooling, but did not cater for keeping track of which investments were coupled to which insurance portfolio. Adding this function required major reworking of the model and caused substantial delay. On a high level, the basic concepts of the *banker* and the *insurer* are practically equivalent in function. Yet, they differ markedly in the representations that they require for their execution, due to one specific requirement that results from a different main goal of one of the underlying local processes.

Another example is one business unit that has chosen "the family" as its primary commercial focus. That is, the concept of *customer* is, deliberately, tightly coupled to the notion of family, as opposed to the notion of (legal) *individual*. This has consequences for the way information is structured throughout the organization. In each of its processes and information systems, an assumption is made that the individual that the organization is dealing with at any one time is probably part of some larger family-like group. Although the concept of an "individual" or a "legal entity" is a much simpler prototype for a company, the concept of a family is, commercially speaking, much more natural and effective. Yet, when this business unit participated in a collective data warehouse project, they were not able to contribute data like "the number of new customers this month" according to the agreed upon definition for that metric, because details were not recorded on the individual level.

The choice of prototype to start with, the path of its adaptation, and the moments of reorganization of the category system, might all be causes of contextuality. Understanding the different archetypes that underlie local processes might enable us to discover salient differences quicker.

### 14.8.2    Co-evolution of competence and trust

A central theme of this chapter is the difficulty of assessing the complexity of problems to be solved, as well as the difficulty of assessing adequacy of the competencies proposed to solve them. Making this assessment is probably one of the more important tasks of management. Trust has a dual meaning: it can mean that parties know that they share an interest in keeping a cooperative relationship, but it can also mean that a party entrusts another party with the task of serving its needs, because it knows the other party has adequate competency to do so.

Often, managers will establish a centralized function that, wholly or partly, executes its activities in parallel with decentralized activities, in the hope that the centralized function will obliterate the decentralized activities when it becomes stronger. In practice, however, such a centralized function will not have, nor gain, the trust of decentralized business units to serve their needs adequately because they are not able to build this competence in close cooperation with their clients. For this reason, it is better not to trust autonomous business units to cooperate willingly, but to force them to do so.

This relationship between competence and trust also works in the smaller context. As described earlier, people tend to build problem solving representations, such as spreadsheets, in a limited context. Whenever such a representation is "trusted" with handling a case outside of its context of development, and fails to do so satisfactorily, it loses the trust-in-competence of its user base. This is aggravated by the fact that cheap information technology allows us to build many such representations; our organizational memory is actually too large. When we lose the overview of which representations adequately handle which situations, this will lead to large volumes of untrustworthy representations.

## 14.9    Effects of standardization on knowledge structure

In the previous section, we have described how knowledge in business processes evolves in the face of change. In the current section, we will elaborate these findings more specifically for a specific kind of change: process standardization.

Standardization leads to a number of structural changes in knowledge structure. Foremost, it leads to disentanglement: isolating context specific distinctions in one defined process step, usually "at the front" of the process.

This is accompanied by a generalization of distinctions in the less context sensitive, concentrated part of the new process. This means process participants have to take distinctions into consideration for decision making earlier than they were used to. This is an instance of disinterleaving. It is most clearly seen in the *document services* case, where workers were used to produce output by trial and error, printing and collecting documents for a client and then checking them as a bundle. Using document services, they now have to be able to guarantee correctness of bits of digital information earlier in the process chain, not yet collected and rendered in concrete form. When checking routines are based on concrete representations, such as a printed bundle of paper, this poses a challenge.

## 14.10   The process of change

### 14.10.1   Origin of transferred knowledge

In each of the projects examined, knowledge constituting the new central process can be said to originate from somewhere. Knowledge items, such as the basic idea behind the new process, the information systems used for it, local representations and the people using them, either came from one of the local processes, came from outside the organization, were created experimentally along the way, or were a mixture of all these possibilities.

There are three levels of process improvement through best practice exchange. For one, process improvement can be autonomous, with no imported knowledge at all. Second, a benchmark can be used to assess *to what extent* a process can be improved, but not knowing precisely how. In practice, not knowing how at all is rare; there is always some piece of information about how an internal or external competitor might have accomplished improvement. Third, best practices can be exchanged by careful studying and copying of behavior and representations. The second form of benchmarking is probably the most often used form of best practice exchange. Knowing that a competitor achieved improvement is a strong means of convincing co-workers that trying some new trick is worth the effort of coping with its disadvantages, whereas, had the trick never been tried before, it is all too easy to argue that the disadvantages will outweigh the benefits.

In the *mortgage center* case, there was strong benchmarking information about competitors that had concentrated their mid-office, and there was even information about the level of performance that they had achieved. The mortgage lending process is a relatively stable domain (if not the competitive landscape in which it has to function). These two characteristics combined made the implementation process highly combinatorial, mixing and matching resources from multiple local processes.

In the *property underwriting* case, multiple forms of best practice exchange were used. As a concrete example, the smaller of the two local processes had a practice of coordinating staff allocation with the sales department through a "mailing plan". This document describes marketing actions planned for the near future, along with a projection of their effects on the volume of customer contacts. The mailing plan would allow the back-office to plan staff allocation. Sometimes, they would contact the sales department to ask for some change in the plan to optimize the planning.

By contrast, the larger of the two organizations did not have such a representation and its associated practice. After a number of contacts with their new peers, they slowly started to develop the same practice. Upon first question, the respondent did not believe this was copying behavior. But when pressed, he did agree that the practice had started some time after he himself had "put a mailing plan on their table". This goes to show that copying behavior is always apparent or explicit; upon seeing that a particular behavior is feasible and effective, it is more natural to adopt it. The socialized knowledge of its existence and effectiveness elsewhere obviates the need for justifying a change of behavior.

In the *pensions* case, both the benchmarking and copying forms of best practices exchange were apparent. As Linderman et al. (2003) points out, Six Sigma is a systematic way of asking two questions: is adequate knowledge available? Is there enough motivation and cognitive discipline to exploit the knowledge available? Different from the other cases was the fact with *pensions* (and, with Six Sigma in general) that willingness to *create* knowledge was much greater. In most cases, a pragmatic, combinatorial approach was chosen with respect to best practice implementation, instead of an inquisitive, experimental approach. As the respondent in the *pension's* case pointed out, Six Sigma is a method you use when other methods have failed to solve some persistent problem. Thus, to separate fact from mere belief, he would hand out stopwatches and time registration forms to gather precise knowledge on process characteristics, rather than relying on expert opinion, which is characteristic of a combinatorial approach.

### 14.10.2    Implementation chores

For this research, we made a conscious choice not to divide our research object into separate "design", or "strategic" issues vs. "implementation", or "practical" issues. We have looked at projects in various phases of development, and have thus gained an overview of the role that knowledge structure plays in various phases of development, one of which is implementation. Implementation is often neglected in the management field, while research shows that thorough implementation of a strategy is at least as important as choosing the right one. In many cases, respondents complained that key ideas from the design phase were inconsequently followed through in the implementation phase. In the worst case, this can lead to a situation where disadvantages of the design are realized but not the advantages. Yet, it is very difficult to assess whether a disappointing outcome is due to design flaws or lack of implementation skill.

Failing to transfer a best practice from one context into another is called *stickiness* by Szulanski (1996). He identifies the factors that influence the probability of success in transferring knowledge, and researches them by surveying some 180 cases of best practice transfer in some large corporations. These factors belong to the categories: ability and effort by the sender, absorptive capacity of the source, and features of the transfer process. Szulanski concludes that cognitive difficulties are a significant cause of failure, even more so than motivational factors. In a later paper (Szulanski, 2001), he zooms in on the process of transfer, and finds out that *replication accuracy* is a variable that mediates cognitive difficulties. That is, the accuracy with which a recipient party copies a practice has a strong influence on success. Attempts by a recipient party to adapt a practice to supposed contextual circumstances usually leads to failure.

Different kinds of replication were observed in the cases. Local processes can be standardized in two ways. One possibility is to require that they adapt their knowledge structure to accord with the features of the proposed best practice that are considered salient or beneficial. The other is to make them function on the basis of uniform, new representations. The first approach is often used in practice, because it requires much less change. Besides, it is quite hard to explain why compliance to quality or efficiency requirements is not enough. Yet, conservation of old, contextual representations greatly complicates standardization.

Examples of such representations are forms and product specifications. In the *mortgage center* case, one of the brands had not understood the idea of "one product portfolio". They thought that their mortgage products would have to be made compliant with such requirements as fitting in a particular information system, and offering certain product features. However, the program manager's understanding of the "one product portfolio" idea was that there was to be only one, highly complete and flexible set of product specifications, one set of customer forms, legal specifications, financial models, and so forth, that could be *trimmed down* as appropriate for each of the brands. The difference in understanding was discovered months too late, leading to a delay and a compromised outcome.

Keeping old representations brings with it inflexibility, double maintenance and mapping activities between new and old representations, but is much easier to attain than starting from scratch. What makes it especially problematic is that, from top management perspective, the *compliance* and *replacement* strategies look similar, whereas in practice they are not.

As a hypothesis, we offer *replacement of representations* as a refinement or perhaps a constituent of *replication accuracy.*

## 14.11   Conclusions

We stated our research problem as explaining the contextual nature of business processes on the basis of features of their knowledge structure. It is too early to summarize strict research findings already. Contextuality, it has been illustrated, is a key concept in knowledge management. In real life cases, similar processes are different in subtle ways. Contextuality of a concept or a process is an evolving matter. The dynamics of the knowledge infrastructure can no longer be ignored.

Standardization, almost by definition, has a limiting effect on contextuality. Standard processes, independent on how much they seem attractive, go in fact against contextuality. As suggested earlier, it is a given and widely accepted that specialization inside a company is a more efficient way of working, but is it also effective? Our observations invite companies to seriously (re)consider the balance of standardization versus contextualization. Knowledge infrastructure is by definition contextual and standardization is much less so. It could be suggested that companies should maybe introduce a preparatory step on the way to standardization, which is the identification of the knowledge infrastructure. In particular with mergers (or acquisitions) this seems of paramount importance. Already on the semantic level (how different units use the same words differently) important problems are encountered. The level deeper, i.e. the knowledge infrastructure merger, which a (merged) company wants to capitalize on, is even more difficult to grasp but precisely very important.

An open question remains whether standardization preserves valuable knowledge and allows it to be easily spread by decontextualising it, or, rather, that standardization destroys contextual knowledge and, consequently, knowledge per se. Further research will have to give more insight into this paradox. What we can observe is that this paradox is an important one in knowledge management that plays a key role in merging units (or companies). Consequently how is knowledge disentangled and decontextualized in order to be transferred into a new context? Or shouldn't this be the purpose of knowledge management?

A suggestion to companies in the process of merging units could be the following. A strict concentration on the processes and merging the processes makes the integration of knowledge infrastructures and knowledge exchange difficult. It could be envisaged that in merger processes, the prime effort should be targeting the integration of the knowledge infrastructures, after which the standardization of processes, based on this integrated knowledge infrastructure, will be much easier. It does highlight again the dichotomy efficiency and effectiveness in a company, and the fact that the two are not necessarily a smooth couple.

# 15. EMERGENT LEARNING PROCESSES IN INNOVATION PROJECTS

Saskia Harkema

## 15.1 Introduction

Innovation is the lifeblood of companies, while simultaneously being one of the most difficult and elusive processes to manage. Failure rates are high – varying between 6 out of 10 (Hultink, 1996) to 9 out of 10 (Ernst & Young, 1999). Against this background it seems appropriate and justifiable to look for an alternative way to approach the innovation process and explore whether it leads to insights and lessons which help the academic and managerial community further.

Based on the practice of a multinational manufacturer of fast moving consumer goods - Sara Lee-Douwe Egberts – companies that have placed innovation and learning high on the agenda; mainstream ideas about learning and innovation will be revealed in the course of this chapter. It will be argued that most learning theories rest on a sender-receiver model of knowledge transmission, and that this affects how people learn from innovation projects. Additionally it will be demonstrated that innovation processes are predominantly managed in a mechanistic way – *i.e.* as a sequence of phases and activities that have to be performed and from which the outcome can be predicted with relative accuracy.

A complex adaptive perspective on innovation and learning forms an alternative perspective on these phenomena. Complex adaptive systems (CAS) consist of an intricate network of agents with highly interdependent relations. The most important characteristics of CAS are non-linearity, dynamic behavior, emergence and self-organization. In the course of this chapter the implications of these phenomena for learning in innovation projects are explained. First of all innovation and learning are dealt with as separate topics and also their interrelationship. Consecutively the main concepts of CAS theory are introduced, and linked to innovation and learning. This chapter also includes the findings of an exploratory multi-agent simulation model, which gives insight into the underlying forces in innovation projects when they are modeled as a CAS.

## 15.2    The constructed dualism between innovating and learning

Despite the fact that working, innovating and learning are related activities, practice shows that in reality they tend to be regarded as conflicting activities (Brown & Duguid, 1991: p.40). According to these authors this has to do with the fact that working is generally seen as conservative and resistant to change; learning is viewed as something which is distinct from working and somewhat problematic in the face of change; and innovation is in most cases regarded as a disruptive but necessary imposition of change on both learning and working (see also Meeus, 2003). According to the authors the source of the conflict between these three phenomena primarily lies in the gap between precepts and practice. Conventional learning theory, for instance, tends to separate learning from working and innovating and – more importantly – learners from workers. Innovation theory on the other hand shows a multitude of approaches and perspectives. However within companies, linear and stage-gate-models like the one developed by Cooper (1987) prevail. The dualism, especially between learning and innovating is the topic of discussion in this chapter. In the next paragraphs the source of the dualism between innovation and learning is discussed via an overview of the theoretical framework wherein these two phenomena are embedded.

### 15.2.1    An overview of the relation between innovation and learning

There are as many definitions as misunderstandings about what innovation actually means. In this chapter innovation is defined as a knowledge process which is geared towards the creation of new knowledge that becomes embodied in new products and services. By implication, the knowledge creation process is geared towards the development of commercial and viable solutions. Learning plays a crucial role in this process.

According to Gieskes (2001) there are basically two streams of thought about the relationship between learning and innovation. The first one looks at product innovation as a natural learning process. The focus lies very much on R&D as the driving force behind innovation, and sees developments in R&D as a natural learning process. The second stream of thoughts puts the emphasis on the product innovation process. Learning is seen as essential for the improvement and dissemination of new knowledge throughout the rest of the organization. In that process organizations use learning experiences of a failure or success to improve new product development projects and avoid mistakes made earlier. This is quite a mechanistic view of learning. In addition, there are many assumptions underlying these two ways of looking at learning within innovation projects. These assumptions will be unraveled in the course of the next paragraphs and an alternative perspective- which links innovation with learning within complex adaptive systems theory - brought forward.

The literature on innovation and learning is hugely fragmented and it would go beyond the scope of this chapter to deal with it extensively. Therefore the focus is on the main issues within that literature to the extent they are relevant. In the next section a description is given of the domain of innovation, to be followed by an overview of learning definitions and paradigms.

### 15.2.2    An overview of innovation perspectives and theories

A broad review of the innovation literature shows there are three streams of thought, namely 1) diffusion of innovation: refers to the spread of an innovation through a population of potential adopters, 2) organizational innovativeness: the objective is to discover the determinants of an organization's propensity to innovate and 3) process theory models: investigates the nature of the innovation process (Wolfe, 1994). Additionally there are three perspectives on innovation: an individualist, a structural and a collaborative perspective (Slappendel, 1996). In the first case, the focus lies on the individuals or innovators within the process, in the second instance the attention is diverted towards the structural aspects of innovation – decision-making, information flows, procedures – whereas, in the latter case, the process is the main topic.

It is in the broad range of theories that the different approaches to innovation clearly come to light. The most predominant of these theories are neo-classical and evolutionary theories. Neo classical theories of innovation are grounded in classical economic theory, whereby innovation is regarded as a variable that can be controlled and predicted. Evolutionary theories regard innovation as an adaptive learning process responding to external circumstances. The ideas of Nelson and Winter (1982) are especially relevant in this respect. Evolutionary theory basically seeks to explain how organizational routines enable the production and reproduction of operations, structures and outcomes. The problem with routines is that they are counter-intuitive to innovation, *i.e.* change, and routines assume a degree of predictability in processes and outcome, while innovation is neither predictable, nor are consequences foreseeable.

Other theories are cognitive oriented theories or knowledge based theories. Knowledge-based theories tend to emphasize the cognitive side of innovation processes. There are two distinct perspectives on knowledge management for innovation according to Swan *et al* (1999). In the cognitive model knowledge is conceived as being captured and codified from individuals, packaged, transmitted and processed through the use of ICT, and subsequently disseminated and used by other individuals in new contexts. The community model on the other hand focuses on social interaction and collaboration and emphasizes the idea of learning.

In general it can be said that most theories place the focus of attention either on structural or individual processes at the organizational level, or on cognitive and behavioral processes at the individual level. This results in a dichotomy at two levels: at the level of the individual between the inner world – cognition – and the outer world – behavior – and the level of the organization between the structural aspects – procedures and decision-making – and the individual aspects – the culture of an organization. This distinction also becomes manifest in learning theories as we will see in the next paragraphs.

## 15.2.3    Definitions of learning

The classical definition of learning is that it is a change in behavior as a result of experience or practice. The emphasis lies on behavior and not necessarily on the transfer of cognition. A more recent definition is the one by Kim (1993) which says that learning is the acquisition of knowledge, whereby he makes a distinction between the (a) acquisition of know-how and (b) acquisition of know-why. The first refers to the physical ability of an individual to produce some action and the latter to the ability to articulate a conceptual understanding of an experience. Other authors, such as, for instance, Argyris and Schon (1978) define learning as the development of knowledge. Fiol & Lyles (1985) describe learning as the process of improving actions through better understanding and knowledge. According to Dodgson (1993) learning can be described as the ways firms build, supplement, and organize knowledge and routines around their activities and within their cultures, and adapt and develop organizational efficiency by improving the use of broad skills of their workforce. Baets & Van der Linden (2000) define learning as the process whereby knowledge is created by the transformation of experience. Learning is not seen as an abstract process but it is contextual: it occurs while the experience is taking place, so that it can be applied immediately.

Knowledge and learning in most definitions are intertwined. Learning is generally understood as a process that transforms an experience into some form of creative capacity that is subsequently geared towards some form of creative action. Definitions of learning largely depend on the perspective from which one looks at the phenomenon and also the level of analysis. These two are connected. A clear distinction in the literature is made between individual and organizational learning; a distinction that, within innovation projects, is also of importance. While a creative idea usually starts at the individual level, innovation gains meaning for an organization when it is shared by more people and is endorsed by top management.

### 15.2.4     Levels of learning – individual versus organizational learning

In the literature an ongoing debate can be witnessed between those who claim that organizations learn, as opposed to those who assert that only individuals can learn. In this research the individual's learning perspective is chosen and organizational learning is regarded as a derivative of the co-operation between learning individuals. In general it can be said that individual learning is defined in terms of individual mental models, which change under the influence of experiences people go through. Mental models are embedded in our brain and body (Varela, 1991) and they are representations of how we perceive the world, in addition to norms, values, emotions, beliefs and rules.

The most influential model on individual learning was developed by Kolb (1984)-The OADI cycle (Observe-Assess-Design-Implement). The cycle works as follows: first an experience is had, then observations and reflections on that experience are created, thirdly abstract concepts and generalizations are formed on the basis of these reflections, and finally, these ideas get tested on the new situation, giving food for new experiences.

Models seem to play an important role in the individual learning process, but also at the level of the organization. Most authors agree that learning starts at the individual level and eventually may become shared and thus organizational. Whereas individual learning refers to individual mental models that change under the influence of experiences people have, organizational learning usually refers to a corporate memory or to shared mental models in which the knowledge that guides organizational behavior resides.

An important aspect of the learning process is how individual and organizational learning are linked with each other and how individual knowledge may become corporate knowledge, or individual models become organizational models. According to Kim the importance of individual learning for organizational learning is at once obvious and subtle – obvious because organizations cannot learn without individuals, subtle because organizations can learn independent of all individuals. He developed an Integrated Model of Organizational learning which addresses the issue of transfer of learning through the exchange of individual and shared mental models. Analogous to individual learning, organizational learning is defined as "increasing an organization's capacity to take effective action" (Kim, 1993: p. 43). The cycles of individual learning – represented in the earlier mentioned OADI cycle - affect learning at the organizational level through their influence on the organization's shared mental models. An organization can only learn through its members, but it is not dependent on any specific member. The transfer mechanism from individual to organizational is the shared mental models. He emphasizes the importance of mental models because, according to him, it is where the vast majority of an organization's knowledge (both know-how and know why) lies.

Argyris' and Schön's (1978) ideas about the relation between individual and organizational learning are the most widespread and important within the field. They regard individuals as the agents of learning, where individual learning experiences may eventually become embedded in organizational memory or in a corporate knowledge repository. The question is how this occurs. In that process they identify three learning types:

1. *Single-loop learning* takes place when errors are detected and corrected and firms carry on with their present policies and goals – they have merely been improved. According to Dodgson (1993) single-loop-learning can be compared with activities which add to the knowledge base, firm specific competencies or routines of an organization without altering the fundamental nature of the organization's activities. Senge (1990) speaks of adaptive learning in this context.
2. *Double loop learning* occurs when, in addition to detection and correction of errors, the organization questions and modifies existing norms, procedures, policies, and objectives. Double loop learning involves changing the organization's knowledge base, firm specific competencies or routines.
3. *Deutero learning* occurs when organizations learn how to carry out single-loop and double-loop learning. This awareness makes the organization recognize that learning needs to occur and says something about how organizations learn to learn. It takes place at the highest aggregate level, where the way of learning is questioned and adapted.

Baets and van der Linden (2000) have adapted the OADI-model and developed a model, which clearly demonstrates that individual mental models cannot be detached from organizational routines and that the former are the agents of change.  27 depicts a graphical representation of their approach.

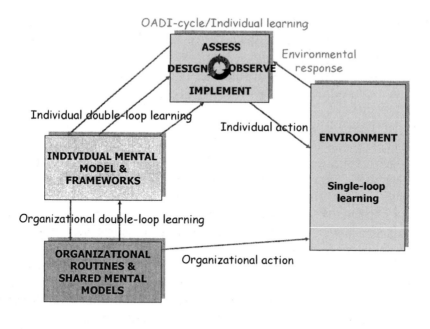

*Figure -27.* OADI cycle as adapted by Baets and Van der Linden

In this model individual single-loop learning similarly takes place when errors are detected and corrected: an individual adapts its behavior within the framework of present policies and goals – actions are merely improved. A second stage of individual learning is however introduced – individual double loop learning - which links individual learning with individual mental models. It includes learning on the basis of external impulses but also learning by connecting what has been learnt from external impulses with individual mental models. In this case errors are not only corrected but are linked to individual mental models, which are eventually adapted. So, in this case the adaptation is not merely at the behavioral level but goes a layer deeper, i.e. at the cognitive level.

The organizational double loop learning process is introduced in the figure in two ways. Comparable to single-loop learning in the individual model, each individual can be part of an organizational action, which may cause an environmental response. This is called organizational single-loop learning (Baets, 1998; p:59). Double-loop learning at this level occurs when individual mental models are brought into relation in order to form shared mental models, which in turn again affect individual mental models. Shared mental models basically refer to institutionalised organizational routines and procedures, *i.e.* the way things are done within a company.

The contribution of the model developed by Baets and Van der Linden is that it makes us aware of the fact that individual mental models and organizational routines are not separate from each other but that the former are the agents of change, while simultaneously being constrained and affected by the same routines wherein individual learning is embedded. In addition it makes us aware of the fact that learning involves both a behavioral and cognitive change and that the two are inseparably linked.

This brings us to the fundamental thinking underlying most learning theories, which according to Stacey (2001), uphold a strict dualism between the individual and the organization or between cognition and behavior. Generally speaking it can be said that the central assumption of mainstream thinking is that learning involves the transfer of knowledge. Underlying this notion is a sender-receiver model of knowledge transmission, which sees organizations as information-processing systems. The individual and the organization are then treated as separate phenomena. According to Stacey, in mainstream thinking the individual learns and creates knowledge, and the principal concern is how knowledge might be shared across the organization and subsequently captured, stored and retained in some sort of corporate memory. A clear distinction is made between knowledge acquisition, which takes place at the individual level and knowledge retention, which takes place at the individual and organizational level.

Before discussing an alternative approach to learning and innovation, it is important to gain insight into the practical effects of this sender-receiver model of knowledge transmission, for learning in innovation projects. In order to illustrate that, I would like to return to practice. Below is an example of a how SaraLee/DE has embedded this type of learning within their company and what the underlying assumptions are of this way of working. It clearly shows how a sender-receiver model of learning is applied in real-life and is used to retain lessons from projects with the aim of extrapolating them to future projects.

### Example: learning within and from innovation projects

The start of an innovation project is usually determined by an idea, which mostly emerges in the mind of an individual, in an R&D department or elsewhere. An idea can be carried forward and embedded within the formal structure of the company after having been evaluated according to a set of criteria defined by management. If an idea is accepted as being interesting, a project team is installed and the idea is further developed in line with the stages defined by the innovation model – idea, feasibility, concept, development, and launch. In this process the activities, gate-reviews and checklists play the role of channelling the interaction and decision-making of people up until the launch phase. Learning is explicitly coupled to the new product development process, with the aim of improving effectiveness – *i.e.* avoid mistakes made earlier - and retain as much knowledge as possible for the future. The underlying assumption is that people are the most important asset since they are the owners of valuable knowledge, and henceforth knowledge related to the new product development (NPD) process has to be made explicit as much as possible and subsequently codified in some form. Teams are gathered together to evaluate the process in terms of the decisions that were taken with pre-defined objectives as a yardstick to measure the success of the process. The idea is that knowledge can be made explicit by asking people to recall what decisions were taken, and why they were taken and how this affected the course of the process. On the basis of this, process lessons are defined to learn from past mistakes and successes. These learnings are subsequently communicated to other employees, with the ultimate aim of thus improving the overall performance of innovation efforts. The thinking behind this way of working is that experiences from the past can be extrapolated to the future to thus avoid mistakes and exert more control over the process so as to increase effectiveness. The focus is on the decision-making process.

Learning in SL/DE clearly fits within a sender-receiver approach to learning. The focus is very much on double-loop learning and trying to identify commonalities in what people say they have learned. The aim is to retain lessons in some sort of database or Intranet, so people can access them and use them in future projects. However, lessons appear to be context and people dependent. A SL/DE employee who was interviewed described it as follows: *"if you try to merely implement lessons from other projects in new projects, whether these lessons will be useful will depend on the composition of the team and the circumstances"*. This touches upon a very fundamental assumption underlying the way many companies work. Mostly this is influenced by a rational-mechanistic view of reality, which supposes that reality can be decomposed in parts and organizations are metaphorically comparable to machines. Knowledge is then objectified and detached from individuals and the context wherein knowledge is shared and developed. To understand how learning theories developed and the predominance of a sender-receiver approach explained, we need to know more about some of the most influential learning paradigms wherein these theories developed and are embedded. This is the subject of the next paragraph.

### 15.2.5     Learning paradigms

The distinction between individual and organizational learning cannot be fully understood without a brief review of the prevailing learning paradigms. In general literature two strands of thought are defined: a behaviorist one and a cognitive one.

The emphasis of behaviorism lies in observable indicators that learning has actually taken place. The father of behaviorism is J.B. Watson (1878-1958), who defines learning as a sequence of stimulus response actions in observable cause and effect relationships. The most well-known example of behaviorism is Pavlov's experiment. Skinner developed Watson's ideas further. According to Skinner voluntary or automatic behavior is strengthened or weakened by the immediate presence of reward or punishment, where the assumption is that new learning occurs as a result of positive reinforcement and old patterns are abandoned as a result of negative reinforcement.

At the individual level learning is regarded as a change of individual behavior resulting from changing stimulus-response mechanisms (see *e.g.* Kolb, 1984). At the organizational level the same process applies: organizations are open systems that change their behavior primarily in response to changes in the environment as a result of previous experiences. Learning is a reactive and adaptive process and results in changed organizational behavior.

Contrary to this view cognitivism places the emphasis on mental processes of the mind. Behaviorists do not deny the existence of these processes; they simply regard them as an unobservable indicator of learning, which cannot be established empirically. Cognition is seen as an important driving and explanatory force for understanding behavior. Jean Piaget (1896-1980), for instance, regarded human development in terms of progressive stages of cognitive development. These four stages – sensorimotor, preoperational, concrete operational and formal operations stage - characterize the cognitive abilities necessary at each stage to construct meaning.

Generally speaking, a clear line separates the behaviorists from the cognitivists. There are, however, alternative views on learning which also try to link individual cognition with organizational behavior. Leroy and Ramantsoa, for instance, argue (1997) that a strict separation between behavior and cognition is constructed, or Nonaka and Takeuchi (1994) couple individual with organizational learning by linking the cognitive with the behavioral component via the externalisation of knowledge and the transformation of tacit into explicit knowledge, and finally Nicolini and Meznar (1995: p. 738) go as far as to argue that the distinction between behavior and cognition is inadequate to serve as the basis for defining organizational learning. According to them *"it narrows the boundaries of organizational learning, leaving aside a number of phenomena that could be included in a broader notion of organizational knowledge and learning"* of which constructivism is the most relevant one in this context. Also Baets (1998) emphasizes the fact that shared mental models develop under the influence of individual experiences, whereby the former can be completely different from the sum of individual experiences. The process of change cannot be dictated, since it is emergent and non-linear, what an organization has to do is let the individual undergo new experiences in a positive atmosphere whereby individuals may decide – since they cannot be forced to do so – to integrate these new experiences into their individual mental models. In this view the emphasis is changed from learning as a transfer mechanism, to learning as emergent and a construction mechanism that starts at the individual level. This idea that learning is a process construction process is laid down in ideas on constructivism. Constructivism is an example of a learning theory that focuses on the mental processes that construct meaning, whereby cognition is regarded as situated. According to Walker (2003) the constructivist approach assumes that individuals impose meaning on the world, rather than meaning existing in the world independent of us. Constructivists believe that all humans have the ability to construct knowledge in their own minds through a process of discovery and problem-solving. Constructivists focus on the learner as the one responsible for learning, and they assume learning takes place via a process of learning-by-doing or via experimentation and practice (McDermott, 1981; Baets & Van der Linden, 2000). The main consequence of a constructivist paradigm is that knowledge and learning cannot be isolated from practice (Brown and Duguid, 1991) and both knowledge and learning are situated. Whereas transfer models isolate knowledge from practice, constructivism primarily sees learning as a process of social construction. From this perspective learners can only develop understanding of a wide range of aspects - including the social relations of the people involved in a project team for instance - through interaction.

We can reasonably conclude from the above that the assumption that organizations learn is, as such, not in question. What is the point of discussion is how this transition from individual to organization takes place, which is particularly important when we think about innovation projects.

Ideas usually emerge in the mind of an individual and eventually have to transcend that individual, to lead to something new for the organization – be it in the form of a new product, a new service or a new technology. In this chapter learning is seen as a process, which starts at the individual level in someone's mind- learning as a consequence cannot be detached from the individual. This assumption raises the question whether learning is seen solely from a procedural perspective does not overlook an essential aspect of learning in innovation projects. By placing the emphasis on the processes, decision-making and information-exchange, the role of the individual is merely regarded as secondary instead of primary. Individuals are not viewed as the agents of change- change is the result of an individual adaptation in behavior to procedures of decision-making with which individuals have to comply.

A gap is assumed in traditional learning theories between the one who knows and the recipient of that knowledge and between individual and context. Within an innovation project this translates into a view of learning as described earlier: learning is then detached from the innovating process and is seen as the outcome of a process instead of as an integral part of it. The question is what CAS theory can contribute towards bridging the apparent existing gap between innovation and learning, which brings us to the subject of the next paragraph.

## 15.3 Learning, complexity and agency

In the previous section it became clear that innovation and learning are classically seen as two separate phenomena which are primarily concerned with the theoretical framework wherein these processes are embedded. This translates into an application in real-life that has repercussions on the way innovation processes are organized and learning is embedded within the organization.

In this paragraph CAS theory is proposed as an alternative approach to innovation and learning in an attempt to bridge the existing gap between these two processes. First of all the main concepts of CAS theory are introduced, to be followed by a conceptual model in which all elements are brought together.

### 15.3.1 The theory of complex adaptive systems

Simply defined complex adaptive systems are composed of a diversity of agents that interact with each other, mutually affect each other and, in so doing, generate behavior for the system as a whole (Lewin and Regine, 1999, p.6). The patterns of behavior are not constant because when a system's environment changes, so does the behavior of the system as a whole. The system is thus constantly adapting to the conditions around it. Chris Langton, one of the members of SFI (Santa Fe Institute) provides a graphical representation of a CAS from the perspective of the agents and how they cause emergent properties of the system.

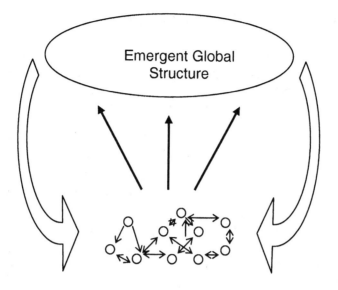

*Figure -28.* Chris Langton's view of emergence in CAS

The heart of complex adaptive systems, as understood by Holland (1998), is formed by agents – which can be individuals, teams or organizations – and their cognitive schemes. Agents are basically entities that show intentional and autonomous behavior; it is a definition stemming from the computer sciences where agents are comparable to a piece of software that is autonomous – in that sense it resembles humans. These agents have cognitive schemata, which enfold their mental models. An agent also has a number of properties that allow it to adapt. Axelrod and Cohen (1999) name a few of the properties of which the most important are: memory - in which lessons from the past are embedded - in combination with specific personal skills and competencies. The way they interact, the strategies they pursue, lead to non-linear, dynamic behavior, emergence and self-organization.

### 15.3.2    Dynamic and non-linear behavior

Linear behavior implies that input and output are causally related in a 1 to 1 relation. As a consequence the future can be predicted with the help of mathematical projections on the basis of experiences in the past. Linear behavior and causality are grounded on the theoretical assumption that systems work best when in equilibrium –one of the pillars of Newtonian theory. The idea of closed systems in equilibrium is one of the most influential ones in traditional economic theory and management thinking. It rests on the assumption of the simple sequence "equilibrium-change a variable-new equilibrium". Translated to management practice this means that in a typical strategy formulation a company will make an assessment of its current position, consider the changes that might occur and develop a point of view on how the industry is likely to change and thus affect the business strategy. This approach is based on three main assumptions: 1) that the industry structure is and can be known, 2) that the law of diminishing returns applies and 3) that firms are perfectly rational.

In a complex adaptive system linearity is not present which makes it highly dependent on the starting conditions; minor changes and variations can lead to highly unexpected and unpredicted effects that exponentially grow in magnitude over time. Lorenz coined the term 'butterfly" effect for this phenomenon as a description for behavior in complex systems. It suggests that a small change at one point in time can lead to larger changes later on, and these in turn can trigger even bigger changes, a dynamic of effects that escalate in time. Non-linear and dynamic behavior is related to each other. The dynamic behavior in a system is caused by the interaction between the individual elements that compose a system, but also between the individual and contextual elements that are part of the system. The context is not a given entity but is formed and transformed in the process of interaction and in that process the duality between object and subject is transcended. Underlying this dynamic behavior is a process of emergence and self-organization that makes a complex adaptive system evolves in an unpredictable way.

### 15.3.3    Emergence and Self-organization

Self-organization and emergence are closely connected. Holland (1998, p.13) defines emergence in the following way:

*"The program for studying emergence set forth here depends on reduction. Complicated systems are described in terms of interactions of simpler systems. I emphasize "interactions" because there is a common misconception about reduction: to understand the whole you analyze a process into atomic parts, and then study these parts in isolation. Such analysis works when the whole can be treated as the sum of the parts, but it does not work when the parts interact in less simple ways. When the parts interact in less simple ways (as when ants in a colony encounter each other) knowing the behaviors of the isolated parts leaves us a long way from understanding the whole. We have to study the interactions as well as the parts. Emergence occurs when the activities of the parts do not simply sum up to give activity of the whole. For emergence the whole is indeed more than the sum of its parts."*

So emergence looks at wholes and parts and especially at the interaction between the two. Holland compares emergence with a game of chess. The rules underlying the game are quite straightforward and simple, the outcome however depends on the people playing, their mental models, the strategies they pursue in response to the strategies chosen by each individual player and how these strategies in turn affect their own and the other player's mental models. A game of chess shows how interactions feed back and forth on each other: players, strategies, mental models, and the course of the game. The process is not only hugely complex, but the outcome is also unpredictable: it emerges bottom-up.

Emergence and self-regulation are connected in the sense that the interaction underlying emergent phenomena tends to behave in a self-organizing way – it is not subject to rules imposed from above, but the rules emerge in the process of interaction and are, as such, self-organizing.

Holland (1995) was also one of the founding fathers of the theory of self-organization. According to him self-organizing theory is an attempt to understand how complicated rules or spatially complex systems with many interacting components produce complex, but organized and patterned, behaviors. Furthermore self-organization is viewed as the capacity of open and living systems to generate their own new forms from inner guidelines, rather than the imposition of form from the outside (Loye and Eisler, 1987). Amabile (1988) speaks about the difference between intrinsic and extrinsic motivation in this context. The former is an innate form of motivation that individuals have, while the latter is external to the individual. It is especially this innate form of motivation that drives people to excel in their performance – be it by being creative and coming up with new ideas, or be it by looking beyond the scope of the boundaries set by organizations and looking for new venues to do business.

According to Axelrod and Cohen (1999) and Holland (1998) self-organization is characterized by four elements:

1. *Aggregation* – In a nutshell aggregation means that the whole is more than the parts. Aggregation and emergence are linked with each other in the sense that aggregation is an emergent property. Non-linearity and aggregation are similarly linked, because the aggregation of disparate events can result in non-linear behavior.
2. *Diversity/Variety* – It is important that a complex system has a significant variety of individuals or agents. In an ecological or biological context, diversity refers to the number of species that inhabit a system. Diversity is a measure of a system's variety: the greater the diversity, the more it is fit.
3. *Flows* – Flows refer to the fact that systems consist of networks of interactions, comparable to the network of cells and neurons in our brain. The suggestion is that complex systems behave in a similar way.
4. *Attractors-* An attractor is a representation of the favored behavioral results of a system at a certain point in time. The attractor is not a force of attraction, nor a goal-oriented presence in the system, but it simply depicts where the system is headed based on the innate rules of motion in the system. It is a product of the system itself, an expression of its dynamics at a particular point in time.

Having explained the main mechanisms within CAS, it is now time to revert to the main topic of this chapter, namely learning in innovation projects. The question is what CAS theory can add in order to bridge the existing gap between these two phenomena.

### 15.3.4    A complex adaptive perspective on innovation and learning

In this paragraph innovation, learning and CAS theory are merged together to create a theoretical framework, which is subsequently translated into a conceptual model. This model forms the basis for the simulation model that was developed and which primarily aims at illustrating what occurs when an innovation project is modelled as a CAS.

The general idea behind a CAS is that reality is holistic and must be examined as such. We saw earlier that two distinctions play an important role both in the domain of innovation and learning. One of them is the distinction at the individual level between the inner and outer world, the other distinction is at the organizational level between the structural and cultural aspects of an organizations. Wilber (2000) designed a model in which the multi-layered aspects of social reality become manifest and which form the basis for the conceptual model that links innovation with learning.

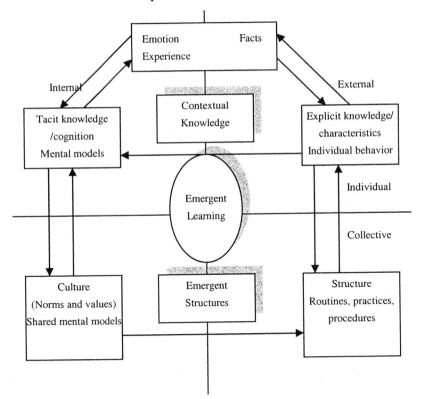

*Figure -29.* Innovation as emergent learning

The conceptual model forms a synthesis between the holistic model of Wilber and the learning model of Baets & Van der Linden. The model of Wilber makes a distinction between the interior and the exterior, and the individual and the collective. According to Wilber we can only really understand social phenomena if we take all dimensions into account. Baets and Van der Linden have translated these thoughts in their learning model, which not only makes us aware of the contextual nature of knowledge, but also of the fact that knowledge is constructed through mutual interaction. If we combine these thoughts and apply them to innovation projects and the underlying innovation process, what emerges is a conceptual model of innovation as an emergent learning process. The frames in the figure refer partly to the elements already identified in the model of Baets & Van der Linden: individual mental models, shared mental models and contextual knowledge. The picture is divided in four quadrants, to show that in principle there are different layers within an innovation process: there is the individualized emotional layer, which is not observable to an outsider; there is the overt behavioral layer; there is the collective layer which manifests itself in the culture of an organization, and finally there is the system layer, which is mainly concerned with structural and formal mechanisms which are observable. The left hand side of the figure has to do with the "inner" world and the right hand side with the "outer" world.

In this model two distinctions are important – the one between the internal and the external and the one between the individual and the collective. In the individual/external quadrant, we discern the individual with his or her specific characteristics, which – given the fact that there is also a distinction between the inner and the outer world – are composed of both non-observable cognitive aspects and overt behavioral aspects. These aspects mainly refer to tacit knowledge and emotions of the inner world and explicit knowledge and facts of the outer world. Innovation processes are influenced by both components, though the tendency is to focus only on external behavior. This external behavior is usually primarily a function of the lower right quadrant - the structural and formal organizational mechanisms at a collective level – and to a lesser extent a sole function of the inner world of an individual. An individual is expected to adapt to organizational mechanisms imposed on him or her.

Emotions and other non-observable aspects at the individual level are often the drivers of human action, in combination with the rules and routines laid down in organizations which are part of what we call the culture and structure of an organization. Organizational culture refers to the shared mental models that develop within companies or are already ingrained within a company. In principle individuals have to adapt to this shared model, since it often forms one of the criteria to hire a new employee: an employee has to "fit" within the organizational culture, or learn what the practices, symbols, and heroes are in order to become a member of the organization (Hofstede, 1988).

If we consider innovation as a learning process, it is the combination of the individual inner and outer world and the culture and structure within a company that in reality drives an innovation process. We already identified agents as the heart of CAS, which implies that in an innovation project it is not the activities that determine the process but the people with their specific characteristics and idiosyncrasies. In addition, we observed that interaction is the main mechanism within a CAS, implying that all elements of the model (cognition, behavior culture and structure) adapt and change under the influence of interaction. Structural and cultural mechanisms are then not imposed, but develop and change through interaction.

The lower right quadrant is where emergence and self-regulation mainly become manifest. Therefore we speak about dissipative temporary structures, since they depend on both the individual and the context wherein they emerge.

Having identified the main elements of the conceptual model, we have arrived at the final stages of the theoretical part of this chapter. The conceptual model frames the holistic approach in combination with the assumption that innovation projects show behavior that is similar to that of complex adaptive systems.

We started this chapter by expressing that the processes underlying innovation projects have inputs, outputs and a transformation process. We are primarily interested in the latter, which we identified as being a learning process which starts at the individual level. Following from the most fundamental assumption in most learning theories is the implication that there is something like an "objective" world out there and that it is the same for everyone. This implies that experiences that are similar are perceived and interpreted in the same way and eventually represented in a similar way in individual mental models. There is an assumed causal relation between experience, interpretation and representation. This same process applies to organizational learning. Complex systems manifest non-linear and dynamic behavior raising the question how this may affect the individual learning process. Within complex adaptive systems everything is relational. Stacey (2002) phrases it as follows: *"what conditions the experience is not just what is received from some presumably unchanging out there, but the interpretations we bring to bear on the experience. How we represent the experience, we symbolize it, and we metaphorize it, has as much influence on the experience itself, as the experience has on the representation, symbols, and metaphors. In essence a recursive relationship occurs between the experience and the representation that cannot be disengaged. Within this context, the causal flow from the object, to the experience, to interpretation breaks down. We cannot separate the experience from the representation, nor the representation from the experience"* (Stacey, 2002: pp.115-116). When we recognize the recursive relationship between experience and representation we are operating in the domain of non-linearity. In so doing we set up an environment that is continuously open and possibly expanding. When we become locked into a closed system in which we generalize from the past to come to conclusions about the future, we cannot break away from the systems we are generalizing about. Nor can we break away from the interpretations that we bring to bear on our experiences. Since our environment constantly changes we remain stuck and co-evolution cannot take place. This process is similar to the process we identified as structural inertia. In that case routines can be compared to the cognitive schemata of organization.

This is as far as the individual learning process is concerned. The distinction between cognition and behavior basically breaks down under the influence of CAS theory, suggesting that cognitive and behavioral processes are fruit of the same underlying mechanisms.

The other matter of interest - given the assumption that individual learning is a non-linear and dynamic process - is how organizational learning manifests itself. It is here that the phenomenon of emergence becomes relevant. Whereas mechanistic models assume that this process is linear, CAS theory suggests that this process is emergent. If we assume that learning is an emergent process, this suggests that the process starts at the individual level and evolves to a collective level through interaction. This process can not, however, be understood by studying individual learning processes, because of the effect of aggregation- the whole is more than the sum of the parts, *i.e.* shared mental models cannot be distilled from a simple sum of individual models.

Another matter of interest is modelling of the processes, since it is through models that companies manage innovation projects and regulate individual and group behavior. The emergent character of complex behavior not only affects the transformation process from individual to organizational learning; it also affects modelling of the process. We saw that models help us make sense of reality. Individuals develop models to reduce complexity and make sense of their surroundings. Organizations have models – shared models – partly for the same reasons; they help organizations make sense of external changes and to develop strategies accordingly. Models are, however, also used internally as a regulatory mechanism to streamline processes, manage projects and control decision-making. These models are usually developed top-down and are, as such, a reflection of the organizational structure of a company. A model that starts at the individual level is built bottom-up, while a model that starts at the organizational level is built top-down. In the next section an agent-based simulation is introduced, which was built bottom-up starting with the characteristics of agents. These characteristics were gathered via the analysis of a large number of innovation projects within the coffee & tea and household and body care divisions of Sara Lee/Douwe Egberts.

## 15.4 An agent-based simulation: creating an open learning environment

In order to run the agent-based simulation software called RePast was used. RePast stands for Recursive Porous Agent Simulator. In RePast the global behavior of a group of agents cannot be controlled directly. All one can do is set up the conditions that one assumes will make the behavior possible, then run the model and see what happens.

The agents in the model represent the people in innovation projects. 6 types of agents were distinguished
   A – R&D managers
   B – Marketing managers
   C – Project managers
   D - Senior managers

E – Technical developers
F – Production managers

The way the agents are modeled closely represents the way an innovation project is organized within SL/DE. The agent hierarchy is visualized as follows in the figure below.

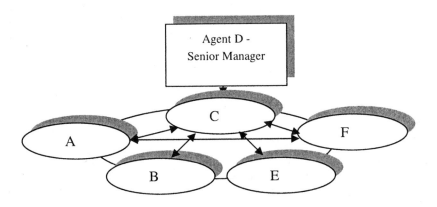

*Figure -30.* Agent hierarchy

In a complex system hierarchies work differently from in other systems. Hierarchies are transformable entities (Cilliers, 2001). In the hierarchy agent D has the highest position. The role of agent D – as it happens in real-life – is to exert control over the rest of the team by, for instance, imposing timelines, budgets, pressing the team to keep to deadlines. Agent C is the spider in the web, since he forms the liaison with the senior managers and the agents. The role of agent C is somewhat different than that of the other agents. Being in a central position in the network, agent C can influence agents A, B, E and F and can in turn be influenced by them. Agent D can influence the project leaders and *vice versa.* The choice has been made to channel the communication of agent D solely via the project manager, though the indirect influence of the senior manager on the rest of the agents can be experienced via the project manager.

### 15.4.1    The simulation- results and conclusions

In developing a simulation abstractions and simplifications of the real-life phenomenon have to be made. A model is more than anything an abstract representation of some aspects of social structures and processes. The simulation developed for this purpose was run under various conditions, with the aim of exploring what the behavior of the system is at an aggregate level following from individual actions. In the first instance some test-runs of the simulation were done in order to get a grasp on the model and gain some insights into the results that emerged from the interacting agents. The test runs were also aimed at identifying possible shortcomings in the model in order to make necessary adaptations. Some of these insights were:

- The initial values of the agents play an important role in the process. This suggests that the specific characteristics of agents seem to determine the behavior of agents and subsequently what the emergent behavior at system-level is.
- Each agent has his or her individual threshold to reach. The decision whether to exchange knowledge with another agent depends on the initial values of the agents and this in turn determines whether learning takes place. Given the fact that each agent has specific characteristics, likewise, each agent reaches his or her threshold on the basis of different criteria. The threshold is reached through interaction, where it depends on who an agent meets, whether learning takes place.
- Each group of agents reaches their thresholds on the basis of different criteria. Where marketing managers reach their group threshold when trust is high enough, R&D managers seemingly only reach their threshold as a group if trust and motivation is high enough.
- Time – represented by the tick counts - plays an important role in the process.
- The project manager and the senior manager play an important role in the process. If there are too many senior managers nothing happens with the project managers, in the sense that their values remain quite static. Similarly if the senior managers are not included in the process, learning in some cases takes place much faster. This suggests that given a certain team composition, the role of the senior manager gets in the way of emergent learning if too much control is exerted.

- The number of times an agent interacts with other agents in combination with the characteristics of the agents determines whether knowledge is exchanged and the speed at which that occurs.
- The number of agents within one category influences the process. When more agents of one type are included in the simulation, this leads to a greater influence of the group on the others.
- An important element of the model is to determine whether self-organization takes place. In the model it was assumed that self-organization can only take place if a senior manager loosens his level of control to the extent that they will withdraw from the interaction process – the team is left to make its own decisions. They, so to speak, withdraw from the process to leave room for self-organization. Graphically this is visualized by the senior-managers withdrawing to their offices (Manager Region) and remaining there. In the long term this occurred – senior managers then loosened their level of control depending on the level of trust for the project manager.
- When senior managers withdraw from the interaction process and exert no control the agents may "fall back" in their values on trust, motivation or orderliness and the senior managers then intervene again in the process. This may suggest that some form of control is required.

In the initial runs it became clear that the initial settings of the model – parameters and initial values of the agents – played an important role in the unfolding of the process in addition to interaction patterns. Therefore an model was constructed in which the initial settings and parameters could be adapted and which also allowed us to trace the interactions between the agents.

The approach chosen to analyze and record the simulation was to develop several scenarios in which the parameters and the initial settings were changed. A total number of 3 scenarios were developed, with a number of variations in the initial scenario.

| *Scenario 1* | 1 Marketing Manager<br>1 R&D manager<br>1 Project Manager<br>3 Senior Managers<br>1 Technical Developer<br>1 Production Manager |
|---|---|
| *Scenario 1a* | The same as 1 except for senior managers who were not included |
| *Scenario 1b* | The same as 1 with high values on trust for all agents |
| *Scenario 1c* | The same as 1a with high values on trust |
| *Scenario 1d* | The same as 1 with lower values on Expertise A, B and C and Functional knowledge A, B and C (75 instead of 100) for respectively agents A, B and C. |
| *Scenario 1e* | The same as 1a with lower values on Expertise A, B and C and Functional knowledge A, B and C (75 instead of 100) for respectively agents A, B and C. |
| *Scenario 2* | 1 Marketing manager<br>3 Project managers<br>5 R&D<br>1 Senior manager<br>1 Production manager<br>1 Technical developer |
| *Scenario 2a* | The same as scenario 2, with high values on trust and motivation for all the agents |
| *Scenario 3* | 3 Marketing managers<br>3 R&D managers<br>2 Project managers<br>2 Senior managers<br>1 Production manager<br>1 Technical developer |
| *Scenario 3a* | The same as 3 with different initial values |

The choice for the scenarios was made for a number of reasons. The first scenario is a close representation of innovation projects within SL/DE. As we already said earlier the choice to vary team composition and initial values was made to determine their effect on the process. The second scenario includes a relatively large group of R&D managers. This was done to determine whether the larger influence they have, due to the fact that they outnumber the rest of the agents, affects the process. Within SL/DE the role of R&D in projects is important; which is the reason for this scenario. The third and last scenario aims to gain insight into the effect of the relatively stronger influence of marketing managers and R&D managers on the process.

## 15.5    Conclusions and practical implications

What we hoped to find out is what would occur if a group of people was gathered together, and were allowed to interact at random with each other like in a CAS? We expected that emergent learning underlies the process of innovation and were interested in finding out what the factors are which underlie this possible emergent learning behavior.

Analysis of several innovation projects within Sara lee/Douwe Egberts showed that there is a dilemma between the organizational structures wherein individual behavior is embedded and an individual wish to have control over events.

One of the main conclusions is that emergent learning did indeed take place but that it depends on the composition of a team and the characteristics of agents whether this takes place, and how fast this takes place. This suggests that team composition may be a critical success factor in determining the success of an innovation project in combination with the extent to which team members are motivated, trust each other, are orderly or not and are influenced either positively or negatively by external control. Team composition is, however, not the only important factor. It is the combination of team composition with the dissipative structures which compose a CAS that forms the key to understanding what the possible implications might be of modeling innovation projects like a CAS, instead of a sequence of events. In a CAS, order is not imposed from above as we said earlier, but structures emerge in the process of interaction. Henceforth they are dissipative. Structure in the model is primarily represented by the senior managers who exert control over the process. The simulation showed that at a certain point senior managers withdrew from the process, and left the group to self-organize. The evidence, however, is not conclusive suggesting that a balance has to be struck between an individual wish for autonomy and a need felt by senior management to exert control over human behavior.

The practical implications of the theoretical ideas presented in this chapter, and the findings from the simulation model, are expected to affect management of innovation projects in several ways:

*Manager' perception of reality* – We saw that the way innovation projects are managed follow from a view of reality that is predominantly rational-mechanistic. The complexity paradigm shows that reality is not static and linear, but complex, dynamic, non-linear and unpredictable. This requires a fundamental shift in the way managers perceive reality, a shift in their mental models.

*The concepts and parameters used by managers* - Besides a shift in mental models, managers will need to acquire a new vocabulary. Instead of speaking of objectives, targets and strategy, concepts like initial conditions, emergent behavior, fitness landscapes and dissipative structures become relevant. The metaphor of the organization as a machine will make way for the metaphor of an organization as a CAS.

*The role of the manager-* Managers usually act as a central authority in decision-making within a top-down chain of command. In CAS theory the emphasis is placed on self-organization and the distributed nature of the structure of a system. According to CAS theory, systems do not have centralized control mechanisms: these are adaptive and dynamic, not rigid an invariable. Consequently the notion of hierarchy is different in these systems. According to Cilliers (2001) the role of hierarchies is simplified in complex systems. Hierarchies are necessary; they only work in a different way. Cilliers argues that hierarchies should be seen as transformable entities, where transformation does not mean that hierarchies are to be destroyed, but that they should be shifted. This implies that authority may shift among people, depending on how the process evolves. This phenomenon will affect the role of the manager, towards a role in which a manager is more a facilitator in creating the right ambiance for self-organization and emergence to occur.

*The decision-making process* – Decision-making takes place at different levels, but we are primarily interested in decision-making within teams and between teams and senior management. In CAS decision-making is similarly distributed among the agents, in line with the role hierarchies play in such systems. In general decision-making processes should not be regulated by rigid and inflexible structures, since the appearance and reappearance of structures are themselves part of the process. Processes should therefore be flexible enough to allow for individual autonomy and creativity, and avoid the danger of structural inertia. Decision-making will be in relation to what the agents within the system feel is important, which implies that the path will not be fixed, but will evolve in the process without a predetermined outcome. Trust plays a crucial role in this process.

*Learning within and from projects*- In complex systems learning is not focused on the procedural aspects of the innovation process, but on the relational aspects. This has to do with the fact that in this case the heart of these systems is formed by people, instead of procedures and activities. This will affect learning in quite a fundamental way. First of all in the sense that learning is not merely a transfer mechanism and an outcome, but an integral part of the innovation process. Product development and learning basically cannot do without each other, since products can only be developed if knowledge is shared and learning takes place. In the long run this will result in people being able to look beyond the scope of their own knowledge area and expertise, thus creating the conditions for truly becoming a learning organization. In the second instance, learning will not only affect people, but also the structure wherein their behavior is embedded. Instead of this being imposed from above, it becomes part of the learning process. In that process the structures are created and transformed by the people themselves.

# 16. THE DYNAMICS OF LEARNING AND INNOVATION

Machiel Emmering

## 16.1    Introduction

Failure rates of product innovations are generally high. Therefore, companies may want to engage in systematic improvement efforts regarding innovative ability. This chapter considers ways to support people annex organizations to develop their ability to innovate.

A general form of support in the approach of any phenomenon is **knowledge** that matters to it. Knowledge can be seen as a mental source that predisposes prudent ways of dealing with a phenomenon, thereby requiring future spending to deal with it more cheaply: knowledge about a *proper* way to get along relieves the necessity of ad hoc deliberation upon and experimentation with *possible* ways to get along, which will usually require more resources (e.g. time, energy, money). This applies e.g. to appropriate action in the face of danger, or to the execution of a task such as innovation: knowing 'it' minimizes offers towards the desirable, and may be critical in achieving the desirable at all.

Langerak et al (2000) found that there is a strong relation between proficiency in product innovation and organizational success. This is an encouraging justification of the argument about the value of knowledge, but given the high failure rates, the general proficiency level seems far from enough – no wonder that the Marketing Science Institute has proclaimed product innovation to be a research domain of top priority (Hultink, 1998). However, this evocation comes at a time when the abundance of literature about the subject is already difficult to survey, so this suggests an impediment in established theory's supportive value for the practice of innovation. This impediment must be pinpointed, not only in order to avoid the same pitfalls, but also to identify clues for desirable support.

## 16.2    Assessment of existing theory of innovation

Against the background of a literature review that has been made, an abstracted account of what one finds when starting to read texts can sum up established theory as a *type* of knowledge that appears to be pursued. At the outset, one reads a text stating that 'X' is important for the practice of innovation, e.g. 'leadership'. Reading more texts, other issues of acclaimed importance appear. These could be anything, so now the reader 'knows' that apart from 'leadership', e.g. 'funding' and 'success factors x/y/z' matter. Having read innumerable texts, the findings become blurred; the many issues of apparent importance come in the most diverse forms, and pertain to the most diverse topics. Their mutual relation is mostly unclear, if they seem compatible and mutually consistent at all.

The ideas all appear as 'prescriptions of specific ideas that matter to the practice of innovation'. They stem from a traditional way of advancing knowledge; they present themselves as 'truthful' insights in innovation. However, although this may intuitively be appreciated at face value regarding an individual idea, it becomes more difficult to accept this claim when viewing a collection of them. One sees a highly dispersed amount of ideas, unordered amongst each other, partially incommensurable, partly inconsistent, and in a variety that leaves no other option but to consider them to be contingent, and therefore not necessarily 'mattering' at all. Even worse than these self-imposed problems of *theory* of innovation (apart from the problem of innovation), it appears that certain suppositions about reality that are implicit in this type of (advancing) knowledge are in disaccordance with the nature of the reality that the ideas aim to cover. This concerns at least the following issues.

- Theoretical ideas about innovation suggest clarity of the topics addressed, while many phenomena in social reality are of an elusive, conceptual nature. The ideas speak of leadership, structure, motivation, etc., as if these refer to clear-cut, ready-made parts of reality. However, while objects in physical reality can be observed, verifiably described,

measured, etc., the 'objects' in social reality are of a nature that makes a clear-cut, unambiguous approach inadequate.
- Theoretical ideas about innovation suggest their prior validity, while the reality concerned is new, and thus unprecedented as regards knowledge about it. The ideas suggest that the task of innovation can be partly determined (by the idea that is advanced), but it is precisely the non-standard and novel change of reality that characterizes the task.
- Theoretical ideas about innovation suggest their external relevance, while the reality of the innovator is characterized by highly specific, internal knowledge needs. The ideas suggest that they are 'answers' to 'the' problem / question of innovation, while ignoring that it is precisely the 'idiosyncratic question' that is the core difficulty of innovation.

The peculiarity that this assessment uncovers is that the ideas in established theory of innovation take too little regard of the nature of the reality that they intend to cover in several important respects. This drawback follows from the implicit reality suppositions hidden in the *type* of knowledge that is pursued annex conjectured. This calls for a closer examination of the established account of proper (ways to get to) knowledge, its limits, and a possible alternative, in particular with regard to innovation.

### Why do settled ideas about innovation fail to be 'knowledge' (what does it mean to 'know')?

Knowledge creation is about stabilizing conceptualizations of reality. De Zeeuw depicts it as follows[23].

---

[23] Personal conversation, 27 June 2003

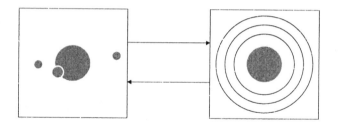

*Figure -31.* what Copernicus saw

The left half of this figure represents which (series of) visual stimuli, harboring reality, Copernicus sensed. The right half represents Copernicus' impressions of the fixed order between these sensations, and thereby the fixed order of the behavior of the phenomenon that was experienced. The stimuli pertain to what was *sensed*: different positions of celestial bodies (this is what Copernicus *saw*). The impression pertains to what was *conceptualized*: invariant patterns of movement of celestial bodies (this is what **Copernicus** saw). This picture distinguishes between a reality that can be *sensed* to some extent, and an actor that *makes sense* to some extent, in the form of stabilizations of impressions (of e.g. components, properties, or behaviors).

In this way, knowledge pursuits are traditionally aimed at the crystallization of conceptualizations that retain their adequate correspondence with the reality that they intend to cover (while reality keeps behaving 'conform' the conceptualizations). The traditional i.e. the established scientific method that has been developed to that end is focused on clarity and detail. Concomitant investigation operations are almost literally clear-cut, including isolation of a phenomenon (towards the discipline it 'belongs' to), decomposition, measurement and description of (e.g. the properties of) parts, and of their influence on others. By iterating such investigation actions on parts, components and previous states about phenomena have been fathomed in ever fuller and clearer detail, with the ideal of tracing back to ultimate building blocks and/or origins.

As attempts to fathom reality were primarily oriented to natural, physical phenomena, the traditional account improved and crystallized in the investigation of phenomena with 'reliability attributes' such as natural, physical, distinct, clear, stable, recurring, 'human independent', reducible, etc. In other words: it got specialized in investigating reality of a certain *type*: with stable order of composition and behavior. This focus predisposes two convictions: reality is already there ('given', it exists independently of mankind), and it 'is' in some way (stable and clear, it can in principle be known unambiguously). It is like an ordered space that can be explored by analysis, and it gets uncovered to a degree by investigation efforts. Therefore, implicit in this account of proper (ways to get to) knowledge is the orderly *nature* of the reality it intends to cover (stable, clear, unchanging). Evidently, not all reality is like that.

Reality contains features that do not fit into the set of characteristics around which the traditional methods were created. Important characteristics of the type of reality at which the traditional account is directed are stability, reducibility, and clarity. The opposites of those demarcate kinds of reality that established methods do not comfortably find their way out with. *Stability* refers to fixed order of composition and behavior (including interaction with other phenomena). Change and especially intentional, unprecedented or irregular change in all these stabilities distresses the possibilities of getting to know the phenomenon under study, for it appears not to remain the same phenomenon while studying it. So the traditional account has difficulty with cases of 'change', 'unpredictability', 'non linearity', and 'contingency'. *Reducibility* is a refinement of the stability feature, and refers to a phenomenon's susceptibility to being fathomed by retracing its components (and ultimately its elementary building blocks) and/or previous states (and ultimately its genesis). It may however be that the phenomenon's properties of interest cannot be carried back to its elements (because of properties of a different order), and/or to where exactly they came from (because the track of history can be erased). So the traditional account finds difficulty with cases of 'emergence' and 'irreversibility'. *Clarity,* as far as it pertains to phenomena themselves, refers to their properties of being clear: e.g. having clear (for instance physical) boundaries, and being describable in non-arguable terms. However, many phenomena are not so clearly discernible, which especially applies to reality of a conceptual nature, on which social reality thrives. So the traditional account has difficulty with cases of 'fuzziness' and 'social constructs'.

A different 'case of reality' where the traditional method runs short concerns the difference between creation and use of understanding. Getting to understand reality does not come by itself; it involves research efforts for which resources such as energy, time and money must be provided. Now, traditional research is mostly occupied with creating knowledge about phenomena, without being actually engaged in dealing with those phenomena. Knowledge is created for the sake of itself, or at least the requirement of its potential use is postponed. The *creation* and the *use* of understanding are disconnected. Because of this lifting of a usefulness obligation, constraints (of the resources that the activity takes) appear to play little part. On a much more daily basis, people *are* engaged in dealing with phenomena in which knowledge would come in helpful. If absent, it has to be created with regard to the specific situation. If feasible, a tailor-made research could be set up, the results of which could be acted upon. In this situation, although directly connected, there is still a separation between creation and use of understanding. The latitude of investigation efforts is tighter: while the research results should compensate the offers, constraints play a part. Gradually shifting, knowledge needs can become more idiosyncratic and more acute, thereby diminishing the possibility of separating the creation and use of understanding. When the limit of this latitude tends towards zero, the creation and the use of understanding coincide. In this situation, you have to distinguish between 'knowing = being able to (proceed)', or 'knowing = acting properly'. For instance: when in danger, if you do not know what to do, there is no time for (extensive, traditional) research of the situation; one has to implement more or less immediate hypothetical understanding in the form of action, which is at the same time the test for this understanding.

When understanding has to be created situationally, issues like time, the number of possible relevant issues in a situation, unclear relations between them, and limited accessibility of phenomena to investigation, are relevant constraints in creating situational understanding. So consideration of understanding as an *activity* (possibly hindered by 'multitude', 'connectedness', and 'intransparency') imposes practical limits on the applicability of the traditional account. The institute of science appears up till now to disregard this link between the creation and use of understanding, or let us say the latitude of investigation efforts in real situations of knowledge needs. This blind spot pertains pre-eminently to the whole domain of novel, intentional action.

It has been demonstrated that certain reality evades the possibilities of scrutinizing it by traditional investigation methods, let alone fathoming it fully. Especially the domain of innovation concerns reality with characteristics in the face of which the applicability of the traditional account is limited. The situation here is that 'understanding' is not aimed at *covering* reality, but at *advancing* and *realizing* it; one aims at bringing about conceptualized reality. This inversion of the relation between reality and understanding makes understanding of novel action situational by definition; the actor (and his domain of action) 'is' the situation to be understood. This developing reality to be understood and brought about only unfolds in the course of action, so the conceptualization latitude is limited by definition – the creation and the use of understanding are tightly connected. This becomes all the more relevant when the innovator is a dispersed group of differently oriented people – they all see and do their own things, while their different understandings must ultimately pertain to the same thing. This calls upon ways of developing harmonious understanding (while the specialized contributors should still understand their own thing). The inadequacy of the traditional account to support the creation of useful, common understanding makes the desirability of alternative ways of developing understanding in situations of limited knowability, or understanding of such situations perse, evident.

### Which alternative conceptualization account does offer a perspective on these kind of cases?

Trans-disciplinary recognition of 'cases' where the traditional account proved to be insufficiently supportive in the face of a certain reality to be understood has led to several initiatives in approaching the reality concerned differently. These could be grouped under the header of 'complexity'. This term is sometimes used in order to refer to an alternative account of obtaining understanding (compared to the traditional), and sometimes in order to refer to kinds of situations. Regarding the first type of use, 'complexity' could be defined as 'the study of roots and approaches of situations where reality does not lend itself to be covered by full knowledge'. Regarding the second type of use, 'complexity' would apply to 'situations where reality does not lend itself to be covered by full knowledge' (the second half of the definition). The traditional and the complexity account are not 'rivals'; they are both useful – in different situations. While the traditional account aims at progress by *dissolving* knowledge impediments, the complexity account is aimed at progress *despite* knowledge impediments. Therefore, the initiatives are aimed at developing conceptual equipment ('language') that offers better suited views on what, from the perspective of the traditional account, appears to be incomprehensible.

Because the complexity realm emerged from a number of different experiences and initiatives originating from different realms of reality, it hosts a number of novel views. Examples are chaos theory (origin: meteorology), cybernetics (origin: engineering), evolution (origin: biology), information theory (origin: thermodynamics), and network theory (origin: neurology). These conceptual realms are all interested in specific 'cases' of reality that the traditional account does not adequately help to understand (roots of knowledge impediments), and in approaching these differently. For example, chaos theory has an interest in unpredictability due to non-linear behavior and high sensitivity of developments to initial conditions, and focuses on patterns of order on other levels, so that the unpredictable development can be understood on those other levels (as dealt with in the earlier chapters of this book). Closely aligned is catastrophe theory, which has an interest in (asymmetric) discontinuity, and focuses on possibilities to represent a phenomenon's whole set of discontinuity transitions in an integrated conceptualization. Note that both do not (want to) specify *what* has characteristics of unpredictability or discontinuity. They offer the meta-disciplinary conceptual equipment by which all possible cases with these characteristics may be approached.

Because these languages are discipline and phenomenon neutral and enable one to describe highly diverging situations with concepts that have a wide range of possible referents, their value resides in their capability to *serve the users' utilization* of the concepts in the improvement of their approach of concrete phenomena, rather than that they, in a fixed manner, designate concrete but not necessarily useful things. Therefore, it is important to realize that complexity language does not *replace* terminology that has been advanced in order to refer to specific phenomena. They offer *abstract* terminology that can be employed in the most diverse situations, helpful as this may be in the recognition and approach of situations which are not fully comprehensible. Complexity concepts help to create understanding by shifting to more abstract levels of understanding. They are like *filters* (or ordering / interpretation moulds) that may help to adjust one's view on more concrete phenomena, so that this view is better accommodated to recognizing annex dealing with e.g. what is important or unclear regarding concrete phenomena. So complexity concepts are the more abstract categories that support an enhanced focus on the concrete phenomena that can be recognized in these categories. This is what complexity terms such as 'stability', 'discontinuity', and 'fuzziness' can be very useful for. In the last instance of a specific situation however, such terms always apply to real phenomena with more concrete terminology. This connection may never be lost from sight, for otherwise the complexity terminology will start drifting: it may then be used while the user is not really aware of what it refers to in more concrete terms of real phenomena. Hence, there are situations of knowledge impediments regarding real phenomena (with concrete terminology) which one does not really know what to do with (yet), and complexity terminology offers more or less invariant focus adjusters that help to recognize and deal with such situations. They are the mediating abstract concepts that help to illuminate more concrete concepts that one may be interested in, thereby facilitating a justifiable or even sensible disregard of other issues in one's situation. So to speak, complexity concepts help to focus or accelerate common sense; they mediate between scientific investigation and unprepared situational experiencing; they help to *direct* this experience.

Now that the complexity stance has been set out and it has been shown that the special theories offer conceptual equipment that help to face complex phenomena, *innovation* as the phenomenon of interest in this research can be re-addressed.

## Which other more particular ideas in complexity theory may support the case of innovation?

Established theory about innovation suggested (external) relevance of the ideas, thereby ignoring the fact that innovators have idiosyncratic knowledge needs and dispositions. It also suggested the (prior) validity of issues which would 'determine' successful innovation, thereby ignoring that the characteristic problem of innovation is that it concerns a new, non-standard change of reality, involving a new, non-standard assembly of a myriad of regulative issues by which the innovation is processed. Furthermore it suggested clarity of the ideas, thereby ignoring that many phenomena in social reality are of a partially unclear, conceptual nature. Regarding theory in general as a 'message', it is often unclear who the addressee is. The innovator is not an individual, but a collective of people who relate to each other in some interaction. Organizations can carry out complex tasks because of some division and reintegration of contributions. This means that 'the' knowledge required for bringing about the task does not reside in some central point; it is distributed over the whole network of contributors (who again have *their own* individual idiosyncratic situation, with idiosyncratic plans, tasks, and knowledge dispositions). So the theory largely ignores the nature of the innovator, and the fact that this innovator (itself – the group of distributed, specialized contributors working on an integral accomplishment) is in fact one of the more important issues to be understood.

These issues point out that innovators themselves – including their idiosyncratic knowledge dispositions – must be the pivot on which the whole quest for improved understanding of the specific situation hinges. They, themselves, form the situation that they subsequently do not fully understand, with a task that they do not fully understand up front. Because this applies to each new case of intending to bring about a new, non-standard change of reality (an innovation), and because different innovations may involve different people, the people must create useful understanding case by case. This understanding pertains to the regulation of everything that influences the realization of the innovation. Since this will involve a mass of different issues by a number of different people, the necessity of safeguarding cohesion becomes an explicit issue of concern. While creating understanding with regard to each innovation, the people involved may make use of ideas that have appeared to be useful earlier, and they may improve the ideas themselves. All in all, there is a necessity that the people involved in an innovation create, via communication, a common conceptualization of a project-specific decomposition of regulative affairs, while prohibiting the cohesion within this assembly of distributed contributors.

Established theory is hardly supportive regarding this necessity, and neither is the traditional account of creation of understanding on which such theories are based. A particular realm in the complexity account that does offer ideas towards dealing with this necessity is cybernetics.

## 16.3    Cybernetics

Cybernetics may be defined as the study of regulation. It offers concepts by which certain phenomena may be seen as 'systems', and it has a particular interest in looking at 'complex' systems, which means: systems that cannot be fully scrutinized. This research has considered how the language of cybernetics may help to illuminate when looking at the practice of innovation. As it is not the aim of this text to set out what cybernetics comprises, below we simply mention which of the ideas were important for the exploration.

An innovation project was, in the first place, conceptualized as a system, layered in a constellation of three levels, related to functions of different types. The levels, annex functions, that were distinguished pertained to:
1. what the innovation should accomplish in the bigger picture of the market,
2. what the organization / innovation team should accomplish in order to support and integrate the distributed specialists' contributions towards the intended integral innovation, and
3. what the disciplinary participants should accomplish to deliver proper contributions.

Regarding those levels, what appeared to be the more interesting issues to remember was explored. The idea was to elicit contributors' stories of a completed innovation, and to interpret those in categories of variables related to regulation. The following categories were regarded:
1. Desired effects / values (E); these pertain to the functions that must be maintained or brought about in order to perform in accordance with intentions.
2. Regulative elements (R); these pertain to practices or means that can carry things into effect.
3. Disturbances (D); these pertain to undesired influences.
4. Contextual characteristics (C); these pertain to the circumstances that clarify why specific issues within the former categories appeared to be relevant.

With these classes of distinctions at different levels, it should become possible to articulate a whole layered network of (un)desired effects or influences, practices that contribute to and/or prevent those, circumstances under which issues appear to be the case, and mutual influences between all these factors. To start working towards that end, the following has been done in practice.

This project was undertaken in cooperation with the knowledge management steering group of Sare Lee/DE, a large multinational with two main activities: coffee, tea and beverages; household and bodycare.

Several 'case analyses'of (Sara Lee/DE) innovation projects were conducted, in which the attempts were aimed at the reconstruction, articulation, and endorsement of collective, distributed experiences concerning issues that project participants considered worthwhile to remember. Several sources were used in order to collect an amount of impressions of experiences. These were cast in the general form 'X <and consequentially> Y', in which the terms could be recognized as being either a circumstance, a disturbing factor, a practice, or an issue that was influenced – all linking up with cybernetic concepts of regulation. These experiences were differentiated towards the strategic level of the innovation, the process level of managing the project, and the level of key disciplinary 'components' (e.g. marketing, R&D) – linking up with recursive levels of 'innovation' viewed as a complex system, as cybernetics enables one to see it. This resulted in a list of 'learnings' per project. The learnings retained as much as possible the terms from the information sources involved in the analyses, and the company was not informed about the cybernetic concepts which governed the representation of the experiences. The key participants were asked if they could subscribe the findings, and adaptations were made until they would. A more strategic committee (monitoring a larger knowledge management program of which these analyses were only one part) would subsequently give a 'definite' approval of the reports, so that the final analyses could bear the status of 'organizational learnings'. Underneath a (random) sample of the roughly 250 learnings that have been created is given for illustrative purpose.

### Lessons learned from various cases

### strategic

- As the *concept* was unclear, specifications of what exactly to develop kept drifting.

- As the *project definition* was unclear and constantly changing, there was a lack of clarity about the project's classification in the innovation portfolio, which implicitly affected criteria for strategic assessment of the project's results. More generally, the large number of different 'general overviews' troubled a real general overview.
- The *concept* had to be *global*, but there were many *culturally different preferences* concerning product variations and taste profiles, which troubled elaboration of what the product should exactly be.
- The market was loaded with *competitors' equivalents*, of which SL/DE was not fully aware. Once noticing this, an urgent need for distinctiveness was sensed. This meant, in practice, development of a *niche product*, with a *limited potential*.
- There was an intrinsic tension between the project's strategic role and assessment criteria. As the Board of Management was committed to highly optimistic *volume projections*, expectations were too high up front. And despite the fact that this project was primarily meant to be an image builder rather than a money-maker, it was terminated because of low volumes.
- process
- As the project itself was unclear, it was difficult to list *required expertise*.
- As the *team composition* initially did not include Inventory, Production, and Finance, this expertise was involved too late, causing delay, re-doing work, and loss of cohesion.
- As no *regular meetings* were planned, communication was considered to be poor.
- As *timings* for the concept, the pack and the formula were not always compatible; they manifested unclear priorities, weak co-ordination, and accomplished facts of delay.
- As the *team changed* many times, the project was slowed down, and it led to problems with dedication and co-ordination.
- As *initial investment* in the line was low, the *capacity* limit of the *production* line was far lower than what a world brand requires.
- *Volumes* were structurally underestimated, causing heavy deviations with real demand, thus making production planning impossible, as it leads to establishing a production line with capacity that is most likely insufficient, but which cannot easily be extended.

- There were a lot of *team changes*, and individual responsibilities were initially not very clear. This had a negative effect on quality of dedication and speed of the project.
- There was *no hand-over* in the case of a team change; this resulted in lack of commitment to decisions already taken, and reinventing the wheel by successors.
- As the time frame was the team's proposal, it was very committed to it.
- The *project organization* and more in particular *responsibilities* were unclear to 50% of the members (central evaluation document), resulting in slow and troublesome progress, obscured priorities and sub-optimal commitment.
- Hierarchical *decision-making* took a long time, on the account of implementation.
- implementation
- As team members tested the product *personally* as consumers, they had immediate insight into its performance, and were more committed to improvement efforts.
- Lack of clarity about a patent pertaining to either the use of some ingredient or the claim about the alleged advantage of that ingredient meant that it was unclear for some time if this imposed a production or a marketing constraint.
- The engineering specification did not mention the requirement of chilled

## 16.4     How can these outcomes be elaborated?

The learnings as they have been created within this research are not meant to be 'final products'; they are rather the raw material for further possibilities of interpretation and representation, which lie in the design of the learnings. Additionally they provide initial content to fill an external repository. Furthermore, some suggestions for the development of such a repository are given.

## 16.5     Options for elaboration

A first, primitive way to use the learnings is to provide distinctions of possible attributes of items of e.g. regulative practices, which people can use as checklists which help to improve the quality of the issues to be accounted for. This option only needs the learnings on the level of the sentences that were created. The attributes are derived from the reported quality problems that appeared to be of relevance in certain learnings, so that people are warned about what they should remeber (e.g. when it appeared that the 'concept' had to be 'global', while the markets concerning the particular product are strongly local). It is also possible to list potential characteristics, and link them (e.g. with hypertext) to learnings to remember when something has this or that characteristic (e.g. when a concept is 'hybrid', special attention should be given to learnings regarding 'in-store location' and to 'clarity of the market proposition'). Furthermore, the quality problems that appeared could also be reformulated positively, in order to come to proper characteristics of regulative practices (e.g. when it appeared that a team line-up was incomplete, the proper characteristic of a team assembly is that it is 'complete'). A possible checklist of attributes is the following.

### 16.5.1   Checklist of attributes

| Concept | Project objectives |
|---|---|
| • Difficult | • Unclear |
| • Unclear | • Neglected |
| • Global (in strongly local markets) | • Changing |
| | • Too broad |
| • Hybrid | • Trivial |
| • Innovative | |
| **Product specifications** | **Team organization** |
| • Not documented | • No clear Project Manager |
| • Unclear | • Unclear |
| • No 'negatives' | • Changing |
| • Conflicting | • Incomplete |

A more sophisticated way of re-using the learnings makes use of the cybernetic concepts that have governed the learnings as they have been drawn, pertaining to *issues (E, R, D, C)) and levels (strategic, process, operational) of regulation*. This could help one to formulate, for instance, what would be desirable effects in an innovation project. All too often, objectives solely relate to the product to be innovated, and consequently (at best) the product characteristics are what one manages for. However, if the innovation team is to deliver a superior performance, this team will have to be managed around certain desired effects pertaining to the team as well. That means that if, for instance, a project manager wants 'motivation' and 'clarity' in the team, these issues will have to be treated as *desired effects* that have to be made explicit and actively *managed* in order to be achieved. Subsequently people could start to think about *regulative practices* that contribute to motivation and clarity. Doing so, people can start to make their span of regulation wider and more sophisticated. A possible way to stimulate people's thought about such distinctions is to create and enrich a table that makes such distinctions explicit – like in the table below (the distinctions given here are random and unrelated; they merely mean to clarify that such an external repository can offer useful suggestions regarding what matters).

*Table -7. Table of regulative distinctions*

|  | **Strategic** | **Process** | **Operational** |
|---|---|---|---|
| **Desired effects** | Clear market proposition Distinctiveness Global product Innovative image | Project transparancy Interdisciplinay cohesion Resource discipline Motivation | Bacteriological stability Unambiguous test results Packaging usp Strong negotiation position |
| **Regulative practices** | Product specifications Project goals Board commitment Corporate | Limit work load List required expertise Regular meetings Delegate decisions | Harmonize test methods Patenting Simplify logistic routes Volume |

|  | **Strategic** | **Process** | **Operational** |
|---|---|---|---|
|  | funding |  | estimations |
| **Disturbances** | Drifting project | Team changes | Dual roles in |
|  | status | International | production |
|  | Competitor's | friction | Weak in-store |
|  | countermove | Projects' | location |
|  | Cultural diversity | conflicting | Partner's low |
|  | 'Political' target | priorities | interest |
|  | setting | Withdrawal | Changes of |
|  |  | corporate support | others' specs |
| **Context** | Competitive | International | Necessity of |
|  | market | cooperation | partnerships |
|  | Unfamiliar | Structural | Decentralized |
|  | market | assignment issues | choices |
|  | Decreasing | Involuntary | Customers' usage |
|  | consumption | "opco" | habits |
|  |  | participation |  |

Alternatively, one could strip the learnings, so that only the distinctions and the relations between them become explicit. This could help to make people aware of possible influences, and could also be used in an analysis of trajectories of effects, possibly revealing interesting loops. This could begin with an overview of 'stripped' learnings, such as in the following table.

*Table -8.* **Table of regulative relations**

| Many team changes | → | project slow down / dedication problems / co-ordination problems → delay |
|---|---|---|
| Unclear project-organization | → | weak project planning / suboptimal individual dedication |
| Unclear individual responsibilities | → | suboptimal dedication / slowdown of project |

| | | |
|---|---|---|
| Many team changes | $\rightarrow$ | project slow down / dedication problems / co-ordination problems $\rightarrow$ delay |
| No dedicated controller | $\rightarrow$ | slow investment decisions / superfluous efforts / Waste of means money control |
| Unclear and changing central financial support | $\rightarrow$ | diminished "opco's" ability and confidence to continue their efforts |
| Sub-optimal use of in-house expertise | $\rightarrow$ | problems that could have been foreseen |
| No risk analysis | $\rightarrow$ | no contingency plan $\rightarrow$ delay in case of any setback |
| Mismatch between marketing and R&D timing requirements | $\rightarrow$ | either low quality or time-wise inappropriate launch |
| Late and unclear estimations | $\rightarrow$ | unclear production requirements |
| No clarity about taste attributes | $\rightarrow$ | unclear what exactly to develop / unclear comparative taste profile |
| Complicated design | $\rightarrow$ | shelf instability / inefficiency |
| Different testing methods | $\rightarrow$ | varying test results / ambiguity about causes of method itself / marketing mix or cultural preferences |
| Unclear testing outcomes | $\rightarrow$ | no clear input for adaptations |

Another way of representing the learnings in a broader overview of the intricate relations between all the regulative issues would be to make graphs of such relations. A small section of the graph of all the learnings that have been created within this research could for instance be represented as follows.

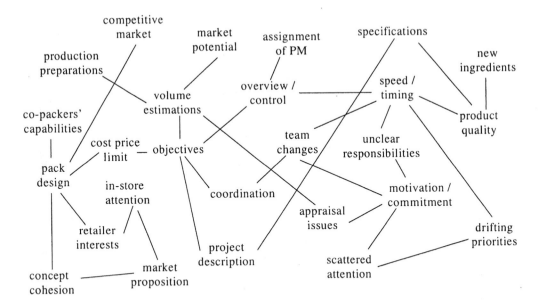

*Figure -32.* Graph of intricate regulation

Such a way of representing learnings can be made even more informative, for instance by combining it with the other options given earlier. Different colors or symbols could indicate whether something is a desired effect, a regulative practice, etc, and indicate what level of regulation it pertains to. Furthermore, possible attributes concerning all the issues could be attached, for instance via a hypertext link. Also, the lines between issues could be made thicker if the learnings appear to be more important or more persistent in different projects. Particularly interesting regarding operational implementation of this kind of representation might be to make use of an automatic (semantic) search and link engine: a software device that selects, links and represents all the concepts that are related to a concept of one's choice that is centralized (a commercial product that can partially account for this suggestion is the 'Aquabrowser') (for details, see chapter 4). In that way, only the selected sections of the whole pool of concepts and relations are triggered. Such a focus becomes indispensable when graphs get larger, containing more concepts and more relations. One could then for instance centralize the desired effect 'motivation', and ask for all the related concepts in the categories 'regulative practices' (what contributes to motivation) and 'disturbances' (what does damage to motivation). Even more specifically one could focus on a particular systemic level of regulation (the strategic, project, or disciplinary level) regarding these issues, or ask for attributes regarding motivation that have been discerned earlier.

Would the practice of creating and reusing learnings become more or less standard, further ways of dealing with the outcomes become possible. One could, for instance, start to list which 'desired effects' ultimately contribute most to the key variable that the company is in the end primarily interested in: innovative success. This could help to pinpoint the relative importance of such effects, so as to discover what would be the more interesting issues to manage with enhanced attention. Similarly, one could list regarding a desired effect what the more influential regulative practices contributing to it seem to be. Or, again similarly, one could list the influences of disturbances on regulative practices and / or on desired effects, or of desired effects on each other, and so on. The scores of such relative influences increase every time an issue reappears in a similar way in a newly drawn learning. The scores could for instance be recorded with a representation as follows.

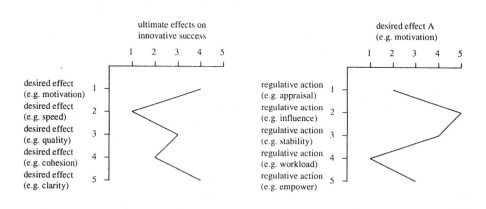

*Figure -33* Diagrams of relative influences

Another possibility to determine relative influences would be to let an artificial neural network (see chapter 4 for detail) process the findings of the continued practice of drawing learnings. Such a device could calculate relative influences of the relations between all the possible issues of regulation on each other in a dynamic way (with changing weights while new learnings are drawn), and discover unrecognized patterns of influences. The establishment of such relations with variable weights of importance between concepts could be depicted as follows.

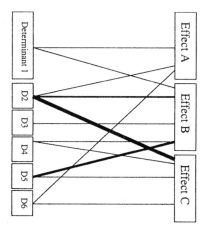

*Figure -34.* A neural net of influences

The findings of such consolidated results could be communicated in many ways. Regarding traditional forms, the more stable findings could be integrated in course material of, for instance, trainings in 'project management' or 'innovation'. Another traditional way would be to send around briefings with 'key principles' that have been distilled from the analyses. Regarding more novel, technology supported, ways of embedding practices and results of learning, several applications that offer people the possibility to stimulate their thought might be developed, such as a semantic hypertext thought stimulator (containing a pool of possibly relevant distinctions, linked with their possibly relevant quality attributes, etc), which could be navigated by an automated search and link engine.

All in all, the learnings as they have been created in an ad hoc way within this research are potentially only the beginning of more advanced ways of interpreting and representing the findings. What would be the more interesting of the ways suggested above is a matter that falls outside the scope of this research – the suggestions merely serve as a demonstration of how the research findings can be further operationalized and elaborated towards very clear-cut practical tools that could be implemented in the standard practice of innovation. Regarding the suggestions themselves, it might well be commendable to embrace different options simultaneously, catering for differences in people's personal preferences of how their thinking might best be stimulated.

## 16.6    Conclusion

The essence of underlying research suggests that 'language' or 'conceptual equipment' can support people in their understanding and approach of the reality that they reside in, are a part of, and contribute to. Conceptual equipment that is advanced in order to go under the name of 'knowledge' traditionally aims to come to invariant, precise descriptions of reality. This kind of knowledge, in which a conceptualization is modeled and stabilized towards the reality that it aims to cover, can be successful in the approach of reality with certain characteristics (important ones of which are 'fixed', 'stable', 'clear' and 'reducible'). This traditional approach finds difficulty with a differently conceived reality however (where features may be 'changing', 'unstable', 'unclear', and 'irreducible'). This applies in particular to innovation. This situation concerns intentionally changed (created) reality, in which reality is modeled and stabilized towards a conceptualization that advances it. This reverse relation between conceptualization and reality compared to the traditional notion of knowledge appeals to a novel account of developing understanding. What appears to be needed here is not conceptual equipment that represents 'reality as it is' (because it is not – yet), but conceptual equipment that supports the variety and the quality of conceptualizations about 'what and how' regarding the creation of reality. It has been demonstrated how concepts from cybernetics can help to highlight potentially useful things pertaining to issues of regulation in a distributed network of contributors. These results could be preserved and built into an external memory, by which people and organizations may improve the quality of their innovation-specific ideas.

# 17. KNOWLEDGE MANAGEMENT AT AKZO NOBEL CAR REFINISHES R&D:IMPROVING KNOWLEDGE CREATION ABILITY

Stefan van Diessen and Robin Gommers

## 17.1 Introduction

Knowledge Management (*KM*) is a "hot item" in today's business environment and is often associated with a "bright business future". But what can knowledge management actually do to improve business success? What first comes to mind are questions like:

- What is knowledge?
- How does it relate to data and information?
- How is knowledge processed?
- What are key determinants in knowledge processing?
- Is knowledge processing manageable?
- Does it all come to: When is new knowledge created?

These are fundamental questions that need to be explored more thoroughly before it is wise to even think about knowledge management and what it can do (or can **not** do) in a business environment.

Beside exploration of these principal questions, it is also critical to realize that a knowledge management system's (*KMS*) main task is to transform, develop, assess, update, transfer, preserve and apply knowledge and data into actionable information [AF02]. What

follows from this is the notion that information can only become actionable through sense-making by the KMS-users themselves. What can actually assess or improve KMS-users' ability to create actionable information?

This immediately brings us to the core difference between first and second generation knowledge management. Basic thought behind the concept of first generation KM is the idea that technology offers the answers. The unspoken assumption behind this concept is the idea that valuable knowledge exists and that the only task is to capture, codify and share it. According to this view KM begins after the knowledge is produced. Therefore first generation KM does not emphasize knowledge production, but it focuses on knowledge integration [Elr03]. Within this framework it is assumed that information technology (solely) can provide solutions to KM [Koc02].

Second generation KM, closely linked to the research theme as covered in this chapter, tries to identify when and how **new** knowledge is created, governed by (personal and organizational) wants and needs, recognizing and preserving its organic nature.

## 17.2    The real life case

Based on this theme, the knowledge creation ability was thoroughly investigated in a real life R&D business environment: Akzo Nobel Car Refinishes. The research question as covered is:

What are key determinants in the way actionable information (=new knowledge) is created in the context of the Akzo Nobel Car Refinishes R&D community?

Akzo Nobel Car Refinishes (CR) is part of the Akzo Nobel Coatings group, which has a global leading position in almost all its businesses with operational bases in 60 countries and 30.000 employees [Akz03]. Being one of the global leaders in the CR coatings market, Akzo Nobel CR has gradually increased R&D efforts over the last few years. It is recognized that the BU's position has to be secured by continuously improving and innovating the product portfolio and associated processes.

Today, R&D or new product development (NPD) processes are being viewed as integrated processes that have to overcome many trade-offs [SR98], [DH00]. None of all associated factors in isolation can guarantee product development success. In order to make these trade-offs effectively, NPD is considered to be an end-to-end process that draws on many different disciplines within the organization. This results in the NPD end to end model which summarizes many of the forces that play a crucial role in the NPD process [DH00]. This NPD model consists of the "NPD funnel" as the concept screening and selection process, including all internal and external forces [MM02].

In many ways the R&D process is an innovation process, in which 'enlightening experiments' are performed [Bro03]. Innovation therefore is one of the central building blocks of R&D. Jacobs & Waalkens have identified that competition in a knowledge-based economy mainly is about capacity to innovate and learn [JW01]. For these reasons our study is focused on innovation, learning and the way knowledge is created. This is done by zooming in more closely on these processes and what drives them.

Again it can be stated that the context as investigated (Akzo Nobel Car Refinishes) is highly determinant in the question if, when and how new actionable information (or new knowledge) is created. In order to determine context specific key determinants in knowledge creation ability, an in depth literature study was performed, serving as a basis for the conceptual research model (see figure 35).

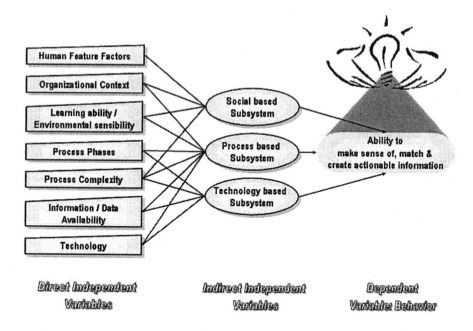

*Figure -35.* Conceptual research model: Knowledge Creation Ability

The direct independent variables as presented in Figure 35 all appear to have their effect on knowledge creation ability. Human feature factors are all personality and personal (background) issues important in knowledge processing behavior. A person's working style and role are determined by both environmental factors (organizational culture, nature and task requirements) and personality based preferences. The Myers-Briggs Type Indicator (MBTI), as a useful tool to understand a person's working style and role, is used in this research setup [CC03], [Dis00]. Other personal (context creating) features as investigated are: experience, demographic data, educational background and personal needs.

Interpreting organizational context in a knowledge processing framework brings us to issues like: sub-cultures, (co-)alignment, cross-functionality, bottom-up versus top-down approach and empowerment. Looking at these topics in the light of complexity theory in real-life innovation management [HB01], we can also state that:

- People are capable of organizing themselves;
- There is no need for tight control;
- People are adaptable;
- People change their patterns of behavior in such a way that they want some kind of order (i.e. a common goal) to arise.

These observations are closely linked to the concept of self organization, as Pyka and Wyndrum have described in the self organization process of innovation networks [PW00]. Self organization theory is based on the principles of thermodynamic openness, local interaction, non-linearity and emergence (see also chapters 1 and 3). These principles have to be taken into account, when looking at the organizational context and the implications for the R&D process. It is also shown that clarity of vision and management support are vital organizational context factors in learning and creation of knowledge [LA00].

As Lundvall called it the dawn of the Learning Economy, today we find ourselves in an economy in which the competitiveness of individuals, firms, and entire systems of innovation reflects their ability to learn [BP98]. Learning, in this context, does not just refer to the acquisition of information or access to sources of information, but to the development of new areas of competence and new skills, based on interaction with the environment [Bae02], [HH86], [Gie02]. Environmental sensibility and learning ability therefore are closely related in this context, as also in the questionnaire used in this research.

Again referring to complexity theory, 'openness' to the environment (environmental sensibility) is a prerequisite for the occurrence of dissipative structures [Hol96], [Hol98], [NP89]. Typically, these dissipative structures (in dynamical systems, at the edge of chaos) can provide improved innovation and creation capabilities. The ability to change behavior in relation to this environment and its dynamics (=learning ability) typically is promoted by the possibility and willingness to make mistakes. The experiential nature of R&D activities makes learning abilities even more important (in order to create new knowledge).

The importance of process phases (as the fourth direct independent variable) is stressed by Albors, who has linked (R&D-) process phases to the well known Nonaka & Takeuchi SECI learning cycle [Alb01], [NT95]. This process phase coupling is as follows:

1. Socialization        → Phase 1: Conceptualization
2. Externalization     → Phase 2: Selection of process variables
3. Combination         → Phase 3: Model formalization
4. Internalization     → Phase 4: Model learning

Prior research has shown that R&D units have significantly different knowledge flow characteristics in the area of knowledge sharing than more conventional knowledge sharing parties. R&D knowledge sharing can be characterized as reciprocal, tacit and nonstructural and is the result of a less specifiable organizational context [LF00]. This results in a relatively high process complexity in a R&D process environment, thus being a significant factor in the way a knowledge system is able to serve its R&D clients.

Another way to look at process complexity is by focusing on structural diversity. Cummings has shown that external knowledge sharing is more strongly associated with performance when work groups are more structurally diverse in terms of differences in geographic locations, functional assignments, reporting managers, and business units [Cum03]. His research also shows that the performance of work groups will improve because of this active exchange of knowledge through unique external sources. Structural diversity is closely related to the level of entropy: the more complex the process, the higher the entropy level. Complexity increases when structural diversity (or entropy) in one or more terms increases.

Information is one of the basic elements in learning and therefore innovating. Five direct independent variable concerns information & data availability. To understand the concept of information and data availability we must first understand **why** information is used.

Format, style, timeliness themselves will not lead to utilization of information [Ric02]. There are other factors that determine the utilization of information. They are enablers or perhaps even qualifiers to use information. It also seems that it is more important who provides the information than what the information actually is. The information source is a significant factor to consider. It is of great influence on the validation of information at first sight. Therefore the "why-question" needs to be taken into consideration when one defines an ideal knowledge management system [Ric02].

Knowing that data, knowledge and information are of major influence in all phases of the R&D process, we must understand that there is a wide variety of formats and media, being used in the delivery of information and they are obtained from many diverse locations. This can result in a number of problems that cannot be resolved simply by investing in Information Technology [CC97]. This would neglect aspects of social interactions and personal sense making in specific contextual situations.

In a setting of R&D and NPD (New Product Development), the environment is changing in several ways: Wider variety of products and product needs, rapid developments, high product performance and competitive costs. Research has shown that information is essential, especially within the early phases of the R&D process (the so called "fuzzy front end"). This is because in these early phases 80% of future costs are determined. The usefulness of specific information in this process is determined by numerous factors [CC97]. From these factors it becomes clear the independent variable "information & data availability" can be interpreted as the availability of useful information, data and knowledge.

The last variable, which is called "technologies & toolboxes", accounts for "artificial vehicles" which have the ability to support the creation of knowledge. Standards like XML, with the possibility to include meta-information, incorporated into ICT solutions enable smooth communication between the information stakeholders. Such technologies are clear examples of how they can support and facilitate the creation of new knowledge, by adding meta-tags to information and thus creating user based filtering and suggestion opportunities.

It is essential that people have the technology and resources they need at the right time and right place. Note that it is also important for people to be familiar with these tools and their functionalities.

An additional effect is that technology drives the type of social interaction a team uses. Different types of interactions are needed at different stages of the NPD process. Different types of technologies will facilitate different interactions, depending on the needs of the project team. One should consider what technology is useful, at what stage of the R&D process [LS98].

## 17.3    The research design

In order to investigate the variables as presented in the conceptual research model, a structured questionnaire was distributed among all Akzo Nobel CR employees, active in the NPD process.

Correctly answered questionnaires were collected from 82 respondents worldwide. The response-rate was 42%.

All (sub-) questions are linked to the different indirect variables and observed project success is added to integrate some kind of success score. Referring to the conceptual model, the questionnaire as used in this research in fact tries to identify three things:

1. Akzo Nobel CR R&D employee personal background;
2. In what way does this personal background influence "R&D behavior", specifically: when is knowledge created;
3. Can certain patterns or clusterings of independent variables (= user specific context) describe different information & knowledge behavior tactics including their success.

Connectionist models, or Artificial Neural Networks (ANNs), have been successfully applied in many different applications related to sensory perception in all different kinds of dynamical systems (see also chapter 4 for a general introduction). Much of the work involved in ANN applications has primarily involved the use of supervised models, networks with a "teacher" who indicates the desired output. Larger and more complex problems would be approachable with unsupervised learning algorithms [Plu91]. Typically, in the conceptual framework as used here, no desired output (named knowledge creation ability or probability) can be known a priori nor can be taught. This makes unsupervised ANN setup the most promising method for analysis of this conceptual model, by using questionnaire results as unsupervised training data. Various researchers have compared the predictive power of neural networks with that of conventional (statistical) techniques. All of this research concluded that ANNs perform better than the traditional techniques. Main reasons for this better performance are [VB94]:

- ANNs make no assumptions about underlying statistical distributions in the data;
- ANNs do not ignore past information;

The unsupervised ANN structure as used for questionnaire results analysis is a Self Organizing Map (SOM) type Kohonen network. This type of ANN develops a map of the feature space by organizing nodes which capture similar features in focused regions. These local connections are made stronger than connections to more distant parts of the feature space. This type of unsupervised ANN is commonly used in tasks where the feature environment can be very noisy [Sch02].

The assumption is made that the questions asked can be used as indicators in the classification of respondent patterns into groups with different knowledge creation abilities. This assumption is based on the link between the questions, the seven independent variables and the ability (or probability) to create actionable information (or new knowledge). Knowing that the questions as asked should be able to classify respondents in named groups, and assuming that these groups are present, you could compare this goal to that of a traditional discriminant analysis [VB94]. In this case a Kohonen SOM analysis with two output neurons could perform this classification (assuming that two groups are present). An interesting next step in the analysis could be to perform another Kohonen SOM analysis with a much larger output map, thus achieving a cluster-like analysis. This next step could identify how many characteristic groups (in a one dimensional map with a width larger than two) respondents could be clustered in, not knowing the number of groups a priori.

For the ANN calculations as performed, object oriented open source & Java-based neural network software has been used, named Joone (http://www.jooneworld.com). Multiple ANN setups were used to analyze the results. Also Principal Component Analysis (PCA) was performed, using a SOM Kohonen ANN, in this case with a transposed input matrix consisting of all respondents' answers to one question as different training cases.

For results interpretation reasons, when using completely different quantities or scales in the questions, normalization preprocessing was performed (on a scale from 0 to 1). The normalization issue is covered on a case-to-case basis, in order to prevent "data-smoothing". However, if you want to compare Kohonen synapse weights in the respondent clustering ANN setup (with answers per respondent as training cases), normalization is necessary [Plu91]. In case of PCA normalization was not necessary.

During the ANN training phase, all respondent answers are used as training input patterns. After having performed the network training phase, the network is fed with all respondent answers once again to collect the projections (0 or 1 when classifying into two groups) for all respondents (thus using the trained Kohonen synapse weights). Extracting the Kohonen synapse's weights after the Kohonen ANN training phase, teaches us which synapse connections are determining the knowledge creation ability classification to what extent. This means that it can be determined which answers (to which questions) are the most determinant in knowledge creation ability, or better: the difference in knowledge creation ability. By comparing Kohonen synapse weights for output neuron [1,1] with those for output neuron [1,2] the difference in importance of certain questions between the two groups can become clear. Actually, this can identify what exactly the difference in knowledge creation ability is based on.

We should keep in mind that neural networks with only two layers, like the Kohonen architecture (disregarding the linear input layer), can only be applied to linearly separable problems [Hea03]. The assumption made in this first step of the questionnaire results analysis therefore is that variables (questions) concerned are linearly separable.

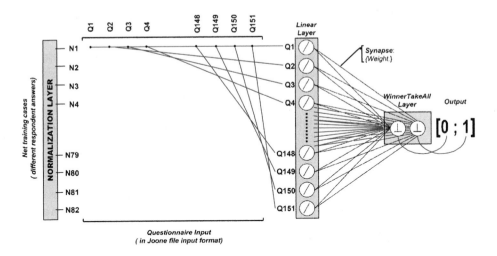

*Figure -36.* Kohonen ANN architecture as used in discriminant-like   analysis of questionnaire results

## 17.4     **Results**

Results concerning different elements of the conceptual model are interpreted and discussed at three different levels:

1. *Level one*     : respondent answers at individual (sub)question level, based on the direct independent variables;
2. *Level two*     : observation of the model as a whole
3. *Level three*   : content based comparison of different variable interdependencies and combinations, which take us at the level of the (hidden) independent variables (see also fig.17.1).

The level three discussions are triggered by the first and/or second level of the questionnaire results analysis.

## 17.4.1     Level One

Employees within the R&D community are more focused on thinking than on feeling. This could be a result of the technical/chemical context in which they operate. It can be concluded that employees share main characteristics resulting in five major MBTI-types. This shows that all individuals share common features that can be identified and used for future customization of knowledge management, because different personality types require different approaches, based on their different personality and working styles (Human Feature Factors).

It can be concluded that there are no signals of insufficient alignment (organizational context). It also remains open whether or not the identified main "goal-setting contribution drivers" can be used by Akzo Nobel to promote alignment further. In the field of organizational context it can also be concluded that the most important external networking sources (non-Akzo Nobel) are Suppliers and Educational Institutions / Universities. These networking sources promote cross-fertilization, share a common goal but look at research items in different perspectives.

Observing the most preferred learning scenarios (Learning Ability / Environmental Sensibility) it can be concluded that "non-static" learning modes are preferred over static learning modes like "instruction type learning" and "rote learning". Dynamic learning modes enhance sense making. Another conclusion can be found in the fact that an open view of the environment triggers you to learn, thus reaching the core of learning. Much of the learning is triggered by external sources, technical information being the most important one.

The results of analysis on process phases show that different process phases have a different local emphasis. Within up-stream activities (at the beginning of the NPD funnel) more "investigative type" people are present. This supports the conclusion on Human Feature Factors and the difference in personality types. Another major conclusion can be found in the fact that per NPD phase different information types are important. Alignment of information source types and position within the NPD funnel are therefore essential.

Looking at information and data availability it must be concluded that information and data availability are not yet optimized to their full extent, considering the average scores on the different criteria (quality, quantity, availability, relevance, accuracy and applicability). Knowing that information and data availability are essential for the creation of knowledge, it provides a basis for further investigation. The only positive outlier can be observed in the field of technical information. Besides being important, this is also a more day-to-day related information type within the R&D context.

In the field of Technology & Toolboxes it must be concluded that e-mail and other interactive communication tools are considered to be of high value by the respondents. The high-end dedicated tools and database applications do not perform sufficiently in serving knowledge clients in the same way as the "communication tools" do.

## 17.4.2    Level Two

It has become clear that in the observed context the use of different information types, including the valuation of different aspects of these information types, is the most important determinant in knowledge creation ability. Note that this conclusion can only necessarily be drawn concerning the variables investigated. Based on the neural network analysis of independent variables, respondents could be classified into two groups:

- Group A (40%); with a relatively low knowledge creation ability;
- Group B (60%); with a relatively high knowledge creation ability.

This statement is based on the following results:

1. Group B respondents are more likely to participate in more successful projects;
2. Group B respondents use more information (internal and external);
3. Group B respondents are more externally oriented (externally triggered learning);
4. Group B respondents experience more experimentation freedom;
5. Group B respondents discuss project success with their superiors more often;
6. Group B respondents experience better alignment with direct colleagues;
7. Group B respondents have a larger "project history".

Note that these key differences were found completely unsupervised (without bias) and are identified by the ANN analysis as the most determinant differences in knowledge creation ability between the two groups. This could be identified by extracting Kohonen synapse weights after the ANN training phase.

Another conclusion that can be justified is that two major "personal needs" patterns could be identified. A relationship is found between these personal need patterns and the ability to create knowledge.

### 17.4.3    Level Three

Firstly, it can be concluded that the homogeneity among specific questions and the way in which they are compiled into several principal components (based on PCA ANN analysis), provides a basis for the existence of several subsystems underlying the direct independent variables. The way people value learning scenarios and their personal needs are related closely, showing the existence of a social subsystem which was identified in the conceptual model a priori. As a result of this, the stimulation of the ability to make sense of, match and create actionable information can only be achieved when process phase, personal needs and learning scenarios, including their interactions, are considered.

Concerning preferred learning scenarios and styles, it can be concluded that this shows a homogeneous and similar pattern for all respondents. Secondly, it must be concluded that all the information types are unique and provide a valuable basis for the design of a technological subsystem. Also all underlying factors (like quantity and quality) are of great importance in the determination of the use and relevance of such a subsystem. As concluded earlier it is found that different process phases have a different local emphasis implication on the existence of a process based subsystem.

## 17.5    Knowledge creation ability

Returning to the basic research question, we can now state that aspects as identified by ANN analysis of questionnaire results are the most determinant ones in the ability to create (new knowledge) in the observed context. Based on these findings the implication for knowledge management system design and optimization is, in fact, twofold:

1. Knowledge management system, including its interfaces, should try to support the key determinants as named. This could help people make the transition from the low knowledge creation ability group (A) to the high knowledge creation ability group (B);
2. Knowing that these two groups do exist, the knowledge management system should be able to support both groups in a (different) way, based on their differences in key determining factors for knowledge creation ability.

How this twofold knowledge management system implication could eventually be accomplished is a whole new research area on its own. What we will try to do in the remainder of this chapter is to highlight the direction where solutions might be found.

Important general result that should be guiding in any further step is the fact that all (sub-) questions (thus indirect variables) as observed have some effect on knowledge creation ability. Keeping in mind that the interconnection (through the hidden subsystems) is this complex and in fact is a result fixed in time, it should imply that connectability and adaptability are definitely elements that any knowledge management system should incorporate.

## 17.6    Bridging the Gap: Complex Adaptive Knowledge Management

Based on the research as conducted, we could conclude that different settings of social, process and technology based subsystems somehow determine the knowledge creation ability. Associated knowledge processing, and specifically creation of actionable information (new knowledge) from data and existing knowledge, is the key element that a knowledge management system should support.

There appear to be a number of key determinants in this knowledge creation ability, but the overall findings have shown that all variables concerned, including their interactions, in some way do have their effect (more or less) on knowledge creation ability.

If it is now considered that these determinants all have their personally different (and changing) effect on the question whether knowledge **really** is created on a case to case basis, it becomes clear that heterogeneity and dynamics are key themes in trying to manage (or better: support) knowledge creation.

At this point it is appropriate to refer to complex adaptive system (CAS) theory again. In all traditional knowledge management activities, as also supported by Manville [Man99], the issue of classification and cataloging of knowledge remains the central challenge. However, it is extremely difficult (if not impossible) to create a classification scheme for any body of knowledge that matches everyone's personal mindset.

You could associate this categorization principle, as the basis for traditional knowledge management programs, with an "engineering mindset" [Man99]. When this engineering mindset is exchanged for the CAS principles of self-organization and emergence, classification of any knowledge form (e.g. by keywords) would by nature be imperfect and immediately outdated. Personal meanings (sense-making) of knowledge elements change from person to person and are different tomorrow from what they are today.

Looking at knowledge management in this light, the challenge is to simulate sense-making and classification as it is done by the ultimate CAS itself: the human mind. Semantic recognition (observing surroundings and context) in an unsupervised way should then be the preferred "categorization-tactics". As mentioned in Holland's Quasi-Homomorphism model, complex systems "invent" their environments through (rule-based) representations. In this way implicit understandings can be externalized and objectified [Hol96], [Hol98].

Based on elements of a knowledge management system as previously implemented by McKinsey, a proposed setup to integrate the CAS-elements could be as follows [Man99]: considering conventional knowledge management solutions as being large knowledge based readings on an intranet or website, four major problems arise. First of all, broad topics can often not be represented by one big website, which makes a breakdown into several units essential. Secondly, an associated problem is that knowledge about a specific topic within the business environment is often messy and overlapping (redundancy). Third is the problem of codifying implicit knowledge. The last theme is that it is impossible to build and maintain an overall classification scheme, as mentioned before.

The major challenge is to overcome these barriers by creating applicable solutions. Therefore, first of all, communities of practitioners (COPs) need to be identified (social subsystem). One could consider the information types deducted from presented analysis as main domains (see also chapter 7). The members of these communities are all people who have in any way a clear connection to these topics. This embodies both personal preferences and professional interest. This is the first step in re-designing the social subsystem into dedicated and empowered smaller COP-like subsystems.

When looking at the technology subsystem, it is essential to embrace a new paradigm, which is based on allowance of redundancy and web-technology (as an enabler). Web-technology could well be supported by semantic search engines and be optimized by genetic algorithms (for generation of connections). Embracing redundancy is contrary to current normalizing procedures within today's ICT. Often entities are "frozen", and therefore become static. Allowing redundancy enables the flexible use of technological tools to support self-organized organic-like structures. It must be stressed that this definitely needs a loosening of the ICT "standardization paradigm" within the different subsystems.

Continuous feedback from the social subsystems towards the classification scheme underlying the knowledge that is put into the knowledge management system is essential. User reports provide a "market-like" feedback mechanism based on self organization. The classification scheme grows as a result and is defined organically.

Some feasible limits on the underlying terms and maps may be desirable. One consideration could be the creation of a steering committee. In addition to such a "McKinsey" setup, such steering committee activities could (partly) be covered by neural network and/or genetic algorithm technology. The applicability of these technologies should be considered to avoid "human bias" in the steering committee function.

The main idea behind this setup, in order to create complex adaptive characteristics into the system, is that dedicated **social** groups (COPs) become responsible for specific parts of the whole system that concerns them directly. Connections of these subsystems and introduced "market forces" by user reports promote adaptation of the subsystems, based on user input and interaction between the subsystems themselves.

The first step in the Akzo Nobel CR context could be to take a look at current technologies & toolboxes (as used in the questionnaire analysis) and observe what should change to start implementing these tools in a (flexible) way as suggested in this chapter. This should be done in parallel with the implementation of COPs in order to make these tools "behave organically". When input and interaction with the specific sub-tools can be connected to the other ones, these sub-systems can "learn" from each other and adapt to a changing context. Isolated "islands" of distributed and non-connected knowledge pools would then become history.

in such a setup neural network technology could provide the self-organizing connections (organizing connection strengths by neural cooperation and competition), while genetic algorithms could organize the "birth" (and "death") of new connections. This could also provide the semantics for searching capabilities. These kinds of setups have recently been used in other contexts [AM02] and would be interesting to observe in a knowledge management system context. Suggested setups should then ideally be operational at three different levels: individual user level, COP level and R&D strategic level.

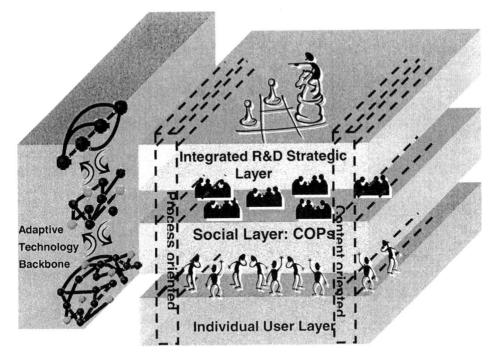

**Adaptation based on: User Reports ▶ Fuzzy Memberships**

*Figure -37.* Optimized Knowledge Management: Complex Adaptive Knowledge Processing in R&D

These three different levels should be "overarched" by an adaptive technology backbone incorporated into an intranet-like solution. This would basically consist of fuzzy based neural networks and genetic algorithm technologies thus incorporating the organic and adaptive nature.

Fuzzy membership functions from different individual users (based on user reports and system use) could construct effective COP compilations. The basic thinking behind this concept is that specific COPs acquire sufficient empowerment and responsibility for certain subtasks in the system. Translating the same mechanism to a higher level, concerning R&D process phase specific strategic issues, could complete the whole to operating as a coherent system. Keep in mind that complex adaptive characteristics across the different "layers" are covered by one "adaptive technology backbone", offering the right functionality to all the "layers".

Knowing that the most important context specific knowledge creation ability "improvers" are identified by the research as performed, the system should focus on these items to start with. It should be noticed that their importance will also change as time proceeds. The basic thinking behind proposed setups is that the system would then be able to adapt its behavior to its experiences.

# References

Arthur B, Positive Feedbacks in the Economy, Scientific American, Febr, pp 92-99, 1990.

Baets W, Organizational Learning and Knowledge Technologies in a Dynamic Environment, Kluwer Academic Publishers, 1998

Baets W, The Hybrid Business School: a four-part fugue for business education, management development, knowledge management and information technology, Inaugural address, June 1999

Baets W, Knowledge Management beyond the hypes, Kluwer Academic, forthcoming 2004(a)

Baets W, Une interprétation quantique des processus organisationnels d'innovation, mémoire HDR, IAE Aix-en-Provence, 2004

Baets W and Van der Linden G, The Hybrid Business School: Developing knowledge management through management learning, Prentice-Hall, 2000

Baets W and Van der Linden G, Virtual Corporate Universities: A matrix of knowledge and learning for the new digital dawn, Kluwer Academic, 2003

Baets W and Venugopal V, *An IT architecture to support organizational transformation*, in Galliers R and Baets W (eds), Information Technology and Organizational Transformation, Wiley, 1998

Cohen J and Stewart I, The Collapse of Chaos: Discovering Simplicity in a Complex World, 1994

Langton C, (ed), Artificial life, Santa Fe Institute in the Sciences of Complexity, Proceedings Vol 6, Addison-Wesley, 1989

Maturana H and Varela F, The tree of knowledge, The biological roots of human understanding, Scherz Verlag, 1984

Nicolis G and Prigogine I, Exploring Complexity, Freeman, 1989

Prigogine I and Stengers I, Entre le Temps et L'éternité, Fayard, 1988

Stewart I, Does God Play Dies: The mathematics of chaos, Blackwell, 1989

Swan J, Scarbrough H, Preston J, Knowledge Management – The next fad to forget people, Proceedings of the 7th European Conference on Information Systems, Copenhagen, 1999

Venugopal V and Baets W, An integrated intelligent support system for Organizational Learning – A conceptual framework, The Learning Organization, Fall 1995

Apostel L en Walry J, Hopeloos Gelukkig: Leven in de Post-modern tijd, Meulenhoff, 1997

Blommaert S, Niets is mogelijk, alles kan, Kritak, 1992

Cahoone L (Ed), From Modernism to Post-modernism: an Anthology, Blackwell, 1996

Feyerabend P, Against Method, Verso, 1975, 1993

Holden N, Cooper C and Carr J, Dealing with the new Russia, Wiley, 1998

Latour B, Science in Action, Harvard University Press, 1987

Le Moigne Jean Louis, Le constructivisme, EME, Editions Sociale Françaises, 1980

Le Moigne Jean Louis, La modélisation des systèmes complexes, Dunod, 1999

Marcuse H, De Eén-dimensionale Mens, Paul Brand, 1968 (vertaling)

McDermott J (Ed), The Philosophy of John Dewey, University of Chicago Press, 1973

Moten A R, Political Science: An Islamic Perspective, MacMillan Press, 1996

Van den Bersselaar V, Wetenschapsfilosofie in veelvoud, Coutinho, 1997

Wilber K, A Brief History of Everything, Gateway, 2000

Baets W and Van der Linden G, The Hybrid Business School: developing knowledge management through management learning, Prentice Hall, 2000

Baets W, Une interpretation quantique des processus organisationnels d'innovatoin, HDR thèse, IAE d'Aix en Provence, Université Paul Cezanne d'Aix-Marseille, 2004

Baets W, Complexity, Learning and Organisations : the quantum theory of business, Routledge, 2005

Baets, W. (1998), Organizational Learning and Knowledge Technologies in a Dynamic Environment. Kluwer Academic Publishers.

Collins, J. (2001), Good to Great: Why Some Companies Make the Leap... and Others Don't. Harper Collins.

Christodoulou, K. (1998), Modelling and simulation of variable structure systems: a way to handle complexity. In: Baets, W. (ed.) *Complexity and Management. A collection of essays, vol. 1.* World Scientific.

Economist Intelligence Unit (1997), Vision 2010. Designing tomorrow's organization. The Economist Intelligence Unit.

Hamel, G. (2002), Leading the Revolution: How to Thrive in Turbulent Times by Making Innovation a Way of Life. Plume.

Kim, D. (1993), The Link Between Individual and Organizational Learning. Sloan Management Review, Fall 1993.

Nonaka, I. And Takeuchi, H. (1995), The Knowledge-Creating Company: How Japanese Companies Create the Dynamics of Innovation. Oxford University Press.

Pirsig, R. (1974), Zen and the Art of Motorcycle Maintenance. Penguin Books.
Woodruffe, C. (1991), Competent by any other name. Personnel Management, September, pp. 30-33.

[AgIS 93] Agrawal, R., Imielinski, T., Swami, A., Mining Association Rules between Sets of Items in Large Databases, Proc. ACM SIGMOD 93 Int Conf. on Management of Data, 1993, pp. 207-216.

[BaRi 99] Baeza-Yates, R., Riberio-Neto, B., Modern Information Retrieval, Addison Wesley/ACM Press, 1999.

[Crof 93] Croft, W.B. Knowledge-Based and Statistical Approaches to Text Retrieval, IEEE Expert 8(2), 1993, pp.8-12.

[FPSU 99] Fayyad, U., Piatetsky-Shapiro, G., Smyth, P., Uthurusamy R., (eds) Advances in Knowledge Discovery and Data Mining. AAAI/The MIT Press, 1996.

[Fuhr 92] Fuhr, N., Probabilistic Models in Information Retrieval, The Computer Journal 35(3), 1992, pp. 243-255.

[Roch 71] Rocchio, J., Relevance Feedback in Information Retrieval, In: The Smart Retrieval System: Experiments in Automatic Document Processing, 1971, pp. 313-323.

Ahuja, M., Carley, K. (1998) Network Structure in Virtual Organizations. *Journal of Computer Mediated Communication*, 3(4).
Ali, I., Pascoe, C., Warne, L.(2002) 'Interactions of organizational culture and collaboration in working and learning'. *IEEE Journal Educational Technology & Society* 5(2).

APQC (2001) *Building and Sustaining Communities of Practice: Continuing Success in Knowledge Management.* American Productivity and Quality Center, Houston, TX.

Davenport, T., Prusak, L. (1998) *Working Knowledge: How organizations manage what they know*, Harvard Business School Press, 1998.

De Moor, A. (1999) *Empowering Communities: A Method for the Legitimate User-Driven Specification of Network Information Systems*. PhD Thesis, Tilburg University, The Netherlands.

Dignum, V., Dignum, F. (2003) 'The Knowledge Market: Agent-mediated Knowledge Sharing'. *Proceedings of CEEMAS*, LNAI 2691, Springer.

Domingue, J. B., Motta, E. (1999) 'A Knowledge-Based News Server Supporting Ontology-Driven Story Enrichment and Knowledge Retrieval'. *Proc. EKAW'99*.

Drucker, P. (1995), *Managing in a Time of Great Change*, Tuman Talley, New York.

Gongla, P., Rizzuto, C. (2001) 'Evolving Communities of Practice: IBM Global Services Experience'. *IBM Systems Journal* 40(4).

Gurteen, D. (1999) 'Creating a Knowledge Sharing Culture', *KM Magazine* 2(5).

Lesser, E., Storck J. (2001) 'Communities of practice and organizational performance'. *IBM Systems Journal* 40(4).

McDermott, R. (2000) 'Knowing in Community', *IHRIM Journal*, March.

Nickols, F. (2000) 'CoP Overview', http://www.kmadvantage.com/cop_articles.htm.

Preece, J. (2000) *Online Communities: Designing Usability, Supporting Sociability*. Wiley.

Talbott, S. (1995) *The Future Does Not Compute: Transcending the Machines in our Midst*. O'Reilly.

van Elst, L., Dignum, V., Abecker, A. (Eds.) (2003) *Agent-Mediated Knowledge Management*, LNAI, Springer, (to appear).

Vidgen R. (1997) Stakeholders, Soft Systems and Technology: Separation and Mediation in the Analysis of Information Systems Requirements. *Information Systems Journal* 7:21-26,.

Weigand, H., Dignum, V., Meyer, J-J., Dignum, F. (2003) 'Specification by refinement and agreement: designing agent interaction using landmarks and contracts'. *Engineering Societies in the Agents World III*, LNAI 2577, Springer.

Wenger, E. (1998) 'Communities of Practice: Learning as a Social System'. *Systems Thinker* 9(2-3).

Wenger, E., McDermott, R., Snyder, W. (2002) *Cultivating Communities of Practice.* Harvard Business School Press.

Alavi, M. & Leidner, D. (2001). "Technology-mediated Learning – A Call for Greater Depth and Breadth of Research." *Information Systems Research,* 12 (1), 1-10.

Alavi, M., Yoo, Y. & Vogel, D. (1997). Using Information Technology to Add Value to Management Education. *Academy of Management Journal,* 40: 1310-33.

Albrecht, W. & Sack, R. (2000). *Accounting Education: Charting the Course through a Perilous Future.* American Accounting Association.

Arbaugh, J. (2000). "Virtual Classroom Characteristics and Student Satisfaction in Internet-based MBA courses." *Journal of Management Education,* 24, 32-54.

Arbaugh, J. & Duray, R. (2002). "Technological and Structural Characteristics, Student Learning and Satisfaction with Web-based Courses: An Exploratory Study of 2 On-line MBA Programs." *Management Learning,* 33 (3), 331-347.

Baets, W. & Van der Linden, G. (2000). *The Hybrid Business School: Developing knowledge management through management learning.* Amsterdam: Prentice Hall.

Bailey, E & Cotlar, M. (1994). Teaching via the Internet. *Communication Education,* 43 (2): 184-93.

Becker, H. & Ravitz, J. (1999). The Influence of Computer and Internet Use on Teachers' Pedagogical Practices and Perceptions. *Journal of Research on Computing in Education,* 31(4).

Berger, N. (1999). Pioneering Experiences in Distance Learning: Lessons Learned. *Journal of Management Education,* 23: 684-90.

Britain, S. & Liber, O. (1999). *A Framework for Pedagogical Evaluation of Virtual Learning Environments.,* University of Wales, UK, http://www.jtap.ac.uk/reports/htm/jtap-041.html

Bovy, R. (1981). "Successful Instructional Methods: A Cognitive Information Processing Approach." *ECTJ,* 29 (4), Winter, 203-217.

Chee, Y. (2002). "Refocusing learning on pedagogy in a connected world." *On The Horizon,* 10 (4), 7-13.

Chong, V. (1997). "Student Performance and Computer Usage: A Synthesis of Two Different Perspectives." *Accounting Research Journal,* 10 (1), 90-97.

Collis, B. (1996). *Tele-learning in a digital world – the future of distance learning*. London: International Thomson Computer Press.

Collis, B. (1995) "Anticipating the impact of multimedia in education: Lessons from the literature." *Computers in Adult Education and Training*, 2 (2), 136-149.

Davis, F. (1989). Perceived Usefulness, Perceived Ease of Use and User Acceptance of Information Technology. *MIS Quarterly*, 13: 319-340.

Davis, F., Bagozzi, R. & Warshaw, P. (1989). User Acceptance of Computer Technology: A Comparison of Two Theoretical Models. *Management Science*, 35: 982-1003.

Dede, C. (1990). The Evolution of Distance Learning: Technology-mediated Interactive Learning. *Journal of Research on Computing in Education*, 22 (1): 247-264.

Dumont, R (1996). "Teaching and Learning in Cyberspace." *IEEE Transactions on Professional Communication*, 39 (4), 192-204.

Ellram, L. & Easton, L. (1999). "Purchasing Education on the Internet." *Journal of Supply Chain Management*, 35 (1), 11-19.

Frand, J. & Broesamle, W. (1996). "Technological Innovation at the Paradigm Shift in Management Education." *Selections*, 12 (3), 1-7.

Freeman, M. & Capper, J. (2000). "Obstacles and opportunities for technological innovation in business teaching and learning." *The International Journal of Management Education*, 1 (1), Autumn. UEA, UK.
http://www.business.ltsn.ac.uk/publications/Journal%20papers/Journal%201/freeman.pdf

Hara, N. & Kling, R. (2000). "Students' Distress with a Web-based Distance Education Course: An Ethnographic Study of Participants' Experiences." *Information, Communication and Society*, 3 (4), 557-579.

Harasim, L. (1990). On-line Education: An Environment for Collaboration and Intellectual Implification. In: L. Harasim (ed.), *On-line Education: Perspectives on a New Environment*. New York: Praeger.

Hiltz, S. (1995). Teaching in a Virtual Classroom. *International Journal of Educational Telecommunications*, 1 (2): 185-198.

Hiltz, S. (1994). *The Virtual Classroom*. Norwood, NJ: Ablex Publishing Corporation.

Hiltz, S. (1993). Correlates of Learning in a Virtual Classroom. *International Journal of Man-Machine Studies*, 39: 71-98.

Ives, B. & Jarvenpaa, S. (1996). "Will the Internet Revolutionize Business Education and Research?" *Sloan Management Review*, 37 (3), 33-41.

Jaffee, D. (2002). Virtual Transformation: Web-based Technology and Pedagogical Change. Presented at: *The Thirteenth International Conference on College Teaching and Learning.* April 2002, Jacksonville, Florida, USA.

Jarvenpaa, S., Knoll, K. & Leidner, D. (1998). "Is anybody out there? Antecedents of trust in global virtual teams." *Journal of MIS,* 14, 29-38.

Jonassen, D. (1996). *Computers in the classrooms: mindtools for critical thinking.* Columbus, OH: Prentice Hall.

Knoll, K. & Jarvenpaa, S. (1995). Learning to work in distributed global teams. *Proceedings of the 28th Hawaii Conference on Systems Sciences,* 3-6 January, 1995, vol. 4: 92-101.

Leidner, D. & Jarvenpaa, S. (1995). "The Use of Information Technology to Enhance Management School Education: A Theoretical View." *MIS Quarterly,* 19 (3), 265-292.

Lenzner, R. & Johnson, S. (1997). "Seeing Things as They Really Are." *Forbes Magazine* 159 (5), 122-129.

Levin, J., Kim, H. & Riel, M. (1990). "Analyzing Instructional Interactions on Electronic Message Networks." In: L. Harasim, (ed.), *Online Education: Perspectives on a New Environment,* pp. 185-214. New York: Praeger.

Mason, R. (1998). *Globalising Education: Trends and Applications.* London: Routledge.

Morrissey, C. (1997). *The Impact of Groupware on the Case Method in Management Education.* Ph.D., Claremont Graduate School, USA.

Nixon T. & Salmon G. (1995). *Spinning Your Web.* Paper presented to the Society for Research into Higher Education, UK.

Paquette, G. (1998). Virtual Learning Centers for XX1st century Organizations. In: F.Verdejo and G. Davies (eds.), *The Virtual Campus.* Gateshead, Tyne & Wear, UK: Athenaeum Press Ltd.

Piccoli, G., Ahmad, B. & Ives, B. (2001). Web-based virtual learning environments: A research framework and a preliminary assessment of effectiveness in basic IT skills training. *MIS Quarterly,* 24 (4): 401-426.

Preece, J. (2000). *Online Communities: Designing Usability, Supporting Sociability.* Chichester, UK: John Wiley & Sons.

Ravitz, J. (1997). An ISD model for building online communities: Furthering the dialogue. *Proceedings of the Annual Conference of the Association for Educational Communications and Technology.* Washington, D.C.: AECT, http://copernicus.bbn.com/Ravitz/isd_model.html

Renzi, S. & Klobas, J. (2002). "Developing Community In Online Distance Learning." *Proceedings of the Xth European Conference on Information Systems*, Gdansk, Poland, 1384-1393.

Renzi, S. & Klobas, J. (2000). First steps toward computer-supported collaborative learning in large classrooms. *Educational Technology & Society*, 3 (3): 317-328. http://ifets.ieee.org/periodical/vol_3_2000/d07.html

Robson, C. (1993). *Real World Research: A Resource for Social Scientists and Practitioner-Researchers*. London: Blackwell.

Romme, A.G. (2003). "Learning Outcomes of Microworlds for Management Education." *Management Learning*, 34 (1), 51-61. London: Sage Publications.

Salmon, G. (2000). "Computer-Mediated Conferencing for Management Learning at the Open University." *Management Learning*, 31 (4), 491-502. London: Sage Publications.

Salmon, G. & Giles, D. (1995). "Moderating Online." *Proceedings of the Online Educa Conference*, Berlin, 29-31 October.

Schank, R. (2001). Revolutionizing the traditional classroom course. *Communications of the ACM*, 44, 12: 21-4.

Schutte. J. (1997). *Virtual Teaching in Higher Education: The New Intellectual Superhighway or Just Another Traffic Jam?* California State University, Northridge, CA. http://www.csun.edu/sociology/virexp.htm

Shoffner, M., Jones, M. & Harmon, S. (2000). Implications of New and Emerging Technologies for Learning and Cognition. *The Journal of Electronic Publishing*, 6 (1). University of Michigan Press. http://www.press.umich.edu/jep/06-01/shoffner.html

Triandis, H. (1971) *Attitude and Attitude Change*. New York: John Wiley.

Turoff, M. (1989). "The Anatomy of a Computer Application Innovation: Computer Mediated Communications (CMC)." *Technological Forecasting and Social Change*, 36, 107-122.

Webster, J., & Hackley, P. (1997). Teaching Effectiveness in Technology-Mediated Distance Learning. *Academy of Management Review*, 40 (6):1282-1309.

Yin, R. (1993). *Applications* of *Case Study Research – Design and Methods*. Newbury Park, CA :Sage Publications.

Kessels, J. en P. Keursten (2001). Opleiden en Leren in een Kenniseconomie: Vormgeven van een corporate curriculum. In: J.W.M. Kessels & R.F. Poell (Red.). *Human Resource Development, Organiseren van leren.* Groningen, Samsom.

Bolhuis, S.M. en P.R-J. Simons (1999). *Leren en werken, opleiden en leren.* Deventer, Kluwer.

Davenport, J. and Davenport J.A. (1985). A chronology and analysis of the andragogy debate. *Adult Education Quarterly, 35,* 152-159.

Holton, E.F. 3e, R.A. Swanson and S.S. Naquin (2001). Andragogy in practice: Clarifying the andragogical model of adult learning. *Performance Improvement Quarterly, 14(1),* 118-143.

Kessels, J.W.M. (1999). ' Het verwerven van competenties: kennis als bekwaamheid'. *Opleiding & Ontwikkeling, 12,* 1-2,pp 7-11.

Kessels, J.W.M. (2001). Learning in organisations: a corporate curriculum for the knowledge economy. *FUTURES, 33,* p. 497-506.

Kessels, J. en P. Keursten (2001). Opleiden en Leren in een Kenniseconomie: Vormgeven van een corporate curriculum. In: J.W.M. Kessels & R.F. Poell (Red.). *Human Resource Development, Organiseren van leren.* Groningen, Samsom.

Knowles, M.S. (1953). *Informal Adult Education.* New York, Association Press.

Knowles, M.S., E.F. Holton and R.A. Swanson (1998). *The Adult Learner: The Definitive Classic in Adult Education and Human Resource Development.* (5th ed.). Houston: Gulf.

Krogt, van der F.J. (1995). *Leren in netwerken. Veelzijdig organiseren van leernetwerken met het oog op humaniteit en arbeidsrelevantie (proefschrift).* Utrecht: Lemma.

Kuijpers, M.A.C.T. (2003). *Loopbaanontwikkeling, onderzoek naar 'Competenties'(proefschrift).* Enschede: Twente University Press.

Kwakman, K. (2001). Leren van professional tijdens de beroepsuitoefening. In: J.W.M. Kessels & R.F. Poell (Red.), (2001). *Human Resource Development, organiseren van het leren.* Groningen, Samsom.

Marsick, V. (2001). Informal Strategic Learning in the Workplace. In: J. Streumer (Ed.), *Perspectives on Learning at the Workplace, Proceedings Second Conference on HRD Research and Practice Across Europe 2001, Supplement.* Enschede, University of Twente.

Marsick, V.J. and K. Watkins (1990). *Informal and incidental learning at the workplace.* London: Routledge.

Nonaka, I. (1994). 'A Dynamic Theory of Organization Knowledge Creation'. *Organization Science, 5, 1*, 14-37.

Nonaka, I. & Takeuchi, H. (1995). *De kenniscreërende onderneming. Hoe japanse bedrijven innovatieprocessen in gang zetten.* Oxford: University Press.

Onstenk, J. (2001). Ontwikkelen van bekwaamheden tijdens het werk. In: J.W.M. Kessels & R.F. Poell (Red.), (2001). *Human Resource Development, organiseren van het leren.* Groningen, Samsom.

Pakkert, M., Kuijpers, M. en Mulder M. (1999). De opleidingsmarkt wordt volwassen, onwikkelingen binnen de branche bedrijfsopleidingen. *Nederlands Tijdschrift voor bedrijfsopleidingen,* september 1999.

Poell, R.F. (1998). Organizing Work-related Learning Projects, A Network Approach (thesis). Nijmegen: Katholieke Universiteit Nijmegen.

Quinn, J.B.(1992). *Intelligent Enterprise: A Knowledge and Service Based Paradigm for Industry.* New York: The Free Press.

Senge, M. (1990). *The Fifth Discipline: The Art and Practice of the Learning Organization.* New York Doubleday.

Rondeel, M. en S. Wagenaar (2001). Van kennismanagement naar kennisproductiviteit: Een actueel overzicht van benaderingen in de literatuur. In: J.W.M. Kessels & R.F. Poell (Red.). *Human Resource Development, Organiseren van leren.* Groningen, Samsom.

Adams, R.S., Turns, J., Atman, C.J. (2003), "Educating effective engineering designers: the role of reflective practice", *Design Studies* 24, Elsevier Science Ltd, pp. 275-294

Armstrong, S (2001), *Engineering and Product Development Management: The Holistic Approach,* Cambridge University Press, Cambridge MA

Barton Cunningham, J. (1993), *Action Research and Organizational Development,* Praeger Publishers, London

Battles, B., Mark, D. and Ryan, C. (1996) "An open letter to CEOs: How otherwise good managers spend too much money on information technology", *The McKinsey Quarterly,* Number 3, pp. 116-127

Bekker, M.M., Long, J. (1998) "User Involvement in the Design of Human-Computer Interactions: Some Similarities and Differences between Design Approaches", In: McDonald, S., Waern, Y. and Cockton, G. (Eds.), *People and Computers XIV- Usability or Else!,* pp. 135 – 148

Beyer, H., Holtzblatt, K. (1998) *Contextual Design: Defining Customer-Centred Systems*, Morgan Kaufmann Publishers, Inc., San Francisco

Bourgeon, L. (2002), "Temporal Context of Organizational Learning in New Product Development Projects", *Creativity and Innovation Management*, Volume 11, Number 3, September 2002, pp.175-183

Bucciarelli, L.L. (2003), Designing and learning: a disjunction in contexts, *Design Studies*, Vol 24, No. 3, May 2003, pp. 295-311

Buchanan, D.A. (1991) 'Figure Ground Reversal in Systems Development and Implementation: From HCI to OSI', in Nurminen, M.I. and Weir, G.R.S. (1991), *Human Jobs and Computer Interfaces*, Elsevier Science Publishers BV (North-Holland)

Cooper, A. (1999), *The Inmates Are Running the Asylum*, SAMS Macmillan Computer Publishing, Indianapolis, p.119

Davenport, T. (1993), *Process Innovation: Reengineering Work through Information Technology*, Harvard Business School Press, Cambridge MA

Dixon, N. (1999) *The Organisational Learning Cycle: How we can learn collectively*, McGraw-Hill International Ltd. Developing Organisations Series, Maidenhead, UK

Dorst, K. (1997) *Describing Design: A comparison of paradigms*, PhD Dissertation, Technical University of Delft (Industrial Design)

Earthy, J. (1998), Usability Maturity Model: Human Centredness Scale, Project report, Lloyd's Register of Shipping, IE 2016 INUSE Deliverable D5.1.4s

Eden, C. and Huxham, C. (1999), "Action Research for the Study of Organizations" In: Clegg, S.R., Hardy, C., Studying Organizations: Theory and Method, Sage Publications, London; Ch. 10, pp. 272-288

Evers, M.L. (2000) "Dynamic knowledge management in intelligent, collaborative virtual environments", *Proceedings of the International ICSC Symposium on Interactive and Collaborative Computing* -- ICC/ISA 2000, Wollongong, NSW

Evers, M.L. (2001), "Human-centered design of intelligent assistance to support collaboration in virtual teams", *Proceedings of the Joint international conference on HCI*, September 2001, Lille, France.

Evers, M.L. (2002), "Mechanisms to support organizational learning: the integration of action learning tools into multidisciplinary design team practice", *Proceedings of the Third European Conference on Organizational Knowledge, Learning, and Capabilities* (OKLC), April 2002, ALBA, Athens, Greece

Evers, M.L. (2003), "Leren van Binnenuit: Kennis en Leren in Multidisciplinaire Ontwerpteams", presentation of research and accompanying workshop using the 'Design and Learning Methodology', SIGCHI.NL Lustrum, June 2003, Amersfoort

Forrester Research (2003), Benchmark North America February Data Overview: Technology Spending Plans, available online at http://www.forrester.com/ER/ Research/DataOverview/Summary/0,2740,16211,FF.html

Garvin, D. (2000), Learning in Action: A guide to putting the learning organization to work, Harvard Business School Press, Cambridge, MA

Gieskes, J. (2001), "Learning in product innovation processes: managerial action on improving learning behavior" PhD dissertation, Universiteit Twente, Enschede

Gill, K.S. (Ed.), (1996), *Human Machine Symbiosis, the foundations of human-centred design*, Springer-Verlag London Limited, London UK

Glass, R. L. (1998) Software Runaways : Lessons Learned from Massive Software Project Failures, Prentice-Hall.

Heygate, R. (1993), "Immoderate redesign", The McKinsey Quarterly, Number 1, pp. 73-87

Homan, T. (2001) Teamleren: Thoerie en Facilitatie, Academic Service, Schoonhoven [English: Team Learning: Theory and Facilitation]

Ishizaki, S. (2003) Improvisational Design: continuous, responsive digital communication, The MIT Press, Cambridge MA

KPMG Consulting (2000). *Knowledge management research report*. London: Atos KPMG Consulting. At: http://www.kpmgconsulting.co.uk/research/othermedia/wf_8519kmreport.pdf [Site visited 24th September 2002]

Laudon, K.C., Laudon, J.P. (2000): *Management Information Systems* (6th edition), Prentice Hall, Inc., Englewood Cliffs, New Jersey

Lawson, B., Bassanino, M., Phiri, M., Worthington, J. (2003), Intentions, practices and aspirations: Understanding learning in design, Design Studies: The International Journal for Design Research in Engineering, Architecture, Products and Systems, Elsevier Publishers, July 2003, pp. 327-339

Lei, L. (1994) *User Participation and the Success of Information System Development: An integrated model of User-Specialist Relationships*, No. 73, Tinbergen Institute Research Series, Erasmus Universiteit Rotterdam

Lloyd, P., Christiaans, H. (Eds.) (2001), *Designing in Context: Proceedings of Design Thinking and Research Symposium 5*, Delft University of Technology, 18-20 December 2001

Malholtra, Y. (1999), Knowledge Management for Organizational White-Waters: An Ecological Framework, Knowledge Management (UK), March 1999, pp. 18-21

Marquardt, M.J., & Revans, R. (1999) *Action Learning in Action: Transforming Problems and People for World-Class Organizational Learning*, Davies-Black Publishers, London

McNeice Filler, S. (2001), "Project Failures Spur Management Back to Basics" Billing World & OSS Today, November 2001, available online at http://www.smu-training.com/Schools/Dallas/PM/Industry_Commentary.htm

Megens, E. (2001), "Toepassen en organiseren van technologie", Management & Informatie, 2001/1, 23-29

Norman, D.A. (1998), 'Want Human-Centred Design? Reorganize the Company', Ch. 10, in The Invisible Computer: Why Good Products Can Fail, the Personal Computer Is So Complex, and Information Appliances Are the Solution, MIT Press, Cambridge MA

Olsen, G.R., Cutkosky, M., Tenenbaum, J.M., Gruber, T. R. (1994), Collaborative Engineering Based on Knowledge Sharing Agreements, Proc. of the 1994 ASME Database Symposium

Rosenbrock, H.H. (Ed.) (1989), 'Designing Human Centred Technology: A Cross Disciplinary Project', in *Computer Aided Manufacture*, Springer-Verlag London Limited, London

Rothwell, R. (1992), Developments Towards the Fifth Generation Model of Innovation. *Technology Analysis & Strategic Management*, 1-4, 73-74

Schwarz, R.M. (1994) The Skilled Facilitator: practical wisdom for developing effective groups, Jossey-Bass, Inc., San Francisco

Sole, D., Edmondson, A. (2002), "Bridging Knowledge Gaps: Learning in Geographically Dispersed Cross-Functional Development Teams", In: Choo, C.W. and Bontins, N. (Eds.), The strategic management of intellectual capital and organizational knowledge, Oxford University Press, Inc., London, pp. 587-605

Standish Research Paper (1995), Chaos Study, available on-line at http://www.standishgroup.com/chaos.html

Steiner, M.W., Gabriele, G.A., Swersey, B., Messler, R.W., & Foley, W. (2001), "Multidisciplinary Project-based Learning at Rensselaer: Team Advisement, Assessment and Change," Proceedings of NCIIA 5th National Conference, March 6-9, 2001

Stowell, F.A. (1995), Information systems provision: the contribution of soft systems methodology, McGraw-Hill International (UK) Ltd, Cambridge

Van Langen, P. (2001) "On the anatomy of design", *SIKS Design Research Seminar*, The Department of Artificial Intelligence, Faculty of Sciences, Vrije Universiteit Amsterdam, July 12th, 2001

Walz, D, Elam, J., Curtis, B. (1993), Inside a software design team: Knowledge acquisition, Sharing and Integration, *Communications of the ACM*, 36(10): 62-77

Weick, K.E., Roberts, K.H. (1993), 'Collective Mind in Organizations: Heedful Interrelating on Flight Decks'. In: *Administrative Science Quarterly*, 38, 1993, pp. 357-381.

Willcocks, L. and Griffiths, C. (1994) "Predicting Risk of Failure in Large-Scale Information Technology Projects", Technological Forecasting and Social Change, Volume 47, pp. 205-228

Wilson, S., Bekker, M.M., Johnson, H., & Johnson J. (1996) "Costs and Benefits of user involvement in design: practitioners' views", In: Sasse, M.A., Cunningham J., Winder, R.L. (Eds.) (1996): *People and Computers XI: Proceedings of HCI"96*, London, Springer, pp. 221-239

Zuber-Skerritt, O. (1997) "Introducing action learning and cultural change in a public sector organization", *ALAR Journal*, Vol. 2, No. 1, pp. 3-12

Adler, N.J. (1991) *International Dimensions of Organizational Behavior*, 2nd ed., Kent Publishing Company, Boston, MA (originally published in 1986).

Bachelard, G. (1934), *Le nouvel esprit scientifique*, PUF, Paris

Baets, W. (1998), *Organizational Learning and Knowledge Technologies in a Dynamic Environment*, Kluwer Academic Publishers, Boston

Baets, W. (2003), *Wie orde zaait zal chaos oogsten*, Van Gorcum, Assen

Benkirane, R., (2003) *La complexité, vertiges et promesses*, 18 histoires de sciences, Ed. Le Pommier, Paris

Berthoin-Antal, A. (1998) 'Le défi culturel de la mondialisation', *Sciences Humaines*, Hors série n.20, mars/avril, pp. 48-51

Browaeys, M-J., (2000) Achieving transcultural competence in management through cases studies, in Browaeys M-J & Trompenaars F. (Eds) , *Cases Studies on cultural Dilemmas: How to use transcultural competence for reconciling cultural dilemmas*, Nyenrode University Press, Breukelen d'Iribarne, P. (1986) Vers une gestion culturelle des entreprises, *Annales des mines - Gérer et comprendre*, No.4, pp.77-85

Dortier, J-F. (1998), *Les sciences humaines,* Sciences Humaines Editions, Paris

Genelot, D., (1998,) Manager dans la complexité, Réflexions à l'usage des dirigeants, 2nd ed., INSEP Éditions, Paris

Granier, F., (2001), Sociologies Pratiques, 2001, No.5

Harzing, A-W, and Sorge, A. ( 2003) ' The relative impact of country of origin and universal contingencies on internationationalization strategies and corporate control in multinational enterprises: Worldwide and European perspectives', *Organization Studies*, Vol.24, No2, pp.187-214

Hofstede, G. (1980) *Culture's consequences: International differences in Work Related Values*, Sage Publications, Beverly Hills C.A.

Koening, G., (1994) 'L'apprentissage organisationnel: repérage des lieux' *Revue française de gestion*, January-February, pp:76-83

Larrasquet, J-M, (1999) *Le Management à l'épreuve du complexe*, Vol II, L'Harmattan, Paris and Montréal

Laurent, A. (1983) 'The cultural diversity of Western conceptions of management' *International Studies of Management and Organization,* Vol.13 No1/2, pp.75-96

Le Moigne, J-L. (1990), Epistémologies constructivistes et sciences de l'organisation, in Martinet, A.C. (Ed.), *Epistémologies et sciences de gestion*, Economica, Paris, pp.81-140

Le Moigne, J-L. (1995) *La modélisation des systèmes complexes,* Dunod, Paris.
*Le Monde* (2003), 7 March

Lissack, M.R, (1999) 'Complexity : the science, its vocabulary and its relations to organizations', *Emergence*, Vol. 1 No.1, pp.110-126

Meschi, P-X, Roger, A. (1994)'Cultural context and Social effectiveness in International Joint Ventures', *Management International Review*, Vol.34 No.3, pp.197-215

Morin, E., (1990) *Science avec conscience*, Nouvelle Edition Sciences, Coll. Points, Editions du Seuil, Paris, originally published in 1982

Morin, E., (1986) *La Méthode. Tome 3 : La connaissance de la connaissance*, Editions du Seuil, Paris

Morin, E., (1990) *Introduction à la pensée complexe*, ESF éditeur, Paris

Morin, E., & Le Moigne, J-L.(1999), *L'intelligence de la complexité*, L'Harmattan, Paris and Montréal

Prigogine, I., (2000) ' Le futur est-il donné ?' in Ricciardelli, M., Urban, S.,

Nanopoulos, K., (Eds), *Mondialisation et sociétés multi-culturelles – L'incertain du futur*, PUF, Paris.

Richardson, K., and Cillers, P.(2001) 'Special Editors'Introduction: what is complexity science?", *Emergence*, Vol. 3 No.1, pp.5-23

Ruigrok,W. and Wagner,H. (2003) 'Internationalization and performance: An organizational learning perspective', *Management International Review*, Vol. 43 No.1, pp.63-83

Sackmann, S.A.(1997), "Introduction", in Sackmann, S.A.(Ed.), *Cultural Complexity in Organizations: Inherent contrasts and contradictions*, Sage Publications, Thousand Oaks, CA, pp.1-13

Schumacher, T. (1997), "West Coast Camelot: The rise and fall of an organizational culture", in Sackmann, S.A. (Ed.), *Cultural complexity in organizations*, Sage Publications, Thousand Oaks, pp.107-132

Søderberg A-M. and Holden, N. (2002) 'Rethinking Cross cultural management in a globalizing business world', *International Journal of Cross Cultural Management*, SAGE Publications, London

Thévenet, M. (1999) *La culture d'entreprise*, 3rd ed., Que sais-je ? PUF, Paris
Wang, C.L. and Ahmed, P.K. (2003) 'Organisational learning : a critical review', *The Learning Organisation*, Vol. 10 No.1 pp. 8-17

Wunenburger, J-J., (1990), *La raison contradictoire*, Albin Michel, Paris

Baets, W. R. J. (1998). Organizational learning and knowledge technologies in a dynamic environment. Dordrecht, Netherlands: Kluwer Academic.

Byron, D. K. & Heeman, P. A. (1997). Discourse marker use in task oriented spoken dialogue. Proceedings of the Fifth Biennial European Conference on Speech Communication and Technology (Eurospeech '97). University of Rhodes, Greece.

Ciborra, C.U. (1993). Teams, markets and systems. Business innovation and information technology. Cambridge, UK: Cambridge University Press.

Clark, H.H. (1996). Using Language. New York: Cambridge University Press.

Clark, H. H., and Brennan, S. E. (1991). Grounding in communication. In L.B. Resnick, J.M. Levine, & S.D. Teasley (Eds.). Perspectives on socially shared cognition. Washington: APA Books.

Davenport, T.H., & Prusak, L. (1998). Working knowledge. How organisations manage what they know. Boston, MA: Harvard Business School Press.

Ericsson, A. & Simon H. (1993). Protocol Analysis. Verbal Reports as Data. (2nd Ed.). Cambridge, MA: MIT Press.

Global Market Information Database: Market Research in the UK. (September,2002). Retrieved May 8, 2003, from http://www.euromonitor.com/gmidv1/TopicList.asp?ID=13410

Global Market Information Database: Market Research in the France. (September,2002). Retrieved May 8, 2003, from http://www.euromonitor.com/gmidv1/TopicList.asp?ID=13332

Hoffman Ponder, N. (2001). The theory of customer intimacy: Towards an understanding of relationship marketing in a professional service setting. Retrieved January 28, 2003, from http://wwwlib.umi.com/dissertations/preview_all/3027353.html

Keursten, R. A. & Bolte, J. J. (2003). Must of marketing tool. Onderzoek naar de geleverde en ontvangen kwaliteit van call centres in Nederland en de rol die call centres toebedeeld krijgen door bedrijven [Mandatory or marketing tool. Research into the provided and received quality of call centres in the Netherlands and the required role of call centres by organisations]. Universiteit Nyenrode, Breukelen, The Netherlands.

Lewis, D. K. (1969). Convention: A philosophical study. Cambridge, MA: Harvard University Press.

Reichheld, F. F. (1993). Loyalty-based management. Harvard Business Review, 71(2), 64-70.

Reichheld, F. F. (1996). The loyalty effect. The hidden force behind growth, profit and lasting value. Boston: Harvard Business School Press.

Sacks, H. (1995). Lectures on Conversation. Edited by G. Jefferson, Malden, NJ: Blackwell Publishers.

Schiffrin, D. (1987). Discourse Markers. New York: Cambridge University Press.

Schourup, L. (1999). Discourse markers. Lingua, 107, 227-265.

Tuomela,R. (2000). Cooperation. A philosophical study. Philosophical Studies Series, Dordrecht, Nederland: Kluwer Academic Publishers.

Winer, R. S. (2001), A Framework for Customer Relationship Management, California Management Review, 43

Amabile, M., 1988, A model of creativity and innovation in organisations, *Research in Organisational Behaviour*, Vol 10:123-167.

Anderson, P., 1999, Complexity theory and organization science. *Organization Science, 10*, 216-232.

Argyris, C., & Schon, D.A.,, 1978, *Organizational learning: a theory of action perspective.* Reading MA: Addison Wesley.

Axelrod, R., & Cohen, M.D., 1999, *Harnessing complexity. Organizational Implications of a Scientific Frontier.* New York: The Free Press.

Baets, W., 1998, *Organizational learning and knowledge technologies in a dynamic environment.* Dordrecht: Kluwer Academic Publishers.

Baets, W., 2000, *The Hybrid Business School: developing knowledge management through management learning,.* Prentice Hall

Brown, S. & Duguid, J., 1991, Organizational learning and communities of practice: towards a unified view on working, learning and innovation, *Organization science*, Vol. 2, Nr. 1, pp. 40-57.

Cilliers, P., 2001, Boundaries, hierarchies and networks in complex systems, International Journal of Innovation Management, Vol. 5(2):135-147.

Clippinger III, J.H.,1999, *The Biology of Business: Decoding the Natural Laws of Enterprise.* San Francisco: Jossey-Bass, Publishers.

Coleman, R. , 1999, What Enables Self-organising Behavior in Business. *Emergence, 1,* 33-48.

Coombs, S. J., Smith I. D., 1998, Designing a Self-Organized Conversational Learning Environment. *Educational Technology, ,* Vol 38, Nr 3, pp 17-28

Cooper, R.G., 1987, *Winning at new products.* London: Kogan Page.

Dodgson, M., (1993), Organisational learning: a review of some literatures, *Organisation Science*, Vol 14:375-394.

Fiol, C.M., Lyles, M.A., 1985, Organizational learning, *Academy of Management Review*, Vo. 10 (4), pp. 803-813.

Fonseca, J., 2002, *Complexity and innovation in organizations,* Routledge, London

Gieskes, J., 2001, *Learning in product innovation processes. Managerial action on improving learning behaviour,* Print Partners Ipskamp, Enschede.

Harkema S.J.M., forthcoming in March 2004, *Complexity and emergent learning in innovation projects,* Dissertation University Nyenrode, Breukelen.

Hofstede, G., 1980, *Culture´s consequences. International differences in work-related values,* Sage Publications, London.

Holland, J., 1998, *Emergence from Chaos to order,* Berkshire, Great Britain: Oxford University Press,

Hultink, E.J., 1997, Vier van de tien producten floppen, *Telecommagazine,* 47-48.

Kauffman, S.A., 1993, *The origin of order: self-organization and selection in evolution.* New York: Oxford University Press.

Kim, D.H., 1993, The link between individual and organizational learning, *Sloan Management review,* October, pp. 37-50.

Kolb, D.A., 1984, *Experiential learning: experience as the source of learning development,* Prentice Hall, Englewood Cliffs, New York.

Leroy, F. & Bernard R., 1997, Cognitive and behavioural dimensions of organizational learning in a merger: An empirical study. *Journal of Management Studies* 34: 871-894.

Lewin,A.Y. & Volberda, H.W., 1999, Prolegomena on Covolution: A framework for Research on Strategy and New Organizational Forms, *Organization Science,* Vol. 10, No. 5 pp. 519-534

Lewin, R., 1998, Complexity Theory and the Organisation: Beyond the Metaphor. *Complexity 3, 4,* 36-40.

Lewin, R & Regine, B., (1999), *The soul at work: unleashing the power of compleity for business success,* Orion Books, London.

Lissack,M.R., 2000, *Chaos and complexity-What does that have to do with management?* www.lissack.com/writings/chaos.htm

Loye, D. & Eisler, R., 1987, Chaos and transformation implications of non-equilibrium theory for social science and society, *Behavioural Science,* Vol 32:53-65.

McDermott, J. J., 1973, *The Philosophy of John Dewe.* Chicago: The Chicago University Press

Meeus, M, 2003, Innoveren en organiseren: over het verklaren van (on)verenigbare grootheden, Inauguratierede Universiteit Utrecht, Utrecht.

Morin, E., 1996, *Introduction à la pensée complexe*. Paris: ESF Editeurs

Nelson, R., & Winter, S., 1982, *An evolutionary theory of economic change*. Boston: Harvard Business Review Press.

Nicolini, D. & Meznar, M.B., 1995, The social construction of organisational learning. Conceptual and practical issues in the field, *Human Relations*, Vol 48(7):727-747.

Nonaka, I., & Takeuchi H., 1994, A dynamic theory of organisational knowledge creation, *Organisation Science*, Vol 5:14-37.

Nonaka, I., & Takeuchi H., 1995, *The knowledge creating company. How Japanese create the dynamics of economics*. Oxford: Oxford University Press.

Parsons, T., 1964, *The Social System,* London, Routledge & Kegan Paul.

Prigogine, I., 1984, *Order out of chaos: man's new dialogue with nature*, Free Press, New York.

Senge, P,, 1990, *The fifth discipline: the art and practice of the learning organisation*, Doubleday, New York.

Sherman, H., & Schultz, R.,, 1998, *Open boundaries: Creating business innovation through complexity*. Reading Massachusetts: Perseus Books.

Slappendel, C., 1996, Perspectives on innovation in organisations, *Organisation Studies*, Vol 17 (1): 107-129.

Stacey, R., 2001, *Complex responsive processes in organisations: learning and knowledge creation*, Routledge, New York.

Swan, J.; Scarbrough, H.; Hislop, D. 1999, Knowledge Management and innovation: netwroks and networking, *Journal of Knowledge Management*, Vol 3(4): 262-275.

Varela, F.J., 1991, *The embodied mind. Cognitive science and human experience*, Massachusetts, MIT Press.

Walker, R., 2003, *An investigation into virtual learner-centred solutions for competency based management education*, PhD dissertation University Nyenrode, Breukelen.

Weick, K.E., 1979, *The social psychology of organizing*, Reading MA: Addison Wesley.

Wheelwright, S., & Clark, K., 992, *Revolutionizing Product Development*. New York: The Free Press.

Wolfe, R.A., 1994, Organisational innovation: review, crituique and suggested research directions, *Journal of Management Studies,* Vol 31(3): 405-431.

Alberdi, E., Becher, J.C., Gilhooly, K., Hunter, J., Logie, R., Lyon, A., McIntosh, N., and Reiss, J. (2001). Expertise and the interpretation of computerized physiological data: implications for the design of computerized monitoring in neonatal intensive care. *International Journal of Human-Computer Studies*, 55, 191-216.

Alberdi, E. and Logie, R. (1998). Applying cognitive theories and methods to the design of computerised medical decision support. *Proceedings of the 20$^{th}$ Annual Conference of the Cognitive Science Society*, pp. 30-35. Mahwah: Lawrence Erlbaum.

Benysh, D.V., Koubek, R.J., and Calvez, V. (1993). A comparative review of knowledge structure measurement techniques for interface design. *International Journal of Human-Computer Interaction*, 5(3), 211-237.

Bevan, N. (2001). International standards for HCI and usability. *International Journal of Human-Computer Studies*, 55, 533-552.

Chipman, S.F., Schraagen, J.M., and Shalin, V.L. (2000). Cognitive Task Analysis: Introduction. In: Schraagen, J.M., S.F. Chipman, and V.L. Shalin (2000). *Cognitive Task Analysis*. Lawrence Erlbaum Associates, London.

Coiera, E. (1994). Question the assumptions. In P. Barahona and J.P. Christensen, (Eds.) *Knowledge and Decisions in Health Telematics*, pp. 67-72. Amsterdam: IOS Press.

Cooke, N.J. (1994). Varieties of knowledge elicitation techniques. *International Journal of Human-Computer Studies*, 41, 801-849.

Corbett-Clark, T. and Tarassenko, L. (1997). A principled framework and technique for rule extraction from multi-layer perceptrons. *Proceedings of the 5$^{th}$ IEE International Conference on Artificial Neural Networks*, Cambridge, 233-238.

Cunningham, S., Deere, S., Simon, A., Elton, R.A., and McIntosh, N. (1998). A randomised control trial of computerised physiological trend monitoring in an intensive care unit. *Critical Care Medicine*, **26**, 2053-2060.

Dubois, D., and Shalin, V.L. (1995). Adapting cognitive methods to real-world objectives:An application to job knowledge testing. In P.D. Nichols, S.F. Chipman, and R.L. Brennan (Eds.), *Cognitively diagnostic assessment* (pp. 189-220). Hillsdale, NJ: Lawrence Erlbaum Associates.

Edworthy, J. and Stanton, N. (1995). A user-centred approach to the design and evaluation of auditory warning signals: 1. Methodology. *Ergonomics*, 38, 2262-2280.

Egan, D.E., Remde, J.R., Gomez, L.M., Landauer, T.K., Eberhardt, J. and Lochbaum, C.D. (1990). Formative design-evaluation of SuperBook. *ACM Transactions on Information Systems*, 7, 30-57.

Fayyad, U.M., Piatetsky-Shapiro, G., Smyth, P., and Uthurusamy, R. (Eds.) (1996). *Advances in Knowledge Discovery and Data Mining*. Cambridge, Massachusetts: MIT Press.

Gray, W.D., John, B.E., and Atwood, M.E. (1993). Project Ernestine: validating a GOMS analysis for predicting and explaining real-world task performance. *Human-Computer Interaction*, **8**, 237-309.

Green, C.A., Gilhooly, K.J., Logie, R.H., and Ross, D.G. (1991). Human factors and computerisation in intensive care units: a review. *International Journal of Clinical Monitoring and Computing*, **8**, 95-100.

Hall, E.P., Gott, S.P., and Pokorny, R.A. (1995). *A procedural guide to cognitive task analysis: The PARI methodology* (Technical Report AL/HR-TR-1995-0108). Brooks Air Force Base, TX: AFMC.

Hayes-Roth, F., Waterman, D.A. and Lenat, D.B. (Eds.) (1983). *Building expert systems*, Reading, MA: Addison-Wesley.

ISO (1998). *ISO 9241-11: Guidance on Usability*. Geneva: International Standards Organization.

Jonassen, D.H., Tessmer, M., and Hannum, W.H. (1999). *Task Analysis Methods for Instructional Design*. Mahwah, NJ: Lawrence Erlbaum Associates.

Kirakowski, J. (1996). The Software Usability Measurement Inventory: background and usage. In: Jordan, P.W., Thomas, B., Weerdmeester, B.A. and McClelland, I.L. (Eds.) *Usability Evaluation in Industry*, 169-178. London: Taylor and Francis.

Kohavi, R. and Provost, F. (2001). Applications of Data Mining to Electronic Commerce. *Data Mining and Knowledge Discovery*, **5**, 5-10.

Langley, P. and Simon, H.A. (1995). Applications of machine learning and rule induction. *Communications of the ACM* 38, **11**, 55-64.

Leddo, J. and Cohen, M.S. (1989). Cognitive structure analysis: A technique for eliciting the content and structure of expert knowledge. *Proceedings of 1989 AI Systems in Government Conference*. McLean, VA: The MITRE Corporation.

Luger, G.F., and Stubblefield, W.A. (1998). *Artificial Intelligence: Structures and Strategies for Complex Problem Solving*. Reading, MA: Addison-Wesley Longman.

Martin, B., Subramanian, G., and Yaverbaum, G. (1996). Benefits from expert systems: An exploratory investigation. *Expert Systems With Applications*, 11(1), 53-58.

McGraw, K.L. (1994). Knowledge Acquisition and Interface Design. *IEEE Software*, 11, **6**, 90-92.

McGraw, K.L. and Harbison-Briggs, K. (1989). *Knowledge Acquisition: Principles and Guidelines*. Englewood Cliffs, NJ: Prentice Hall.

Morgan, C.J., Takala, J. DeBacker, D., Sukuvaara, T., and Kari, T. (1996). Definition and detection of alarms in critical care. *Computational Methods and Programs in Biomedicine*, **51**, 5-11.

Patel, S., Drury, C.G., and Shalin, V.L. (1998). Effectiveness of expert semantic knowledge as a navigational aid within hypertext. *Behavior and Information Technology*, **17**, 313-324.

Setiono, R. (1997). Extracting rules from neural networks by pruning and hidden-unit splitting. *Neural Computation*, **9**, 205-225.

Sommerville, I. (1995). *Software Engineering*. Reading, MA: Addison-Wesley.

St Amant, R., and Riedl, M.O. (2001). A perception/action substrate for cognitive modeling in HCI. *International Journal of Human-Computer Studies*, **55**, 15-39.

Stillings, N.A., Weisler, S.E., Chase, C.H., Feinstein, M.H., Garfield, J.L., and Rissland, E.L. (1995). *Cognitive Science: an introduction*. Cambridge, Massachusetts: MIT Press.

Tarrassenko, L. (1998). *A Guide to Neural Computing Applications*. New York: John Wiley.

Vora, P.R., Helander, M.G., and Shalin, V.L. (1994). *Evaluating the influence of interface styles and multiple access paths in hypertext*. Proceedings of CHI '94, ACM/SIGCHI, Boston, MA.

Williams, K.E., Hultman, E., and Graesser, A.C. (1998). CAT: A tool for eliciting knowledge on how to perform procedures. *Behavior Research Methods, Instruments, and Computers*, **30**, 565-572.

Williams, K.E., and Kotnur, T.G. (1993). *Knowledge acquisition: A review of manual, machine-aided and machine-learning methods* (Technical Report on Office of Naval Research contract N00014-91-J-5-1500). Blacksburg, VA: Virginia Polytechnic Institute and State University, Management Systems Laboratories.

Winston, P. H. (1984). *Artificial Intelligence.* Reading MA: Addition-Wesley.

Witten, I.A. and Frank, E. (2000) *Data Mining.* San Diego: Academic Press.

**General**

Richardson, J.T.E. (ed.) (1996), *"Handbook of Qualitative Research Methods"*, publisher??, 1996.

Dennis, A.R., Carte, T.A., and Kelly, G. (2002), *"Breaking the Rules: Success and Failure in Groupware-Supported Business Process Reengineering"*, Technical Report/in preparation, Kelley School of Business.

Nohria, N., Joyce, W., Roberson, B. (2003), *"What really works"*, Harvard Business Review, July, Pages 42—52.

**Synergy, integration**

Bakker, H., Helmink, J. (2000), "Successfully Integrating Two Businesses", Gower Publishing Limited, London.

Veltman, J. (2002), "Post-fusie integratie van informatiesystemen: een methode voor alignment van business- en ICT-integratie", PrimaVera working paper series, Universiteit van Amsterdam.

Nadler, D.A., Gerstein, M.S., Shaw, R.B. (1992), "Organizational Architecture – Designs for Changing Organizations", Jossey-Bass.

Nadler, D.A., Limpert, T.M. (1992), "Managing the Dynamics of Acquisitions: Successfully Moving from Decision to Integration", in: Organizational Architecture – Designs for Changing Organizations, Jossey-Bass.

Zollo, M., and Singh, H. (submitted), "Post-acquisition Strategies, Integration Capability, and the Economic Performance of Corporate Acquisitions", under review at the Strategic Management Journal, March, 2003.

Swagerman, D.M., and van Steenis, J. (1998), "Shared services in accounting and finance", Organizational Virtualness – Proceedings of the VoNet-Workshop, April 27-28, Bern.

**Organizational scripts**

Gioia, D.A. and P.P. Poole (1984), "Scripts in organizational behavior", Academy of Management Review, Vol. 9, No. 3, pp. 449—459.

**Organizational processes**

Weigand, H., van der Poll, F., and de Moor, A. (2003), "Coordination through Communication", 8th International Workshop on the Language Action Perspective on Communication modelling (LAP´03), July, Tilburg.

**Variety, nature of knowledge**

Vidgen, R. (1998), "Cybernetics and Business Processes: Using the Viable System Model to Develop an Enterprise Process Architecture", Journal of Knowledge and Process Management, Vol. 5, No. 2, pp. 118—131.

Eppler, M.J., Seifried, P.M. and Röpnack, A. (1999), "Improving Knowledge Intensive Processes through an Enterprise Knowledge Medium", in: Prasad, J. (ed.): *Proceedings of the 1999 ACM Conference on Managing Organizational Knowledge for Strategic Advantage*, New Orleans (USA), April 8th-10th, 1999.

Zack, M.H. (2001), *"If Managing Knowledge is the Solution, then What's the Problem?"*, in: Knowledge Management and Business Model Innovation, Yogesh Malhotra (ed.), Idea Group Publishing, April.

Kock, N., McQueen, R.J. and Corner, J.L. (1997), *"The Nature of Data, Information and Knowledge Exchanges in Business Processes: Implications for Process Improvement and Organizational Learning"*, The Learning Organization, Vol. 4, No.2, Pages 70—80.

Regev, G. Alexander, I., Wegmann, A. (2003), *"Use Cases and Misuse Cases Elegantly Model the Regulatory Roles of Business Processes"*, Business Process Management Journal, submitted.

## Processes and knowledge

Crowston, K. (1997), "A Coordination Theory Approach to Organizational Process Design", *Organization Science*, Vol. 8, No. 2, pages 157—175.

Grant, R.M. (1996), "Toward a knowledge-based theory of the firm", *Strategic Management Journal*, Vol. 17 (Winter Special Issue), 109–122.

Davenport, T.H., Jarvenpaa, S.L., and Beers, M.C. (1996), "Improving knowledge work processes", *Sloan Management Review*, Vol. 37, Summer, 53—645.

Kock, N. and Murphy, F. (2001), "Redesigning acquisition processes: a new methodology based on the flow of knowledge and information", Defense Acquisition University Press, Fort Belvoir, VA.

Linderman, K., Schroeder, R.G., Zaheer, S., Choo, A.S. (2003), *"Six Sigma: a goal-theoretic perspective"*, Journal of Operations Management, March, Vol. 21, No. 2, Pages 193—203.

Postrel, S. (2002), *"Islands of Shared Knowledge: Specialization and Mutual Understanding in Problem-Solving Teams"*, Organization Science, Vol. 13, No. 3, May—June, Pages 303—320.

Choenni, S., Bakker, R., Baets, W. (2003), "Effects of workflow management ...", ....

## BPR, process redesign heuristics

Reijers, H.A. (2002), "Design and Control of Workflow Processes: Business Process Management for the Service Industry", Ph.D. dissertation, Technische Universiteit Eindhoven, 2002.

de Bruin, B., Verschut, A., and Wierstra, E. (2000), "Systematic analysis of business processes", *Journal of Knowledge and Process Management*, Vol. 7, No. 2, 87—96.

Nissen, M.E. (1998), *"Redesigning reengineering through measurement-driven inference"*, MIS Quarterly, Vol. 22, No. 4; pp. 509—534.

Buzacott, J.A. (1996), *"Commonalities in Reengineered Business Processes: Models and Issues"*, Management Science, Vol. 42, No. 5, May. (ook: variëteit)

Dietz, J.L.G., Mulder, H.B.F. (1996), "Integrating the strategic and technical approach to business process engineering", *Proceedings of the International Symposium on Business Process Modelling*, Springer-Verlag, 1996.

## Knowledge transfer as a manageable object

Zollo, M., Winter, S. (2002), *"Deliberate Learning and the Evolution of Dynamic Capabilities"*, Organization Science, Vol. 13, No. 3, May—June, Pages 339—351.

Szulanski, G. (2000), *"Appropriability and the Challenge of Scope"*, in: The Nature and Dynamics of Organizational Capabilities, Dosi, G., Nelson, R.R., and Winter, S.G. (eds.), Oxford University Press.

Dosi, G., Nelson, R.R., and Winter, S.G. (eds.) (2000), "The Nature and Dynamics of Organizational Capabilities", Oxford University Press.

Linderman, K., Schroeder, R.G., Zageer, S., Choo, A.S. (2003), *"Six Sigma: a goal-theoretic perspective"*, Journal of Operations Management, Vol. 21, Pages 193—203.

Nooteboom, B. (1999), *"The Combination of Exploitation and Exploration: How does it Work?"*, EGOS colloquium, Warwick, 3-6 July.

## Contextuality and strategy

Porter, M.E., and Biggelkow, N. (2001), "Contextual Interactions within Activity Systems and Sustainable Competitive Advantage", working paper, Wharton School.

Cotteleer , M.J. and Frei, F.X. (2003), "Enterprise-Level Packaged Software Adaptation: An Empirical Study of Firm-Initiated and Vendor-Initiated Strategies", Harvard Business School Working Paper 02-049, under review.

## Contextuality and stickiness

Szulanski, G. (1996), "Exploring Internal Stickiness: Impediments to the transfer of best practice within the firm", Strategic Management Journal, Vol. 17, Winter 1996.

Szulanski, G., and Jensen, R.J. (2001), "Facilitating Knowledge Transfer: an Empirical Investigation of the Role of the Template", working paper #2001-05, The Wharton School.

Van Stijn, E., Wensley, A.K.P. (2001), "Organizational Memory and the Completeness of Process Modeling in ERP Systems: Some Concerns, Methods and Directions for Future Research", Journal of Business Process Management , Vol.7, No.3, Pages 181—194.

Robey, D., Ross, J. W., and Boudreau, M.-C. (2002), "Learning to Implement Enterprise Systems: An Exploratory Study of the Dialectics of Change", Journal of Management Information Systems , Vol. 19, No. 1, Pages 17—46, Summer.

Boudreau, M.-C. (2003), "Learning to Use ERP Technology: a Causal Model", Proceedings of the 36th Hawaii International Conference on System Sciences, Jan. 6—9, Hawaii.

## Process-evolution and the role of knowledge

Nooteboom, B. (1996), "Towards a Cognitive Theory of the Firm: Issues and a Logic of Change", EIASM conference on organisational cognition, Stockholm.

Nonaka, I. (1994), "A Dynamic Theory of Organizational Knowledge Creation", *Organization Science*, Vol. 5, No. 1, February.

Halverson, C.A., Ackerman, M.S. (2003), *"Yeah, the Rush ain't here yet – Take a break: Creation and use of an artifact as organizational memory"*, Proceedings of the 36th Hawaii International Conference on System Sciences, Jan. 6—9, Hawaii.

Correia, M.F., Patriotta, G., Brigham, M.P. and J.M. Corbett (1999), *"Making sense of telebanking information systems: the role of organizational back ups"*, Journal of Strategic Information Systems, Vol. 8, No. 2, Pages 143—156.

Patriotta, G. (2002), *"Sensemaking on the shopfloor: narratives of knowledge in organizations"*, Journal of Management Studies, Vol. 40, No. 2, Pages 349—375.

De Landtsheer, B., and van Loenhoud, H. (2003), *"Stadiamodel voor het testproces"* (in Dutch), Informatie, juni.

Lassila, K.S., Brancheau, J.C. (1999), *"Adoption and Utilization of Commercial Software Packages: Exploring Utilization Equilibria, Transitions, Triggers, and Tracks"*, Journal of Management Information Systems, Vol. 16, No. 2, Pages 63—90, Fall.

## Modularity and abstraction

Orton, J.D., and Weick, K.E. (1990), *"Loosely Coupled Systems: a Reconceptualization"*, Academy of Management Review, Vol. 15, No. 2, Pages 203—223.

Sanchez, R., Mahoney, J.T. (1996), *"Modularity, flexibility, and knowledge management in product and organization design"*, Strategic Management Journal, Vol. 17(Winter Special Issue), Pages 63—76.

## Business processes under consolidation, change logic

Baskerville, R., Pawlowski, S., and McLean, E. (2000), *"Enterprise Resource Planning and Organizational Knowledge: Patterns of Convergence and Divergence"*, Proc. of the 21st International Conference on Information Systems.

Leroy , F. (2002), *"Socialization Processes During the Post-Merger Integration Phase: Conditions for Tacit Knowledge Sharing and Construction of Common Narratives"*, Third European Conference on Organizational Knowledge, Learning, and Capabilities, Greece.

Van Leijen, H. and Baets, W.R.J. (2003), *"A Cognitive Framework for Re-engineering Knowledge-intensive Processes"*, Proceedings of the 36th Hawaii International Conference on System Sciences, January 3-6, Hawaii.

Amabile, M., 1988, A model of creativity and innovation in organisations, *Research in Organisational Behavior*, Vol 10:123-167.

Anderson, P., 1999, Complexity theory and organization science. *Organization Science, 10*, 216-232.

Argyris, C., & Schon, D.A.,, 1978, *Organizational learning: a theory of action perspective.* Reading MA: Addison Wesley.

Axelrod, R., & Cohen, M.D., 1999, *Harnessing complexity. Organizational Implications of a Scientific Frontier.* New York: The Free Press.

Baets, W., 1998, *Organizational learning and knowledge technologies in a dynamic environment.* Dordrecht: Kluwer Academic Publishers.

Baets, W., 2000, *The Hybrid Business School: developing knowledge management through management learning,*. Prentice Hall

Brown, S. & Duguid, J., 1991, Organizational learning and communities of practice: towards a unified view on working, learning and innovation, *Organization science*, Vol. 2, Nr. 1, pp. 40-57.

Cilliers, P., 2001, Boundaries, hierarchies and networks in complex systems, International Journal of Innovation Management, Vol. 5(2):135-147.

Clippinger III, J.H., 1999, *The Biology of Business: Decoding the Natural Laws of Enterprise*. San Francisco: Jossey-Bass, Publishers.

Coleman, R., 1999, What Enables Self-organising Behavior in Business. *Emergence, 1*, 33-48.

Coombs, S. J., Smith I. D., 1998, Designing a Self-Organized Conversational Learning Environment. *Educational Technology,* , Vol 38, Nr 3, pp 17-28

Cooper, R.G., 1987, *Winning at new products*. London: Kogan Page.

Dodgson, M., (1993), Organisational learning: a review of some literatures, *Organisation Science*, Vol 14:375-394.

Fiol, C.M., Lyles, M.A., 1985, Organizational learning, *Academy of Management Review*, Vo. 10 (4), pp. 803-813.

Fonseca, J., 2002, *Complexity and innovation in organizations,* Routledge, London

Gieskes, J., 2001, *Learning in product innovation processes. Managerial action on improving learning behavior,* Print Partners Ipskamp, Enschede.

Harkema S.J.M., forthcoming in March 2004, *Complexity and emergent learning in innovation projects,* Dissertation University Nyenrode, Breukelen.

Hofstede, G., 1980, *Culture´s consequences. International differences in work-related values,* Sage Publications, London.

Holland, J., 1998, *Emergence from Chaos to order*, Berkshire, Great Britain: Oxford University Press,

Hultink, E.J., 1997, Vier van de tien producten floppen, *Telecommagazine,* 47-48.

Kauffman, S.A., 1993, *The origin of order: self-organization and selection in evolution*. New York: Oxford University Press.

Kim, D.H., 1993, The link between individual and organizational learning, *Sloan Management review*, October, pp. 37-50.

Kolb, D.A., 1984, *Experiential learning: experience as the source of learning development*, Prentice Hall, Englewood Cliffs, New York.

Leroy, F. & Bernard R., 1997, Cognitive and behavioral dimensions of organizational learning in a merger: An empirical study. *Journal of Management Studies* 34: 871-894.

Lewin,A.Y. & Volberda, H.W., 1999, Prolegomena on Covolution: A framework for Research on Strategy and New Organizational Forms, *Organization Science*, Vol. 10, No. 5 pp. 519-534

Lewin, R., 1998, Complexity Theory and the Organisation: Beyond the Metaphor. *Complexity 3, 4,* 36-40.

Lewin, R & Regine, B., (1999), *The soul at work: unleashing the power of compleity for business success*, Orion Books, London.

Lissack,M.R., 2000, *Chaos and complexity-What does that have to do with management?* www.lissack.com/writings/chaos.htm

Loye, D. & Eisler, R., 1987, Chaos and transformation implications of non-equilibrium theory for social science and society, *Behavioral Science*, Vol 32:53-65.

McDermott, J. J., 1973, *The Philosophy of John Dewe*. Chicago: The Chicago University Press

Meeus, M, 2003, Innoveren en organiseren: over het verklaren van (on)verenigbare grootheden, Inauguratierede Universiteit Utrecht, Utrecht.

Morin, E., 1996, *Introduction à la pensée complexe*. Paris: ESF Editeurs

Nelson, R., & Winter, S., 1982, *An evolutionary theory of economic change*. Boston: Harvard Business Review Press.

Nicolini, D. & Meznar, M.B., 1995, The social construction of organisational learning. Conceptual and practical issues in the field, *Human Relations*, Vol 48(7):727-747.

Nonaka, I., & Takeuchi H., 1994, A dynamic theory of organisational knowledge creation, *Organisation Science*, Vol 5:14-37.

Nonaka, I., & Takeuchi H., 1995, *The knowledge creating company. How Japanese create the dynamics of economics*. Oxford: Oxford University Press.

Parsons, T., 1964, *The Social System,* London, Routledge & Kegan Paul.

Prigogine, I., 1984, *Order out of chaos: man's new dialogue with nature,* Free Press, New York.

Senge, P,, 1990, *The fifth discipline: the art and practice of the learning organisation,* Doubleday, New York.

Sherman, H., & Schultz, R.,, 1998, *Open boundaries: Creating business innovation through complexity.* Reading Massachusetts: Perseus Books.

Slappendel, C., 1996, Perspectives on innovation in organisations, *Organisation Studies,* Vol 17 (1): 107-129.

Stacey, R., 2001, *Complex responsive processes in organisations: learning and knowledge creation,* Routledge, New York.

Swan, J.; Scarbrough, H.; Hislop, D. 1999, Knowledge Management and innovation: netwroks and networking, *Journal of Knowledge Management,* Vol 3(4): 262-275.

Varela, F.J., 1991, *The embodied mind. Cognitive science and human experience,* Massachusetts, MIT Press.

Walker, R., 2003, *An investigation into virtual learner-centred solutions for competency based management education,* PhD dissertation University Nyenrode, Breukelen.

Weick, K.E., 1979, *The social psychology of organizing,* Reading MA: Addison Wesley.

Wheelwright, S., & Clark, K., 992, *Revolutionizing Product Development.* New York: The Free Press.

Wolfe, R.A., 1994, Organisational innovation: review, crituique and suggested research directions, *Journal of Management Studies,* Vol 31(3): 405-431.


[AF02]    Aragão, M.A.T., Fernandes, A.A.A., Inductive-Deductive Databases for Knowledge Management, Proceedings of the Workshop on Knowledge Management and Organizational Memories, 15th ECAI, Lyon, July 221-26, pp.11-19, 2002.

[Akz03]   Akzo Nobel, Company – Organization, Company Website: http://www.akzonobel.com, 2003.

[Alb01]   Albors Garrigós, J., Knowledge Creation and Management in a SME Environment: A Practical Case, Knowledge and Innovation: Journal of the Knowledge Management Consortium International, Inc. (KMCI), VOl.1, No.2, January 2001.

[Bae02] Baets, W.R.J., Wie orde zaait zal chaos oogsten – Een vertoog over de lerende mens, Assen, Koninklijke van Gorcum, 2002.

[BP98] Belussi, P., Pilotti, L., Knowledge Creation and Learning within the Governance of the Italian Local Production System, Working Paper, http://www.liuc.it, October 1998.

[Bro03] Brockhoff, K., A Utopian View of R&D Functions, R&D Management, Vol.33, Iss.1, pp.31-36, January 2003.

[CC03] Columbia State Community College, Career Services, MBTI types, http://www.columbiastate.edu/careerservices/, 2003.

[CC97] Court, A.W., Culley, S.J., McMahon, C.A., Influence of Information Technology in New Product Development: Observations of an Empirical Study of the Access of Engineering Design Information, International Journal of Information Management, VOl.17, No.5, pp.359-375, Pergamon, 1997.

[Cum03] Cummings, J.N., Work Groups, Structural Diversity, and Knowledge Sharing in a Global Organization, PhD thesis, Carnegie Mellon University, USA, July 2003.

[DH00] Dahan, E., Hauser, J.R., Managing a Dispersed Development Process, in: Handbook of Marketing, B. Weitz, R. Wensley (eds.), USA, 2000.

[Dis00] Dishman, P., Where does CI fit into what I already know? – Where do I fit into CI?, http://cob.isu.edu/dishpaul/scip, February 23, 2000.

[Elr03] Mc.Elroy, M.W., The New Knowledge Management – Complexity, Learning, and Sustainable Innovation, Knowledge Management Consortium Int., Elsevier Science, 2003.

[Gie02] Gieskes, J.F.B., Managerial Action on Improving Learning Behaviour in Product Innovation, Alba – OKLC 2002 Conference, 2002.

[HB01] Harkema, S.J.M., Baets, W.R.J., The Application of Complexity Theory in Real-life Innovation Management, Conference: Transcending Organisational Boundaries with Chaos and Complexity, October 17-18, Lage Vuursche, The Netherlands, 2001.

[Hea03] Heaton, J., Programming Neural Networks in Java, http://www.jeffheaton.com/ai/, 2004.

[HH86] Holland, J.H., Holyoak, J., Nisbett, R.E., Thagard, P.R., Induction Processes of Inference, Learning & Discovery, Computational Models of Cognition and Perception, Cambridge: MIT Press, 1986.

[Hol96]   Holland, J.H., Hidden Order – How Adaptation Builds Complexity, Helix Books, 1996.

[Hol98]   Holland, J.H., Emergence – From Chaos to Order, Oxford University Press, 1998.

[JW01]    Jacobs, D., Waalkens, J., Innovatie2: Vernieuwing in de Innovatiefunctie van Ondernemingen, Research for the 'Adviesraad voor het Wetenschaps- en Technologiebeleid' (AWT), Deventer, Kluwer, 2001.

[Koc02]   Koch, C., The Emergence of Second Generation Knowledge Management in Engineering Consulting, International Council for Research and Innovation in Building and Construction, Conference proceedings CIB w78 – Distributing Knowledge in Building, paper ID cib02-55, Denmark, June 2002.

[LA00]    Lynn, G.S., Akgun, A.E., Accelerated Learning in New Product Development Teams, Working Paper, Xerox Co., 2000.

[LF00]    Loebbecke, C., Fenema, P.C., Virtual Organizations that Cooperate and Compete : Managing the Risks of Knowledge Exchange, Knowledge Management and Virtual Organizations, Y. Malhorta (ed.), Idea Group Publishing, Hershey, USA, pp.162-180, 2000.

[LS98]    LaBrosse, M.A., Schneider, A., Collaborative Innovation in a Global Research Development Environment, International Counsel of Systems Engineering, Australian Conference, November 1998.

[Man99]   Manville, B., Complex Adaptive Knowledge Management – A Case from McKinsey & Company, Chapter 5 in: The Biology of Business: Decoding the Natural Laws of Enterprise, J.H. Clippinger III, Jossey-Bass Books, USA, 1999.

[MM02]    Massey, A.P., Montoya-Weiss, M.M., O'Driscoll, T.M., Performance-Centered Design of Knowledge-Intensive Processes, Journal of Management Information Systems, Vol.18, No.4, pp.37-56, 2002.

[NP89]    Nicolis, G., Prigogine, I., Exploring Complexity – An Introduction, W.H. Freeman and Company, New York, USA, 1989.

[NT95]    Nonaka, I., Takeuchi, H., The Knowledge-Creating Company: How Japanese Companies Create the Dynamics of Innovation, Oxford Press, 1995.

[Plu91]   Plumbley, M.D., On Information theory and unsupervised neural networks, technical report, CUED/F-INFENG/TR.78, http://www..ee.kcl.ac.uk, Cambridge University, UK, 1991.

[PW00]  Pyka, A., The Self-Organisation of Innovation Networks, MERIT: Maastricht Economic Research Institute on Innovation and Technology, Research Memoranda Series, No.020, 2000.

[Ric02]  Rich, R.F., Keynote Address: The Knowledge Inquiry System: Critical Issues & Perspectives, Centre for Knowledge Transfer, 2002 Spring Institute: 'Champions, Opinion Leaders and Knowledge Brokers: Linkages between Researchers and Policy Makers', http://www.nursing.walberta.ca/knowledgetransfer/, May 2002.

[Sch02]  Schwartz, G., Topics in Machine Learning: Neural Nets, Web project based on Richard P. Lippmann's article: An Introduction to Computing wit Neural Nets, first appeared in the April 1987 issue of the IEEE magazine, http://www.cs.brandeis.edu, July 2002.

[SR98]  Smith, P.G., Reinertsen, D.G., Parallel Architectures for Artificial Neural Networks, Chapter One (J. Torresen), IEEE CS Press, 1998.

[VB94]  Venugopal, V., Baets, W., Neural Networks and Statistical Techniques in Marketing Research: A Conceptual Comparison, Marketing Intelligence & Planning, MCB University Press, VOl.12, No.7, pp.30-38, September 1994.